THE POLITICS OF UNEMPLOYMENT POLICY IN BRITAIN

Class Struggle, Labour Market Restructuring and Welfare Reform

Jay Wiggan

First published in Great Britain in 2024 by

Policy Press, an imprint of
Bristol University Press
University of Bristol
1–9 Old Park Hill
Bristol
BS2 8BB
UK
t: +44 (0)117 374 6645
e: bup-info@bristol.ac.uk

Details of international sales and distribution partners are available at policy.bristoluniversitypress.co.uk

British Library Cataloguing in Publication Data
A catalogue record for this book is available from the British Library

ISBN 978-1-4473-6611-9 hardcover
ISBN 978-1-4473-6613-3 ePub
ISBN 978-1-4473-6614-0 ePdf

Cover design: Robin Hawes
Front cover image: istock/antishock
Bristol University Press and Policy Press use environmentally responsible print partners.
Printed and bound in Great Britain by CPI Group (UK) Ltd, Croydon, CR0 4YY

FSC
www.fsc.org
MIX
Paper | Supporting
responsible forestry
FSC® C013604

Contents

List of figures and tables

Figures

Tables

About the author

Jay Wiggan is Senior Lecturer in Social Policy in the School of Social and Political Science at the University of Edinburgh. Jay's research focuses on employment and social security policy and governance.

Acknowledgements

My interest in the politics of social security and employment policy can be traced to discussions with the late Dr Alan Pratt of the University of Central Lancashire, who I thank for introducing me to the work of John Saville and Michal Kalecki and for engaging conversations about full employment and New Labour. The Work, Economy and Welfare research group in the School of Social and Political Science at the University of Edinburgh has provided space for reflection on various aspects of active labour market policy over the years and I thank colleagues for creating an environment conducive to constructive discussion. Thank you also to the anonymous referees for their valuable comments, and to Anthony Rafferty for helpful feedback along the way. Any errors, of course, remain mine alone. Closer to home, Lyndsey's support has been unstinting, bearing with me as unexpected events meant the completion of this journey took longer than anticipated. Thank you. The topic of the book has its origins in a study into welfare reforms and claimant activity supported by the Independent Social Research Foundation. I thank the ISRF for the time and space this provided for research and reflection. Finally, thank you to the editorial team at Policy Press for their assistance and patience.

1

Introduction

From full employment to full employability

The ideas and policy orientation of successive British governments after 1945 and up to the late 1970s indicate a general orientation of state managers to the pursuit of a high and stable level of employment as first expressed in the 1944 White Paper on Employment Policy of the wartime coalition Government (Peden, 1988). The paper implied that, when presented with a deteriorating economic situation, governments should deploy counter cyclical fiscal and monetary policy to arrest a decline in aggregate demand (Thatcher MSS: 1/5/1: 16). Public sector capital expenditure would expand and the rate of interest be reduced to offset and discourage further declines in private investment, while social security would help sustain a higher level of personal consumption than might otherwise occur (Thatcher MSS: 1/5/1: 22–5). Ernest Bevin MP, Minister of Labour in the wartime coalition Government, for example, argued that this broke with past policy approaches to recognise that unemployment was a political matter, which the state could choose to resolve or not (Hansard, 1944: cc 214–19).

The feasibility of achieving and maintaining a high and stable level of employment was premised upon an expansion of world trade, the competitiveness of business to compete effectively to grow exports, and a willingness among employers and workers to moderate wage demands and price increases to mitigate inflationary pressure (Thatcher MSS: 1/5/1; Peden, 1988). In the event, the years following 1945 proved favourable to economic growth and the level of unemployment in Britain rarely breached 3 per cent until the 1970s (Denman and McDonald, 1996: 7).[1]

The state, it seemed, had hit upon a strategy for growth that, with full employment at its core, was mutually beneficial for labour and capital alike. Muysken and Mitchell (2009: 6) provide a stylised depiction of this full employment policy approach as flanked by economic, (re)distributive and collective pillars. The economic pillar encompassed the articulation of monetary and fiscal policy with expansion of state employment and tri-partite discussion between state, capital and labour representatives. The distributive pillar included action to mitigate market-generated inequalities through expansion of social welfare interventions, including working age out-of-work benefits. The collective pillar referred to the expansion of social rights and an entitlement-based approach to social protection, with provision largely delivered by public bureaucrats.

Similarly, Jessop's (2002a, 2002b) notion of the Keynesian Welfare National State (KWNS) draws attention to the (relative) coherence and mutual support of post-war economic and social policy. In particular, the use of Keynesian techniques to sustain (largely male) full employment, generating demand for the goods produced, and financing publicly provided welfare, that fostered national cohesiveness and reproduction of labour (Jessop, 2002b: 350). The expansion of welfare and corporatist forms of government also worked to legitimate the post-war social order, co-opting and integrating the political and industrial representatives of organised labour into managing and improving the conditions for capital accumulation. Stability, however, proved destabilising, with growing expectations among labour for improved living standards and control over everyday life, increasingly in tension during the 1960s and 1970s with the authority and profitability that employers and parts of the political class deemed necessary for private investment and capital accumulation (Smyth and Deeming, 2016: 678–9; Gough, 1981; see also Chapter 2).

The account of what happened next is well known to those familiar with political and economic history of the welfare state and need not detain us long. In 1973 the unemployment rate was around 3 per cent (Figure 3.3) and, in a final flourish of full employment, state managers expressed an interest in how employment and training programmes might tackle labour shortages by raising skill levels and improving job matching, establishing a tripartite body – the Manpower Services Commission (MSC) – to oversee training and employment services and labour market planning (King, 1995; Price, 2000). By 1975 economic stagnation and rising unemployment shook the confidence of policy makers that full employment remained achievable, and the Labour governments of the second half of the 1970s abandoned expansionary fiscal and monetary policy as a means to reduce unemployment, amid persistently high inflation and pressure on public spending (Wickham-Jones, 1996).

Chapter 4 discusses these developments in detail but in brief; the priority shifted to reducing the rate of inflation, with the centre of the 1974–79 Labour Government's economic strategy an agreement with trade union leaders that promised improved social welfare in exchange for moderation in collective bargaining to restrain the pace of wage increases (that is, a voluntary incomes policy). With the possibility of counter cyclical reflationary fiscal interventions abandoned, but needing to conciliate trade union leaders, the Government enacted a suite of 'special' training and employment programmes, building on the nascent active 'manpower' policies that had moved to the fore as a social democratic supply-side response to labour market challenges (King, 1995; Webb, 2003: 94; Weishaupt, 2011).

With the pivot to the political right that accompanied the election of successive Conservative governments during the 1980s the notion of the state actively intervening to support full employment as a key policy goal was abandoned. Deemed incompatible with restoration of a competitive market, control of public spending and the monetary policy action required to lower the rate of inflation (Holmes, 1985; Gallas, 2016), the consequence was the rise and persistence of high levels of unemployment into the 1990s. The electoral success of the Conservative Party showed that high unemployment did not necessarily lead to punishment at the ballot box, and could be functional in the sense of weakening organised labour and facilitating the creative destruction of capital. With de-industrialisation and the shift to a post-industrial labour market (see Chapter 3) the apparatus for organising labour commodification was ripe for reform.

The structures and logic of social security and employment services had been shaped by (and shaped) the role of full employment and rights-based social protection in the post-1945 Fordist economic growth model of a social democratic industrial society (Jessop, 2002a; Koch, 2006). Given the abandonment of full employment and changed economic strategy, these were no longer aligned to the politics and economic organisation of society. The Conservative Party's time in office provided ample opportunity to remake labour market policies and institutions to expunge them of the influence of organised labour, embed business influence and diminish the protection social security provided against market pressure to commodify labour (as Chapters 5, 6 and 7 elaborate).

Full employability and the activation turn

Gradually, the state labour commodification apparatus was reconstructed around the advance of what Finn (2000) has termed 'full employability'. This refers to a focus on supply-side policy to improve the job readiness and availability for work of unemployed and non-employed working-age people, as governments sought to maximise competition for labour market participation (Berry, 2014a; Osborne, 2014). This shift to a focus on employability has taken the form of what McQuaid and Lindsay (2005) eloquently depict as a narrow reading of employability, in which transitions into paid work are largely treated as a matter of individual attributes – be these certified education and skills, or 'pro' employment attitudes and behaviour, such as active job seeking, appropriate discipline in the work place and willingness to accept job offers irrespective of sector or wage level. Active labour market policies to address unemployment, and increasingly, the absence of waged work among the broader population of non-employed people claiming working-age benefits on grounds of caring for young children or ill health, have become primarily concerned with modifying individual attitudes and behaviour, and fostering compliance with employer demands (Lindsay and Pascual, 2009; Deeming, 2015; Wiggan, 2015a; Jones et al, 2024).

A useful way of grasping the broad nature of changes to social security and employment programmes in the UK since the 1980s is Clasen and Clegg's notion of 'triple integration', involving processes of: 'homogenisation'; 'risk-recategorisation' and 'activation' (Clasen and Clegg, 2006: 532). Here homogenisation refers to the erosion of the differences that traditionally existed between insurance-based unemployment benefits and means-tested unemployment benefits, with the marginalisation of the former and narrowing of eligibility for the latter contributing to a more residual system concentrated on the very lowest income groups. Risk recategorisation refers to how non-employed lone parents in receipt of out-of-work benefits on grounds of caring, and people in receipt of benefits paid on grounds of illness or disability have been recategorised as capable of waged work, or engagement in work-related activity previously restricted to unemployed claimants.

Finally, activation[2] captures the shift from provision of income supports via benefits or 'waged' job-creation schemes as compensation for income interruption to structuring interventions so that they cajole (thus activating) all working-age benefit claimants to prepare for and actively seek employment (Clasen and Clegg, 2012). To this we can perhaps add *managerial marketisation* to capture the shift in the governance of employment services, programmes and social security administration. The demise of corporatist arrangements in labour market policy in the late 1980s (see Chapter 6; Price, 2000: 256; Weishaupt, 2011: 134–6) was accompanied by the transformation of the 'statist' public administration of labour commodification found in Jessop's (2002b) KWNS by the precepts of New Public Management, with its focus on cost control and performance-management techniques geared towards incentivising, monitoring and evaluating attainment of output or outcomes. The managerial turn has in turn been conjoined to a gradual expansion and refinement of quasi-markets dedicated to competitive outsourcing of the delivery of employment programmes for unemployed and non-employed benefit claimants (Finn, 2011; Wiggan, 2015b; Greer et al, 2017; McGann, 2023).

As subsequent chapters contend, together these changes have radically remade the capacity of state managers in the core of central Government to hold (para) state employees to account for policy delivery, and use market rationality imbued by competition to drive spending containment and organisational innovations parallel to, and supportive of, the broader application of activation pressure to participating claimants (Raffass, 2017; Redman and Fletcher, 2022; Wiggan, 2015a; Greer and Umney,

2022). Whereas the labour market policy approach in Britain during the heyday of social democratic industrial society was geared to what Bonoli characterises as occupation preservation, commensurate with developing and protecting the core labour force, the policies that have followed the market-liberal politics that have dominated Britain's post-industrial society have centred more on incentive reinforcement and basic employment assistance (Bonoli, 2010: 440–1; Bonoli, 2013). The cohering of activation, managerialism and marketisation is indicative of what Murphy (2016: 432) characterises as a 'low road' to activation in which relatively inexpensive policy tools that promote insecurity and strengthen state control are used to raise the pressure on claimants to apply for any vacancy, irrespective of preferred job, or claimant capabilities (Peck, 2001; Finn, 2003a, 2011; Dwyer and Wright, 2014; Fletcher and Wright, 2018; Fletcher, 2019).

Accounting for the 'activation' turn in labour market policy

The 'activation turn' in labour market policy is in part justified by policy makers on the grounds that to (engage in waged) work and to seek work is a duty, an economic necessity, a social good and, increasingly, a health outcome due to associations of waged work with 'wellbeing' (Carter and Whitworth, 2017: 797; Sage, 2019: 207). Let us leave aside how this depiction of employment flattens the diversity of jobs and job quality, occluding how the social, financial and health benefits that accrue from waged work are differentially experienced in a segmented and stratified labour market (Sage, 2019). Irrespective of the veracity of policy maker claims, they are nonetheless relevant to the extent that they indicate how, despite the abandonment of full employment, the central and most pressing concern remains imposition of paid 'work', and work-like activity that disciplines labour (Cleaver, 2017: 66–7; Greer, 2016).

The development of a post-industrial labour market has though changed the nature of work (see Chapter 3), and the power relations between labour and capital (Altunbuken et al, 2022). During the shift to a service-dominated economy many workers found themselves stranded in unemployment as demand for their capabilities shifted, or ill health pushed them into inactivity, severing them from potential employment and raising the caseload for incapacity-related sickness and disability benefits (Sainsbury, 2009). With state managers viewing public spending and labour as a production cost to be minimised to maintain international competitiveness (Jessop, 2002b; Koch, 2006), incentive reinforcement and basic employability assistance have, as previously noted, been favoured as a low-cost means to bear down upon wage expectations of claimants, impose authority and rework the relationship between unemployment and other forms of economic inactivity (Peck, 2001; Bonoli, 2013; Berry, 2014a; 2014b; Greer, 2016).

Umney et al (2018), citing Kalecki's (1943) prescient argument that sustained full employment would empower labour to such an extent that capital, fearing its domination was under threat would abandon full employment, likewise contend that contemporary activation is primarily about preserving the authority of capital. Here they link the particular emphasis in Britain on a low-cost, work-first approach with the financialisation of the UK economy over the last 40 years (see Norfield, 2016; Oren and Blyth, 2019).[3] While finance capital may operate in a seemingly abstract realm, the (expected) value of its investments is rooted in businesses employing workers and so the profits of finance, as is the case for capital in general, depend in the last instance on the ability to extract surplus value from the labour force (Sotiropoulos, 2011: 109). As Sotiropoulos (2011: 106) notes, this suggests a commonality of interests in labour subordination irrespective of the fraction of capital. The liquidity of finance capital though means state managers are increasingly sensitised to how negative perceptions of business, state flexibility and competitiveness may threaten investment and raise the cost of borrowing, which intensifies the competition between businesses and between states. Awareness of these issues means that financialisation strengthens the incentive for state managers to adapt labour market regulations, social security benefits and public employment services in ways that reduce unit labour costs, limit exits from waged work and (re)activate non-employed labour to compete for jobs as the means to signal and retain business confidence. In this account the turn to activation is a structural feature of the organisation of capitalism in contemporary Britain (Umney et al, 2018: 338–46).

Examining developments in Britain since the 1970s, Koch (2006: 124) similarly argues that policy makers have pursued a 'capital-oriented growth strategy' in which aggressive de-industrialisation cleared the decks for an economic reconstruction built around the (immediate) interests of capital with state managers re-regulating state institutions to contain unit-labour costs and facilitate flexibilisation of employment forms and working hours. The result, contends Koch (2006: 36–40), was that rather than a focus on the development and intensive utilisation of the existing labour force, the state shifted to extensive utilisation of labour (that is, full employability) as a mechanism for driving growth.

The above depiction of the road taken to the early 2000s is not one from which I demur, and the analysis of developments in the final years of New Labour and 13 years of Conservative (led) governments between 2010 and 2023 (Chapters 8 through 11) point to continued travel along this highway. The extensive labour-utilisation approach to accumulation has matured, being informed by and informing successive activation reforms, geared to strengthening labour discipline through benefit retrenchment, greater conditionality and workfare-like employment programmes (Peck, 2001; Deeming, 2015; Greer 2016; Raffass, 2017; Fletcher and Wright, 2018; Fletcher, 2019). These in turn have responded to, and continued to encourage, low-paid and insecure work, occasioning development and refinement of 'in work' benefits, that in turn have incentivised reproduction and development of low-paid, flexible employment (Grover and Stewart, 2002; Grover, 2016a).

The approach to understanding these developments in subsequent chapters however takes a more agency oriented perspective. This is informed by the analysis outlined by the radical political group and magazine, Aufheben (1998), of the emergence of activation reforms, or 'workfare' (Peck, 2001) during the 1980s and 1990s, and its effect on claimants and political activity. Positing a connection between the rise of industrial militancy during the 1960s and 1970s and the attack on the condition of labour reproduction and commodification, Aufheben argued the viability of the latter was undermined by the difficulty faced by state managers in mobilising claimants, given the structures of post-war social security enabled a form of what they refer to as 'dole autonomy' (Aufheben, 1998). Consequently, workfare, in part, emerges as a response to 'dole autonomy' and conjoins with broader shifts in the state, such as the introduction of new public management reforms, to undermine solidarity and the organisational capacity of unemployed claimants.

The aim here is to develop this argument through a detailed account of how the remaking of employment and social security policy and governance under successive governments, beginning in the 1970s, and extending through to 2023, have been shaped by, and shaped the nature and tempo of class struggle, facilitating a shift in the (re)composition of labour. The notion of 'dole autonomy' (Aufheben, 1998) is expanded here to encompass the autonomy of workers, and unemployed and non-employed claimants in the term labour autonomy. This orients analysis to the interdependence of employed labour, the reserve army of labour and the relative surplus population (Marx, 2013; Wiggan, 2015a) and how struggles to expand or constrain autonomy altered the relationships between them as labour markets and the state apparatus were reconfigured.

The examination of the salience of labour autonomy in active labour market policy reform draws on Gallas (2016), whose work has examined how state managers articulate strategies to impose domination and accumulation as they seek to secure the reproduction of capital. While successful strengthening of domination may, for example, work to permit intensification of exploitation, over the medium term this may weaken social cohesion, exhaust labour power and undermine accumulation. The interaction between accumulation and domination strategies, and the particular form taken, varying with whether state managers adopt an offensive stance against labour, consolidate their position, or offer concessions to labour (Gallas, 2016).

The discussion of the co-evolution of active labour market policy and governance reforms with the tempo and form of class struggle and transformation of the labour market is organised into two parts. The first part encompasses Chapters 2 and 3. The former introduces the underlying Marxist concepts concerning labour–capital relations, the role of the state in the management of labour commodification and outlines the analytical approach drawn from Gallas (2016). The second part includes Chapters 4 through 12 and proceeds in chronological order from 1973 to 2023. These chapters are dedicated to examination and periodisation of the struggle over the articulation of a politics of domination and accumulation, and how this has shaped active labour market policy and governance to curtail labour autonomy. The chapters do not align neatly with changes of government as the intention, as with the work of Gallas (2016), is to capture the tempo and unfolding of changes in the orientation of labour market policy. This is somewhat subjective, but the structuring conditions of capitalism and contingency of class politics are brought to the fore in a way that hopefully helps understand the journey labour market policy has taken since the 1970s, and why we have arrived at a punitive, regressive and market-liberal orientation in labour market policy and governance.

2

Labour commodification, the state and class politics

Value, labour autonomy and capitalist development

The underlying material basis for the antagonism between labour and capital arises from the role of the former in the creation of value. For Marx, the 'value' of an object for capital rests not on the use value of a given product or service for the holder, but on its ability to be exchanged for another product/service within the market at a level greater than the cost of its creation (Marx, 2004: Loc 2157). At the risk of simplification Marx posited that only part of the total amount of the time employed (necessary labour time) in production is used to create the value labour requires to subsist and reproduce itself. The goods produced in the remainder of the time spent employed ('surplus labour') is extracted and appropriated by capital ('surplus value') for exchange in the market at a profit sufficient to enable accumulation and reinvestment in pursuit of a new round of accumulation (Huws, 2014: 174).

Exploitation of labour is then endemic to capitalist economies, but is obscured by the notion that individuals rent their particular endowment of skills, attitudes and experience – that is, their labour power – to an employer for a defined period of time at a price, agreed between two ostensibly equal parties (Marx, 2004: Loc 4053; Adkins, 2017). For labour, maximising the price paid for its labour power and its influence over how and with what intensity capital is able to deploy its capacity to produce are key to securing an income beyond subsistence level, and avoiding exhaustion or destruction of the capacity to labour. Conversely, competitive pressure encourages capital to minimise the price it pays for labour power, while intensifying use of labour power to maximise the value created (Cleaver, 2000: 99). The different objectives embed antagonism at the core of capitalist economies and mean that negotiation over wage levels and the hours and conditions of employment are central to capitalist development. The exact price capital pays for labour power ultimately varies with prevailing custom and practice, material conditions, demand for specific skills and the overall balance of power between labour and capital (Ginsburg, 1979: 23; Marx, 2004: Loc 4113).

In the absence of labour having access to an alternative means of securing its subsistence the equality of contracting parties is notional, meaning that struggle over the price of labour power is weighted in capital's favour. The autonomist Marxist tradition, which emerged out of the Italian workerist movement of the 1960s (Wright, 2002; Cuninghame, 2015), however, argued that the centrality of labour to the generation of value means capital is functionally dependent upon labour for its reproduction (Cleaver, 2000; Burgmann, 2013; Cleaver, 2017). Conversely, labour's capacity to produce goods and services with use value exists independent of capitalist social relations. The potential of labour to exit, subvert or contest exploitation consequently implies a latent threat to capital and structurally underpins the bargaining power of labour (Tronti, 2008/1966: 31).

From an autonomist perspective this endows labour with the power to refuse the authority of capital (Tronti, 2008/1966: 29–31), and inverts the assumption of the primacy of capital (Negri, 1991: 116; Tronti, 1964; Weeks, 2011: Loc 1727). A rejection of the (paid) 'work' ethic then is the deadliest threat labour can present to capital. Negri (1988: 75) posits that action which weakens the work ethic, and which ultimately threatens paid work cannot be permitted by capital, for in doing so it would do away with the society organised around the creation of exchange value. As capital must secure the subordination of labour as a condition of exploitation and accumulation, the exercise of resistance to domination by labour drives capital to develop new means for organising the process of production. Consequently, class struggle over the imposition of labour commodification and the work of reproducing labour power acts as a motor of capitalist development.

> The increasing organisation of exploitation, its continual re-organisation at the very highest levels of industry and society are, then, again responses by capital to workers' refusal to submit to this process. It is the directly political thrust of the working class that necessitates economic development on the part of capital, which starting at the point of production reaches out to the whole of the social relations. But this political vitality on the part of its adversary, on the one hand indispensable to capital, at the same time is the most fearful threat to capital's power. (Tronti, 2008: 31-2)

The seeming powerlessness associated with reliance on wages in fact endows labour with a permanent capacity to contest the supremacy of capital (Holloway, 1995: 177–8). Of course, in socio-economic contexts marked by lower levels of industrial action and weaker collective social bonds then contesting domination may take individualised, or unorganised forms, manifesting as micro-resistance to evade, or subvert the authority of employers. Spicer and Fleming (2016: 127) point to unannounced 'go slows', misuse of company equipment and symbolic sabotage of business identities and narratives as examples of low-level resistance that imposes costs on capital. This chimes with Holloway's (2010) argument that there are always gaps where the drive for commodification and control can be evaded by individuals, or blocked by collective action. As subsequent chapters elaborate, the 'creeping conditionality' applied to working-age benefits (Dwyer, 2004: 269) under successive UK governments is understood here as an attempt to prevent social security functioning as a redoubt from the pressure to sell one's labour power, and facilitator of labour autonomy.

The class composition of labour

The potential fragility of capital's dominance results in recurring attempts to diminish a reliance on labour power for value creation, in parallel with moves to strengthen capital's ability to compel the sale of labour power on the terms it favours (Cleaver, 1994: 123; Holloway, 1995: 178–9; Wright, 2002: 37). The effects of the drive to flee and harness labour power on the organisation of production co-constitute with the making and remaking of the industrial and political form of labour as a class, or what autonomists have conceptualised as class composition (Pitt, 2022).

The term class composition encompasses the *Technical Class Composition* (TCC) of labour and the *Political Class Composition* (PCC) of labour. The TCC, as Pitt (2022) elaborates, specifies the organisation of the labour force and production; that is, the technologies and organisation of (un)waged work and accompanying stratification under a given configuration of accumulation and social reproduction (for example, Fordism and the breadwinner model of the family). Dalla Costa and James (1972) for example, drew attention to both the gendered nature and the importance of (unwaged) social reproduction work for sustaining capitalist social relations and how conflict over the organisation of social reproduction is integral to class conflict and capital's development (see also Weeks, 2011: Loc 1752; Tepe-Belfrage and Steans, 2016: 310–11). How a given TCC is individually and collectively experienced intersects then with how ascribed social characteristics, such as gender and age manifest as social divisions in labour market position and participation in (un)paid work, and which shape experience of, and access to income supports and welfare services (Williams, 2015; Dowling, 2016; Nunn, 2016).

In contrast to the TCC, the PCC refers to the form and relative unity (division) within labour, and how this affects solidarity, collective action and means by which it challenges the preferences of capital, or not. The PCC and the TCC are internally related, being both a product and producer of the other (Bowman, 2012; Burgmann, 2013; Dyer-Witheford, 2015: 29). A cohesive and combative PCC of labour, willing to act autonomously of official channels of representation, provides a potent challenge to capital, but also an incentive for capital to co-opt, or repress labour, and reorganise the TCC. To the extent a transformation of production, working conditions and labour markets (that is, the TCC) occurs this begins to dissolve the foundations of the extant PCC. The capacity of labour to cohere and operate effectively as an autonomous collective actor in the political and industrial sphere subsequently weaken (Burgmann, 2013: 179). Capital's response to combative action arising from a given PCC–TCC does not end class antagonism; instead the new TCC–PCC alters the balance of class forces and how labour is integrated into waged work, or more or less excluded from exploitation.

Domination, accumulation and the Relative Surplus Population

To understand the connection between labour's variable inclusion/exclusion from paid work and domination, exploitation and accumulation we turn now to a discussion of the concept of the Active Army of Labour (AAL), Reserve Army of Labour (RAL) and the Relative Surplus Population (RSP). The AAL essentially refers to the portion of labour engaged in formal employment, but the AAL is itself highly differentiated, reflecting the stratification and segmentation of activity related to the production and circulation of goods and services. Consequently, wage levels, industrial relations, job security, promotion prospects and inequalities vary considerably within the labour force, which in turn is linked to the form and extent of the labour supply and organisation of social reproduction activity (Rubery, 1978; Grimshaw et al, 2017).

Segmented labour market theory conceptualises this through the notion of a core and periphery, or primary and secondary labour market,[1] with the former consisting of the businesses endowed with comparably high productivity, wealth and market share and possessing the incentive to maintain their competitive position by investing resources in new technologies and employee skills to enhance productivity. Employers in the core labour market also have scope to offer better terms and conditions of employment and benefit from stability in the labour force as they seek to realise returns on their investment (Rubery, 1978: 20; Harrison and Sum, 1979: 693; Peck, 1996: 51; McTier and McGregor, 2018).

As employers are not solely competing on 'price' and benefit from labour force stability this encourages the institutionalisation of collective bargaining processes between management and trades unions, with the former ceding a degree of power to worker representatives to reduce the risk of disruption and the latter accepting moderation in action for a regularised forum for negotiating the price of labour power. The core is further segmented by the extent and form of worker autonomy and whether or not specific occupations require a higher level of qualification, or vocation-specific skills. What might be thought of as 'good' working-class jobs – namely, those which are well paid, but require lower qualifications and offer limited autonomy – differ in this way from professional occupations (Harrison and Sum, 1979: 689).

The periphery is also internally divided between a secondary (formal and waged) labour market, irregular paid work (informal segment), social security (welfare segment) and work-oriented education and employment programmes (training segment) (McTier and McGregor, 2018: 23–5; also, Harrison and Sum, 1979: 699). Business in the secondary labour market is understood to be especially sensitive to the costs of complying with regulation, not least around the terms and conditions of hiring/firing, and working hours (Rubery, 1978: 20; Peck, 1996: 51). The profile of the jobs within the secondary labour market more typically requires, from the viewpoint of the employer at least, only limited job-specific training and so the labour power of individuals with what capital deems basic skills appear as functionally interchangeable. Low wages and labour flexibility are consequently incentivised, while expenditure on employee development minimised. Given the relatively larger pool of labour available to draw upon, the risk of employee dissatisfaction leading to high levels of labour force turnover appears an acceptable cost of doing business (McTier and McGregor, 2018: 23–5).

The structural segmentation of the labour market generates space for patterns of employment participation and occupational opportunities to be conditioned by ascribed social characteristics. Employer expectations of how a job should be done, under what conditions and for what price can, and has, for example, negatively affected access to employment among disabled people (Morris, 2020: 253–4). Conversely, breaking down a full-time job into two or three part-time jobs to promote flexibility in staffing is likely attractive to young people combining work with study, or to people with health conditions, or caring responsibilities that constrain availability for full-time paid work. To the extent this occurs, however, it reinforces the association between ascribed group characteristics and suitability for particular jobs that then deepen and reproduce social divisions within the labour market (Rubery and Piasna, 2016: 9). The gendered organisation of social reproduction means working age women bear a disproportionate share of care work and domestic labour that absent of sufficient private resources, or public supports, constrains participation in full-time jobs in the core labour market. Conversely, part-time jobs in the secondary labour market present as relatively accessible and feasible to combine with unpaid care work, which points to how unwaged social reproduction and secondary labour market jobs are entwined (Rubery, 1978; Grimshaw et al, 2017). In turn, such connections reinforce implicit gender coding of particular forms of work, which may then shape individual worker preferences and employer perceptions of suitability that then help structure the organisation of the AAL.

Whether in the primary or secondary sectors of the employed labour force the loss of employment for a period of time as the individual finds themselves suddenly surplus to their employer's requirement for labour power means they are without their usual means of securing their subsistence (Marx, 2013: 439–40). Depending on overall demand for labour and the particular sets of skills the individual possesses, this entry into the RSP may be brief or go on for some time. Moreover, some sections of labour, whether due to age, health or caring commitments may, at best, be partially connected to the labour market. The depiction of the surplus population by Marx was broadly disaggregated into four forms: *a floating segment*; *a latent segment*; *a stagnant segment*; and *a 'pauperised' segment* (Marx, 2004: Loc 11333–111400; Wiggan, 2015a: 374).

The floating segment of the RSP includes those with the skills and attributes that capital currently demands and who therefore may move rapidly back into waged work (that is, they are a labour reserve) and is understood here as akin to short-term unemployment. In describing the latent segment Marx discussed populations not integrated into the core wage relation, paying particular attention to the mass of the then rural population engaged in agricultural work as peasants. With capital expanding in urban areas and reorganising agricultural production the need for this form of labour declined creating a growing population with limited means of realising their subsistence in the traditional way that capital could gradually draw upon to meet rising demand for labour power in urban industry (Marx, 2013: 449). On this definition the notion of the latent segment of the RSP has limited utility in an advanced (post) industrial economy. Those engaged in full-time unwaged reproductive labour in the home, or claimants of out-of-work benefits on grounds of temporary ill health, however, could be regarded as a contemporary example of a latent source of labour power.

Marx represents the stagnant segment of the labour force as occupying a weak position, participating in irregular marginal forms of employment, such as day labouring or domestic service work typified by underpayment of (low) wages and hence a need to 'overwork' where possible to make up for a low income. For Jamil Jonna and Bellamy-Foster (2016: 28–9) the stagnant segment is redolent today of work on the margins of the formal economy and crossing over into the informal economy, but we might also consider the perennial insecure, underemployed worker in the formal economy. Finally, the pauperised segment is a somewhat eclectic grouping for Marx encompassing four distinct strata. People who previously participated in waged labour, but who have been plunged into abject poverty due to a cyclical collapse in economic demand. Those who due to 'redundant' skills, age, impairment or illness are unlikely to participate in waged work again; along with the children of 'paupers' and orphans and finally various groups Marx termed the 'lumpen proletariat' (for example, criminals, sex workers and homeless people) (Marx, 2013: 450).

For the stagnant and pauperised segments securing subsistence is depicted as primarily involving more/less illicit informal economy activity which may involve waged labour or micro-business activity involving the selling of various goods or services (Marx, 2013: 449–51; Jamil Jonna and Bellamy-Foster, 2016: 30; Neilson and Stubbs, 2011: 442). Translated into a contemporary context in which social security, albeit increasingly policed, has been accessible for working-age individuals and families outside employment the 'pauperised' segment is used subsequently to conceptualise the position of people of working age with long-term absence from formal paid work, in recognition that long-term reliance upon social security in the UK is pauperising. The contention advanced in subsequent chapters is that successive welfare reforms have been concerned with sorting the latent and pauperised segments of the RSP in order to expand the floating labour reserve, or the stagnant segment of workers engaged in intermittent, low-intensity paid work.

For terminological clarity subsequent chapters adopt a narrow treatment of the term RSP as the 'pauperised' and 'latent' segments, to differentiate it from the reserve army of labour, which is used to encompass the floating segment and the stagnant segment of the surplus population. The rationale of the division being that it provides a means to identify labour that is semi-permanently 'detached' from the wage relation, and that which is in comparably close proximity to and/or partial engagement with some form of paid work. In short, this positions the surplus population as a holding area for labour deemed ill suited to commodification, but from which some labour may be mobilised and (partially) integrated into paid work, depending on changes in the economic cycle, social expectations and the organisation of (re)production.

For Marx the generation and maintenance of an RSP and labour reserve co-constitutes the expansion and renewal of accumulation, acting as a mechanism by which labour's capacity to exercise power is constrained. As economic expansion takes place capital is presented with the problem of securing labour power to increase production. In response employers may seek to poach the staff of competitors, extend working hours of existing employees or (re)integrate those deemed relatively employable, but who are currently in the labour reserve, or the broader surplus population, as the perceived cost of hiring less job-ready workers falls relative to the rising price of the labour power of existing workers (Wiggan, 2015a).

At the same time capital is presented with the problem that expansion in the demand for labour strengthens the bargaining position of workers. A refusal to acquiesce to worker demands for better terms and conditions carries the risk of recruitment problems and existing workers quitting to sell their labour power elsewhere, or of facing costly industrial action that disrupts production. Marx suggested that employers could consequently be expected to seek to reduce their reliance on labour power via mechanisation, and/or reconfiguration of production so that one person's labour power is more easily substitutable for that of another. To the extent this is successful and provides a competitive advantage then, market pressure incentivises the swift dispersal of the new production practice to all. With uncompetitive laggards driven out of business and the revolutionising of production there is a fall in demand for labour power within a sector. A recurring feature of the struggle over the creation and distributiuon of surplus value is, then, that a portion of labour is demobilised, refreshing the labour reserve and surplus population even during periods of growth, while during periods of acute economic contraction the surplus population grows as employer demand for labour power declines (Marx, 2013: 437–41).

The expansion of the labour reserve is not simply an economic matter, as it is enmeshed with the class politics of domination and accumulation. For as the labour reserve and surplus grows the ability of workers to bring pressure to bear upon employers weakens, providing an opportunity for the latter to go on the offensive and roll back the concessions enacted during a tight labour market (Marx, 2013: 446). Put simply, as the economy slows and vacancies decline, there are fewer outside options and greater competition amongst the sellers of labour power, which induces worker moderation. Demands for a greater share of surplus value, or say over production wither as the threat of dismissal and destitution loom large (Ginsburg, 1979: 24; Byrne, 2005: 41–3).

Yet, while an engorged labour reserve and surplus population may be beneficial to the articulation of domination and accumulation, there are also tensions that arise. The exclusion of a portion of the working-age population from formal employment creates a potential source of social and economic destabilisation. In advanced capitalist economies, this is mitigated by the provision of various forms of income assistance that buffers social cohesion and the legitimacy of the socio-political order. To the extent the state imposes costs on capital to collectively provide such support for labour outside of waged work, however, then this may act, or at least be perceived to act, as a drag on accumulation (Gough, 1981; Smyth and Deeming, 2016).

Moreover, as Grover (2012: 285) drawing on Offe (1984: 98–9) reiterates, capital experiences the perennial problem that reliance on impersonal market forces to compel labour to sell its labour power is far from certain. The existence of a surplus population does not guarantee capital can mobilise additional labour power during an economic upturn, or that the labour reserve is replenished when it depletes. If labour that is dismissed from employment flows into the surplus population and is not deemed suitable for waged work at the price employers are willing to bear, then the labour reserve is not replenished when it depletes, potentially hampering future expansion of production. The latent threat of replacement that might encourage moderation and strengthen labour discipline also diminishes.

The attention given by UK governments since the 1980s to expand the supply of labour meaningfully competing for paid work, implicitly recognises this problem within the labour commodification process (Grover and Stewart, 2002: 19–21).

Revisiting neo-Marxist accounts of the state and social welfare

This brings us to the role of the state in creating labour market institutions (that is, social security benefits, employment services and labour regulations) and consideration of class power, state legitimacy and accumulation in how these variously discipline, mollify, sort, mobilise and train labour as a means to regulate and police labour commodification (Byrne, 2005: 42; Grover and Piggott, 2005). Das (1996: 52–4) suggests that despite the theoretical and methodological variety within Marxist thinking about the nature of the state (Barrow, 1993) there are overlaps and elements of convergence on Marx and Engels' (1985: 82) proclamation that, 'the Executive of the modern state is but a committee for managing the common affairs of the whole bourgeoisie'. Gough (1981: 62–3), posited the state is the apparatus through which different capitalist actors reconcile and coordinate their varying interests, establish hierarchies of domination and relative subordination, and set (temporally contingent) priorities for preferred courses of action that contribute to the general reproduction of capital as a system (Ginsburg, 1979: 28).

Miliband's (2015) classic work on the state pointed to how the core decision-making and repressive institutions of the state are typically populated by people drawn from elite social and economic strata. Shared social norms and expectations imbue the state with a common outlook and preference for policies that advantage elite class fractions and prioritise the needs of capital as a socio-economic system (Gough, 1981: 46; Umney, 2018: 99). Within the constraints of an overall commitment to reproducing capital this does not rule out, though, a number of ways that such activity may be undertaken, making possible a multitude of policy prescriptions (Miliband, 2015: 67; Ginsburg, 1979: 28).

Nor does it presuppose the state as homogenous entity, leaving an opportunity to draw on Poulantzas' insight that conflict between social forces is not solely external to the state, but is carried into the ensemble of institutions that make up the state apparatus (Rooksby, n.d.; Poulantzas, 2014: Loc 2535–45). So, while the centre of state authority, such as the core executive, senior civil servants, military and judicial positions (that is, state managers) are likely staffed by people from elite social class backgrounds, more peripheral apparatus and frontline delivery of state services will more likely be drawn from subordinate classes.

The class heterogeneity within the state hierarchy consequently opens up the possibility that decisions taken by the centre meet resistance in different arms and levels of the state from subordinate class forces. It is not that class background of the latter automatically translates into action that is pro-labour. Rather that this interacts with the material conditions of a given job or occupation, which may involve commitment to professional ethics and adherence to established bureaucratic practices, together with sufficient autonomy in everyday work to open up space within the state for sympathetic, if not solidaristic, action with labour (Poulantzas, 2014: Loc 2610–32). To the extent opposition develops within the state which frustrates the will of the centre we can expect attempts to reconfigure the state to circumvent, blunt or directly eliminate the relevant institution (Rooksby, n.d.: 25–6). State managers can, and do, respond to (perceived) obstruction, by abolishing troublesome, pro-labour sites within the state, and create new organisational forms and practices to foster frontline employee adherence to the goals of the centre (Soss et al, 2011; Greer et al, 2017; McGann, 2023), an issue returned to in subsequent chapters.

For Block (1977: 27) the elite class origin of state managers is advantageous for capital, but neither necessary, nor sufficient to explain the priority given to securing conditions favourable to business, irrespective of partisan political position. Nor why state managers have been willing to overrule the preferences and perceived interests of individual capitalists, or occasionally instigate the destruction of particular forms of production.

Block (1977) suggests these are explicable in terms of state managers' perceptions as to the policies required to successfully run a capitalist economy and maintain state legitimacy. Perceiving that the jobs and income of the populace and the resources of the state depend upon private investment, state managers favour policies and institutions believed, in a given set of conditions, to be favourable for capital. This does not mean the most optimal policy approach is taken, but rather one deemed sufficient to be compatible with securing, or at least, not threatening the somewhat amorphous notion of 'business confidence'. Business confidence being not simply about direct 'costs' that might reduce profits, or threaten competitiveness, but also, as noted in Chapter 1, about policies which threaten employer authority, even if this would potentially enhance the profitability of one or more sectors of capital (Block, 1977: 15–16; Umney et al, 2018: 337; Kalecki, 1943: 324–26).

The broader non-Marxist academic literature has also long identified that policy makers can be constrained by a belief that certain policies put at risk private sector investment. As this is perceived to effect economic growth and employment it also impinges on state revenue, public opinion and electoral prospects of incumbent governments. Policies that are interpreted as a risk to business confidence may consequently be automatically positioned outside the parameters of what is deemed a feasible policy option. Where this is not so, business lobbying, and threats of disinvestment, may rapidly remind state managers of the structural power of capital and encourage adoption of a more favourable approach (Lindblom, 1977: 175; Young et al, 2018).

Such acquiescence is not guaranteed though and what is deemed necessary to secure business confidence, or willingness to override the sectional interests of a given set of businesses, is temporally and spatially contingent. Sustained disruption due to war, economic depression or some other crisis may, for example, create greater space for action that (temporarily) disempowers capital as state managers pursue initiatives deemed to advance the long-run security of capital in general (Block, 1977). To the extent that social movements to advance the position of labour generate sufficient disruption to the social order and accumulation, they can also encourage state managers to adopt policies that may clash with short-term business confidence, but stabilise the reproduction of capital in general, as accounts of the development of the welfare state have detailed (Saville, 1957; Valocchi, 1989; Navarro, 1991; Matthews, 2018).

Gough (1981: 13), for example, positions the provision of welfare as a 'contradictory process through time'. Improvements to social welfare, such as working-age social security may promote wellbeing and assist the reproduction of labour power, stabilise demand for goods and services and improve conditions for accumulation. Yet, the creation of an alternative income source to waged labour weakens the incentive to sell one's labour power and sets a floor under wages. Capital's ability to enhance competitiveness via wage cuts is eroded, while the cost of such provision in public spending raises the prospect of higher tax and social insurance contributions that eat into the profitability of business (Gough, 1981: 12–13). The keenness with which individual businesses and business organisations deploy resources to lobby, staff and elect pro-capital individuals to state institutions, and propagate their ideas among the public points to the continued salience of agency in the policy process, and the value for capital in securing dominance within the state apparatus (Hacker and Pierson, 2010; Bell and Hindmoor, 2014). The form and development of the state labour commodification apparatus and attendant labour market and TCC–PCC are, then, understood here to be conditioned by class struggle within and outwith the state (Peck, 1996: 75). Policy actors may move between what Cleaver (1977: 95) termed strategies of development and underdevelopment as struggle unfolds overtime. In the former the state deploys its resources and orients interventions to support investment in and protection of workers. The goal is to improve the capabilities of labour power as a factor of production and drive the attainment of a higher level of output. With rising output and demand from workers soaking up additional products, higher (money and social) wages can be sanctioned without squeezing capital's share of surplus value, provided the increase does not outpace overall improvements in productivity. Wage and welfare demands are, in short, co-opted, cohered and harnessed to create complementarity between class struggle, productivity, output and profit (Cleaver, 1977: 88; Wiggan, 2015a: 373).

Conversely, underdevelopment abandons recognition of labour as an investment and the prospect of harnessing class struggle to drive productivity. Instead, it seeks relative impoverishment of labour so as to weaken labour's autonomy, control labour costs and enhance the ability of business to compete on price (Cleaver, 1977: 94). Underdevelopment is a deliberate dis-investment in, and destruction of human capital as part of a political project to protect the stability of capitalist social relations themselves. Drawing on Cleaver's conceptualisation, Byrne (2005: 49), analysing New Labour's social policy approach, deemed the strategy of underdevelopment as analogous to the active production of social exclusion, and intrinsic to labour commodification in post-industrial Britain (Wiggan, 2015a: 377). I do not demur from this judgement and Chapters 4 through 12 detail how the state labour commodification apparatus was progressively reconfigured in ways broadly commensurate with underdevelopment, periodising its unfolding as state managers struggled to curtail labour autonomy and facilitate transformation of the class composition of labour.

The primacy of class politics: an analytical framework

As noted above, state managers preferences and (perceived) interests vary, and the position adopted here is that they enjoy relative autonomy in policy decisions (Gough, 1981) that enables them to navigate intra-capital disputes and respond to the tempo, form and intensity of class struggle, and problems emerging in a prevailing form of accumulation. At their core, however, capitalist states are concerned with securing the subordination of labour and the supply of labour power, as it is this which enables the extraction of value, exploitation of labour and accumulation of capital to proceed (Gallas, 2016: 92). For Gallas (2016), this means that state managers are, when it is deemed necessary, willing to accept a destabilisation of social cohesion and legitimacy of the state, and will tolerate the destruction of individual businesses, and sectors of industry, and undermining of accumulation in the short term to restore authority over labour. Active destruction may also contribute to the long-term viability of capital by opening new sites for investment, reordering how fractions of capital are integrated into the economy and remaking the coalition of social classes dominating the political sphere. Should a fracturing of societal order persist, however, Gallas argues this will encourage state managers to reprioritise policy to foster social cohesion as a means to stabilise and improve the functioning of a given pattern of exploitation and accumulation (Gallas, 2016: 30–4).

In order to unpack and examine the complexity and co-constituting dynamism of this process, Gallas outlines a multi-level theoretical framework organised around an analytical distinction between political (Class Political

Regime) and economic (Economic Order Politics) strategies. The political strand, deemed to bear directly upon class domination, foregrounds state managers' concerns with establishing conditions whereby labour is compelled to rent its labour power. To the extent that state activity to this end is relatively coherent across policy fields (for example, regulation of working hours and wages; the social security system and employment services; legislation regarding trade union activity and the use of coercive measures), it is said to represent an 'Extraction Strategy' (ES). The advance of a given ES is conjoined with a strategy for securing consent sufficient to govern the populace, with this termed a 'Mode of Leadership and Domination' (MLD) (Gallas, 2016: 49; Wiggan and Grover, 2022: 718–19).

Gallas sets out five types of MLD, which variously include or exclude class fractions and utilise consensual and conciliatory, or more divisive and coercive, mechanisms to secure the power of the dominant class coalition. First, a one-nation strategy oriented to securing mass and active consent to the preferences and actions of the government, with policy and institutions oriented towards facilitating and embedding such an integrative cross-class approach (Gallas, 2016). Second, a two-nation approach whereby policy seeks to foster division and secure active consent among segments of the population deemed important, teamed with, at best, passive acceptance of this by the broader population. Third, the pursuit of measures commensurate with achieving passive acceptance across the population rather than any active consent to the governing strategy. Fourth, the selective use of policy, power and other material resources to attain the support of key groups in society only. Finally, the open use of coercion through the repressive apparatus of the state to impose authority of the dominant coalition (Gallas, 2016: 29; Wiggan and Grover, 2022: 718–19). The articulation of a particular form of MLD with a given ES representing the class–politics approach of a government (that is, the CPR) (Gallas, 2016: 49).

Although the terminology of 'regime' conjures a sense of permanence and intention the very entanglement of the MLD and ES means that any CPR is always contingent, subject to political contestation, and whether a given CPR is buttressed or destabilised by changes occurring in the realm of Economic Order Politics (EOP). The EOP refers to how state managers concern themselves with crafting conditions conducive to economic growth via Accumulation Strategies (AS) and State Strategies (SS) (Gallas, 2016: 49). In the former, policies and institutions are enacted to develop and/or to support a particular form of production and growth (for example, Fordist, export-oriented), that crafts a particular (social) division of labour within (re)production.

An SS meanwhile refers to the institutional supports enacted by state managers, which are (more or less) attuned to an established, or emergent production process such as, corporatist state planning, or the turn to market liberalisation and rise of regulatory state activity. To the extent the AS and the SS are complementary, a particular EOP exists, which if satisfactorily coherent with the prevailing class politics, coalesces into what Gallas terms a 'Regime of Condensation' (RoC).[2] In short, the RoC encapsulates the supremacy within state apparatus of a preferred approach to securing labour's subordination, the conditions for exploitation and their relative alignment with a given approach to (managing) accumulation (Gallas, 2016: 50).

The cohering of class and economic order politics are, in turn, the product of collective political action. To trace and explain this Gallas differentiates between policy and institutional reforms that represent *offensive, defensive* or *consolidating* 'steps' in the class struggle (Gallas, 2016: 57). For example, when a ruling coalition perceive their authority over labour to be at risk, or in the absence of countervailing pressure seek to press their advantage, this is understood as an offensive step. In the event the offensive proves successful (it may not), attention may refocus on economic order matters, as the 'threat' to capital recedes, especially if the offensive undermined the reproduction and mobilisation of labour power and/or the fallout is contributing to new political antagonism deemed a threat (Gallas, 2016: 57–61).

Gallas suggests that this gives rise to a particular temporal rhythm in the interaction of class and economic order politics. The former being more closely attuned to the rhythm of class conflict, understood to be more variable in the short term than the latter, which is conditioned by perceptions of the medium-term conditions for the accumulation of surplus value. Each however being informed by, and informing developments in the other, meaning they are moments and elements of the same process (Gallas, 2016: 59–60). The concepts of class and economic order politics are subsequently applied in Chapters 4 through 12 to examine the emergence of distinct labour market policy strategies, how these shaped, and were shaped by the struggle of state managers, claimants and workers over labour commodification and how this intersected with transformations in the PCC–TCC. To contextualise the labour market conditions and class relations, in which successive waves of reforms to social security and employment policy has taken place, Chapter 3 maps changes in the sectoral distribution of jobs, growth and decline of occupations, employment participation, and the organisation of labour and patterns of industrial action (that is, the technical and political class composition over time).

3

Labour market restructuring and the changing composition of labour

Changing patterns of labour market participation

Following the stagflation of the mid-1970s and prior to the COVID-19 pandemic in 2020 the British economy experienced three economic recessions (1980–81, 1990–91 and 2008–09) (Jenkins, 2010). These punctuations in economic growth have been accompanied by a considerable restructuring of the labour market over the last four decades. The Notes from Below collective have investigated the changing composition of employed labour in the UK, and produced an excellent dynamic depiction of industrial and occupational change focused on the years 2005 to 2020 (Notes from Below, 2023). The following sections, build on this and Koch's (2006) work to extend the mapping of shifts in the technical and political class composition of labour from the early 1970s through to the early 2020s.

Transformations in the distribution of employment

The industrial shake out during the 1980s was vigorous and deep, but deindustrialisation did not begin, or end, in that decade. Figure 3.1 provides a snapshot of the changing share of jobs held by each sector in select years since 1979 and helps convey the rapidity and extent of de-industrialisation, and the steady growth of the share of employment related to social reproduction activity.

By the late 1990s, the share of total jobs held by manufacturing and mining had fallen to around 14 per cent and by 2019 had almost halved again to just under 8 per cent of total workforce jobs. While the proportion of total workforce jobs in sectors such as transportation and storage, and construction, remained relatively consistent across this period, other sectors experienced greater oscillation. Financial and insurance activities saw a rise in share of total jobs from 3 per cent in 1979 to 4 per cent during the 1990s, but by 2019 had fallen back to 3 per cent. Similarly, from a 15 per cent share of total jobs in 1979, the wholesale and retail trade sector rose to a share of just under 17 per cent in the late 1990s, dropping back to a 14 per cent share by 2019.

Figure 3.1: Changing share of total workforce jobs by industrial sector

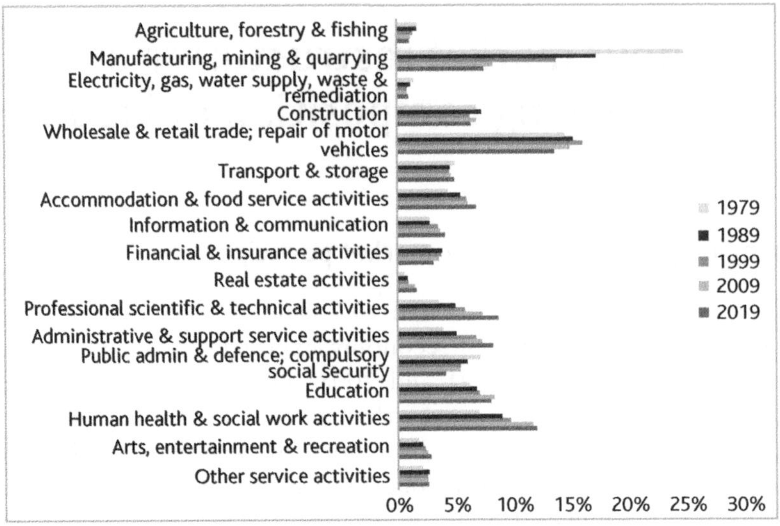

Source: Office for National Statistics (2023e). Open Government Licence v3.0.

Conversely, the share of total jobs more than doubled for the professional, scientific and technical activities sector, rising from just under 4 per cent in 1979 to 9 per cent in 2019, pointing to the growing importance in the economy of employment deemed to require higher skills. More striking perhaps is the general growth in the share of total workforce jobs among the various sectors concerned with aspects of social reproduction. The accommodation and food services sector, which includes hotels and the restaurant trade, expanded its share of total jobs from around 4 per cent in 1979, to 7 per cent in 2019. The share of total jobs held by the education sector sat at around 8 per cent in 2019, up from around 6 per cent in 1979. Similarly, the share of total jobs found in the human health and social work activities sector increased from just over 7 per cent in 1979 to over 12 per cent in 2019 (ONS, 2023e). The share of total jobs found in the health sector eclipsed manufacturing during the early 2000s, and is set to surpass the wholesale and retail sector. As Wren (2013) pointed out, much of the work in these sectors tends to be labour intensive and cost sensitive, which drives business and the state to press down on wages. It is notable that the median hourly pay in health and social work; accommodation and food services; arts, entertainment and recreation; and the administrative and support service sectors indicate many people engaged in these sectors work for comparably low pay (ONS, 2022c: Table 4).

The transformation of the labour market also draws attention to change and continuity in the nature of gender segmentation in employment. Though

Figure 3.2: Employee jobs March 1979 and March 2023

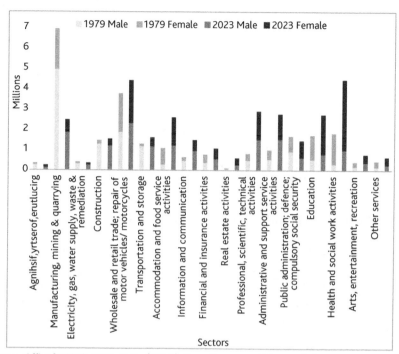

Source: Office for National Statistics (2023f). Open Government Licence v3.0.

women were not absent from industrial jobs, the majority of employee jobs in manufacturing, mining and quarrying; construction; and transportation and storage were held by men in 1979 (Figure 3.2). The process of de-industrialisation has reduced the number of jobs in these sectors held by men and women, with a slightly greater drop in the jobs held by women in mining and manufacturing relative to 1979, but the proportion of all employee jobs held by women in the transportation and storage sector rose from 9 per cent in 1979 to 27 per cent in 2023, while the proportion of jobs held by women in the construction sector had risen from 12 per cent in 1979 to 21 per cent in 2023.

Conversely, the proportion of all employee jobs held by men in the accommodation and food service sector has risen from 26 per cent in 1979 to 47 per cent in 2023. While women continue to hold the majority of employee jobs in the health and social work sector, the proportion of the jobs held by men in this sector is up from around 17 per cent in 1979 to 23 per cent in 2023 (ONS, 2023f). Overall, around four in five employee jobs held by women in March 1979 were located in the service sector, compared with just under half for all male employee jobs. In comparison in March 2023, more than nine in ten employee jobs held by women and more than four fifths of the employee jobs held by men were in services (ONS, 2023f). Gendered patterns of labour market segmentation persist, but the integration of men and women into paid work has been transformed.

As Figures 3.1 and 3.2 attest, the technical class composition of labour has shifted to technical, professional and communication work on the one hand, and to social reproduction work on the other (that is, health, education, social care; leisure). This is redolent of autonomists conceptualisation of the 'mass worker' of industrial society, giving way to the 'socialised worker'; reflecting how work, class relations and possibilities for class struggle, have been transformed by the 'communication and sociability' permeating (re)productive work in post-industrial society (Cleaver, 1993: 41–4; Burgmann, 2013: 183).

Occupational change and labour market stratification

The expansion of information and communication, and commodified social reproduction employment, captured by the avatar of the 'socialised worker', has been accompanied by a change in the occupational structure of the labour market that has fragmented experience, strengthened division and has made securing a good price for labour power, more difficult. Analysts depict this as a polarisation, resulting from a decline in the relative share of employment in middle-skill (pay) jobs, occurring alongside growth in low-skill (pay) and high-skill (pay) jobs as a share of all employment (Cirillo, 2018; Salvatori and Manfredi, 2019: 12). Explanations for job polarisation have identified automation as a principal causal factor, with the offshoring of jobs to other countries, and changes to employment protection regulation and social security policies also playing a role (Goos et al, 2014; Cirillo, 2018). Or in Marxian terms, a substitution of dead labour (machines) for living labour (workers), relocation of production from the 'metropole' to the 'periphery' of the Global South and reform of the state apparatus concerned with labour commodification.

Analysis of job growth across occupations in the UK labour market between 1975 and 1999 indicated the highest percentage change in employment levels during this period were concentrated in relatively well-paid, 'high-skilled' managerial, finance and technology occupations. Substantial growth also occurred in low-paid work in health, care and education and in retail- and sales-related occupations. In contrast, the middle-paying jobs declined, with this particularly concentrated in energy, mining and manufacturing-related occupations (Goos and Manning, 2007: 124–5; also Goos et al, 2014: 2512). Subsequent analysis of the occupational structure of the UK labour market since 2000 notes similar trends, albeit with subtle variation over time (Plunkett and Pessoa, 2013; Gardiner and Corlett, 2015; Clarke and Cominetti, 2019).

In the years leading up to the financial crisis the low-paid end of the labour market experienced relative stagnation, meaning low-paid occupations did not increase their share of overall employment, in contrast to high-paid occupations whose relative share of overall employment did grow. The immediate post-crisis period going into the early 2010s, however, was marked by a resumption in the expansion of low-paid jobs and decline in middle-income jobs (Plunkett and Pessoa, 2013: 8–11; see also Gardiner and Corlett, 2015: 9; TUC, n.d.: 11). Taken as a whole the structure of the labour market in the decade following the 2008 financial crisis was marked by asymmetrical polarisation, as employment in the managerial and professional occupations expanded, accompanied by weak growth in caring and leisure, and elementary occupations, with (small) declines in skilled trades and administrative and secretarial occupations (Clarke and Cominetti, 2019: 37).

The changing structure of the labour market has itself shaped, and been shaped by, the availability of particular types of labour power. For example, young people's weaker entitlement to social security benefits, and the lower payment rates for those aged under 25 has diminished the viability of out-of-work benefits as a potential source of subsistence. Alongside this the extension of young people's time in education, including higher education, has also generated a supply of young people seeking easily accessible and flexible jobs, such as part-time and temporary employment to fit with study (Furlong et al, 2017: 40). As a growing proportion of young people hold higher levels of education qualifications this has also squeezed opportunities for young people with fewer, or no qualifications (Ainley, 2013; George et al, 2015: 14–16).

George et al's (2015: 18–19) analysis of the labour market participation of successive cohorts of young people shows that whereas around four in ten employees aged 16–25 in 1993 were low paid, this was around half in 2013. Similarly, Clarke and Cominetti's (2019: 41) analysis of the period between 2001 and 2018 indicates occupational change for young people was marked by a greater clustering among low-skill work than for the overall working-age population. Employees under 25 concentrated in low-paid entry-level occupations, particularly in elementary and sales and customer service roles, and sectors associated with low rates of pay, such as accommodation, retail and food service industries (ONS, 2018b: 7; ONS, 2019d: Table 3).

While we should be cautious of implying there was a golden age of secure and desirable employment for young people, the intersection of age, education and the transformation in the technical composition of labour has affected the employment open to young people. For some this has worked to channel them into repeat transitions between unemployment benefits, state employment programmes and the secondary labour market (Furlong et al, 2017: 28), facilitated by the rise of non-standard work.

Similarly, the exclusion of disabled people from the labour market of industrial society in the post-1945 period (Baumberg, 2012; Roulstone and Prideaux, 2012: 143–8) has diminished since the 1980s following enactment of equalities legislation and measures to improve state support for job entry and retention, in part a response to disabled people's campaigns (Roulstone and Prideaux, 2012: 87–8). Yet, there has remained a gap between the employment rates for disabled people and non-disabled people (Powell, 2019c: 10), and a pay gap with disabled workers on average earning less than non-disabled workers (ONS, 2019c). The proportion of disabled people concentrated among occupations such as sales and customer services; caring, leisure and other services; and elementary occupations has also been greater than the proportion of non-disabled people (ONS, 2019b: 14). What this suggests is that integration of disabled people into the post-industrial labour market has been into forms of work that are relatively low paid.

Atypical employment and labour market restructuring

A somewhat amorphous category, atypical employment refers to work that differs from full-time paid employment, typically encompassing self-employment, part-time work, temporary contracts, agency jobs and zero-hours contracts (ZHCs). An exhaustive investigation of atypical employment can be found in Choonara (2019), but a brief discussion of its key features follows, as it is a striking feature of labour market transformation, and one that has facilitated changes in the composition of the labour force and relative liquidity of the labour reserve.

The use of ZHCs has, for example, seemingly accelerated since the early 2010s with their use fluctuating around 0.8 per cent of all people in employment between 2001 and 2012 then steadily increasing to reach 3 per cent in 2019, plateauing during the pandemic, before increasing again during 2022 to reach 3.6 per cent in 2023 (ONS, 2023c). There are considerable sectoral variations in the use of ZHCs with just over 40 per cent of all people on a ZHC in 2018 found in the accommodation and food services sector and the health and social work sector. In comparison fewer than 10 per cent of all people on a ZHC were working in the manufacturing, agricultural and construction sectors of the economy combined (ONS, 2023c).

Moreover, use of ZHCs is concentrated among relatively low-paid occupations with more than three in ten people on a ZHC in 2019 working in elementary occupations and a fifth in the caring, leisure and other service occupations. Fewer than 5 per cent were in managerial occupations or in skilled trades (ONS, 2023c). The 16–24 age group is most affected with 7–9 per cent of the people in employment in this age group on a ZHC between 2015 and 2019, rising throughout the pandemic and reaching 13 per cent in the second quarter of 2023. Conversely, this compared with between 2–3 per cent or less for the 25–64 age groups (ONS, 2023c). Yet while a majority on ZHCs consistently report they are not seeking more hours, between a fifth and a quarter since 2019 have indicated a desire for additional employment in some form indicating a not inconsiderable level of underemployment among people on ZHCs (ONS, 2023c) and what we might term indicative of a 'stagnant' segment of the labour reserve.

The uneven patterning of ZHCs by age points to how social characteristics contour experience of the labour market segmentation and stratification of atypical work more broadly (see Schwander and Hausermann, 2013: 254–6). Clarke and Cominetti (2019: 50) suggest that in 2018 almost half of employed women were in atypical work (49 per cent up from 47 per cent in 2008) and for lone parents the proportion in non-standard paid work was even greater rising from 36 per cent to 56 per cent between 2008 and 2018. Trends in both full-time and part-time self-employment between 2001 and 2015 and the stated preferences of self-employed people also provide a further indication of the intersection of gender and age in shaping labour market participation. Between 2001 and 2015 full-time self-employment, for example, remained more common among men than women and more prevalent among those in middle age and older age with the proportion of people in full-time self-employment in 2015 highest among those aged over 45 (ONS, 2016c: 34).

For men and women, the proportion of people across the age range in part-time self-employment in 2015 was greater than in 2001, though there was clear variation between the sexes as to the point at which they engaged in this form of work and why. In 2015 the proportion of women part-time self-employed was concentrated among those aged between 25 and 54 in contrast to men where participation in part-time self-employment was much greater for those aged 54 and above than for all younger age groups (ONS, 2016c: 15). Moreover, the propensity to report participation in part-time self-employment because a full-time job was not desired was greater among working-age women than working-age men, with the latter more likely to report an inability to find a full-time job as a reason for self-employment (ONS, 2016c: 20). Such differences reflect the continuing inequity in the division of unpaid domestic and care work between men and women, and how a gender-segmented and stratified labour market integrates a segment of women workers into paid employment via long-term part-time work (Choonara, 2019: 148).

Given that a greater proportion of disabled people than non-disabled people find work in low-wage occupations such as sales and customer services (9.4 per cent to 7.4 per cent); caring, leisure and other services (12 per cent to 8.7 per cent) and elementary occupations (12.6 per cent to 10.2 per cent) (ONS, 2019b: 14), it is not surprising that in 2018 48 per cent disabled people in work were in atypical employment, a five percentage point increase on 2008 (Clarke and Cominetti, 2019: 50). Not all atypical work is poorly paid and insecure, and the professional and managerial occupations are strongly represented among self-employed, temporary and part-time work indicating that atypical work is itself highly stratified (see Schwander and Hausermann, 2013; Koslowski and McLean, 2015; ONS, 2018c).

Some of the self-employed are themselves employers and have a material position distinct from waged employees, arguably more aligned, though not synonymous with, the concerns of employers in general. Many self-employed people, however, do occupy a precarious labour market position where pressure to reduce service fees translates into a low and/ or unstable income and whose condition is closer to that experienced by low-paid employees in the secondary labour market (ONS, 2018c). As the growth of self-employment since the early 2000s has been concentrated among self-employed people without employees there is some indication that a growing portion of the self-employed are more akin to employees themselves (ONS, 2018c; Choonara, 2019: 12). As such we would expect the expansion of this group to contribute to greater flexibilisation and insecurity as contracting services implies an internalisation of discipline required for entrepreneurial flexibility.

Choonara (2019) suggests however that the structural shift to part-time employee work, self-employment and temporary employment occurred during the 1980s and 1990s. We see this in the expansion and contraction of the proportion of people working part time or in temporary jobs. In January to March 1993 temporary employees equated to 6.3 per cent of all employees; this then rose to a peak of 7 per cent of total employees in 2000, fell to 5 per cent at the end of 2019 and has fluctuated at 5–6 per cent of all employees up to 2023 (Clarke and Cominetti, 2019: 47 – Figure 29; Choonara, 2019; ONS, 2023b).

Similarly, while more than four in ten temporary employees during the last quarter of 1994 reported they could not find a permanent post, this fell away as the economy recovered in the late 1990s and early 2000s, climbed back up to four in ten during 2012–13 and then declined to around a quarter at the end of 2019, before dropping to around one fifth of temporary employees in 2022–23 (ONS, 2023b). For part-time workers the proportion who could not find full-time employment stood at 14 per cent in the middle of 1994, declined to around 7–8 per cent in 2004–05, before increasing up to 17–18 per cent during 2011–14 and then gradually recovering to a pre-pandemic low of 10 per cent in 2019. A small rise during the pandemic was then reversed with under 10 per cent of part-time workers reporting they could not find full-time work from the middle of 2022 (ONS, 2023b).

In terms of participation in part-time employment, recent trends point to an increase in the proportion of men working part time, and a decrease in the proportion of women working part time. Whereas, around 90 per cent of all part-time employment in 1983 was held by women, by 2022 this had fallen to around 70 per cent. As a proportion of all women employed, part-time work also declined from 40 per cent in 1983 to 33 per cent in 2022, while for men, the proportion of male employees working part time rose from 3 per cent in 1983 to 12 per cent in 2012, and oscillated around this share through to 2022 (OECD, n.d.). We see here traces of how the changing technical composition of labour has been altering the gendered nature of labour market participation, but also that engagement in paid work remains strongly contoured by gender.

Given the gendered division of labour with respect to care and domestic work, Choonara (2019), suggests the expansion of part-time jobs has been the means by which capital has expanded the integration, and retention of working-age women with children in the labour force. Certainly, the 'breadwinner' employment patterns of the post-1945 years have eroded in the early 21st century, but the organisation of family social reproduction continues to structure when, and how, women engage in paid work (Koch, 2006; Daly, 2011; Fraser, 2016; ONS, 2018a). Data for England on employment hours and parenting indicate that while about half of all women with dependent children worked more than 30 hours per week in 2018, this compared with more than nine in ten fathers, and more than two thirds of women without dependent children (ONS, 2018a: 5). In Northern Ireland, Wilson (2019: 54) has detailed how one fifth of working-age women without children were employed part time in 2016, compared with two fifths of women with one or more children. The concentration of women in part-time work contributes, in turn, to the persistence of a gender pay gap, weaker occupational mobility and prospects for pay progression (D'Arcy, 2018: 35; Powell, 2019b: 12). The growth and persistence of temporary and part-time work has, in turn, provided a rationale for the state to limit the access of lone parents to out-of-work benefits on grounds of caring responsibilities for children, as it has sought to mobilise a portion of the 'latent' non-employed surplus population, an issue returned to in subsequent chapters (Grover, 2005; see also Freud, 2007).

How to conceptualise and map occupations into broader social classes has, not surprisingly, been much debated over time, but in the UK the official tool used to record and group people by occupation is the

National Statistics – Socio-Economic Classification (NS-SEC) (Payne, 2013; Harrison and Scott, 2020). For the purpose of indicating relative size of different occupational layers amongst the population aged 16 plus the NS-SEC is helpful. As an illustrative example, the ONS analysis of Census 2021 data for England and Wales, records that employers in larger organisation and higher managerial, administrative and professional occupations equated to a 'class' of about 13%, with a further 20% in less senior managerial, administrative and professional roles. Small employers and own account workers, and the intermediate occupations that involve no meaningful supervisory role, each making up around 11%, with the lower supervisory and technical occupations about 5%. The semi-routine and routine occupations together covering around 24% with a further 9% assigned to the category never worked and long term unemployed and a further 7% classed as full time students (Nomis, 2021).

The relative size of the professional and managerial occupations is indicative of a growth in social groups situated in what Wright (2023: 43) depicts as "contradictory locations within class relations". This captures how a reliance on selling one's labour, co-exists with greater autonomy in the workplace, and control over subordinates, to position the interests of such groups as partly aligned to the general interest of labour and capital (Wright, 2023: 87–9), and consequently alters the possibilities for, and nature of struggle. Amid the fragmentation and polarisation of the post-industrial labour force, and attendant divergence in socio-cultural experience and preferences, the shifting occupational structure has made forging a pro-labour intra and inter class industrial and political unity more challenging (Devine and Sensier, 2017; Evans and Tilley, 2017; Morrison, 2022; Vlandas, 2019).

Employment, inactivity and unemployment

The decomposition and recomposition of the labour force during the last 40 years is further indicated by changes in levels of employment participation, unemployment and economic inactivity and the intersection with various social divisions. The rate of economic inactivity (that is, not in employment or actively seeking a job) among women aged 16–59[1] fell throughout the 1970s and 1980s, from about 40 per cent in 1971 to about 28 per cent at the beginning of the 1990s. Following the economic recession during 1990–91 (Jenkins, 2010: 30), the rate remained around this figure before falling to around 25–6 per cent, then plateaued at around 26 per cent following the financial crisis and subsequent recession of 2008–09 (Jenkins, 2010: 30; ONS, 2018d).

With the gradual increase in the State Pension Age for women since 2010 the notional span of 'working age' for women has increased, and this is reflected in the higher inactivity rate reported for women aged 16–64, which stood at 30 per cent at the end of 2010. Having declined to around 25 per cent by the beginning of 2020, inactivity then oscillated around 25 per cent into 2023 (ONS, 2023a). For men aged 16 to 64 years old, the pattern has been the reverse. An economic inactivity rate of around 5 per cent in 1971 steadily increasing and reaching over 17 per cent in 2011, as the effects of the financial crisis and recession fed through into the labour market. Inactivity then fell back to a low of around 16 per cent in 2019, before rising to a peak of around 18 per cent by the end of 2022 (ONS, 2023a).

A convergence in economic inactivity rates for men and women is mirrored in changes in employment rates. Participation rose from 56 per cent in 1971 to 69 per cent by 2018 among women aged 16–59 (ONS, 2018d), and for women aged 16–64 had crept up from 65 per cent in 2010 to 71–2 per cent between 2018 and 2023 (ONS, 2023a). For men aged 16–64 the employment rate of 92 per cent at the beginning of 1971 had dropped to 75 per cent by the beginning of 2010, recovered to 80 per cent by 2018, only to fall back during the pandemic, before rising again to just under 80 per cent at the beginning of 2023 (ONS, 2023a).

With respect to unemployment, this has oscillated for men and women aged 16 and over, with the unemployment rate increasing rapidly in the early 1980s amid recession and de-industrialisation. A similar spike occasioned by the recession of the early 1990s was, however, marked by a greater divergence, between the male unemployment rate, which peaked at almost 13 per cent in 1993, and the rate for women, which reached 8 per cent (ONS, 2023a). As indicated in Figure 3.3, the rates then narrowed until the 2008–09 recession where they widened again, albeit peaking at a lower level, stabilising and then steadily declining and converging through to 2019. The moderate rise during the acute phase of the COVID-19 pandemic in 2020–21, likely reflected the labour market stabilisation policies introduced (Wiggan and Grover, 2022; Clegg et al, 2023; see Chapter 11), and that fewer people were actively seeking employment amid pandemic-related 'lockdowns'. As the economy opened up and labour market activity increased the unemployment rate for men and women declined to just under 4 per cent in 2022 (ONS, 2023a; see Figure 3.3).

The scale of the early 1980s and early 1990s downturn in the labour market is striking. Between the beginning of 1983 and middle of 1987 three million people aged 16 and over were unemployed, and peaked just below this level during 1992–1993 (ONS, 2023a; Figure 3.4). Jenkins (2010: 31) notes that a rapid fall in manufacturing jobs accompanied the 1980s and 1990s recession, with the latter also affected by a collapse in jobs in the construction sector. Given the gendered nature of employment participation

Figure 3.3: UK unemployment rate aged 16 and over

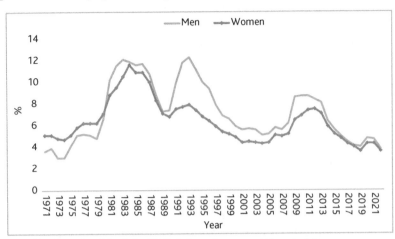

Source: Office for National Statistics (2023a). Open Government Licence v3.0.

and labour market segmentation of the time it is perhaps not surprising that the absolute numbers of unemployed men during the first half of the 1980s, and the early 1990s, was higher than the absolute numbers of unemployed women. With the rise of the services economy, and remaking of the technical recomposition of labour into the 2000s, the changing patterns of labour market participation for men and women has arguably moderated the scale of this somewhat, though differences remain (Figure 3.4).

Despite the 2008–09 recession and 2020–21 COVID-19 pandemic the number of unemployed people has been trending down. With long-term unemployment a consequence of short-term unemployment the pool of people at risk of long term unemployment has also shrunk. The overall numbers of people unemployed for 12 months plus declined from over 1 million in 1992 to 1995 to below 300,000 in 2004. The post-2008–09 rise in long-term unemployment in turn peaked in 2013 at 900,000, before falling back below 300,000 by the end of 2019 (ONS, 2023g).

The experience of unemployment is not evenly spread among the active army of labour, but striated by occupation, with some occupations more sensitive than others to shifts in the economy. Table 3.1 provides a snapshot of changes in unemployment rates over time by occupation of last job, which points to the connections between the active army of labour and labour reserve. For example, the unemployment rate in 2003, during a benign economic environment, for people whose last job was in an elementary occupation, was 7.9 per cent, and for sales and customer services 5.5 per cent.

In 2013, amid austerity and a sluggish economy the unemployment rate for people with an elementary occupation as last job reached 13 per cent,

Figure 3.4: Numbers of unemployed people aged 16 and over

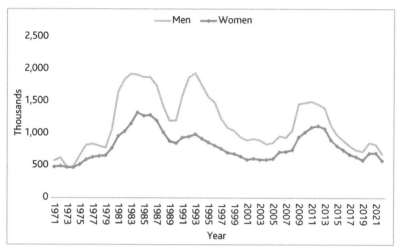

Source: Office for National Statistics (2023a). Open Government Licence v3.0.

Table 3.1: Unemployment rate by occupation of last job

	Q1 2003	Q1 2008	Q1 2013	Q1 2018
Managers, directors & senior officials	2.4	2.1	2.6	1.4
Professional occupations	2.0	1.2	2.3	1.4
Associate professional & technical	2.8	2.2	3.6	1.9
Administrative & secretarial	2.9	3.3	4.6	3.3
Skilled trades	4.3	4.1	6.0	2.8
Caring, leisure & other services	3.4	3.9	5.7	3.4
Sales & customer services	5.5	6.2	10.0	5.1
Process, plant & machine operatives	6.5	5.3	7.4	3.4
Elementary occupations	7.9	8.3	13.2	6.4

Source: Office for National Statistics (2018e). Open Government Licence v3.0.

and 10 per cent among those from a sales and customer service occupation, before falling back again as the labour market improved through to 2018. Conversely, the unemployment rate for people whose last job was in the professional, managerial or associate professional occupations oscillated between 1 and 3 per cent throughout the same period. These overall patterns were reflected in long-term unemployment rates, with people whose last job was in managerial and professional occupations having the lowest long-term unemployment rates between 2001 and 2018 (ONS, 2018e). The prevalence of unemployment, and whether this is of shorter or longer duration, also

Figure 3.5: Unemployment rate and long-term unemployment rate

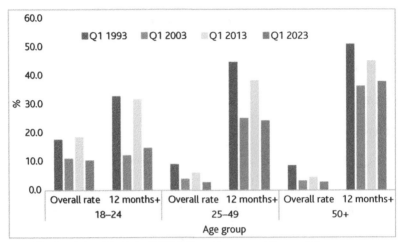

Source: Office for National Statistics (2023g). Open Government Licence v3.0.

intersects with characteristics such as age. Figure 3.5 provides a snapshot of unemployment for different age groups, along with the proportion of unemployed people for each age group that are long-term unemployed for select years. The rate of unemployment has consistently been highest among the 18–24 age group, with lower unemployment rates among the 25–49 age group and the over-50s. The unemployment rate for young people in the first quarter of 1993, for example, was about 18 per cent, compared with around 9 per cent for the the 25–49 age group and the over-50 age group. Thirty years later in quarter one of 2023 the unemployment across all age groups was lower, but the pattern remained with young people's overall unemployment rate just under 11 per cent, compared with just under 3 per cent for older age groups (Figure 3.5).

Older people are better positioned with regard to having had longer to establish a record of labour market participation and the associated skills, experience, references and social networks that mitigate risk of job loss. Young people transitioning into the labour market lack such accumulated endowments, and are often located in entry-level and less secure jobs (Furlong et al, 2017), placing them at greater risk of being let go, or frozen out of the labour market when employers curtail hiring during downturns. Yet, relative to older age groups a lower proportion of unemployed young people experience unemployment as a long-term state. Although the proportion of unemployed people experiencing long-term unemployment varies with the economic cycle and has trended downwards over the last 30 years, the rate remains higher among older age groups (Figure 3.5).

Understandably, older unemployed workers will likely seek jobs that are a good fit with occupational experience, their health, existing financial commitments and socially situated perceptions of what counts as appropriate work, which may constrain what jobs are deemed desirable and feasible (Wiggan, 2015a: 377). Meanwhile, employer demand for older unemployed people is seemingly constrained by perceptions that such workers carry higher labour costs and lack up-to-date skills and flexibility (Phillipson et al, 2016: 196–8; Axelrad et al, 2018: 3). Age, then, not only affects opportunities to enter 'core' employment, but also the risk that exit from wage work will be followed by temporary membership of the labour reserve, or extended leave in the relative surplus population.

Stratification and segmentation of the active army of labour is, then, reproduced in the patterning of entry to the labour reserve and surplus population, which in turn feedback into the constitution of the labour force. The differing experience of unemployment also creates opportunities for state managers to discursively depict the interests of claimants and non-claimants as inherently counterposed, and warrant the residualisation of social security. The development of the post-industrial labour market, as others have pointed out, has in this way both informed, and been informed by, the transformation in benefit and employment policy since the 1980s, towards what has been deemed a more workfare-like approach to the management of labour commodification and reproduction (King, 1995; Peck, 1996, 2001; Grover and Stewart, 2002; Greer, 2016; Briken and Taylor, 2018).

The remaking of the political composition of labour

The pursuit and evolution of this policy direction during the last 40 years has been eased by the decline in the unity of labour and its ability to act collectively in the industrial and political sphere as counterweight to capital. In short, the political class composition that accompanied the organisation of industrial society, and the social democratic corporatist state, has decomposed. Trade union membership peaked at just over 50 per cent during the late 1970s and early 1980s before going into decline (Bank of England, 2017: Table A52b). By 2022 overall trade union membership, as a proportion of all employees, had fallen to a low of 22 per cent with membership among private sector employees at 12 per cent, compared to 48 per cent among public sector employees (DBT, 2023b: 6–8).

In addition, there has been a concentration of trade union membership in fewer industry sectors. As a proportion of employees, trade union membership, in 1995, was greater than 30 per cent in ten industry sectors, with membership rates of above 50 per cent in sectors related to utilities (that is, electricity, gas, water, sewerage and waste management sectors);

public administration; education; and transportation and storage (DBT, 2023b: Table 1.8). By 2022 only four sectors of industry had trade union membership rates above 30 per cent and no sector had levels of membership above 50 per cent. The three sectors that remained relative bastions of union membership in 2022 were education (47 per cent); public administration, defence and compulsory social security (38 per cent); and human health and social work activities (38 per cent). These sectors often involve work activity related to the social reproduction of labour (DBT, 2023b: Table 1.8), and in education, and the health sector, their share of overall employment has been growing. The transportation and storage sector had the next highest proportion of employees with trade union membership, yet even here this had fallen from 50 per cent in 1995 to 34 per cent in 2022 ((DBT, 2023b:Table 1.8).

The decline in membership is matched to a shift in the composition of membership. Three in ten women employees were trade union members in 1995, compared with 35 per cent of men. By 2022 the proportion of male employees who were trade union members had fallen to just under one fifth (19 per cent), and to around one quarter (26 per cent) among female employees ((DBT, 2023b: Table 1.6). If we take age, one quarter of members were aged under 35 in 2022, while two fifths (39 per cent) were aged over 50, indicating weaker connections among younger workers to organised labour (DBT, 2023b: Table 3.1). Prior to the pandemic trade union membership in 2019 as a proportion of employees within different occupational groups was greatest among professional occupations (41 per cent), and weakest among managers and senior officials (12 per cent), sales and customer services (14 per cent) and elementary occupations (16 per cent) (DBT, 2023b: Table 1.7b).

The representation among the professions accords with the relative strength of unions among the education, health and social work, and the public administration sectors. With the retreat to a base in the professions and public sector the ability of organised labour to project power across the economy has diminished. Yet, it also means that among state employees a sizeable portion have remained relatively well organised. Given that workers in education, health, social care and public administration are confronted by the negative social and economic consequences of exploitation and market failure in their everyday activity this may generate pro-labour sympathies within parts of the state apparatus concerned with labour reproduction and commodification. As noted earlier however, the supervisory activity and bureaucratic and managerial practices of professionals and managers have long been recognised as a source of antagonism with other workers and service users that makes solidarity and unity of political action difficult (Ehrenreich and Ehrenreich, 1977).

The atrophying of the political combativity of organised labour is aptly, if crudely, indicated in Figure 3.6 which shows the days lost to industrial

Figure 3.6: Days lost to industrial action 1945 to 2023[1]

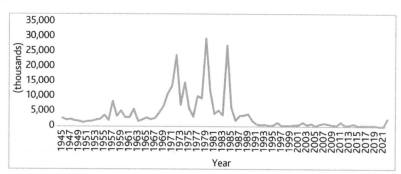

[1] Data collection for 2020–21 disrupted by the COVID-19 pandemic.
Source: ONS (2023d). Open Government Licence v3.0.

action from 1945 through to 2022. The peaks of industrial action in the 1970s coincide with the final flourish of the social democratic, industrial society era, as this destabilised amid economic stagnation and distributional conflict in the 1970s (Jessop, 2002a: 74–90). The final peak marks the defeat of the year-long strike of the National Union of Mineworkers in 1984–85 as the class offensive of the Conservative Government gathered pace (Gallas, 2016). Beginning in the 1990s industrial action plateaued through to 2020, with the second half of the 2010s dropping to post-1945 lows. The decay of the political composition of industrial labour into a weaker post-industrial form was consequence and facilitator of successive reforms to industrial relations legislation that undermined the feasibility of industrial action and the attractiveness of union membership (Gallas, 2016; Etherington, 2020).

An uptick in worker combativity accompanied the post-pandemic tightening of the labour market and I return to discuss this, and the attempt of state managers to undermine it, in Chapter 12. Of course, not captured by data on days lost to industrial action are other forms of extra-parliamentary collective organisation and action, though focus, extent and intensity of such activity has varied over time also (Bailey, 2014; Bailey et al, 2018). The Claimants Union (CU) movement, for example, which emerged in the late 1960s as organisations run by, and for, benefit claimants had expanded rapidly in the 1970s (Marsland, 2018; Stevenson, 2020). By the end of that decade the National Federation of Claimant Unions, which acted as a loose body for information sharing and coordinating activity amongst autonomous local CUs, numbered around 100 affiliated CUs across the UK (GB243 T/ SOR, 3-C.197; Yamamori (2014: 4). While active through the 1980s, by the early 1990s the number of active CUs had declined. A report on the 1988 autumn conference of the Federation of Claimant Unions noted that 100 delegates attended, representing 35 organisations (The New Scrounger, 1988a; 1988b). Conversely, a report on a 1992 national conference indicated only six organisations in attendance, with the report noting that "many groups were experiencing centre/funding problems" (Hassle, 1992: 4). In short, the shifting politics in the broader labour movement was also removing the institutional supports for CU activity, not least in terms of access to unemployed workers centres and their local authority and trade union funding.

Indeed, the TUC linked Unemployed Workers Centres which expanded in number during the 1980s to around 200, began to disappear in the 1990s, and in the 2010s only around 40 remained (Bagguley, 1991: 117; TUC, 2015: 27). Attempts to reanimate national action by still active claimant groups in the middle of the 1990s to oppose the introduction of Jobseeker's Allowance and workfare programmes were patchy (see Chapter 7) and claimant led organisation activity shrunk and plateaued through to the financial crisis in 2008.

The rejuvenation of claimant led organisations in the 2010s followed the state's pivot to the more aggressive imposition of benefit retrenchment, sanctioning and workfare. The (re)emergence of pro-claimant campaigns and organisations providing valuable support to claimants to navigate the social security system and working to disrupt the everyday operation of work-for-your-benefit schemes, and benefit policing. Despite some success, they were unable however, to garner sufficient support to derail the disciplinary drive in active labour market policy (Grover and Piggott, 2013; Weghmann, 2019; Griffin, 2021; Coderre-LaPalme, 2023).

Concluding remarks

The impact of de-industrialisation in advanced economies is well known (Benanav, 2019a), but the decline in industrial employment in Britain over the last 40 years is nonetheless arresting for its scale, speed and seemingly relentless nature. Given the concentration of working-age men in industrial jobs and the relative positioning of men and women with regard to waged and unwaged work it is not surprising that the rapid mass de-industrialisation during the 1980s and 1990s was accompanied by a swelling of male unemployment in particular. Industrial workers in 'core' jobs found their skills and experiences increasingly surplus to requirements and ill-suited to the demands of employers in the expanding service sector. The prevailing composition of industrial society, with its strong gendered division of waged and unwaged work, however, meant a (latent) reserve of women's labour existed which could be drawn upon to meet rising demand for workers, particularly in jobs relating to the circulation of commodities (for example, in retail and customer services) and classic social reproduction-related work (for example, education, health and social care), and forms of reproductive work, such as the food service industry, which provide a commodified solution to changing family arrangements and patterns of labour market participation.

This is not to say the shifts in employment participation were inevitable. The creation of a socially heterogeneous labour force was fought for by women and disabled people, long subordinated and marginalised in formal waged labour of the industrial society (Fraser, 2016). Yet, although inclusion in the labour market created new opportunities to secure an 'independent' income, thereby bolstering individuals' autonomy from family and state, it has remained the case that participation in the primary and secondary labour market and between people in employment and people who remain outside of it is striated by, and works to (re)inscribe and reproduce, broader social divisions and patterns of stratification, domination and exploitation. While the proportion of women in the labour market working full time has increased over time, many women continue to work part time for extended periods. As in the case of care work, this in turn may help free the time of other women, enabling capital to purchase their labour power for more highly paid jobs, pointing to the interdependence that underpins stratification of the labour market (Goos and Manning, 2007; Morel, 2015).

The shift to the service sector, however, has been marked by growing concerns regarding scope for productivity improvements and the turn to additional labour power to drive increases in output while holding down labour costs (Benanav, 2019b: 126–8). The problem though is that this potentially disincentivises labour to willingly sell its labour power, undermining the scope for expansive utilisation of labour power to expand output, and capital's ability to exercise domination. The resolution of this dilemma cannot be found by individual businesses alone, but instead depends on state managers' recognition and interpretation of this as a 'problem' requiring policy intervention. The transformation in the technical and political class composition, as previously laid out, should, in this regard, be viewed as informing, and informed by, the struggle over the remaking of the state labour commodification apparatus.

4

Labour autonomy, conciliation and the emergence of Special Employment Measures: 1973–79

The problem of labour subordination

The institutions that govern the operation of the labour market are core to regulation of the antagonistic social relations between labour and capital that drive accumulation (Peck, 1996: 10; Aglietta, 2000: 398–402; Koch, 2006: 21). In the post-1945 'Fordist' model of mass production and consumption the state cohered market expansion, labour utilisation and social protection into a complementary self-reinforcing dynamic of accumulation (Koch, 2006: 38). With high levels of economic demand sustaining high employment, regularised struggle between workers and employers over wage demands became a driver of industrial innovation and modernisation (Cleaver, 2000: 27). This was facilitated by institutionalisation of trade unions as legitimate partners in pay bargaining, improving employers' ability to reach pay agreements with union leaderships who would police adherence to agreements among their members. Capital could tolerate rising wages so long as productivity improvements allowed output and profits to outpace labour costs (that is, intensive labour utilisation) (Koch, 2006: 27–8).

The development and maintenance of this expansionary 'Keynesian' and corporatist model of growth was in turn co-constitutive with 'social democratic' welfare provision (Ross and Jenson, 1986; Jessop, 2002a: 56–9; Wiggan, 2015a). The gradual expansion and improvement of social security stabilised consumption and fostered social cohesion, albeit of a form in which women were positioned as dependent by partial exclusion from and/or marginalisation within the labour market by the gendered structuring of unwaged social reproduction work. The attendant inscribing of a male 'breadwinner' family model within the social security system meant many working-age women found themselves subordinated to and dependent on male partners, and at greater risk of material hardship (Millar, 1989: 314–15; Koch, 2006: 25–31). At the same time, with the intersection of gendered social and technical divisions striating the labour market this contributed to maintenance of a pool of labour power 'outside' full engagement in paid work, but potentially available for mobilisation if required (that is, a latent surplus population).

By the late 1960s full (male) employment gave workers greater power to exit jobs or engage in official (or unofficial) industrial action to advance their interests, creating a perennial threat to employer (and government) authority that pointed towards diminishing acquiescence to the subordinate status of workers that undergirds accumulation (Wiggan, 2015a: 373). The expansion of social security had also generated a constituency of influential experts and campaign groups pressing for additional resources to support low-income families (Whiteley and Winyard, 1983). In parallel, claimant unions (CUs) had emerged, formed as autonomous organisations of social security benefit recipients, with the aim of harnessing collective numbers to increase claimant power. Infused with a libertarian socialist perspective the CU favoured horizontalist forms of organising, and while supportive of organised labour, were critical of the Labour Party and trade unions for their productivism, bureaucratic paternalism and prioritisation of sectional, rather than broad class interests. The CUs were active in organising claimants to challenge the policing of benefit entitlements, and used their expertise to maximsie support that might be provided via the discretionary aspects of social security, while also campaigning for a universal income guarantee that would break the link between paid work and income. (Rose, 1973; 184–5; Marsland, 2018: 107; Jordan, 1973). While critical of public bureaucrats in the social security apparatus of the state, the CUs engaged in solidarity work with striking workers and found commonalities with the Women's Liberation Movement with respect to addressing patriarchal aspects of the social security system, particularly the state's prying into the relationship status of lone parent claimants, most of whom were women (Rose, 1973; Yamamori, 2014; Stevenson, 2020: 114–20).

Though different in form, activity and objectives the struggle of the poverty lobby and claimant organisations were complementary to action in the industrial sphere in terms of class–power relations. After all, working-age benefits alleviate the cost of social reproduction and to the extent they permit claimant autonomy they weaken the threat of unemployment and the general pressure to sell one's labour power.

The rebalancing of power towards labour, however, was generating problems for employers in terms of their day-to-day ability to exercise control over the labour process, and for state managers who perceived creeping welfare expansion as a threat to social control and drag on growth that imperilled the conditions deemed conducive to stable capital accumulation. Trade union power in the workplace was perceived by policy elites as the key factor in inflationary wage-price spirals that necessarily involved repeated bouts of distributional conflict, contributing to economic stagnation and political instability (Ross and Jenson, 1986: 27). Rapid rises in the rate of inflation were deemed to undermine business confidence and a willingness to invest as it increased uncertainty in the real rate of return that might be expected. Senior members of the Labour Government, for example, implied this hampered efforts to reconfigure British industry, raise productivity, maintain (non-inflationary) full employment and generate the resources for public spending (Wilson, 1975a: 182; Wilson, 1975b). In response, successive administrations in the 1970s sought to bind Britain's relatively decentralised organised labour movement and wage bargaining with incomes policies that sought to cap permissible increases in pay. The attempt by the 1966–70 Labour Government to impose greater legal constraints on trade union activity fell apart however, due to cabinet division and union opposition (Wickham-Jones, 1996: 133; Lopez, 2014: 7–9).

The subsequent Conservative Government (1970–74) similarly pursued new industrial relations legislation and a statutory incomes policy via the Industrial Relations Act 1971 (Gallas, 2016). The Act sought to strengthen legal regulation of industrial disputes, limit trade union power and alter the opportunity cost of unofficial industrial action, thereby titling the balance of power towards capital and government, and weakening the wage-price spiral dynamic (Edwards, 1985: 88–90; Gallas, 2016). Yet, the Industrial Relations Act 1971 stoked the militant activity it sought to contain and was made unworkable by the non-compliance adopted by individual unions and the Trades Union Congress (TUC), and autonomous industrial action and protests (Thomson and Hunter, 1978: 125). Faced with labour's strength the leadership of the Conservative Government enacted a defensive turn in the realm of class politics in 1972, retreating into an accommodating stance of seeking their goals via an expanded incorporation of trade unions via a renewal of corporatism, but following an industrial confrontation with the National Union of Mineworkers (NUM) found themselves out of office after the 1974 February General Election (Lopez, 2014; 9; Gallas, 2016: 85–7). The Labour Party emerged as the largest single party at the election and on this basis formed a minority administration. A second general election was subsequently held in October of 1974 and Labour increased its number of seats, enabling it to remain in office until 1979 (Thomson and Hunter, 1978: 131; Lopez, 2014).

Labour ministers were ostensibly committed to state–trade union social concertation to improve industrial relations and the social wage as a way to puruse their ostensible political objectives for a fairer society and contain inflationary pressure within the economy. A conciliatory approach to leadership in office was prefigured by the TUC–Labour Party Liaison Committee. For trade union leaders, the committee offered a space to influence the party leadership, and the party leadership a means to bind trade unions to its (anti-inflation) strategy. There was also a hope that the link with the trade unions would signal to the public that the party was well placed to secure social peace and economic renewal if elected to government (Wickham-Jones, 1996: 131; Fawcett, 1999: 161–2).

The TUC–Labour Party paper – *Economic Policy and the Cost of Living* – for example, laid out an analysis of the problems arising from weak investment, fractious industrial relations and the seemingly entrenched high levels of price and wage inflation (TUC–Labour Party Liaison Committee, 1973). The answer to the problems identified was for the trade union leadership to help moderate and police wage demands. In return the Government would restore free collective bargaining by repealing the Industrial Relations Act 1971, deliver improvements to the welfare state (the social wage) and oversee an expansion of industrial planning and investment (TUC–Labour Party Liaison Committee, 1973; 1974).

Restoring free collective bargaining, however, made securing wage moderation across industry difficult as the practice of comparability between occupations and maintaining established pay differentials provided a conduit through which concessions to powerful groups of workers in key industries created a 'going rate' that cascaded through the labour force (CAB/129/183/16: 7–13). Trade unions' leaders were acutely aware of rank-and-file disaffection with incomes policies and their willingness to challenge their leaders (Lopez, 2014). Hugh Scanlon, General Secretary of the Amalgamated Engineering Union (AEU), and Jack Jones, General Secretary of the Transport and General Workers' Union (TGWU), indicating in a meeting with Henry Ford II of the Ford motor company, for example, that they carried only limited weight with their members on the shop floor (PREM 16/1483).

With Labour taking office in 1974, the package of measures outlined in *Economic Policy and the Cost of Living* was put into effect, as part of the first in a series of agreements under the rubric of the 'Social Contract' (Fawcett, 1999: 193). Within the prevailing class and economic order politics of social democratic corporatism the Social Contract offered an alternative means for state managers to reconcile tensions between political legitimacy, social cohesion and medium-term economic renewal (CAB/129/196/15; CAB/129/183/16). In 1975 the Prime Minister identified the continuation of the Social Contract as central to the economic strategy of the Government (TUC–Labour Party Liaison Committee, 1975b), and in subsequent years this was echoed by the Chancellor of the Exchequer in memos to cabinet colleagues (CAB/129/196/15; CAB/ 129/203/1) – the TUC and the leadership of individual unions being relied upon to secure compliance. Annual guidance from the TUC was provided to union negotiators to direct settlements across and within industries to accord with a government-stipulated inflation target (CAB/129/183/16; Fawcett, 1999: 161).

The Government and the TUC, for example, agreed to seek voluntary adherence to a wage cap of 10 per cent (Healey, 1975: col 51) with the agreement made in 1976 placing a cap on wage rises of 5 per cent to last through to August 1977. The first Social Contract agreed in 1974 though failed to prevent annual wage rises reaching 30 per cent and increases in the Retail Price Index of about 25 per cent for 1974–75. Growing economic difficulties and acceptance of a loan from the International Monetary Fund in 1976, which required reductions in public expenditure, in turn weakened the Government's ability to improve social welfare in exchange for pay restraint (Ainley and Corney, 1990; Rogers, 2009). The leadership of the Labour Government were unwilling to pursue demand-side reflationary economic measures to stimulate employment, fearful of the negative impact on inflation. A move towards welfare state retrenchment, meanwhile, limited scope for expanding public sector employment (Wickham-Jones, 1996: 94–101; 141–8). By July 1977 inflation was still running at around 18 per cent, but annual wage increases were just under 9 per cent, indicating the subordination of labour's bargaining capacity via the Social Contract was beginning to have the desired effect (Thomson and Hunter, 1978: 130). The decision to continue to pursue a pay ceiling of 5 per cent, amid fragmenting social cohesion, however, generated a strong push back from workers, erupting in late 1978 in the so-called 'Winter of Discontent' that presaged the electoral defeat of the Labour Government at the following June 1979 General Election (Lopez, 2014).

The period 1974–79 arguably marked the high point of social democratic-corporatist class and economic order politics. The Social Contract, together with ministers' ostensible commitment (albeit shifting to the medium term) to full employment, was manifestation of a One Nation mode of leadership that sought to bind workers and citizens to capital through articulation of common rights, interests and shared material gains. The One Nation governing approach complemented an, albeit gendered, developmentalist extraction strategy geared to investment in labour as a factor of (re)production, including recognition of its right to input in the workplace and protection outside of it. Despite the spending retrenchment there was no break with the general organisation of working-age social security benefits as a social right, albeit one which offered greater protection via social insurance-based Unemployment Benefit to more stably employed workers.

Moreover, a state strategy of corporatism prevailed, as the establishment of the Manpower Services Commission (MSC) in 1973 (discussed later), to manage training and employment programme provision, indicates (King, 1995). The latter in turn augmented the One Nation mode of leadership and developmentalist extraction strategy, being ostensibly geared to support skills development among new labour market entrants, the temporary unemployed and those seeking to change careers. In practice, most of these employment programmes are better understood as primarily a performative policy action undertaken to demonstrate the benefits of the Social Contract and societal

Table 4.1: The social democratic-pacificatory labour market policy orientation

Class politics	Economic order
Labourist	(Weak) Keynesian-corporatist
Extraction strategy	**Accumulation strategy**
Pacificatory-developmental	Intensive labour utilisation
Mode of leadership & domination	**State strategy**
One Nation	Corporatist social planning

Source: Author's creation, informed by Gallas (2016: 64).

salve for the burgeoning problem of unemployment in the mid-1970s. That is, expansive state experimentation with supply-side employment programmes (detailed later) emerged as a defensive step by state managers struggling to respond to labour militancy, fracturing social cohesion, economic pressure and the need to (re)produce labour power within the extant Fordist model of growth (Ross and Jenson, 1986; Lopez, 2014; Koch, 2006: 27–30). This was not a path departure though as the goal of state managers remained the dampening of capital and labour antagonism and their reconciliation within a state cohered project of stabilisation and renewal of the profitability of British capital, which would then provide the means for subsequent improvements in money and social wages. Given the salience of the Labourist infused conciliatory class politics and weak Keynesian-corporatist economic order politics the resulting orientation of labour market policy and governance is conceptualised here as social democratic-pacificatory (Table 4.1). The former manifest in continued commitment to a developmental-pacificatory extraction strategy articulated with a One Nation mode of leadership and domination. The latter in an accumulation strategy rooted in intensive industrial labour utilisation and a state strategy geared to integration of social partners in governance of socio-economic policy. It is to unpacking the component elements of the class and economic order politics of labour market policy and governance and their connection to labour autonomy that we now turn.

Social security for an industrial society

A brief account of social security provision for unemployed people during the 1970s indicates how the configuration of insurance and means-tested benefits offered protection to the segment of the labour force who were full time, had experienced fewer interruptions of employment and enjoyed higher wages; those we might regard as the (largely male) core of the active army in the primary labour market. Upon becoming unemployed and assuming a sufficient record of national insurance contributions such workers could receive 12 months of contributions-based Unemployment Benefit (UB). Though required by the Social Security Act 1975 to look for work, job offers that paid below the prevailing local rate could be declined. The penalty for failing to make oneself sufficiently available for work, for being dismissed or voluntarily leaving a job was disallowance of benefit for six weeks (Brown, 1990: 189–96).

Claimants of the insurance-based UB were also entitled to receive an Earnings-Related Supplement (ERS) for the first six months of a claim; the rationale being to mitigate the drop in income that would otherwise be experienced, enabling more skilled workers to wait for an appropriate vacancy to arise, thereby improving job allocation and mitigating risk of exacerbating skills shortages. The ERS paid an additional percentage of previous earnings up to state-specified limits and topped out at a maximum value of 85 per cent of previous earnings (Brown, 1990: 46). The logic of the UB and ERS were in keeping with the notion that temporary support as a worker moved into short-term unemployment not only protected worker incomes, but also the investment into their development as usable labour power. The social protection extended to core workers experiencing short-term unemployment was in this sense commensurate with intensive labour utilisation, being geared towards maintaining worker skills and readiness, commensurate with fluctuations in the business cycle – redolent of the floating segment of the labour reserve.

UB was though often complemented (or replaced) by means-tested Supplementary Benefit (SB) for workers with weaker contribution records, lower wages or who were experiencing long-term unemployment (Ginsburg, 1979: 68). SB covered a broader range of the non-employed population, including older people, lone parents and sick and disabled people, in addition to unemployed claimants. The unemployed people claiming SB were limited to a lower payment than the other groups – the short-term rate – and from 1975 this was uprated only in line with prices rather than prices or earnings, whichever was higher, for the long-term rate available to more 'deserving' non-employed claimants (Brown, 1990: 71).

Lone parents and people claiming SB due to sickness were entitled to claim a higher rate of benefit reflective of the long-term nature of their claim and social expectations about 'legitimate reasons' for not being in paid work. As alluded to earlier this could be accompanied by intrusive state monitoring of entitlement, with lone parents, for example, often subject to investigation of their relationship status (Ginsburg, 1979: 87–8; Peck, 1996: 71). Conversely, little support to enter or sustain paid work was provided, indicating an implicit positioning outside of the labour reserve and reproduction of a portion of the SB population as surplus to capital's requirement for labour power.

The configuration of entitlements and the conditions of their policing were though 'permissive' for unemployed workers, relative to what would follow in subsequent decades. Workers engaged in industrial action and lacking an income through employment were, for example, eligible to claim SB for their dependants, meaning that the state partially cushioned the impact of a withdrawal of labour power and underwrote participation in action against capital (Ginsburg, 1979: 77). A rise in the school leaving age to 16 in 1972–73 also meant all young people upon leaving school became eligible to claim SB if unemployed, providing a new 'outside option' to paid work. Inadvertently, this raised the number of potential unemployed benefit claimants and stimulated concerns about diminishing the work ethic of young people that would intensify under subsequent Conservative administrations (Brown, 1990: 103–6).

The point is not to suggest that people did not want a job, but rather that the availability of state income support did diminish the intensity of pressure acting on an individual to take any job, which in collective terms strengthens the bargaining power of claimant and worker, relative to employer. Similarly, the 'Wage Stop', under which income from SB could not exceed the pay a worker would usually receive through employment, was also abolished in 1975 by the Labour Government. Abolition removed a measure within social security intended to sustain incentives for claimants to take low-paid work (Brown, 1990: 65–8). Working age social security by the middle of the 1970s embodied the developmentalist, One Nation logic of Labourist social democracy in Britain. As configured it provided some space for claimant autonomy that in turn helped undergird the power of labour as a collective political actor in and outside of formal paid employment.

Accumulation to legitimation: modernising training and employment services

A recurring theme within policymaking circles throughout the 1950s and 1960s was recognition of the challenges of fostering greater investment in upskilling labour and improving labour allocation. A lack of sufficient skilled workers being detrimental to realising productivity improvements, while incentivising employers to pay higher wages to 'poach' skilled workers employed at other companies, thereby hampering the scope to sustain higher rates of non-inflationary economic growth (Ainley and Corney, 1990: 13–14; King, 1997: 394). In the mid-1960s tentative steps to rework the structure of training and employment services increased via corporatist initiatives, such as the Industrial Training Boards, and placing a levy on all employers to finance training provision to mitigate the problem of freeriding by some on the investments of others (King, 1997: 385–6; Weishaupt, 2011).

Here, economic order politics were to the fore with state managers seeking to secure conditions conducive to raising the long-term productive capacity of the economy by enjoining large employers and trade unions to focus on developing the skills of the labour force (King, 1997). This reflected the cohering of a hierarchical corporatist state strategy with a developmental extraction strategy that in turn was commensurate with an accumulation strategy rooted in the intensive use of (male) industrial labour. As King has detailed though, the existing intra- and inter-class divisions hampered the policy shift. Engineering and trades reliant on skilled employees were more committed to training than employers reliant upon low-skilled workers and cost-conscious small employers. Meanwhile, trade unions favoured the apprenticeship system and its associated pay differentials for skilled workers, limiting support for broader development of employed and unemployed labour (Ainley and Corney, 1990: 14–17; King, 1993: 216–20; King, 1995: 128–31; King, 1997: 393).

State managers, however, continued to try to resolve problems in the development of labour power 'quality' through state intervention and the tools of corporatist governance. Both the political and industrial wings of labour (the Labour Party and the TUC) and capital (the Conservative Party and the CBI) were in support of an organisation that would link up job creation, training and labour allocation (TUC–Labour Party Liaison Committee, 1973, 1974; Ainley and Corney, 1990: 18–19). The Employment and Training Act 1973, brought into being the MSC. At arm's length from the Department for Employment (DE), but reporting to the Secretary of State, the day to day operations were overseen by representatives from employers, trade unions, local authorities, the education sector and government. The MSC represented a corporatist, developmentalist approach to governance of active labour market policy (MSC, 1980; King, 1995: 131; Weishaupt, 2011: 99).

Improved utilisation of existing workers permeated employment policy. Policy makers, for example, favoured a public employment service that would be attractive to employers and workers; as well as serving unemployed people. The goal being to improve job matching across the labour force with the assumption that unemployed people would eventually benefit (Employment Committee, 1980: 9; Price, 2000: 188–90).

The MSC suggesting that putting forward candidates deemed less suitable would undermine employer confidence and consequently the share of vacancies employers would place with the public employment service (MSC, 1981b: 16). In a context of intensive labour utilisation, improving the state's job-matching function held out the prospect of mitigating upward pressure on wages by better allocation of skilled labour. Similarly, the turn towards active labour market policy interventions during this period was commensurate with the desire to create space for non-inflationary growth by raising the quality and quantity of skilled labour power (Mukherjee,

1974; Weishaupt, 2011: 87). The Training Opportunities Scheme (TOPS), in operation from 1972, was, for example, oriented to upskilling the labour force to help prevent shortages of skilled workers (MSC, 1977; King, 1995; Price, 2000). While unemployment resurged in the mid-1970s the expectation of a return to growth and commensurate risk of skill gaps later in the decade (Healey, 1975: cols 70–4) seemed to warrant the further development of active training and employment programmes. Amid rising inflation and (youth) unemployment, such medium-term priorities were though secondary to the priority afforded to securing union and worker compliance with ministers' anti-inflation strategy.

Managing labour pacification: the Social Contract and Special Employment Measures

Acquiescence of the trade union leadership to government pay caps rested in part on the perception that the Labour Government was fulfilling its commitments under the Social Contract, or at least moving in the right direction. At the 1975 Labour Party conference, Dave Basnett, General Secretary of the General and Municipal Workers Union, pointed to falling employment rates of young people and argued that government failure to address unemployment would imperil the Social Contract (Labour Party, 1975: 163).

The dilemma facing ministers in the 1974–79 Labour Government was how to resolve the tension between political pressure to address unemployment and legitimate trade union support for the Social Contract with an anti-inflation stance that rejected expansionary fiscal policy and adding to long-term spending which expanding public sector employment would imply (CAB/129/184/21). Against a backdrop of constrained resources and growing unemployment, ministers turned to development and expansion of a suite of training and employment initiatives under the rubric of 'Special Programmes' at the MSC and 'Special Measures'[1] at the DE. Edwards' (1985: 128–33) characterisation of Special Employment Measures (SEMs) as palliatives to sooth concern about unemployment within the labour movement is given support by a memo in September 1975 from the then Secretary of State for Employment, Michael Foot MP.

We know the Trades Union Congress and our supporters in Parliament and in the country are gravely perturbed by these figures. Public opinion generally will rightly revolt against the idea of rising unemployment; and we will come under great pressure to reflate the economy. I think it essential for us to show that we fully share the deepening concern about unemployment, and that we are taking significant steps to slow down the increase, to mitigate the effects of unemployment for those already unemployed and to reduce unemployment among young persons. This can be done at a fraction of the cost of a full reflation and it would be a price well worth paying to maintain our general strategy. But the amounts involved must not be trivial. (CAB/129/184/20)

The result was a flowering of policy innovation as the MSC and DE adopted a variety of instruments including job and wage subsidies, work experience and provision of basic general training as ministers sought to address unemployment at the margins. In this the SEMs reflected tensions arising from a class politics focused on (re)securing the quiescence of organised labour to wage repression through conciliatory corporatist interventions and an economic order politics that, while sensitive to fracturing social cohesion, prioritised spending restraint as necessary to deliver medium-term stabilisation and renewal of the existing political-economic model.

Lingering notions that a high-employment, comparably equitable, labour-intensive system of growth was feasible manifested in the roll out of employment programmes to help protect existing labour power against degradation, or help to develop it as a more valuable factor of production. Yet, this developmental view of labour market policy was also joined by growing concern that the expectations of some, particularly younger job seekers, were too high relative to their capabilities, which hampered job entry. Alongside SEMs targeting and protecting the older 'core' labour, there emerged various youth programmes that in functional terms were a mix of warehousing of otherwise unemployed young people and (downward) repricing of youth labour power as the state began to seek a reworking of transitions within and between social security, employment services and entry-level jobs in the secondary labour market.

Varieties of SEMs

Subsidising jobs and wages

In the mid to late 1970s, the public subsidisation of employment and/or wages through programmes such as the Temporary Employment Subsidy (TES) emerged as an important component of the Labour Government's SEMs. Through subsidising jobs and wages the Government advanced a strategy for extracting value that protected and pacified developed labour power, placating unions and working with the grain of a One Nation mode of leadership and accumulation strategy rooted in intensive utilisation of industrial labour. Introduced in 1975 and closed in 1979, the TES provided a subvention to employers to retain ten or more workers threatened with redundancy. The TES received over 10,000 applications during this period and supported over 540,000 jobs at a total cost of more than £500 million (Metcalf, 1982: 6) giving some indication of the Labour Government's prioritisation of the *prevention* of job loss among the active army of the core labour force. Most jobs (90 per cent) protected via the TES were in the manufacturing sector with a particular concentration in the footwear, clothing and textiles industry (50 per cent), and in engineering (33 per cent) (Metcalf, 1982: 59; Lindley, 1987: 14). The TES was abandoned in 1978 following arguments from the European Commission that its support for domestic UK producers amounted to protectionism and the exporting of unemployment (see Hansard, 1978; Metcalf, 1982: 7–8; CAB/128/63/2).

The TES was subsequently replaced by the Short Time Working Compensation Scheme (STWCS), which ran from 1978 through to 1979. Whereas the TES provided support that allowed employers to maintain existing levels of production, the STWCS supported retention of workers at a lower level of employment and production by subsidising a portion of wage costs (up to 75 per cent for 12 months) that enabled redistribution of working hours across employees in place of an employer enacting a programme of redundancy congruent with a decline in demand for a company's products (Metcalf, 1982: 52; Webb, 2003: 96–7). Irrespective of the form of subsidy the common objective was to prevent an outflow of labour into unemployment, which cohered with a logic of protecting valuable labour capacity ready for an expected upswing in the economy. In moderating pressure upon domestic producers such initiatives were also a concession to business and trade unions in labour-intensive industries, commensurate with a One Nation approach to governing via broad consent.

Concerned to placate the TUC and convey demonstrable action on youth unemployment, subsidises for recruitment of young people were introduced to lower the effective price of youth labour to employers; first, in the form of the DE's Recruitment Subsidy for School Leavers (RSSL), and then in 1976 by its replacement, the Youth Employment Subsidy (YES). The YES broadened eligibility but restricted payment of subsidies to young people under 20 and unemployed six months plus. The aim being to reduce the incentive for employers to prefer recruitment of recent school leavers over other groups – something that had marked the RSSL. As Walker (1988: 28) points out, this did mean though that the YES incentivised recruitment of longer, rather than shorter, duration unemployed claimants. The MSC was somewhat ambivalent about substitution effects, noting that redistributing experience of unemployment could have socio-economic benefits (MSC, 1977: 29). Subsidies targeted at longer-term unemployed claimants could mitigate the proportion sinking into labour market detachment and inactivity; a less pressing concern for new labour market entrants and short-term claimants, many of whom would flow into a job of their own accord.

An additional recruitment subsidy was also introduced by the DE in 1977 – the Job Release Scheme (JRS) – to promote early exit from the labour force of workers approaching the state retirement age of 65 for men and 60 for women. The JRS would pay each participant older worker an allowance until state pension age on condition their employer hired an unemployed young person in their stead, though this could be to an entry-level position rather than a direct replacement into the role held by the exiting JRS participant (MSC, 1981b: 23). Between January 1977 and March 1980 there were about 100,000 participants in the JRS and a DE survey of participants in 1979 suggested those deemed unskilled, semi-skilled and reporting ill health and/or low pay were over-represented relative to the broader labour force (Metcalf, 1982: 47).

The common aspect of this panoply of SEMs subsidy schemes was to lower (youth) labour costs for employers, and in the case of the JRS to subsidise a sifting and replacement of labour power on the verge of 'exhaustion' and migration into the older surplus population with integration of new labour power. A class politics of placating organised labour and broader publics was, in essence, articulated with economic order concerns to mitigate threats to youth socialisation into waged work and protect labour deemed valuable in the prevailing industrial technical class composition.

Job creation in the social economy

The DE's package of job and wage subsidisation was complemented by the MSC's programmes for engaging long-term and young unemployed people with social economy (environmental and community-oriented) work and work experience and preparation courses. The Job Creation Programme (JOCP) was introduced in 1975 and funded temporary work for under 25-year-olds and over 50-year-olds, with wages at the local trade union rate for the job. Placements were typically run by local authorities and the voluntary and community sector, and were intended to demonstrate community value (MSC, 1977: 18; Casson, 1979: 110). Over the course of the JOCP about 200,000 people participated in the scheme with the majority (72 per cent) aged under 25 (MSC, 1979: 51).

The closure of the JOCP in 1978 was accompanied by the roll out of its replacement – the Special Temporary Employment Programme (STEP). The STEP retained payment of a wage at the local rate for the job with the MSC reimbursing placement sponsors, who again were generally sourced from local authorities and the voluntary and community sector. Unlike the JOCP, the STEP placements were only open to those aged over 19 and sought to prioritise placement for six months unemployed people aged 19–24 and people 12 months unemployed and aged 25 plus (MSC, 1979: 28–31). Initially 25,000 placements were made available on the STEP and by the end of 1979 just under 20,000 had participated in the scheme, with 54 per cent aged 19–24 and men making up three quarters of total participants. The total number of unemployed people aged 19–24 and six months unemployed, or 25 plus and 12 months unemployed in April 1979 numbered close to 400,000, however (MSC, 1979: 28–31), indicating the limits of the STEP as a means to soak up 'surplus' labour power.

At the same time the voluntary nature of SEMs participation, the provision for short-time work and waged placements in the social economy were supportive of labour autonomy rather than seeking to diminish it. This was commensurate with perceptions of the economic benefits from protecting labour power as a valuable factor of production within the prevailing Fordist industrial model of growth and the attendant political class composition of labour. State managers recognised that organised labour was strong enough to pose them economic and political problems and the SEMs provided a means within self-imposed spending constraints to mollify union and public concerns, legitimate the Social Contract and buy time for ministers' anti-inflation strategy (TUC–Labour Party Liaison Committee, 1975a; Edwards, 1985).

Young people and the work experience turn

For young people, the introduction of subsidises to increase employer demand for youth labour power was matched with an expansion in basic training and work experience schemes. These marked the first steps in the development of supply-side interventions targeted at (perceived) weaknesses in young people's experience, behaviour and expectations given the entry jobs typically available to school leavers (Ainley and Corney, 1990: 40; Brown, 1990: 102–7). The introduction in 1976 of the Work Experience Programme (WEP) for unemployed people aged under 19, for example, signalled state managers' growing interest in individual 'employability'. The WEP paid a weekly training allowance to participants and sought to instil in participants attitudes and behaviour deemed essential to easing transition into formal paid employment (Edwards, 1985: 107; Evans, 1992: 29). The standalone WEP only lasted until 1978, being replaced in that year by the Youth Opportunities Programme (YOP), which as in the WEP paid participants a training allowance rather than the wage paid to participants of subsidised work schemes (MSC, 1979: 36). In this the YOP was about marshalling and developing labour power in the training segment of the labour market, while the various job and wage subsidy measures were geared towards inducing or sustaining participation in the active labour force.

Targeted at unemployed people aged 16–18 years old, the YOP brought together two streams of provision – work preparation and work experience. The work preparation path included three options: Employment Induction, Short Training and Work Induction. While each was based around full-time participation in training or education, the different options were intended to meet the varied needs/capacities of participants, sifting and sorting young unemployed people by perceived capability and potential for labour market integration. Employment Induction provided a two- to three-week course targeted at young people deemed to lack a clear idea of possible future employment opportunities or the basic skills to secure and retain a job. In contrast, the Short Training course focused on occupational skill-based provision in sectors such as construction, engineering and office administration that would be sufficient to train up a participant to semi-skilled level in a period of 13 weeks. Participants regarded by the MSC as possessing weak job-related skills and attitudes were directed to Work Induction courses. Lasting up to 13 weeks, these interventions were geared towards inculcating basic employability skills.[2] Additional work preparation courses to facilitate moves into paid work were also run in the MSC's Employment Rehabilitation Centres for disabled people aged 16–18 (MSC, 1979: 22–4; Walker, 1988: 30).

The work experience path included four strands: a work experience placement on employer's premises with release for training agreed between employer and the MSC and mainly with private sector business; participation in a community project run by local authorities or voluntary groups, involving various work to deliver social, environmental and community benefits; project-based work experience supervised by MSC staff often, though not exclusively, taking place in the public sector; and, finally, the option of engagement in a training workshop contracted to make and sell various goods and services (MSC, 1979: 18–21). The work experience on employer premises placement could last up to six months while the remaining options were for up to 12 months. During the first year of operation 162,000 people entered the YOP with the majority (55 per cent) engaged in the work experience on employer premises pathway (MSC, 1979: 13 and 18).

As with the preceding WEP and various job subsidies, substitution remained an issue, but one that was tolerated (Holland, 1981: 296; Walker, 1988: 33). In the context of rising (youth) unemployment in the latter half of the 1970s (Whiteside, 1991) and doubts about the employability of young people, the YOP was a politically useful intervention for Labour ministers. Low cost, but demonstrative of the Government's concern, the YOP provided a means to occupy the time of young people in activity intended to variously improve technical skills and acculturation to the employment environment. Importantly though, the YOP was voluntary and continued to be flanked by an entitlement to benefits as an alternative. While young people's opportunities were constrained by the structure of the labour market, availability of jobs and training placements, the state labour commodification apparatus did not constrain, whether by mandated participation or aggressive benefit sanctions, youth autonomy over transitions between training schemes, social security and paid work. In effect the configuration of class and economic order politics that infused social security and employment policy and governance fostered a degree of claimant autonomy and buttressed the power of the industrial political class composition of labour.

Concluding remarks

Between 1974 and 1979 as Labour governments responded to the combativity of industrial labour, Britain experimented with forms of active labour market policy that remained rooted in a developmental extraction strategy, but which legitimated abandonment of active prioritisation of full employment. As Edwards (1985) identified, the SEMs were intended as a stopgap and reassurance to trade unions as ministers repositioned full employment as a medium-term objective subordinate to, and dependent on, a reduction in the rate of inflation (Hansard, 1976: cc 1122). This required co-option of labour into the policing of its own (re)subordination if restoration of conditions conducive to stable patterns of exploitation and domination was to be secured. We can reasonably identify SEMs as a means to secure compliance of organised labour, mollify public concern with youth unemployment and develop labour capabilities for an expected economic upturn. In hindsight they also heralded the emerging embrace of supply-side tools (for example, YOP) by which subsequent governments, pivoting to an offensive class politics, would divide and discipline the labour reserve and remake the labour market.

Here then we have the complex political-economic role played by the SEMs during this period. On the one hand the expansion of training and employment programmes was a tactical defensive step by the leadership of the political and industrial wings of organised labour to placate (potential) grassroots opposition to a strategy of wage repression via pay-award caps instituted under the Social Contract. The SEMs provided ministers with an opportunity to proclaim action against unemployment in line with a One Nation approach to governing that sought to reconcile inter- and intra-class interests. That wage rises above stipulated targets were permissible where commensurate improvements in productivity were achieved indicates that intensive labour utilisation continued to be understood as the basis for driving growth (that is, accumulation strategy). To the extent the SEMs helped the Government to impose and maintain wage restraint it contributed indirectly to a rebalancing of class forces that favoured employers' ability to extract value and accumulate capital.

Yet, as anyone who sells their labour power for a living can attest the conditions under which one does so, or the means by which one is supported when unable to do so, matter greatly. The JOCP/STEP of the MSC and various job and employer subsidies of the DE, the voluntary nature of training schemes, orientation of employment services and structure of social security indirectly supported labour as a collective political actor by sustaining people in waged work and sheltering unemployed and non-employed claimants from the pressure to enter the (labour) market. In short, encoded within the state labour commodification apparatus was space for autonomy commensurate with the prevailing political and technical class composition of labour and its intersection with the class and economic order politics of One Nation conciliation, pacificatory development and intensive labour utilisation. The ascent of the Conservative Party to Government in 1979 heralded the end for this social democratic-pacificatory orientation in labour market policy (Table 4.1).

5

Decomposition, disorder and policy transition: 1979–85

The New Conservatism, political instability and cautious reform

As the Labour Party and trade union leaderships sought to stabilise the social democratic-corporatist state, a more radical rejection of the post-war class compromise was manifesting in the rise to power of the 'New Right' faction of the Conservative Party (Dorey, 2022: 100). From the perspective of a 'New Conservativism' that was expressly committed to market liberal ideas (Lawson, 1980), the growth of the state sector, weak regulation of trade unions and an expansive welfare state meant a pro-labour orientation was encoded within the institutions of the state. Robertson (1986: 278–80) conceptualised the social democratic-corporatist approach to managing labour commodification as a 'Guardian' model in which labour market regulation, trade union power and expansive social protection limited employer authority over the extraction of value, prevented the exhaustion of labour power and socialised support for its reproduction.

In effect, the 'Guardian' model erected a series of redoubts within the state that buffered labour autonomy. The New Right rejected the suitability of these arrangements (Thatcher MSS: 2/6/1/156; Joseph, 1980) depicting them as having empowered an obdurate labour movement, diminished work incentives, weakened the ability of employers to make profit-maximising decisions and undermined the competitiveness of industry (Joseph, 1980; Holmes, 1985: 35; Thatcher, 1995: 105). The result being a deleterious cycle of economic stagnation, inflationary pressure, state intervention and escalating social conflict (Conservative Party, 1977: 28; Joseph,1980: 8–9; Walters, 1986; Tebbit, 1989: 238; Thatcher, 1995: 421; Lawson, 1980).

Consequently, as Gallas (2016) elaborates in depth, the New Right adopted a new strategy, built around a dis-embedding of the prevailing class and economic order politics and a pivot to an offensive step in the class struggle. The goal being to secure the (re)subordination of labour to the authority of state and capital, and wring inflation out of the system, both deemed necessary for the long-term stabilisation and improvement of conditions for accumulation. In place of social pacts and negotiations with organised labour, inflation would be curbed by reducing the growth of the money supply, raising the price of credit and curtailing public spending. Reduced spending was intended to mitigate upward pressure on interest rates and the negative effect this would have on private sector investment and economic growth in the short term (Thatcher, 1995: 92–4).

By signalling to employers, investors and workers the state's determination to bring down inflation, ministers expected that expectations and behaviour would also adjust, creating an environment conducive to entrepreneurialism, investment and accumulation (Holmes, 1985). Inefficient and unproductive businesses would be driven out of the market, while market signals would drive the reallocation and repricing of labour power, enabling innovative and competitive enterprises to expand and profit rates to rise. Here, the New Right was willing to override the interests of individual businesses and fractions of industrial capital in favour of creative destruction as the motor of renewal and with the election of the Conservatives to Government in 1979 they did just that (Gallas, 2016: 63–4).

The Conservative Government's pursuit of a deflationary economic strategy led, for example, to a shake out of industry. Any sense that the Government should prioritise maintaining a high and stable level of employment went with this as the count of registered unemployed people rose from about 1.2 million in September 1979 to 2.9 million by September 1982 (Unemployment Unit, 1987: 2). Though the scale of the disruption was perhaps unexpected, New Right ministers held to their position, but faced growing disquiet with their strategy into the early 1980s. Divisions within the governing class were indicated by the opposition of the 'One Nation' faction within the Government and Conservative Party, who warned of the electoral dangers of abandoning full employment and who favoured a more ameliorative strategy (THCR 1/15/6 f3; Holmes, 1985). Similarly, the Confederation of British Industry, tending to represent larger businesses and manufacturing, was also initially critical of the deflationary economic strategy for damaging productive capacity and generating risky social dislocation (Holmes, 1985: 156–8).

By 1981 unemployment was becoming the dominant political issue as public concern about its negative social and economic effects increased (Moon and Richardson, 1985: 56). The outbreak of rioting across British cities during the spring and summer of 1981, as simmering tension between young people and the police erupted into open confrontation in the streets, gave impetus to concerns about youth unemployment stoking social disorder (Solomos, 1985; Waddington and King, 2009: 247; Marren, 2016). Although ministers dismissed connections between the riots and the level of unemployment, they were aware that newspaper polling indicated burgeoning youth unemployment was widely perceived by the public to be a contributing factor (THCR 2/11/9/32 f119). Similarly, the results of 'A national survey of the political mood' conducted in May 1983 recorded that 51 per cent of respondents agreed with the statement that 'The current level of unemployment is largely due to the present Conservative Government's policies' (THCR 2/11/9/37 f4). The British Social Attitudes Survey 1983 also recorded that 69 per cent of respondents regarded unemployment as their policy priority, compared with 27 per cent who identified inflation as the priority (Edgell and Duke, 1991: 79).

Conscious of the risk unemployment poses to the power of organised labour and with its parliamentary wing out of Government the trade unions moved to channel extra-parliamentary opposition. A 'People's March for Jobs' was supported by the TUC in 1981 (a second occurred in 1983)[1] and a network of Unemployed Workers Centres expanded, linking the unions with the broader claimant movement and becoming nodes of advice for unemployed people and more or less miltant opposition to government policy. Unions, such as the Transport and General Workers Union (TGWGU), also made some effort to organise and unionise participants in state-run employment programmes for unemployed people (Marren, 2016; Bagguley, 1991; Griffin, 2023a; 2023b). The scale of unemployment, social disorder, public concern and activity from organised labour and claimants meant unemployment was sustained as a political problem and threat to government stability, and this militated against radical reconfiguration of social security and employment services in the short term.

Work incentives and the sundering of solidarity

Attentive to how the collective strength of labour could hamper employers in determining the price of labour power, a key concern of the New Right was that out-of-work social security benefits inflated the price a claimant wanted for selling their labour power (that is, their 'reservation wage'). Consequently, incentives to take or retain paid work had eroded, meaning the supply of labour and its potential (downward) effect on wage bargaining of employees was lower than it might otherwise be (Joseph, 1980: 11; Hansard, 1980a: cc1457–63). The Conservative Government's initial package of working-age benefit reforms set out in the Social Security Act 1980 and the Social Security (No. 2) Act 1980 were intended to begin to address these issues. The preceding Labour Government's decision to raise benefit payments in line with earnings or prices, whichever was the greater, was changed to uprating with price inflation only. The new indexing created a ratcheting effect, whereby income differentials would gradually increase, assuming wage growth outpaced the rise in prices. Instead of binding claimants into the gradual rising prosperity of society (that is, a One Nation approach), benefit retrenchment would progressively deepen the material division between benefit claimants and people in paid work (Mesher, 1981: 122–3; Atkinson, 1990: 584; Brown, 1990: 51).

The Earnings-Related Supplement (ERS) for unemployment and sickness benefits was also abolished, with no new claims from January 1982 (Hansard, 1980c: col 1660). Abolishing the ERS struck at attempts by preceding governments to mitigate the drop in income experienced by new claimants and provide time for people to seek a better job match, as the state sought to promote the efficient allocation of skilled labour (Hansard, 1980a; Mesher, 1981: 124; Brown, 1990: 45). Making unemployment benefit less protective of previous status was commensurate with discouraging claims, expediting benefit exit and crafting divisions between workers and claimants, and marked a first step in residualisation of out-of-work support. It signalled a shift away from a strategy of intensive labour utilisation, in which the state apparatus sought to protect core workers and mitigate risk of labour shortages and skills gaps contributing to inflationary pressure that hampered economic expansion. The reorientation of the state apparatus was now towards enabling the market to price labour 'freely' and instituting a repressive class politics geared towards curtailing claimant autonomy and disciplining labour more broadly.

The 1980 Social Security (No. 2) Act, for example, restricted the conditions under which workers taking part in industrial action could claim any income assistance through the social security system. Conservative politicians had long objected to the payment of benefits to workers involved in industrial action and while workers themselves were not generally entitled to receive means-tested benefits except in cases of urgent need,[2] they were entitled to claim Supplementary Benefit (SB) for 'dependants' (Lasko, 1975; Booth and Smith, 1985). In the period between January and November 1980, income assistance had been claimed on behalf of just over 2,000 individual workers on strike and about 53,500 families of striking workers (Hansard, 1981a). That state support might partly substitute for wages and strike pay was perceived to weaken the leverage of employers and moderate trade union leaders, creating an environment conducive to the trade union militancy deemed to be contributing to Britain's relative economic decline (Conservative Party, 1979; Hansard, 1980a: cc1457–63; Thatcher, 1995: 55).

In practice, many workers could not claim as a working partner, or savings affected eligibility and no claim was permissible until a period passed equal to the duration for which a normal wage was expected to last, ruling out claims for shorter actions (Lasko, 1975; Booth and Smith, 1985: 367). In 1975–77, around one quarter of all strikers were estimated to have been eligible to claim SB, while during the year 1976–77 about nine in ten strikes had been settled within three weeks (PREM 19–121 f88).[3] On its own this reform might be regarded as somewhat symbolic. Yet, it is reasonable to note that past length of industrial disputes and patterns of take-up were no guide to future duration, not least when the Government was anticipating (potentially drawn out) confrontations with organised labour (Dorey, 2013;

Gallas, 2016: 99–113).[4] A pre-emptive curtailment of material support to workers engaged in industrial action weakened the resources available to workers and helped shift power to the state and employers.

The remaking of the technical and political class composition of labour was also facilitated by channelling older workers (see later) and claimants out of the floating segment of the labour reserve of unemployed claimants and into the surplus population of 'inactive' claimants. The higher rate of SB that was paid to long-term non-employed claimants was not available to unemployed claimants, but a partial exception to this was introduced in 1981. Claimants aged 60 and over were permitted in the years prior to receiving the basic state pension to move to the long-term rate of SB after 12 months, provided they ceased registering as unemployed, and after 1983 became eligible to claim the long-term SB rate immediately (Brown, 1990: 75; Wells, 2001: 248).

Irrespective of whether or not these measures were a good use of available labour power there was a complementarity here between the short-term class politics and medium-term economic order politics of the New Right. First, supporting the exit of older unemployed workers had the attraction of depressing the politically sensitive headline figure of registered unemployed at a moment when unemployment remained elevated and ministers remained concerned about the electoral consequences. Second, it pacified and expedited removal of (exhausted) workers acculturated to the power relations, social expectations and working forms of industrial society, helping to remake the the class composition of labour for the form of post-industrial labour market envisaged.

Ministers had yet to embrace the extensive labour utilisation strategy that would be developed in the 1990s to reach into, and activate, portions of the surplus population. At this moment they were willing in fact to reduce the ability of the state to chivvy unemployed claimants to seek paid work. At the time, to establish availability for work unemployed claimants were required to attend a jobcentre and sign the unemployment register. Signing on at the Unemployment Benefit Office (UBO) was also a condition of benefit receipt and, if receiving SB, a claimant would also have dealings with the Social Security Office (SSO). The jobcentres and UBO were part of the Department for Employment (DE) while the SSO was under the Department for Health and Social Security (DHSS) (Price, 2000; PREM 19–1841 f116). The requirement to register at the jobcentre as a condition of benefit receipt was brought to an end in 1982, with the decision originating in a review commissioned into the efficiency and effectiveness of the civil service (Price, 2000). Concluding that registration had little use as a benefit control measure, its abolition sought to rationalise the governance of unemployment, delivering a reduction in state employee headcount (Price, 2000: 203–12; PREM19–1841 f116).

The diminishment of checks did not mean the abandonment of benefit policing, however, as indicated in the DE introduction of Regional Benefit Investigation Teams (RBITS), though the number of RBITS staff was relatively modest (93 in 1984) (Hansard, 1984a). The RBITS were modelled on the Specialist Claims Control teams of the DHSS, which were geared towards seeking out evidence of fraudulent claims. The effectiveness of the 'anti-fraud' teams was, at times, hampered by sympathetic local staff, willing to share information with claimant organisations, who then used this to take direct action to disrupt benefit-policing activity (Foxton, 1982; Bell, 1984; Aufheben, 1998; Marsland, 2018: 90).[5] One claimant union member, active at the time, recalled:

> 'through our contact, it was leaked that this special fraud squad were operating and we were able to go out and work out who the snoopers were, hanging around at bus stops and so on outside the benefit office … I don't know what they thought they were doing but we worked out who they were and confronted them and photographed them and stuff like that. Yeah, that was a particularly successful action. Yeah, it's coming back to me, there used to be these special dole snooper squads that were like hit squads that went round different unemployment benefit offices and did a kind of blitz on people. And we had opposition to this particular squad when they came to town'. (Malcolm, Lothian Claimants Union)

While policing benefit access and receipt remained an issue of concern, the Government was primarily preoccupied with managing the destabilising effects of rapid de-industrialisation and this led to an expansion of the types of pacificatory employment programmes pioneered by their Labour predecessors, along with some new liberal innovations commensurate with the New Right's particular class and economic order politics.

Continuity pacification: expanding Special Employment Measures

With unemployment rising, ministers sought to 'educate' the public that long-term employment growth would only come about through controlling inflation and public spending, so as to create an environment conducive for investment (Hansard, 1980b: col 1758; 1981b).

> At the last election we analysed the greatest single cause of unemployment as being the rate of inflation. We have attacked the rate of inflation directly and have halved the rate of increase. We are well on course to cut the root that is the cause of unemployment, by

bringing down the rate of inflation. (Michael Allison MP, Minister of State, Hansard, 1981b: col 148)

As a memorandum by the Central Policy Review Staff (CPRS) in October 1980 to the Ministerial Committee on Economic Strategy (E Committee) reminded ministers, the shake out of industry and attendant rising unemployment were the logical consequence of the Government's macroeconomic policy. Restoration of a competitive market order necessitated a period of extensive disruption that had to be endured (Wiggan and Grover, 2022: 721). Though ministers were advised to remain alert to the political challenges and the risk of collateral damage this posed to viable parts of the nation's industry and labour force (CAB 134/4446; CAB 134/4442-a). Similarly, the CPRS, in a memo to the Prime Minister, suggested that lack of wage work among young people in particular was a potential threat to future growth prospects, and that additional investment in youth-training initiatives could foster a more pliable labour force (CAB 134–4446).

Strikingly, upon taking office the new Conservative Government's 1979 budget had sought reductions in spending on Special Employment Measures (SEMs) (Hansard, 1979: col 247), as part of its broader economic strategy (PREM19/293 f17). Curtailing the state-resourced and corporatist-delivered activity of SEMs was, after all, consistent with the liberal market preferences of ministers to expose labour to the competitive pressure of the market, and their broad understanding of how to improve the conditions for accumulation in the medium term. Yet, as noted, this risked excessive destruction of productive capacity and posed challenges to securing the legitimacy of the new Government and social cohesion that risked the New Right's project running aground. Managing the tensions embedded within the articulation of the New Right's economic order and class politics was a pressing issue. A briefing note to the Prime Minister in the summer of 1981, for example, implied that recent riots in the Toxteth area of Liverpool were an added reason to take swift policy action in the areas of employment (PREM 19–525 f30). Resources for SEMs were soon increased to facilitate mass expansion and development of SEMs with the Manpower Services Commission (MSC) retaining a central role in their governance (Ainley and Corney, 1990: 54).

The renewed commitment to SEMs was accompanied, however, by the New Right taking senior positions in the pinnacle of the state labour commodification apparatus. Norman Tebbit MP taking up the post of Secretary of State for Employment, and David Young[6] – formerly advisor to Keith Joseph at the Department of Industry – being appointed as chair of the MSC (Tebbit, 1989: 232; Ainley and Corney, 1990). The New Right's pro-liberal market preferences and willingness to adopt a robust approach in dealings with organised labour (Thatcher, 1995: 150–2) would now be represented in the DE/MSC, eliminating the possibility of the DE acting as ally to labour within the upper reaches of the state. As with their emergence during the 1970s, the SEMs were seemingly re-embraced as a means to address problems in the field of class politics – in this case the threat that social unrest and public disquiet posed to the stability of the Government and leadership of the New Right within it. That SEMs could also contribute to the protection and preparation of labour power for an anticipated economic upturn and transformed labour market was a secondary matter. In short, the seeming incompatibility between the SEMs/MSC and a liberal market and anti-corporatist economic order politics was balanced against the desire to stabilise the political environment upended by the more confrontational class politics of the Government (PAC, 1983: 16; Moon and Richardson, 1985: 59; Tebbit, 1989: 242; CAB/134/4442-b; Wiggan and Grover, 2022: 723). Though as subsequently detailed, the gradual reconfiguration of SEMs under the Conservatives also weakened the institutional supports for claimant and worker autonomy, and reproduction of the technical and political class composition of industrial labour.

Regulating the flow and stock of (un)employed labour

The last chapter laid out how the 1974–79 Labour Government had used job retention subsidies to reduce outflow from the labour force into the labour reserve, and foster trade union acquiescence to the Social Contract. From the perspective of the New Right, state intervention to shield business experiencing lower demand distorted the operation of market signals regarding business competitiveness and the quality and price of labour power. Yet, upon taking office the Conservative Government maintained such subsidies in the form of the Temporary Short-Time Working Compensation Scheme (TSTWCS). Introduced in April 1979, the TSTWCS was to last until March 1984 (Webb, 2003: 97). Where an employer was planning to make ten or more staff redundant, they could apply to the TSTWCS to support a redistribution of working time across their labour force to avoid redundancies. The state would subsidise employers placing affected workers on short time (for example, a three-day week) who would then receive 50–75 per cent of normal wages for their non-working days. The duration for which an employer could claim the TSTWCS subsidy was initially 12 months, but as the state sought to contain spending and limit market distortion, this was amended so that over the course of its existence the maximum duration varied between six and nine months (Metcalf, 1982: 57; Richards, 1987: 111; Wiggan and Grover, 2022: 722).

The majority of claims submitted were typically by large employers, with support concentrated in the manufacturing sector (Richards, 1987: 116), and in early 1981 almost one million workers were supported in short-time working by the TSTWCS, reflecting the high level of demand in

1980–82 (Hansard, 1985f: col 77w; Wiggan and Grover, 2022: 722). The considerable intervention that the TSTWCS represented points to how policy continuity addressed tensions within the class and economic order politics of the Government. As previously noted, a commitment to high interest rates, reductions in the money supply and curtailment of public spending (Holmes, 1985: 53–5) as essential to improvement in the conditions for accumulation in the medium term came up against ministers' fear that unemployment undermined public support and risked electoral disaster (Tomlinson, 2017: Ch 6). The TSTWCS was a readily available means to moderate the pace and scale of job destruction, when the threat to New Right dominance was greatest. The TSTWCS was brought to a close in 1984 with the Government's politico-economic strategy stabilising, as indicated by the parliamentary majority of 144 that the Conservatives secured at the 1983 General Election and the decline in the annual retail price index rate of inflation from 18 per cent in 1980 to 5 per cent in 1984 (ONS, 2020; Wiggan and Grover, 2022: 722).

The TSTWCS by its nature offered no assistance to people who were already unemployed. To address the politically sensitive issue of youth unemployment the Job Release Scheme (JRS), Job Splitting Scheme (JSS) and the Young Workers Scheme (YWS) provided subsidies to integrate young people into employment. The JRS was a continuation of the programme introduced in 1977 to support older workers to exit the labour market and be replaced by a young unemployed person. An initial drive to save money by raising the eligibility age to 64 (Hansard, 1980b: col 1755), after it had been lowered to 62 prior to the General Election in 1979 was reversed, and in 1983 a part-time version of the JRS was introduced to support partial withdrawal from the labour market (Gregg, 1990: Webb, 2003: 96). The numbers participating in the JRS increased from around 14,500 in 1977–78 to 45,000 in 1983–84, with a commensurate rise in programme expenditure (Hansard, 1985f: col 77–8; Lindley, 1987: 6–7).

In July 1982 the JSS was announced which would pay a grant to employers for each full-time job they agreed to reorganise into two part-time positions and to which at least one unemployed benefit claimant, or employee facing redundancy, would be recruited to (Hansard, 1982a: col 950; Hansard, 1982b: col 372). The take-up of the JSS was limited and the sums expended relative to other SEMs expenditure was low (Hansard, 1985f; Turner et al, 1987: xxvii), arguably indicating how gendered segmentation of the labour market, in which part-time work was dominated by women, but unemployed claimants were predominantly men (see Chapter 3), also affected operation of SEM.

Whereas the TSTWCS/JRS/JSS bore the hallmarks of the social democratic-corporatist state predilection for protective developmental interventions, the YWS expressed a market-liberal approach to unemployment. In 1981 the Prime Minister's economic advisor Alan Walters had questioned the package of SEMs proposed by the then Secretary of State for Employment, Jim Prior MP, as costly and assuming a fixed number of jobs to be distributed, rather than concerned with how to increase vacancies for young people. Following the rise in the school-leaving age in the 1970s, policy makers had identified a compression in the wage differential between young and older workers as a problem (PAC, 1983: 19). With young people able to access SB the perception was of the state underwriting a reservation wage higher than it would otherwise be (CAB 134/4446). For the New Right long-term reductions in unemployment depended on removing labour market 'rigidities' and lowering the reservation wage of young people and long-term unemployed people (Walters, 1986: 183; PREM 19–293 f7; THCR 1/14/4 (153)). For Walters a cost-effective way to progress this approach was to incentivise employers to change their hiring practice through a targeted youth-wage subsidy that would reduce the real wages paid to young people (PREM 19–525-f5).

Introduced in 1982, the YWS resembled the Walters' target group of under-18s and goal of lowering the price of youth labour power to widen pay differentials among the labour force according to age. A subsidy (for up to 12 months) towards the pay of a new employee could be claimed provided the recruit was aged under 18. In keeping with the aim of reducing the price of labour, the level of subsidy varied with level of pay so that it was higher at a lower level of pay and ceased above a given amount per week (Metcalf, 1982: 26; Moon, 1983: 320). At its peak, the YWS was subsidising over 100,000 young people in 1982–83, though some of this was a deadweight, as employers would have hired the young person irrespective of the subsidy (PAC, 1983: 20; see also Lindley, 1987: 19). Irrespective of value for money however, the YWS was commensurate with a class politics geared towards reorganisation of the labour force. It implicitly promoted the switching out of older, expensive workers for new labour market entrants and if successful in broadening competition for jobs would potentially weaken the bargaining position of workers and their unions, facilitating a broader adjustment in wage levels (PREM 19–525-f5: 8). The YWS was in this regard an early indication of a pro-market state strategy for reworking the operation of the state labour commodification apparatus. Lowering wages for young people implied that out-of-work benefits should fall, eligibility narrow and work-related conditions of entitlement be tightened relative to older groups. In this the YWS aligned with a gradual shift to an extraction strategy of underdevelopment, in which devaluing of labour power intersected age as a category entitlement, to deepen divisions within the labour force and labour reserve and differentially apply disciplinary pressure upon claimants.

Policy continuity: the unemployed 'waged' worker

Whereas the YWS signalled the emergence of a new policy response to unemployment, there remained much continuity with the type of job creation and training programmes of the previous Labour administration. Upon taking office the Conservatives initially curtailed spending on the Special Temporary Employment Programme (STEP) and concentrated placements in areas of high unemployment, focused on 19–24-year-olds unemployed for six months plus, and those aged 25 plus and unemployed 12 months or more (Hansard, 1980b: col 1755; Taylor, 1982: 16). Faced with a rising number of unemployed working-age adults at risk of sinking into the surplus population the then Employment Secretary, Jim Prior MP, pressed colleagues for a scaled-up replacement for STEP (CAB 134/ 4446). This came in 1981 in the form of the Community Enterprise Programme (CEP), which operated nationwide with sponsors from public, private and third-sector organisations and support for 30,000 placements, expanding on provision available through the STEP (Hansard, 1981c; MSC 1981a: 34; 1981b: 30). CEP participants were placed within work intended to be of benefit to the community at full-time hours and paid a wage equivalent to the rate for similar local work (Metcalf, 1982: 21; Moon, 1983: 309).

The CEP was superseded in late 1982 by the Community Programme (CP), which again paid participants a wage to (voluntarily) work on a project of benefit to the community, sponsored by a public, private or third-sector organisation (MSC, 1983: 186). The CP, though, marked a pivot to massive expansion of subsidising social economy work as a means to occupy unemployed claimants. The number of CP places announced by Geoffrey Howe MP, the then Chancellor of the Exchequer in 1982, was 130,000 (Hansard, 1982a), but by the middle of the decade this had increased to over 200,000 (Gregg, 1990; Jones, 1996: 142). Correspondingly, expenditure increased from just over £500 million in 1983–84 to over £1 billion in 1987–88 (Disney et al, 1992: 155).

Ministers were less than enthused with state-subsidised social economy work, especially at union-linked wage rates. The CPRS, advisors within the No. 10 Policy Unit and the Chancellor, Geoffrey Howe, all favoured delinking pay to participants from the going rate, or only paying benefits plus a small additional top-up to participants (PREM 19–524 f52; PREM 19–526 f113; PREM 19–525 f30). The institutional architecture of the state, however, remained social democratic-corporatist. To implement the CP on the scale envisaged meant willing engagement from local authorities and voluntary and community organisations, and passive support of trade unions whose objections, the MSC noted (MSC, 1981b: 30), could obstruct the sourcing and organisation of placements. The Government's preference to withdraw eligibility of 16–17-year-olds for SB in 1982, for example, was delayed by the fear that social partners would withdraw the cooperation that ministers required to roll out their new Youth Training Scheme (YTS) (see later) as a replacement for the YOP, with negative financial implications for the Treasury and management of youth unemployment (PREM 19–0837 f346; Finn, 1987: 156–8). With respect to the CP, the tension between social partners' support for keeping a wage equivalent to local rates and ministers' goal of an 'affordable' expansion of placements was resolved by placing a limit on the average weekly wage payable in a sponsored project (initially £60), following a suggestion from David Blunkett, then a Labour councillor in Sheffield, to David Young at the MSC (Price, 2000: 225).

While there was some opposition by trade unions and local authorities to the CP this was limited. There was a recognition that action to obstruct placements in one locality risked losing resources to areas amenable to placements (Paine, 1983: 8). More broadly, the TUC conceded ground on full-time waged work to protect the influence of organised labour within the state through tripartite structures of the MSC (Finn, 1987: 151).

The wage ceiling, though, meant that the CP supported part-time placements, which affected the composition of programme participants, as the part-time wage compared unfavourably with social security support for an unemployed person with children. A reluctance to regularly raise the pay ceiling also meant the differential grew over time and so it is perhaps not surprising that a greater proportion of CP participants were younger people (MSC, 1983: 184; Disney et al, 1992: 165). A survey of CP participants in 1985 recorded that, whereas 37 per cent of the targeted client group of long-term unemployed were aged 18–24, this age group accounted for 62 per cent of CP participants. Conversely, one quarter of CP participants were aged 25–44, but made up over one third of the target group for the programme, while people aged 45 plus made up almost 30 per cent of the CP target group but only 14 per cent of participants (Normington et al, 1986: 27–8).

Entry to the CP involved a process of selection by local sponsors and the result was to channel into the CP those deemed among the employable strata of long-term unemployed people. Disney et al (1992), drawing on survey data of participants noted that the proportion of surveyed CP participants holding academic and technical qualifications was also double the proportion among the broader long-term unemployed population. In terms of outcomes, the survey data suggested around one third of all CP participants were engaged in employment eight months after leaving the programme, while half had returned to unemployment (Disney et al, 1992: 168–9). Interestingly, Normington et al (1986: 37) suggested that immediate employment entry was higher among women CP participants than men, perhaps due to the propensity for women to enter part-time jobs, indicating the complex intersection between programme structures and gendered labour markets. The effective limit on working hours for CP participants also aligned with ministers' broader attempts to encourage part-time work and a flexible workforce (for example, through the JSS) (Hansard, 1982a). So, while there was a concern that the job-creation programmes might weaken the downward pressure unemployment brought to bear upon wages (PAC, 1983: 14), the CP aligned with a remaking of the technical class composition of labour and the broader promotion of labour market flexibility and the repricing of labour power.

Young people and the training turn

The YOP grew from 162,000 participants in 1978–79 to 553,000 participants in 1981–82, before giving way in 1983–84 to the new YTS (PAC, 1983: 23; Hansard, 1985f: cols 76–7). The introduction of the latter followed perceptions, that with its expansion, the YOP was failing to produce young people with the technical proficiency, social attitudes and wage expectations suited to the new labour market. The position of the TUC of cooperating with and supporting the YOP was also coming under pressure from its members, as the YOP came increasingly to be seen as a source of cheap labour, undercutting older workers. Support grew for a more developed, comprehensive training intervention that would combine work placements with on-the-job and off-the-job training (Finn, 1987: 150–1).

The YTS was the result and was introduced as a voluntary programme,[7] with participants paid a training allowance initially set at a level comparable with the allowance for the YOP (Freedland, 1983: 224). All school leavers aged 16, unemployed people aged 17 and disabled people aged up to 21 were offered a 12-month (subsequently two years from 1986) work-based placement with at least three months spent in training outside the workplace. Provision was organised into three strands: Mode A, Mode B1 and Mode B2.[8] The Mode A provision involved placement with a private or public sector employer. The Mode B1 pathway involved placements by public and voluntary sector organisations that were often continuations of community work and training options from the YOP. Mode B2 was targeted at participants the MSC identified as requiring additional support, such as young disabled people (NAO, 1985: 6). Mode A attracted a lower level of public funding as employers were expected to benefit from the output generated by their YTS participants, while the Mode B strands attracted higher funding reflecting their engagement of participants deemed less employable (NAO, 1985: 14; Finn, 1987: 145).

The space for the young person to gain basic skills was intended to improve their overall ability to compete for a variety of jobs within the labour market. For policy makers, the YWS and YTS were complementary interventions. The YWS would open up new demand among employers for young people's labour power by lowering wages, while the YTS would act as a conveyor belt of employable young people ready to transition from the training segment of the labour market to meet the anticipated rise in demand for youth labour (Public Accounts Committee, 1983: 40; DE, 1984: 9), while socialising employer recruitment costs.

Between 1983 and 1984 over 370,000 young people entered the YTS, with around two thirds engaged in Mode A, a quarter in Mode B1 and the remainder in Mode B2 (NAO, 1985: 8). Survey data of YTS providers for June–August 1984 showed two fifths of placements were in the 'retail, hotel and catering and repair of consumer goods' sectors of the economy, with over one fifth located in the 'other service sector' and one fifth located in 'manufacturing and engineering sectors' (Hansard, 1987b: col 297).[9] In terms of occupation, a higher proportion of placements in Mode A were found in administration and clerical occupations and in the personal services and sales occupations, which accounted for 41 per cent of Mode A placements, compared with 16 per cent for Mode B1, and 17 per cent of Mode B2 placements (NAO, 1985: 9). It would be a mistake to conclude the YTS offered few prospects and simply warehoused participants, as the different strands of YTS provision worked to channel young people to more/less desirable positions in the labour market. Raffe (1987: 17–19), for example, suggested the YTS involved four types of provision – Sponsorship, Credentialism, Contest, and Detached – and attendant routes into the labour market. The first referred to where a strong likelihood of progression into employment accompanied job- and sector-specific training with a well-established sponsoring employer. The 'Credentialist' path involved equipping participants with the ability to compete for jobs through certified training that signalled value to employers in particular local labour markets. The 'Contest' type of placement relied on soft-skills development and access to employer information networks with inside knowledge of vacancies – the YTS itself becoming a window in which participants displayed their abilities and value to potential employer(s), but with no guarantee of a job. The 'Detached' category referred to the journey and destination of participants identified as the least qualified and/or motivated, and directed to community work, training workshops or placements provided by employers as part of their contribution to the commonweal.

The young people subjectively judged more employable tended to be directed to Mode A provision, while young people perceived to lack sufficient skills or motivation were directed to Mode B1 (Bradley, 1995: 38). It is not surprising, then, that given the relatively limited pathways into the core or secondary labour market and with participants perceived to have greater employment constraints, that Mode B1 placements were associated with weaker post-programme job outcomes than Mode A placements (Droy et al, 2019: 7). The YTS effectively served to corral, sort and selectively channel an engorged supply of new labour power to different labour market destinations, its operation contributing to the shaping of, and being shaped by, the changing technical class composition of labour and weak labour market of the time.

Concluding remarks

With the return to office of the Conservatives in 1979 we see the changing articulation of class and economic order politics with a deflationary monetary and fiscal policy moving to the fore as part of a broader market-liberal remaking of the economic order to improve medium-term prospects for accumulation (Lamont, 1981; Holmes, 1985; Thatcher, 1995). Conversely, the very same strategy generated a level of socio-economic disruption that undermined social cohesion and led senior ministers to fear the issue of unemployment might threaten their electoral prospects and foreclose the possibility of resubordinating labour. The inherited policy legacies, intense political and economic disruption of this period and the struggle for supremacy consequently manifested as a transitional orientation to labour market policy and governance (Table 5.1). Rather than an immediate pivot to an aggressive offensive step against labour a cautious Conservatism prevailed. The continuation of SEM associated with the preceding Labour governments indicating how New Right ministers were willing to adopt pacificatory interventions at odds with their professed liberal market convictions to shore up their position and buy time (Richardson and Moon, 1984: 29–31; Tomlinson, 2017; Wiggan and Grover, 2022).

A general hostility to corporatist arrangements was overcome by recognition that the capacity of the MSC and co-option of unions, charities and local authorities in the governance and provision of placements aided the Government's immediate concerns (that is, reluctant corporatism). Similarly, the focus on (male) unemployment and the core labour force was indicative of continuity in terms of an intensive labour utilisation approach

Table 5.1: The transitional-pacificatory labour market policy orientation

Class politics	Economic order
(Cautious) Conservativism	(Emergent) Market-liberal
Extraction strategy	**Accumulation strategy**
Pacificatory-underdevelopment	Intensive labour utilisation
Mode of leadership & domination	**State strategy**
Cautious two nation	Reluctant corporatism

Source: Author's creation informed by Gallas (2016: 64).

to accumulation, albeit one that was weakening, with deindustrialization and the dissolving of its attendant technical and political class composition of labour.

The more market-liberal-oriented social security and employment programme reforms, such as the YTS/YWS, sought to accelerate this transformation. Deepening age-related labour market divisions to undermine the cohesiveness of the labour force and power of organised labour in bargaining over wage setting being commensurate with a pivot to a two-nation approach to governing. Scope remained, however, for social partners to obstruct particular policy preferences and opposition to unemployment and-regressive benefit reforms meant ministers could not go as far as they wanted as quickly as they wanted. Compulsory participation in the YTS, for example, remained off the table (Finn, 1987).

Nevertheless, restrictions on entitlement to social security for striking workers, abolishment of the ERS and erosion of the value of out-of-work benefits were indicative of a concerted medium term strategy to weaken insurance-based benefits and the potential of social security to function as a redoubt from market pressure. As with the YWS and YTS, these were commensurate with a strategy of underdevelopment (Cleaver, 1977; Byrne, 2005: 48) in which eroding the protection and autonomy of claimants and workers provided the means to reimpose the authority of capital and state over the extraction of value. The second half of the 1980s was to open up space for a more thorough reconfiguration of social security and employment policy and governance though, as the balance of forces and political-economic context changed in favour of the Conservatives and capital in general.

6

The end of conciliation and concertation: dis-embedding labour: 1985–89

Introduction

From the mid-1980s, the terrain of class struggle and balance of power, while in flux, was moving in favour of capital, as the political class composition of industrial labour fractured. The defeat in 1985 of the year-long strike by the National Union of Mineworkers was conjoined with the Conservative Government tightening control over local government, which curtailed the ability of municipal socialist councillors to resist the centre or channel resources to pro-labour organisations (Gallas, 2016: 194–6). As the power of the industrial and political wings of organised labour was curtailed the Government pivoted away from the pacificatory labour market policy regime of the early 1980s and adopted a more offensive position. A concerted, albeit gradual, attempt commenced to modify, displace or convert the institutions, practices and expectations within social security and employment services that were associated with the social democratic-corporatist state.

To this end, a repressive extraction strategy moved to the fore, reflected in a strengthening of work-availability testing and a move away from waged social economy employment programmes to unwaged 'training' programmes and a tightening of the policing of the benefit claims of unemployed people. These were commensurate with a two-nation approach to governing which involved deepening divisions between those in and out of paid work and between segments of the non-employed population, implicitly contrasting a new individual entrepreneurialism with state dependency. O'Grady's (2022: 122–4) detailed account of parliamentary discourse during the late 1980s and early 1990s, for example, indicates Conservative discourse drew together what we might conceive of as a rational-technical and moral problematisation of unemployment. On the one hand the institutional configuration of social security was said to create financial disincentives to taking low-paid work, implying claimants were rational economic actors. On the other, the failure to take such work was implied to reflect a moral weakness and abdication of social obligations, with failure to take any job available unfair to other low paid workers (O'Grady, 2022: 124–6).

The desire for re-regulation of labour market policy and governance (as discussed later), also included the removal of the last vestige of social concertation and institutional resource for organised labour in the state apparatus with the abolition of the Manpower Services Commission (MSC). As the Government accelerated its clearing away of the social democratic-corporatist apparatus, a new enterprise state strategy moved into view, rooted in the promulgation of entrepreneurialism and labour market institutions that privileged relationships between state and employers while excluding labour (Coffield, 1990; Mitzen, 1994).

The emphasis on enterprise, entrepreneurialism and market forces was not simply a ideational preference, but a response addressed to the material problem of securing authority over the conditions under which labour was commodified and valued extracted. Institutional reconfiguration was a strategic manoeuvre to remove a pro-labour actor embedded within a subordinate arm of the state and create mechanisms through which greater pressure might be brought to bear against claimants and frontline (para-)state employees to comply with government policy. As ministers proceeded with reform, they continued to encounter collective and individual opposition within, and outwith the state, which frustrated their capacity to act and the pace of reform. Yet, obstruction also confirmed that re-regulation of labour market governance to secure greater coherence between social security, employment services and economic strategy and transform (class) power relations necessitated a reconstruction of the state apparatus. Policy developments were not pre-ordained, but contoured by the tempo and form of class struggle. Each successful reforming step taken by ministers during this period eroded the institutional resources labour could draw upon to cohere and sustain collective opposition to government strategy, contributing to the remaking of labour's technical and political class composition and a path-reinforcing policy dynamic of further benefit retrenchment, conditionality and pro-business market oriented reforms to labour market policy and governance.

Social security, work incentives and social divisions

In-work benefits and labour mobilisation

As Grover (2016a: 112) points out, the provision of benefit payments sufficient to meet the needs of unemployed and non-employed people, especially families with children, has been a perennial concern of state managers attuned to the perceived risk that this will discourage job seeking, acculturate people to a life outside of waged work and require higher levels of taxation. Disinvestment in social security to strengthen work incentives, however, risks undermining the reproduction of labour and destabilising the social order. During their first term in office, Conservative ministers had avoided transformative change to social security benefits, allowing the system to buffer the social order amid widespread economic disruption. Yet, they remained highly critical of what they deemed an overly complex, discretionary system that contributed to inefficient use of resources, discouraged job seeking and fostered 'dependence' on the state (Lister, 1991: 96; Drakeford and Davidson, 2013: 367).

Handily, this aligned with the Government's desire to contain public spending as part of a broader fiscal strategy to ease pressure on interest rates and foster investment by signalling to business that sudden tax rises would not be required in the future to pay for rising spending in the present (Bennett and Millar, 2009: 13). The medium-term accumulation strategy aligning with what is conceptualised here as an emergent extraction strategy of repressive underdevelopment.

The 'Fowler Review' of social security set out a process of rationalisation and reconfiguration as the means to improve work incentives and the efficient use of resources. At the core of reform for working-age claimants were changes to the in-work benefit – Family Income Supplement (FIS) and the means-tested out-of-work social assistance payment – Supplementary Benefit (SB) (Secretary of State for Social Services, 1985a: 1–2; Fowler, 1991: 212). By 1985 the numbers claiming FIS had risen to around 200,000 (Dilnot and McCrae, 1999: 2) and the Government's *Reform of Social Security* Green Paper[1] identified that the proportion of working-age families with children in the bottom fifth of income distribution had increased in the decade to 1982 (Secretary of State for Social Services, 1985a: 13).

Ministers regarded FIS as a poor instrument for encouraging low-wage work, however, as rising income could be offset by withdrawal in support provided by FIS and other benefits when taken together with tax and National Insurance contributions (Hoynes and Blundell, 2001: 9). The payment of FIS to the primary carer in a couple family was, assuming the 'breadwinner' model, also misaligned with minsters' anti-inflation strategy. The replacement for FIS – Family Credit (FC) – was originally intended to address this issue by directing income through wages (Secretary of State for Social Services, 1985a: 29), making total income more visible and thereby reducing worker incentive to push for inflationary pay rises to secure a 'family wage' (Grover, 2016a: 122).

The gendered segmentation of the labour market and social reproduction would be refracted through FC to buffer (male) wage moderation. In effect, improvement in support for social reproduction amongst low income working families was entwined with managing (down) the price of labour power, though FC was in the end paid to the main carer rather than via the wage packet (Grover, 2016a). The FC payment was calculated on the basis of net rather than gross income in order to mitigate the problem that a wage rise could be completely cancelled out by a reduction in FIS payment.

Also, in contrast to the 30-hour eligibility rule in FIS for working–couple families with children, this was reduced to 24 hours per week in FC for working–couple and lone-parent families with children (Secretary of State for Social Services, 1985b: 49; Hoynes and Blundell, 2001).

The introduction of FC helped undergird participation in low-wage employment (Bryson and Marsh, 1996: 56–61) and remained, Grover (2016a: 122–4) suggests, compatible with the Conservative Party's preference for a 'traditional' gendered division of labour within couple families. The structure of FC militated against dual working as the earnings of the second earner would be eroded by reductions in FC as family income rose, and it is notable that a majority of FC couple families in the 1990s remained sole-earner families (Bryson and Marsh, 1996: 64). Given second earners at the time were more likely to be women, the FC worked in this way to position partnered non-employed women as a latent surplus population, which was commensurate with a continued ministerial focus on claimant unemployment at the time. However, FC also marked a move towards improving incentives for non-employed lone parents to move into paid work at below full-time hours, priming employers to create more atypical employment opportunities. The transition from FIS to FC is understood here as one component of a proto-extensive labour utilisation accumulation strategy in which the state remained pre-occupied with the 'traditional' problem of (male) unemployment, but was beginning to alter income-assistance mechanisms to channel a greater portion of the latent surplus population into the labour market in support of flexibilisation and wage repression (Grover and Stewart, 2002; Koch, 2006).

Out-of-work benefits, rationalisation and the reassertion of state control

Reform of SB was tied up with a desire to prune the plethora of additional payments that could be claimed to meet costs, such as heating and laundry, and irregular one-off single payments to assist individuals experiencing exceptional needs. Three fifths of all claimants of SB in 1986 were in receipt of some form of additional payment (Dilnot and Webb, 1988: 34) and by 1985 expenditure on single payments equated to 5 per cent of total spending on SB, compared with less than 1 per cent of total spending on SB in 1968 (Huby and Dix, 1992: 1). From the perspective of state managers, rising demand was exacerbating an already complex system that was beset by wrangling over discretionary assistance (Hansard, 1985b).[2] The growth of claimant unions (CUs) and welfare rights organisations had, for example, helped claimants navigate social security and access 'discretionary' provision, enhancing the protection and decommodifying potential of out-of-work benefits (Alcock, 1990: 97–8; Marsland, 2018: 92–3), and buffering claimant autonomy, something which the state was keen to curtail.

Here we see the complex interaction of class and economic order politics. The rising expenditure on SB claimants (Secretary of State for Social Services, 1985b: 13) being partly a consequence of higher unemployment, which was deemed the corollary of lowering inflation and allowing market pressure to shake out industry to restore competitiveness. The problem was that extended decommodification of claimants risked eroding motivation to seek waged work, while the inadequacy of SB, which helped maintain differentials between benefits and wages and contain public spending, raised demand for discretionary support amongst low income families (Secretary of State for Social Services, 1985b: 12; Grover, 2011: 125). As Grover (2011: 140) points out, this provision of additional support meant the gap between the income of non-employed working-age claimants and low-waged families narrowed, eroding the return on paid work (see also Secretary of State for Social Services, 1985b: 22). The autonomy-enhancing expansion of access to entitlements in this way worked against attempts to subordinate labour to market pressure, and added to the fiscal demands placed on the state. The structure of SB was consequently at odds with the broader pursuit of spending control; lowering the inflation rate and incentivising private sector investment (Grover, 2011: 146).

The response from ministers was to replace SB with a new means-tested benefit – Income Support (IS) – that did away with short- and long-term rates of support and additional payments in favour of a single payment determined by category of claimant (for example, unemployed, lone parent, ill or disabled person and presence of dependants, or not). In broad terms the reform favoured families with children over single unemployed and younger claimants (Bennett and Millar, 2009: 16), though who benefitted and lost out was complicated (Dilnot and Webb, 1988).

Accepting there remained a need for supplemental assistance as a safety net for those with exceptional and/or urgent need, ministers legislated for a cash limited loan-based system of discretionary payments – the Social Fund – in the 1986 Social Security Act, which went operational in 1988[3] (Grover, 2011). The structure of the Social Fund was intended to enable ministers to (re)gain control over discretionary support spending, the cash limited nature of the scheme encouraging frontline staff to closely manage demand and curtail bottom-up pressure for expansion (Alcock, 1985; CAB/129–219b: 276; CAB/129–219a: 83; Grover, 2011). A subsequent review of the expansive literature on the administration of the Social Fund for the National Audit Office suggested loan-based discretionary support tended to be offered to lone parents and unemployed applicants, while Community Care Grants were channelled to disabled people and older people (Buck and Smith, 2005: 4). The structure of the Social Fund worked to manage down and control demand in ways commensurate with the segmentation and stratification of the labour reserve and surplus population, and drive to widen the income differential between waged work and out-of-work benefits (Grover, 2008: 482).

In keeping with a broader class politics of labour subordination the Government also took a step to deepen age-related divisions by introducing a lower rate of benefit for unemployed people aged under 25 in 1986 and largely removing entitlement to out-of-work benefits for young people aged 16 and 17 years old in 1988. The reform was enacted as part of a drive to control spending and channel school leavers through the YTS, strengthening the state's ability to inculcate pro-job-seeking attitudes and behaviour appropriate to the work environment (Harris, 1988: 202–6; Alcock, 1990: 91; Brown, 1990: 168–71). The backbench Conservative MP, Ralph Howells, for example welcomed differential treatment of young people on the basis that the availability of out-of-work benefits, by providing an alternative source of support, had discouraged employment and weakened the disciplinary function of the family (Hansard, 1985a: col 214). As with the YWS/YTS, discussed in the preceding chapter, the logic of the reform worked towards encouraging a repricing of youth labour and wage discipline among older workers. The erosion in the value of benefits, and their removal from the youngest age group, point to how the erosion of claimant autonomy and underdevelopment of labour was moving centre stage as ministers sought to strengthen their authority and that of employers over the labour commodification process.

Benefit policing and the activation turn

The benefit-eligibility restrictions and lower payment rates for young people were paralleled by a move to greater policing of benefit claims amid concern that the earlier decision to end mandatory registration at the job centre, taken on grounds of efficiency and economy, had weakened administrative checks on eligibility and availability for employment, contributing to a rise in claimant numbers (Fowler, 1991; Young, 1991; Price, 2000: 239–41). A note by the Secretary of State for Employment to the Prime Minister in August 1985, stated that reviews of registered unemployed people in Crawley indicated three in ten were not actually seeking a job (PREM19–1839 f400). Moreover, as Price (2000) points out, the Rayner Review of 1981 had suggested 8 per cent of unemployment benefit claimants were working informally, and ministers cited findings of subsequent anti-fraud investigations in various locales as confirmation that fraudulent claims were a problem (Fowler, 1991: 297; Young, 1991; Price, 2000: 239; PREM 19–1839 f327; PREM 19–1839 f366). A memo to the Prime Minister in September 1985 noted that action by anti-fraud investigation teams had led one in four of the claimants questioned to withdraw their claim. The conclusion drawn was that an expansion of benefit-policing activity alone could reduce the number of unemployed claimants by 100,000 by the time of the next general election (PREM19–1839 f376). The more thorough and regular testing of availability for work consequently re-emerged in the form of the 'Restart' initiative, intended to engage and activate claimants deemed to have reconciled themselves to unemployment and weed out those working in the informal economy (Price, 2000; Reigler, 2018: 654–55).

Initially targeted at claimants unemployed for 12 months plus, Restart was launched as a pilot at the beginning of 1986 and involved inviting claimants to a Restart interview at the jobcentre with a claimant advisor to discuss employment goals, availability for work and employment support programmes (White and Lakey, 1992: 191). The results pointed to around one fifth of the claimants contacted subsequently leaving unemployment for various destinations, including government employment and training programmes, other working-age benefits due to sickness and/or impairment, new jobs and a portion who were deemed not entitled due to being unavailable for work (Disney et al, 1992: 203). Around 12 per cent of people contacted during the evaluation of the pilots were referred for a review of their claim on grounds such as non-attendance at interview, refusal of employment or suspected lack of availability for work. Ministers interpreted these results as vindication of their belief that many claimants were not engaged in job search and that undeclared working was taking place (Price, 2000: 244). The Restart interview process was rolled out nationally later that year and in 1987 expanded to include unemployed benefit claimants at six months. In 1988 repeat interviews were required every six months after the first interview to sustain the pressure on claimants to exit unemployment benefit (White and Lakey, 1992: 191).

At the Restart interview a claimant could avail of one of five employment or training options, including: placement in the Community Programme (CP) or Enterprise Allowance Scheme (EAS); participation in a week-long course to improve confidence and motivation; attendance at a Job Club to assist with job-search activity; or entitlement to the 'Job Start Allowance' if the claimant took a (low-paying) job (Price, 2000: 242). By the beginning of October 1986, the number of claimants invited to interview had reached 522,668, with the proportion of claimants who brought a claim to an end following invitation to a Restart interview being around 14 per cent of the total. Although it was unclear why these claims were closed, or subsequent destination of claimants (Hansard, 1986a), the outcome was in line with perceptions that introduction of Restart would dislodge fraudulent claimants from the system (PREM19–1839 f327).

Subsequent research in 1989–90, which compared Restart participating claimants with a control group of non-participants, found that on the cusp of the 1990s the Restart interview process was having the desired effect of activating job-search and training-scheme engagement. The participating group of claimants reported less time claiming unemployment benefits (about 5 per cent) and earlier exits from unemployment (White and Lakey, 1992: 158–9). However, many of the jobs lasted only a short time and were relatively low paid, in the end leading back to a new benefit claim (White and Lakey, 1992: 115–16). Disney et al (1992: 205) also suggested that while the employment effects were not clear, the Restart process was associated with a rise in exits from the claimant count among long-term unemployed people. In the light of these assessments, we might regard the Restart initiative as an early example of how active benefit policing fostered transitions between welfare, training and the secondary labour market.

Action to contain labour autonomy was also pursued through tightening up the 'availability for work' test in 1986 via the form (UB671) that claimants for unemployment-related benefits had to complete as a condition of benefit receipt. The then Paymaster General, Ken Clarke MP,[4] presented this as a relatively innocuous administrative reform while making clear the Government's position that a portion of unemployed people were, in practice, economically inactive and as such should not be in receipt of unemployment benefits. The form was ostensibly to help establish correct entitlement to unemployment benefit and induce non-'genuine' claimants to cease claiming, or facilitate disallowance of their entitlement (Hansard, 1986b: col 175). Ministers reported that areas piloting the UB671 showed 3–4 per cent of claimants had withdrawn their claim when tasked with completing the questionnaire and a further 2–3 per cent had their claim disallowed (Hansard, 1986c: col 423).

The changed process attracted opposition from Claimant Unions and some frontline state employees who sought to blunt its impact. A former worker in an Unemployment Benefit Office in Edinburgh[5] recounted how staff felt the form was intended to trip up 'genuine' claimants who did not understand the implications of the questions being asked. In response staff shared information with the local CU as to the 'correct' response claimants should provide. An action confirmed by members active in the local CU at the time, who noted the role played by some frontline workers.

'the day before they introduced the scheme, or it might have been forty eight hours, we got a copy of the handbook that the people that worked in the dole office got which had all the answers in. The answers which if you gave you were okay, and the answers if you gave them you were in trouble. And they were pretty tricky questions. They looked innocuous but they weren't, they were designed to trip you up. And what we did was we photocopied it, wrote in the answers, turned that into a printing plate and printed off all the answers. The day it was released in the Lothians we were at the dole office handing out saying "These are the answers. Give these answers and you'll be alright."' (Malcolm, Lothian Claimant Union)

'We had contacts inside the DHSS, as it was then, who were feeding us information. And we organised to give out information at the dole office, we'd be down the various dole offices in Edinburgh and Leith and out to the west and in Midlothian. Giving people the information saying "this is what the government's doing, this is why we think they're doing it, and this is the way you can resist." Things like don't go on your own, don't say this, give this sort of answer.' (Ben, Lothian Claimant Union).

While we should be careful not to overplay the level of pro-claimant action, nor ignore continuing tensions between claimant organisations and frontline staff over the application of benefit rules, similar solidarity and oppositional activity to heightened benefit policing occurred in various locales.

'So the Restart, we were very strong in campaigning against the whole Restart agenda. We did copies of the forms with a template of how to fill it in, we would give that to people if they came to our offices. Sometimes actually we'd just leaflet outside and say "here's how to fill out the form"'. (Derek, Tottenham Claimant Union)

Such activity did not go unnoticed, with one Conservative MP taking exception to the distribution of leaflets that were intended to obstruct the operation of more stringent benefit policing (Hansard, 1987a: col 801). The everyday local activity of claimant organisations assisted claimants in navigating the changing conditions attached to benefit receipt, but as Reigler (2018: 659) notes, the salience of unemployment as a matter of public concern was ebbing by the late 1980s as the labour market improved (see Chapter 3). State managers however, were nothing if not persistent in their drive to alter the settings of policy instruments that augmented labour autonomy. In 1988, the ineligibility period for unemployment benefit for people deemed voluntary unemployed was increased from 13 to 26 weeks, as was the penalty for refusing a 'reasonable' job offer (Knotz and Nelson, 2018: 18–19). These changes to social security, however, were only one half of an emergent proto-labour activation agenda. The other half was to be found in a move away from state-supported waged jobs in the social economy towards an expansion of training-oriented programmes for adult claimants. This followed government scepticism as to the utility and cost of subsidised job-creation programmes and the belief that employment creation depended on lowering labour costs, improvements in claimant job-search activity and development of skills relevant to the emerging post-industrial labour market (PREM19–1839 f366; Hansard, 1987e).

Dismantling the house that labour built

Transforming young unemployed claimants into trainees

The attempt to mould labour to fit the changing economic order and its cohering with a class politics geared towards degrading alternatives to open market employment was, as before, most evident in youth employment policy. The proportion of 16-year-old school leavers entering the YTS rose from 46 per cent in 1983–84 to 54 per cent in 1985–86 (Hansard, 1987b: col 295) and in 1986 school leavers aged 16 years old became eligible for a two-year YTS. The new two-year YTS provided for up to 20 weeks of training outside of the workplace with participants paid a training allowance (Ainley and Corney, 1990: 88). The scale of the change is indicated by the rise in YTS expenditure from £380 million in 1983–84 to over £800 million by 1987 (Hansard, 1987c: col 328). The Mode A and Mode B categorisation of placements was brought to an end with Government emphasising employer-led training placements, though public and voluntary sector-run placements were retained for participants judged less well equipped for private sector work (Hansard, 1985c; Finn, 1987: 172–3).

Although some YTS placements functioned similar to first-year apprenticeship routes into 'good' jobs, placements could be more akin to the temporary warehousing of otherwise unemployed young people in make work activity (Roberts and Parsell, 1992: 79–82). Not surprisingly, the best options were not equally available to all, with patterns of participant allocation contoured by gender and ethnicity as well as educational qualifications (Youthaid, 1985: 57–8; Wrench, 1986; Raffe, 1987; De Sousa, 1989: 23;). For example, using MSC administrative data to examine allocation of young White and young Black people in Manchester to different strands of the YTS, Freathy (1991: 90–2) identified how, despite similar educational attainment, a greater proportion of young Black people were directed to public and voluntary sector-led schemes compared with young White people. The latter were predominantly enrolled in the employer-led placements associated with better post-YTS employment outcomes (Finn, 1987: 186).

Shaping variation in YTS engagements, Freathy (1991) suggested, was a complex articulation of discriminatory practices, racialised socio-cultural expectations and how minority ethnic group populations had been incorporated into post-war labour markets and locales that were hit hard by de-industrialisation. For young women a greater portion of placements were located in service-oriented sectors rather than industrial work,[6] suggesting the YTS reproduced gendered patterns of labour market segmentation (Cockburn, 1987: 90; De Sousa, 1987: 69; Freathy, 1991: 92). However, as entry-level jobs within the manufacturing industries declined the risk of disrupted employment transitions post-YTS for young men rose (Youthaid,

1985: 66). In a sense the YTS was both reflecting and undermining the gendered patterning of labour market participation as it helped to constitute the transformation of the technical class composition of labour as the economy shifted towards services at the same time as its operation was being shaped by this.

The extension and operation of the YTS post-1985 involved the participation of hundreds of thousands of young people, but it was often perceived as a second-best option if a job could not be secured, or continuing into further education was of no interest (Raffe, 1987). This is indicated in the low take-up relative to the number of places available and high pre-completion drop-out which marked the first years of the YTS (NAO, 1985: 8–12; Youthaid, 1985). A survey of participants with a two-year entitlement to YTS recorded that among scheme leavers in the first year only 35 per cent left for a full-time job, with the majority citing absence of appropriate training, inadequate money or lack of satisfaction with the scheme's operation (Unemployment Unit, 1988a: 5). Mizen (1994) suggests this was indicative of an everyday form of resistance flowing from disaffection with the YTS, which continued to dog the operation of youth training into the 1990s (Mizen, 1994: 106).

Irrespective of young people's ambivalence towards the YTS its extension to all young people aged under 18 provided the warrant for eventual removal of entitlement to SB for 16- and 17-year-olds, as intimated by the Prime Minster in 1985:

> When the full YTS scheme is in place, I believe that it would be right to say to young people, 'You have the choice of a job, education or training.' Unemployment should not be an option. That can only be considered when that scheme is in place. (Hansard, 1985d: col 981)

Subsistence via social security would no longer be an option as the category of unemployed benefit claimant for the under-18 group was being eliminated (Secretary of State for Employment, Norman Fowler MP, Employment Committee, 1988: 6). It is perhaps not surprising that in addition to non-take-up and drop-out more collective opposition was also mounted against the YTS. Perhaps the most spectacular occurred in April 1985 when thousands of school pupils walked out of their classes to protest against the Government's intention to remove access to benefits and make YTS compulsory (Chorlton and Dunn, 1985; Finn, 1987: 182; Johns, 2015). In contrast, the TUC sought to improve the YTS experience, arguing the presence of member unions in the Area Management Boards of the MSC, which oversaw placement approval, acted as a check on placement quality at local level (Wrench, 1986; Ainley and Corney, 1990: 63 and 79). Where collective bargaining was in place, individual trade unions were at times able to improve upon the terms and conditions offered to YTS participants (Ryan, 1995: 17), and placements with large companies, or in the public sector, tended to offer greater scope for this. Union concerns about exploitation and job substitution arising from the YTS also manifested in a widespread, if uneven, pattern of objections to the scheme, albeit one which failed to coalesce around a clear, unified position and strategy of obstruction (Woodall, 1986: 434; Wrench, 1986: 7–9).

Ryan's (1995) review of TUC-affiliated trade unions' position with respect to cooperation with the YTS over the period 1983 to 1988, for example, showed that although only 12 per cent of TUC member unions outright opposed the YTS consistently over this five-year period, 46 per cent of TUC-affiliated unions had voted to oppose the YTS at their annual conference at least once during this period. In addition, one fifth of member unions endorsed a boycott of the scheme in support of this, or in the case of the Civil and Public Services Association civil service union in 1987, had supported industrial action (Ryan, 1995: 11–13). Though sustained industrial action was not forthcoming, the roll out of the YTS in the civil service was obstructed by union opposition and demands for improvements to the scheme (Harper, 1988; Ainley and Corney, 1990: 79), as recalled by an ex CPSA member.

'They tried to bring YTS into the civil service, and we took industrial action against it. We took industrial action in Liverpool, we took industrial action in Glasgow, we took industrial action in London. And we had a set of demands including that once the term of YTS was finished they were taken on full time, that they had to be paid the rate for the job. And we put these demands, we took strike action'. (Jeff ex CPSA member and UBO worker)

On occasion, operation of the scheme was also disrupted by industrial action, including at the MSC itself, where workers walked out in objection to the deployment of a YTS participant in their office on the grounds the person was not being paid a wage (The Times, 1988a). This was, of course, the point of making YTS the only option for young people and pitching the YTS training allowance below the wage a young person might command in employment, as ministers sought to lower the price of labour power – something many employers welcomed. A survey of 1,000 employers involved in YTS placements, recorded that among reasons given for involvement, almost one third cited, 'savings on labour costs', while just over four in ten identified 'screening for good employees', though a similar proportion also indicated 'they wanted to do something to help young people' (Unemployment Unit, 1988a: 4).

With the expansion of the YTS, the Young Workers Scheme scheme was transformed into the New Workers Scheme (NWS) with eligibility altered to focus on unemployed young people aged 18–20. The NWS lasted until 1988 and, under this, employers hiring workers aged 20 or under could receive a wage subsidy provided the level of wages was not above a given level (Webb, 2003: 98). That is, the NWS precluded support for higher wages thereby structurally promoting a lowering of young people's wage levels and expectations (PREM19/1839 f327). In parallel, a consultation was launched on reform or abolition of the Wage Councils that, since 1909, had regulated the wage-setting process in particular sectors of the economy. The New Right contended the Wage Councils distorted pay setting for young people and older 'unskilled' workers, which exacerbated unemployment and discouraged engagement in the YTS (Hansard, 1985e: col 1018). The review signalled the direction of travel to abolition of the Wage Councils in 1993, but in the short term ministers limited themselves to removing the authority of the Wage Councils to set the wage rates of people aged under 21 (Machin and Manning, 1994: 320).

The cultivation of enterprising individualism

The erosion of labour autonomy as extraction strategy was flanked by a discourse heavy with entreaties to free enterprise and entrepreneurialism that was carried into various aspects of training and education, but whose clearest manifestation in unemployment policy was the Enterprise Allowance Scheme (EAS) (Rees, 1988; Coffield, 1990; Greene, 2002). The EAS offered a temporary income allowance to working-age unemployed benefit claimants aged over 18 who had been unemployed for at least 13 weeks. As long as a claimant had access to £1,000 with which to capitalise their proposed business activity then they were eligible to receive a £40 per week payment for a year while they set up and ran their own business (Allan and Hunn, 1985: 313). Although the EAS was never to reach the scale of the YOP/ YTS for young people, or the CP of the over-18 age group of unemployed people, it was not an insignificant scheme. At the end of April 1984, the number of participants in the EAS stood at 29,455 (Hansard, 1984b). The scheme was though to receive additional funding which allowed its gradual expansion, with a target of 110,000 EAS participants announced in 1987 (Hansard, 1987g: col 1334). By the end of October 1989, the Government could point to 470,000 people having participated in the EAS since its inception (Hansard, 1989b).

With the EAS, the Government recast a portion of unemployed claimants as small business entrepreneurs – the individualising logic of the EAS contrasting starkly with the waged social economy work of the CP. The latter with its corporatist origins, public bureaucrats and 'dependent' unemployed claimants called to mind the state regulation and trade union power criticised as hampering the free operation of the labour market and constraining private sector innovation. The EAS in contrast reflected a conviction among senior Conservatives that small businesses were the dynamo of the economy and jobs growth, and fostering an enterprise culture would help displace statist dependency. The EAS was also politically attractive in that it aligned with broader two-nation governing narratives around individual initiative and freedom via the market, while removing recipients from the count of unemployed benefit claimants (PREM 19–1836 f366; Young, 1991; Greene, 2002: 322).

As qualitative research into the experience of EAS participants indicated (MacDonald, 1996), its take-up should also be viewed as a manifestation of the desire of claimants to escape the drudgery and hardship of unemployment, and enhance their autonomy over the working environment. With the dynamism of small businesses animating the vision of ministers, the EAS in this regard provided a means to co-opt and channel claimant desire for autonomy in a pro-capital direction that affirmed the centrality of individual risk taking, rather than collective struggle as the route to liberation from exploitation (Allen and Hunn, 1985; Rees, 1988). A survey of EAS participants indicated that by the summer of 1985 around one quarter of EAS participants were women and one quarter aged under 25, with the majority of participants aged 25–45. Around two thirds of businesses established were located in the service sector, and although a minority were able to command a comparably high income, it was more common for EAS participants to be on low pay (Allen and Hunn, 1985: 314–16).

Subsequent qualitative research conducted into the experience of EAS participants in Teesside in the late 1980s and followed up in the 1990s noted that many participants were working full time for little, if anything more, than their EAS payment. Moreover, of the businesses that survived past the end of the 12 months of EAS, the majority remained low-income sole traders, eking out a precarious existence in which their business was itself threatened by new EAS facilitated businesses (Macdonald, 1991, 1996). As Renga (1991: 175) pointed out, the EAS accorded with a broader rise in self-employment in the British economy. A confluence of factors underlay this, including large companies contracting out aspects of their business, but state support for self-employment provided one means for unemployed people to escape their predicament by creating a job for themselves (McDonald, 1991).

Though the EAS could enhance individual autonomy, for many the experience of the EAS was not of an ascent into the business class, but akin to swapping the hardship of exclusion from exploitation by others for the experience of becoming the manager of one's own self-exploitation. The EAS fostering, as Evans (2023) points out, the type of precarious employment relationships, individualist ethos and competitive practices commensurate with supplanting parts of the industrial working class and its collectivist ethos with an army of (small) independent contractors, contributing to the broader transformation of the technical and political class composition of labour.

The employability shift for unemployed 'adults'

For older workers this period was also marked by the gradual displacement of waged social economy work, despite initial continuity of job creation schemes. In March 1985 the Government announced the expansion of the Community Programme from 130,000 to 250,000 places per year and continuation of the Job Release and Job Splitting schemes (Hansard, 1985e: 1021), but as previously indicated supply-side interventions in the form of strengthened financial incentives, benefit conditionality and unwaged (basic) training placements were moving to the fore (PREM 19–1839 f366). The JobStart Scheme, for example, was introduced in 1986 as an option for Restart interviewees. Running for almost five years, the scheme provided for a weekly £20 wage top-up to be paid for a period of six months to long-term unemployed people electing to take a full-time job for less than £80 per week (Young, 1991: 172). The availability of a £20 payment to take up a vacancy was intended to provide a test of a claimant's willingness to take available jobs, and encourage employers to lower wages (Ainley and Corney, 1990: 108).

Between July 1986 and 1989 around 35,000 payments were made under the JobStart Scheme, with 39 per cent of wages of jobs covered paying below £70 (Hansard, 1989a: 870), suggesting a good portion remained below the eligibility threshold. Disney et al (1992: 193), reporting on an evaluation of participants taking up the JobStart Allowance in 1987 and 1988, noted the majority of recipients were under 30 years old and tended to work for small private companies in the clothing and footwear, manufacture, retail and construction sectors of the economy. Ostensibly, once an unemployed person had been 'priced back' into the labour market the assumption was that such individuals would then be able to maintain their job or secure another (Young, 1991: 172).

Of greater long-term significance was the pursuit of a break with the practice of paying a wage to participants in state job-creation schemes. The White Paper – *Training for Jobs* – set out the case for modernisation of skills provision, as new technologies and sectors grew and old areas of employment declined (DE, 1984: 11–12). The principal work-training scheme for people aged 19 and over had been the Training Opportunities Programme (TOP). Introduced in 1972 the TOP was a carryover from an attempt to raise productivity and promote labour mobility to mitigate sectoral labour shortages and wage-push inflation, and continued in parallel to the SEMs of the DE/MSC until replacement in 1985 by the Job Training Scheme (JTS) and the Wider Opportunities Training Programme (WOTP). The former was intended to meet demand for new higher-level training and improve alignment of training with service sector employment. The latter in contrast was concerned with basic training (literacy and numeracy, for example) targeted at long-term unemployed people (NAO, 1987: 11–13).

In 1987 the unimaginatively titled New Job Training Scheme (NJTS) was introduced for 18–24-year-olds who had been unemployed for six months. Under the NJTS, participants were placed with an employer, but also required to take part in off-the-job training. Eligibility for the CP was amended to align with the 12-month threshold for over 25-year-olds, meaning that for young people aged under 25 with less than 12 months' unemployment, the NJTS was the main programme. Lord Young likened this change to the replacement of the YOP by the YTS for young people, as ostensibly the NJTS was a move towards expansion of employer-based placements and on-the-job training, perceived to be lacking in the CP (Employment Committee, 1986: 16). In the NJTS, unemployed adults aged 18–25 were paid a training allowance equivalent to whatever a participant would otherwise be entitled to receive through out-of-work benefits (Hansard, 1987d; Ainley and Corney, 1990: 108; Brown, 1990: 183; Disney et al, 1992: 175). Having pioneered the training drive among the youngest unemployed claimants, the Government extended this approach up the age range, breaking with the practice of subsidised work, paid at local rates for the job, to unemployed adults aged over 18.

With the NJTS, the Government was not responding to a general problem of long-term unemployment, but the manifestation of unemployment among young men with no 'dependants' and few educational qualifications. The decomposition of industrial labour and the elimination of mass vacancies in manufacturing struck particularly at the job opportunities for young working-class men due to the segmented and stratified nature of the British labour market. Among entrants to the CP in the 12 months leading up to April 1987, for example, almost three quarters were men, almost eight in ten were recorded as 'single' and six in ten had been unemployed for 12 months or longer. Moreover, just under nine in ten were engaged in part-time CP work and CP participants remained predominantly younger adults with around six in ten aged under 25 (Unemployment Unit, 1988b: 3).

The Government tasked the MSC with making 110,000 places available on the NJTS by September 1987 (Hansard, 1987e: col 607), but in the event take-up was much lower than expected, with only 24,418 participating by the end December 1987 (Hansard, 1988b: col 791). Young unemployed people, it turned out, were determined to extract a higher price for their labour power than ministers had allowed for. Looking back on this period, Norman Fowler, who had been the Secretary of State for Employment at the time, regarded this refusal of training as 'perplexing' (Fowler, 1991: 297).

Yet, while something of a policy setback, ministers interpreted such 'refusals' as evidence that out-of-work benefit payments, informal working and lack of motivation to prepare for work meant a portion of claimants were not seeking formal employment and therefore not really unemployed (Fowler, 1991: 297–8).

Conscious that the MSC gave labour a voice within the state apparatus with respect to the organisation and management of labour commodification, the Conservative Party went into the 1987 General Election pledged to downsize the MSC and transform it into a national training authority. The composition of which would be reweighted to give employer representatives a dominant position (Conservative Party, 1987; Ainley and Corney, 1990). Following their re-election in the 1987 General Election, the momentum for remaking labour market policy and institutions was with the Government. The MSC was renamed the Training Commission and shorn of various functions, including oversight of employment and training programmes at the local level. In parallel, job creation and training programmes were reconfigured to focus attention on *all* of the long-term unemployed and make a final break with waged temporary jobs. Ministers viewed the CP in particular as doing little to improve participant employability, or incentivise older unemployed workers with families to participate (Hansard, 1987f: col 1068).

The 1988 White Paper – *Training for Employment* – set out the rationale for the replacement of CP/NJTS/JTS and WOPTS and various smaller initiatives with a unified training and employment programme (known as Employment Training – ET) beginning September 1988 (Secretary of State for Employment, 1988: 21). The new ET programme would involve a mixture of work experience on employer premises and off-the-job training for up to 12 months, or placement with a project run by a public or voluntary sector organisation, prior to moving into an employer placement. Categorised as trainees not workers, participants would be paid an allowance equivalent to benefits plus a top-up (basic rate set at £10) and expenses rather than a wage (Secretary of State for Employment, 1988: 22–7). The introduction of ET marked development of large-scale 'employability'-oriented policy geared towards acculturating unemployed claimants (predominantly men) to employment opportunities in the post-industrial landscape.

Not surprisingly, the nature of ET meant that it drew opposition from individual Labour MPs and trade unions on the grounds that ET eliminated trade union consultation on placements and the shift to a training allowance would place a downward pressure on wages (Hansard, 1988c: col 1384-85). The Secretary of State for Employment, taking the view that the Training Commission would continue to provide a state-sanctioned platform for organised labour to criticise government policy, responded by abolishing the Training Commission, replacing it with the Training Agency run from within the DE (Ainley and Corney, 1990; Fowler, 1991: 300; Jones, 1996; Price, 2000: 271). The Claimant's movement was acutely aware that while the new training programme remained 'voluntary' there was a drift towards retrenchment and coercison taking place. National 'days of action' were mounted, with local rallies in city centres and demonstrations and leafletting outside of job centres in an attempt to discourage claimants from participation, and state workers from directing people to the schemes (The New Scrounger, 1988a; 1988b). Some local authorities also chose not to participate in ET (Finn, 1989: 140), at least in part due to the implied exploitation of labour, but attempts to put financial muscle behind an active boycott, such as Liverpool City Council's motion to withdraw council funding from organisations participating in ET, was blocked in the courts (The Times, 1988b). With collective opposition weakening, the way was opening up for state managers to take another offensive step and this would unfold in the 1990s in a series of measures geared to further curtailment of labour autonomy.

Concluding remarks

Until well into the second Thatcher administration, the Conservative Government had adopted a defensive stance with respect to provision of employment services and access to unemployment benefits. Programmes seemingly inimical to ministers' general political outlook served to buttress the broader goal of remaking the balance of class power relations. The problem, however, was that while the rise in unemployment might have 'chilled' the confidence of organised labour, the conditions of entitlement to benefits, the availability of 'waged' subsidised jobs, weak availability testing and an institutionalised pro-labour presence in the state policymaking apparatus partially shielded claimants from the disciplinary pressure of the market and created space for autonomy and channels through which to contest, or evade government policy objectives.

By the middle of the second term, with the terrain of class struggle moving in its favour, the Government drew up a package of reforms that pivoted towards stronger benefit policing and activation of the claimant population. The target group for activating reforms between 1985 and 1989 remained the politically important unemployed claimant population rather than mobilisation of the broader surplus population of non-employed claimants.

As before, a key social characteristic in policy reform remained age with younger claimants the first to experience benefit restrictions and expansion of employability initiatives that sought to construct a new demand among employers for claimants and induce a shift in wage-setting practices and expectations, geared to advancing a new technical class composition of labour. By the end of the period supply-side employability reform had moved centre stage for older unemployed claimants as ministers sought to curtail claimant autonomy to trim the numbers of unemployed people and activate claimants into job search or training activity. The tightening up of conditionality did foster exit from unemployment benefits, at least temporarily, but the shift to unwaged training schemes was accompanied by a notable lack of claimant engagement, suggestive of a willingness to engage in quiet evasion of 'training' programmes whose material rewards were limited.

Though one may recoil from depicting the state as simply acting at the behest of capital, this period did mark a concerted move to deconstruct the last vestiges of the social democratic-corporatist labour market policy regime, conceded to industrial labour at the height of its power. The dispensing with the MSC in response to trade union obstruction of the ET programme, not only evicted pro-labour class fractions from the state apparatus but, as discussed in the next chapter, heralded the emergence of a new state strategy built around the privileging of 'enterprise' and a new managerialist rationality. That is, a sector-specific version of the 'authoritarian managerial strategy' conceptualised by Gallas (2016: 160–1) as defining the New Right's approach to the public sector and which brought together the Government's class politics of labour subordination and economic order politics of market liberalism.

On the offensive – enterprise, employability and exclusive activation: 1989–97

A new state apparatus

The *transitional-pacificatory* labour market policy regime, conceptualised in preceding chapters as the approach of the Conservative Government as they sought to manage high unemployment, a fracturing of social cohesion and political opposition, was transforming by the end of the 1980s into something new. With their political supremacy secure and earlier reforms having weakened the institutional coherence of the social democratic-corporatist, state labour commodification apparatus, ministers moved onto the offensive with a conservative re-regulatory project focused on reshaping social security and employment policy and governance (Peck, 1996).

In short, between 1989 and 1997 new steps were taken to diminish the discretion of frontline state employees and curtail claimant autonomy. The intensification of a repressive form of 'activation' during this period continued to prioritise unemployed people however, and so is conceptualised here as *exclusive*, with limited attention given to activation of the broader non-employed claimant population.

The exclusive form of activation for unemployed claimants was also *exclusionary* in that the threat of denial of access to income assistance grew in importance as a mechanism for cajoling claimants into job search and participation in employment programmes. A pejorative depiction of claimants whose lifestyles were presented as outside acceptable social norms, also moved to the fore in social security policy and political discourse (O'Grady, 2022), indicative of a strengthening of a confrontational, socially conservative and authoritarian two-nations approach in labour market policy.

These developments in the class politics of labour commodification were articulated with an economic order politics in which new management techniques, business involvement in delivery and championing of entrepreneurial individualism were placed at the core of labour market governance. The intent being to use market rationality and employer knowledge to drive up efficiency and improve the channel between welfare-training and secondary labour markets to facilitate the growth in low-paid service sector employment and labour market flexibilisation (Peck, 1996;

Table 7.1: The conservative market-liberal labour market policy orientation

Class politics	Economic order
Social conservativism	Emergent market-liberal
Extraction strategy	**Accumulation strategy**
Exclusive, emergent repressive	Proto-extensive labour utilisation
Mode of leadership & domination	**State strategy**
Confrontational two nations	Managerialism & enterprise

Source: Author's creation informed by Gallas (2016: 64).

Jones, 1999). New performance management and insertion of business into local governance of employment programmes in order to harness the entrepreneurial spirit and know-how of local business offered new tools for reshaping the expectations, outlook and behaviour of subordinate (para-)state employees to accord with government goals. The growing use of incentives to foster compliance of frontline workers and claimants was an early example of what has since been termed 'double activation' (see McGann, 2023: 22), which from a class power perspective can be understood as an organised attack on labour autonomy. Overall, by the time the Conservatives left office in 1997 the articulation of their class and economic order politics had given labour market policy and governance a (socially) conservative and market-liberal orientation that aligned with, and contributed to, the ongoing transformation of the technical class composition, and dissolution of the political class composition of industrial labour (Table 7.1).

Working-age social security benefits

The disciplinary turn intensifies

While the introduction of Restart had tightened up the requirements placed on unemployed benefit claimants to demonstrate availability for work, the coexistence of vacancies alongside persistent unemployment was interpreted as an indication the system allowed some claimants to become habituated to unemployment. For ministers this meant that vacancies went unfilled and claimants flowed from short- to long-term unemployment, generating upwards pressure on public expenditure that risked hampering the pace of economic growth (Fowler, 1991: 298; Hansard, 1990b: 1092–93; Young, 1991; Hansard, 1993b: col 217–18). Medium term economic prospects and short term class domination were entwined and this manifested in successive reforms to the benefit system to curtail benefit onflow, constrain claimant autonomy, reduce transitions from short term to long term unemployment and increase benefit exit. To tighten up requirements placed on claimants the 1989 Social Security Act specified claimants would be limited to a maximum period of 13 weeks in which they could limit job-search activity to their usual occupation. After this period, a claimant could no longer restrict their search and would be required to consider and accept a wider range of jobs, irrespective of previous occupation, training and wages. In the same year, new social security regulations implied a spatial broadening of job-search activity by specifying that a one-hour commute each way was acceptable (Knotz and Nelson, 2018: 7). The 1989 Act also required claimants demonstrate their activity to frontline staff through recording activity, such as responding to job adverts, attending interviews or going on courses to help with job seeking (Price, 2000: 269–70).

The Government's imposition of new performance-management practices also sought to incentivise staff to align their behaviour with ministers' goals for identifying 'fraud' and policing job search more aggressively (Bryson and Jacobs, 1992: 47–51). The discretion of claimant advisors consequently grew in importance regarding how unemployed people experienced what has been termed the 'Stricter Benefits Regime' (Blackmore, 2001; Wiggan, 2007b: 661). As such, unemployed claimants were incentivised to adopt performative compliance in their reporting of job-search activity in order to comply with the new rules, irrespective of their actual behaviour in practice (Bryson and Jacobs, 1992: 65; see also Blackmore, 2001).

Perhaps not surprisingly, as the 1990s progressed ministers introduced further changes to make claiming a more onerous experience, with restrictions introduced in 1992 to prevent the hardship rate of Income Support (IS) being received by those denied the full rate (Hansard, 1992b: col 1025). Although this particular change affected all working-age claimants without children it was initiated in a context of political panic about 'New Age Travellers'. The 'New Age Traveller' moniker was the label applied by media and political elites to a group of nomadic people, whose peace movement proclivities and embrace of an eclectic mix of environmentalism, 'alternative' spirituality and the free festival scene troubled Conservative social mores, private property rights and the (waged) work ethic (Clark, 1997: 129–39; Martin, 1998; Martin, 2002). The post-1988 rise of 'rave' music, with its culture of mass outdoor events, brought the prospect of a fraction of the urban youth population traversing Conservative voting areas of the English countryside and mixing with 'New Age Travellers' at unsanctioned festivals. The combination of nomadism and a new unruly, hedonistic youth movement gestured towards a potential reinvigoration of the commons and anarchic alternatives to the (re)ordered world of repressive social conservatism, labour discipline and the commodification of everything, everywhere. Claiming that such activity and lifestyle was a threat to social order and one that was financed by the 'taxpayer' through social security, pressure from Conservative MPs to curtail nomadism by preventing gatherings and clamping down on benefit eligibility[1] gained impetus (Buck, 1993; Halfacree, 1996: 54; PREM 19/4733).

The Income Support (General) Amendment (No. 3) Regulations 1992, which come into effect on 3 December, will remove entitlement to income support from most unemployed single people and childless couples who fail to seek work actively. So-called new age travellers and others who make no effort to look for work will no longer be able to support themselves at the taxpayer's expense. (Hansard, 1992c)

As a visible manifestation of antagonism to the logics of the New Right project the 'New Age Travellers' found themselves and their nomadic lifestyle incorporated into ministers' crafting of divisions between workers and unemployed claimants in a confrontational two-nations approach to governing (Gallas, 2016; see also Hansard, 1992b: col 1029; Halfacree, 1996: 47). Although, as Clark (1997: 133) points out, many travellers found it difficult to claim benefits, given the system's orientation towards 'settled' populations with their (expected) patterns of (relatively) stable employment (Clark, 1999). Moreover, the lack of 'fixity' of the traveller population and their varied forms of work was, in many ways, aligned with the post-industrial vision of labour mobility, entrepreneurialism and casualised labour markets (Halfacree, 1996; Clark, 1999). The mobility and intermittent (self-)employment of 'New Age Travellers' appeared, however, disruptive of established administrative practice and anathema to the benefit-control and work-availability checks (Buck, 1993; Halfacree, 1996; Clark, 1999), connected with ministers' broader concerns to restrict labour autonomy (Hansard, 1992b: col 1023; Hansard, 1993c: col 3).

Speaking in a House of Commons debate regarding the proposed replacement of Unemployment Benefit (UB) and Income Support (IS) for unemployed people with a new benefit– Jobseeker's Allowance (JSA) (Department of Employment/Department of Social Security, 1994), Peter Lilley MP, though conveying indifference to the living arrangements of 'New Age Travellers', noted that tightening up the policing of claims would prevent the system being exploited by people not fixed to one location (Hansard, 1994: col 642). The subsequent introduction in October 1996 of the JSA saw the National Insurance contributions-based UB and the means-tested IS benefit for unemployed claimants replaced by JSA (C) (the contributions-based version) and JSA (IB) (the income-based version). Following the reform the amount payable to claimants, whether in receipt of JSA (C) or JSA (IB), was aligned, and duration of eligibility for insurance-based support, previously 12 months under UB, was reduced to six months with JSA (C). After this period a claimant reliant on JSA (C) would have to claim JSA (IB) if they remained unemployed, though the means-testing of household savings above a particular threshold and/or the earnings of a partner would adversely affect eligibility (Novak, 1997; Clasen, 2011).

The shift to JSA further diminished the protective and autonomy enhancing aspect of unemployment benefits compared with the 1970s (Novak, 1997: 102). For the Government, though, changes to duration of entitlement had the attraction of removing a portion of JSA (C) unemployed people from the claimant count after six months, which residualised support and aligned favourably with ministers' goal of containing public spending (Finn, 1995: 8; Clasen, 2011). To satisfy conditions attached to benefit receipt, JSA claimants were required to be available for 40 hours' work per week and agree a Jobseeker's Agreement. The latter institutionalised a 'back to work' plan, strengthening the state's ability to direct, monitor and penalise claimants for non-compliance (Hansard, 1994: col 637).

Were a claimant deemed insufficiently active in their job search, to have turned down a job, or engaged in behaviour that undermined their likelihood of securing a job, they could be subject to sanction. Refusal to participate in work-related activity courses also risked a benefit sanction. For claimants refusing a reasonable job offer, or who had voluntarily left their employment, or been sacked for misconduct, then denial of JSA for a period of 26 weeks without access to hardship payments[2] remained the deterrent (Knotz and Nelson, 2018; Department of Employment/Department of Social Security, 1994: 25; Novak, 1997: 106). With the Government gradually ramping up activation pressure on unemployed claimants, frontline state employees sought to balance the tension arising between activation goals, the negative effect of economy drives on organisational capacity and an understanding that sanctioning and sending reluctant candidates to employers risked claimant and employer disengagement – leading, as already noted, in some cases to frontline workers using their discretion at the local level to hold back from imposing a more aggressive regime of benefit-policing (Blackmore, 2001: 156–9).

The expectation of minsters though was that JSA, together with low-cost job-search courses and employment schemes, would intensify competition for jobs, mitigating employers' need to offer higher wages to recruit, providing greater scope for additional hiring at the margins (Department of Employment/Department of Social Security, 1994: 10). Taken together these changes sought to reduce the numbers of new claimants drifting into long-term unemployment and promote exit from the claimant count into paid work. Wells (2001) has argued this can reasonably be judged a success, as outflow rates from unemployment benefits improved in the 1990s, following the introduction of Restart interviews, intensification of anti-fraud activity and tightening of eligibility and conditionality with the 1989 Social Security Act and Jobseeker's Act 1995. Exit from the claimant count need not necessarily translate into formal paid employment, however, with some people remaining unemployed, or making claims for benefits paid on grounds of sickness or disability (Manning, 2009: 240). Nevertheless, the JSA marked a step change in the reorientation of social security towards a more controlling, coercive form of activation for unemployed people.

Following more than a decade of relentless Conservative advance in the industrial and parliamentary sphere, the opposition of the trade unions and the Labour Party to the JSA was limited. Individual Labour MPs expressed disdain for the JSA, but by 1996 the leadership were not willing to scrap the JSA (Novak, 1997: 108), which aligned with their developing enthusiasm for supply-side active labour market policy (see Chapter 8). As Aufheben (1998) detailed, there were attempts to disrupt the introduction and roll-out of the JSA and other workfare-type initiatives, including the Conservative's Project Work scheme by autonomous claimant organisations, cohered in the Groundswell network.[3] Groups in various locales provided advice and support to claimants to help navigate the new JSA conditions (Groundswell, n.d.), protested against organisations providing work placements and took direct action at job centres to disrupt and discourage frontline state employees imposing benefit sanctions on unemployed claimants (Aufheben, 1998).

In an echo of longstanding CU antipathy towards officious policing of benefit claims (Marsland, 2018) some Groundswell groups, including Edinburgh and Nottingham experimented with a 'three strikes' policy in which a warning would be issued to a frontline worker to cease aggressive benefit policing. If this was ignored subsequent warnings were given and if no change was forthcoming this eventually escalated to a naming and shaming of the worker through a local flyer and poster campaign. The action was controversial within the Network and with the relevant trade unions[4] and points to the tensions arising from the growing divergence in interests of claimants and staff (Education and Employment Select Committee, 1997: 21; Nottinghamshire Jobs not JSA, 1996; Aufheben, 1998; Groundswell, 1997: 3; Counter Information, 1996/97: 1). In the political-economic conditions of the mid-1990s solidarity between claimants and job center staff, with few exceptions, proved difficult to achieve (Subversion, 1996a, 1996b). Despite their actions the Groundswell groups were unable to foster a level of claimant engagement and mass action sufficient to translate local activity into a national political problem for the Government (Counter Information, 1995/96: 3; 1996: 4; Rogers, 2002). With the embedding of activation reforms, individuals were consequently left to develop their own means of navigating the new terrain of the state under the growing pressure to commodify their labour.

Although the emphasis throughout this period was on retrenchment and conditionality to mobilise unemployed claimants to seek paid work, Grover and Stewart (2002: 111) note that, in 1996, the piloting of the in-work benefit known as the Earnings Top-Up (ETU) extended availability of wage top-ups to single and couple families without children. The pilot implicitly recognised that even with greater benefit policing the expansion of low-wage jobs weakened the financial returns from paid work. Using a policy instrument such as the ETU meant the state could raise the return from paid work even without stipulating a minimum wage, or re-empowering trade unions to bargain wages up. This was commensurate with preserving the role of capital in setting the price for labour power and disregarding policies that might strengthen the autonomy of labour. The ETU was paralleled by tweaks to Family Credit (FC) for couple and lone-parent families with children. A disregard in FC was introduced to offset some of the childcare costs that claimants incurred upon moving into paid work, and the minimum hours requirement to qualify for FC was changed from 24 hours per week to 16 hours per week (Dilnot and McCrae, 1999: 4; Grover and Stewart, 2002: 87).

The changes to FC and other minor advice initiatives signalled a growing interest in measures to entice non-employed lone parents into jobs, but these remained underdeveloped. With no requirement for lone-parent IS claimants to seek paid work, the orientation of the state apparatus remained weighted to maintaining non-employed lone parents as a latent surplus population, rather than channeling them into the floating labour reserve, or employed labour force. In this regard a desire for public spending restraint as a core part of the government's accumulation strategy seemingly clashed with developing policy tools suited to facilitating transition from an intensive to extensive model of labour utilisation, in which all claimants were subject to activation measures.

An opportunity you might (not) refuse: the reconfiguration of employment schemes

With the number of young people aged 16–17 expected to decline in the 1990s (Department of Employment, 1990: 13) and growing employer demand for technically proficient labour and motivated workers suited to service-sector work (Department of Employment, 1990: 29–38), the Youth Training Scheme (YTS) was replaced by Youth Training (YT) (Hansard, 1989c). The YT involved a work placement with off-the-job training and payment of a training allowance. The intention was to provide a route to at least a Level 2 National Vocational Qualification for under-18s and improve employer perception of, and engagement with, youth training. The management of the training provided was devolved to business-led Training and Enterprise Councils (TECs – see later) in England and Wales and their equivalent Local Enterprise Companies (LECs) in Scotland. The DE steered delivery at the operational level through funding arrangements focused on the securing of qualifications (level) gained and jobs entered (Bennett et al, 1994: 156; see later).

In addition to YT, the Conservative Government also launched the Youth Credit (YC) pilot scheme in 1991, following in the wake of a proposal outlined by the CBI in 1989 for a system of training credits. The YC involved careers advice, development of a training-related action plan and provision of training vouchers to participants. Young people as consumers would now have the power to purchase services from an employer willing to offer appropriate training, or a range of approved providers within a nascent training (quasi-)market (MacDonald and Coffield, 1993). Commensurate with a developing market-liberal state strategy the Government anticipated training vouchers would use financial incentives and choice to craft a training market that would better align training provision with employer demands (Hansard, 1990a; 211).

Croxford et al's (1996) analysis of the first year of the YC pilot indicated a positive effect on employment-oriented training and attainment of vocational qualifications, which helped mitigate inequity among young people arising from differential access to non-state supported forms of training. Yet, as Felstead (1995) pointed out, there remained a power imbalance between YC participants and employers. As unemployment rose in the early 1990s and the YC programme expanded the imbalance grew with employers operating in a 'buyers' market for labour power (Hodkinson and Sparker, 1994: 9). The level of resources directed to support YT/YC by the Government was also curtailed with expenditure falling from over £800 million in 1990–91 to under £650 million by 1994–95 (Hansard, 1996d: col 373). The performance-related funding structure, which incentivised action that delivered positive returns quickly, also did little to discourage training that aligned with 'traditional' gendered occupational and sectoral segmentation (MacDonald and Coffield, 1993: 8–9; Felstead, 1995: 194–6).

Parallel to YT/YC, the roll-out of Employment Training (ET) marked the convergence of programmes for older unemployed groups with the services offered to the under-18 age group (King, 1993: 226). The priority ET groups were unemployed claimants aged 18–24 and claimants under 50 unemployed for two years plus. However, disabled people, and some lone-parent recipients of IS, could also participate if available for paid work. Following referral, completion of an individual action plan would inform[5] the mix of training and work placement, with participants receiving an allowance plus expenses (see Chapter 6) (Finn, 1989; Gregg, 1990).

Jones (1996: 139) astutely referred to the gradual shift in employment programmes under the Conservatives as 'creeping trainingfare'[6] (that is, training for benefits), which aligned with the New Right's goal of reconfiguring the state apparatus to induce claimants to lower their reservation wage. The Unemployment Unit, a campaign and research organisation, pointed out that Manpower Services Commission (MSC) survey data regarding the income of Community Programme (CP) participants in 1985 showed that more than nine in ten had an income at least £15 per week higher under CP than they would have received in social security alone. Relative to CP the ET eroded the real value of participation (Unemployment Unit, 1988c: 4), but like CP remained relatively exclusive in its orientation towards activating working-age men at risk of becoming permanently detached from employment. Between September 1988 and April 1989, seven in ten of all ET entrants were men; around a third had been unemployed for between six and 12 months, and over one third had been unemployed for more than two years (Hansard, 1989d: col 867 – also cited in Finn, 1989: 10).

Participation in the core adult training and employment schemes was not made mandatory for claimants, however (Tonge, 1999: 221), thereby limiting cost commitments amid high unemployment. In the event, the Government overestimated the number of unemployed claimants willing to engage in ET (Brown, 1990: 185). More than 40 per cent of people referred to an ET place by the Employment Service in the first year did not go on to commence a placement with a provider (Employment Committee, 1989: 4).

An initial flow of 600,000 participants passing through a stock of 300,000 ET places had been envisaged, but subsequently this was lowered to an expected flow of 560,000 people, and then a flow of 450,000 people through a stock of 265,000 places. By the beginning of December 1989, the Director General of the Training Agency within the Department of Employment (DE) estimated 210,000 ET places had been filled out of the 250,000 available at the time (Employment Committee, 1989: 2). The Unemployment Unit argued that the Government's own research indicated limited claimant enthusiasm was itself a consequence of ministers' desire to contain programme costs and reduce the reservation wage of claimants by shifting to 'benefit plus' payment. A portion of potential ET participants were, as with the New Job Training Scheme (NJTS) and YTS, electing to evade this form of activation as the financial attractiveness declined (Employment Committee, 1996b: xxviii) – something that, as noted previously, claimant organisations worked to encourage by emphasising to claimants that participation was voluntary.

In 1991, with a general election on the horizon, the then Secretary of State for Employment, Michael Howard MP, announced the introduction of Employment Action (EA) to complement the ET scheme (Hansard, 1991; Jones, 1999: 142). The EA programme targeted six-month unemployed claimants aged over 18. In contrast to ET, which focused on private sector training and work experience, the EA resurrected the type of community benefit projects found in the earlier CP (Secretaries of State for Employment, Scotland and Wales, 1992: 55). Unlike the CP, the EA was smaller in scale – up to 60,000 people a year – and did not pay a wage, but rather an allowance as with ET (Hansard, 1991; Price, 2000: 292). The EA scheme was the type of work for benefit activity floated by ministers during the early 1980s, but deemed impractical at the time given the priority ministers afforded to depoliticisation and their dependence on the cooperation of trade unions and local authorities through the MSC. With this no longer the case, the Government was free to institutionalise lower costs through a benefit-plus expenses payment (Jones, 1999: 109).

Indicative of the struggle over the conditions of labour commodification, the low take up of training places was followed by the DE altering the claimant review process to tighten monitoring of work availability, and initiate interviews with claimants who did not enrol in employment schemes, following initial expressions of interest (Price, 2000: 289). The ET and EA were in turn replaced from April 1993 by Training for Work (TfW) (Hansard, 1992a: col 130-31). Similar to ET, the TfW[7] scheme aimed to place participants in training and work experience with an employer, or off-the-job training courses and prioritised (albeit not limited to) 18–24-year-olds unemployed for six months plus. Potentially, TfW supported training to NVQ Level 3 or 4, but a more outcome-oriented funding system again incentivised lower-level training and job entry (Felstead, 1994; Jones, 1999: 152; Gray, 2000: 318).

The then Secretary of State for Employment, Gillian Sheppard MP, rejecting a role for the state in creating jobs, argued that the state should instead construct the best environment for growth and act as an intermediary between labour and capital by helping the former via training and employment services compete for existing job vacancies (Hansard, 1990a: col 130). The pivot to training programmes paid at benefit-plus rates also addressed the concern that 'make work' activity could provide an alternative to the formal labour market, hampering the reallocation of resources to new growth areas (Employment Committee, 1996b: xxxiii and xxxv–xxxvi).

The effectiveness of the new schemes in terms of promoting entry into paid work is questionable. In 1990–91 when ET was in operation the post-programme destination of around one third of participants was employment, whereas over half (53 per cent) moved back into unemployment, and around 15 per cent left for other destinations. For 1995–96, with the labour market improving and TfW in operation, around four in ten (39 per cent) participants entered employment, just under half (47 per cent) returned to unemployment and 14 per cent left for other destinations (ONS, 1998: 69).

Ministers' professed commitment to upskilling unemployed claimants belied the concern that training programmes struggled to secure claimant participation[8] or employer placements, and were often not necessary for the jobs many claimants would enter (Hansard, 1992a: col 128; Towers, 1994: 382; Gray, 2000: 308–9; Price, 2000: 291–2). They were also costly, with Fletcher (1997: 176) noting the cost per place of YT (£2,831) and TfW (£2,475) in 1994–95 was substantially greater than job search, advice and motivation initiatives (for example, job clubs, job plan and job search seminars) run by the DE's Employment Service, which cost between £75 and £200 per place (Fletcher, 1997: 177).

Given the relatively high cost of the training programmes and the reluctance of some claimants to participate, it is perhaps no surprise that more coercive, low-cost interventions moved to the fore of active labour market policy. In 1994, through the Workwise and 1-2-1 schemes the DE trialled mandated participation in job-search activity, backed by threat of benefit sanctions for non-engagement. The Workwise scheme involved enrolment in a four-week-long employment assistance course, while the 1-2-1 scheme involved 'directed job-search activity', undertaken during attendance at a series of interviews with a claimant advisor. These strengthened availability for work checks on claimants unemployed for 12 months plus, and aged 18–24, who had declined options offered during Restart interviews (Webb, 2003: 102; see also Jones, 1996: 148).

These initiatives were in keeping with a repressive class politics geared towards curtailing claimant autonomy and in 1996 were followed by the roll-out of the Project Work pilot scheme. Involving two locales and up to 6,000 people, Project Work targeted long-term (two years plus) unemployed benefit claimants aged 18–60 and involved two distinct stages that followed referral at a Restart interview. First, claimants entered a 13-week period in which they could engage in various job-search and advice supports (Jobclubs, 1-2-1 scheme); contracted training (TfW); short work placements (Work Trials); or potentially avail of a subsidy (Workstart) claimable by employers hiring long-term unemployed people. Second, private- and third-sector organisations provided a work experience placement for up to 13 weeks, which was mandatory for claimants failing to move off benefit in phase one. Project Work also operated a 'stop the clock' approach. So, participants exiting the claimant count, but making a new claim within the six-month period of the pilot, would rejoin the scheme instead of being treated as short-term unemployed, which closed off the possibility of a 'tactical' signing-off from benefit. Non-engagement could also lead to benefit disallowance for two weeks and four weeks if repeated (Department for Education and Employment, 1996: 34–5).

By the end of 1996, ministers had announced the expansion of Project Work to cover 100,000 unemployed people, and the 'Contract for Work' pilots – a trial of a new quasi-market in return-to-work services for long-term unemployed people (Hansard, 1996c: cols 175–6). The roll-out of Workwise and 1-2-1 to police claimant compliance with work availability and Project Work shows the gradual shift towards an exclusionary approach to activation that paralleled the introduction of JSA as ministers sought to enhance the state's domination of claimants and deliver cost savings in training and employment schemes (Hansard, 1995a) that aligned with their broader liberal economic strategy. As before, a more liquid labour reserve being the priority, rather than a sorting and mobilisation of the broader non-employed claimant population. Activation remained relatively exclusive, geared towards increasing the transitions of unemployed claimants from benefits, through training and into the secondary labour market.

The new managerialist turn in employment and social security governance

Complementing the activation drive was the authoritarian managerialism Gallas (2016) identifies as a hallmark of the Conservatives state strategy during this period. This was manifest in the creation of the Employment Service and Benefits Agency as operationally independent agencies of the Department of Employment and Department of Social Security, respectively. The reform crafted a ostensibly clearer divide between delivery and policy formulation with each agency headed by a Chief Executive, and given greater autonomy in budget management and service delivery (Considine, 2001: 42). A quasi-contractual agreement governed relations between agencies and departments, with the centre using performance indicators and targets to steer and regulate delivery activity (Price, 2000: 277–8; Talbot, 2001: 291; James, 2003; Talbot, 2004).

What is of interest here is the growing reliance on performance management and (quasi-)contracts as the mechanism for steering the activity of delivery organisations and their frontline workers. Moreover, the governance reform did not challenge the division between services for unemployed claimants and services for working-age economically inactive claimants. That is, the different approach taken by the state to the organisation of the labour reserve, and the broader surplus population remained institutionally embedded. Successive Employment Service performance agreements during the 1990s, for example, were geared towards 'activation' of unemployed claimants, and lowering the claimant count. Conversely, the Benefits Agency was charged with ensuring payment accuracy not the mobilisation for paid work of lone parents and sick and disabled people in receipt of Income Support (IS), or Incapacity Benefits (IB) (Price, 2000: 277–8; Wiggan, 2007a: 414).

Following the changes to the governance of employment services and benefit administration, the job (in)security of frontline state employees came to be more closely linked to organisational performance in strengthening activation and benefit policing. By implication, this imposed new pressures and constraints on state employees, as their interests were structurally repositioned to weigh against facilitating claimant autonomy, or undertaking solidaristic action. In this regard the managerialism and market rationality (Considine, 2001) of the new state strategy cohered with the exclusionary, repressive extraction strategy being pursued through reform to benefits and employment programmes, and worked to reproduce the divisions within and between the labour reserve and surplus population.

Private enterprise and (quasi-)market-managerialism

The emergent market-managerialist turn was also evident in the reorganisation of employment programme delivery following the dissolution of the MSC. As Jones (1999: 102–11) details, a new enterprise-oriented approach was developed through the creation of Training and Enteprise Councils (TECs)/Local Enteprise Companies (LECs) (England and Wales/ Scotland),[9] which revolved around a bi-partite relationship between the Department of Employment and local business leaders (see Bennett et al, 1994; Peck, 1996: Jones, 1999). Just over 100 TECs/LECs were established in Britain and operational by the end of 1991, with four-fifths located in England and Wales and the remainder in Scotland (King, 1993: 231; Jones, 1996: 144; Lourie, 1997b). The TECs were indicative of the Government's boosterist depiction of 'enterprise' as the key ingredient for driving economic and jobs growth (Thatcher, 1989; Young, 1991).

The new organisations were constituted as private companies and controlled by a board of directors consisting of local business leaders and/ or business organisation representatives (two thirds of board members), with trade unions, civil society and other state and sub-national government actors taking up the remainder of places. This downgraded and limited the influence of organised labour, and other state and civil society actors, as ministers sought to give business greater authority to direct labour commodification at the local level (Jones, 1999: 241). A rescaling of the management of labour commodification was in this way combined with a change in the class composition of actors embedded within the (para-)state apparatus – the TECs marking a shift away from dialogue at the national level with representatives of large capital to engagement of a middling strata of local entrepreneurial business leaders. What Jones (1999: 116 and 195) implies marked the incorporation into the (para-)state of core constituents of the Conservative's political support coalition, the small and medium sized employers sensitive to the 'price' of labour power and the cost of state regulation.

Initial expectations were for TECs to assist local economic development by fostering and coordinating local enterprise- and employer-led training for the already employed, with administration of programmes for unemployed people a secondary activity (Peck and Jones, 1995: 1378). With respect to state employment and training, notably ET/TfW/YT, the TECs were not service providers themselves, but rather coordinating and contracting organisations who sub-contracted delivery to other state and non-state actors (Education and Employment Committee, 1998; Jones, 1999: 117–18). From a market-liberal perspective, the focus of each TEC and their domination by business leaders rooted in the area offered a means to improve the capabilities of the state to function as a 'knowledge apparatus' (Stutzle, 2011; Brand, 2013: 435). The gathering, sifting, generating and utilising of local labour market information providing for a fine-grained understanding of (local) employers' requirements for labour and helping to identify opportunities and challenges to growth and accumulation in the medium term.

Giving power to business did not automatically translate into buy-in from employers, alignment of employment programmes with the local labour market, or an improved local economic environment however. Peck (1996) points out that the TECs proved to be poorly suited to the tasks they were charged with and in part this flowed from the same market-liberal preferences that informed their creation. As there remained no regulation to compel employers to resource training, for example, there was little reason for individual employers, particularly small businesses, to increase their spending on training, and TECs struggled to encourage them to do so (King, 1993; Jones, 1999). Concern with the future productive capacity of the economy led some TEC leaders to lament that the voluntary approach of peer encouragement envisaged by Government as sufficient to induce investment in training, was, in practice, a failure (Coffield, 1992: 21). In short, the TEC experiment pointed to how capitalists could not be relied upon to make decisions that were in the long term interests of capital in general.

The deep economic recession Britain experienced during the first half of the 1990s compounded this, as employers required fewer staff and the resources available for investment in training diminished. In any case, rising unemployment meant a wider and deeper pool of talented applicants became available to employers (Coffield, 1992: 21–3; Peck, 1996). The Department of Employment's annual survey of employer recruitment indicated that in 1990 around one fifth of those surveyed reported 'hard to fill' vacancies, suggesting a need for investment in the labour supply to overcome shortages and damp down pressures for wage inflation. By 1993 the proportion of employers indicating they had vacancies that were proving hard to fill had dropped to 6 per cent (Dale, 1994: 123). In this context the TECs, like the MSC before, became converted into organisations primarily concerned with organising the warehousing, sifting and (re)mobilisation of unemployed people with little or no experience of employment (that is, young people), and those deemed at risk of losing the motivation to sell their labour power (that is, long-term unemployed people) (Peck and Jones, 1995; Peck, 1996). Given the importance of delivering state training and employment schemes to the funding of TECs, their ostensible autonomy became heavily conditioned by Government and the operation of its employment and training service quasi-market (Felstead, 1998: 29; Felstead and Unwin, 2001: 93).

The actual funding arrangements within the quasi-market were somewhat complicated (see Felstead, 1994; Lourie, 1997b: 22–3), but in broad terms the DE agreed with each TEC the resources available; the unit costs, the number of people to be served and what the state would pay for particular 'results' achieved. The total funding varied between areas and over time (Hansard, 1995a: col 806; Hansard, 1995b: col 615; Hansard, 1996b: col 1129-30w), but typically included a number of distinct payments by the state to TECs. These included: a management fee, fees relating to programme starts (inputs), completions (outputs), attainment of educational qualifications and/or securing of employment (outcomes), and extra resources were made available to TECs achieving greater performance in efficiency (that is, lower unit cost price) compared with their peers. The level of outcome fee could vary depending upon participant characteristics and associated levels of attainment and employment. Additional weight was given to outputs/outcomes for participants whose ascribed group characteristics placed them at a relative labour market disadvantage (for example, low level of literacy or numeracy; being from a minority ethnic group). The aim being to offset the risk that the market would position such participants as too costly to engage (Employment Committee, 1996a; Lourie, 1997b: 22–3; Felstead, 1998: 32).

Overtime the 'Output Related Funding' became a greater share of funding in the core programmes (Youth Training and Training for Work) (Felstead, 1998: 33). A consequence was that TECs and sub-contracting organisations were incentivised to press down on service delivery costs and maximise programme throughput of participants most likely to attain output and outcome fees. Lower-cost training options and placements that did not require higher-skill competencies were, therefore, more attractive than sectors and occupations with greater (that is, expensive) resource demands. Consequently, how the quasi-market was constructed and regulated worked to shape what employment transitions were open to participants (Felstead, 1994: 31–40; Peck and Jones, 1995: 1385; Peck, 1996: 220) and this intersected with participant-ascribed characteristics.

The Equal Opportunities Commission and the Commission for Racial Equality in evidence to the then House of Commons Employment Select Commitment noted that as training and employment schemes were for unemployed claimants this excluded many women without a job, as fewer women claimed unemployment benefits. Moreover, qualifications and jobs secured by participants categorised as 'Asian' and 'African-Caribbean' in 'youth' and 'adult' employment and training programmes lagged those of 'White' participants (Employment Committee, 1995). Overall, incentives to direct TECs and providers to serve 'disadvantaged' participants were overwhelmed it seems by incentives to concentrate attention on participants deemed likely to quickly secure a favourable outcome (Employment Committee, 1995: 172–87; Employment Committee, 1996a: xxxviii).[10]

As previously alluded to, the necessary attention to cost pressures also meant that the TECs and contracted providers were structurally disposed to work with the grain of labour market segmentation and stratification, rather than the financially risky path of seeking to diversify the occupational/sectoral destinations of participants (Bennett et al, 1994: 165; Felstead, 1995: 196). The business-led and marketised form of active labour market governance worked in this way to reproduce prevailing patterns of labour market exclusion/inclusion, segmentation and stratification (Peck, 1996: 221). Felstead (1995: 183–5) noting that among women participants in YT, over three quarters were engaged in training related to sales or office work, with only around one in 20 training for work in construction, engineering and electrical, metal work or vehicle trades occupations. Similarly, the ET scheme tended to line up participants on gendered pathways, with male trainees dominating transport, manufacturing, construction, engineering, science and industry occupations, and women strongly represented among health, childcare, personal services and textiles-related trades (Felstead, 1995: 184). The seeking of economy and efficiency in employment programmes, in line with the Government's broader liberal market preferences, worked against realignment of claimants' socially situated job preferences at the point when the technical class composition of industrial society, was passing into history.

In practice, the TECs were indicative of the articulation of a developing market-managerialist state strategy with an accumulation strategy beginning to signal an interest in extensive labour utilisation, and an extraction strategy geared to the curtailment of labour autonomy. Whereas the early to mid-1980s had seen the Conservative New Right tactically adopt the labour market policy regime it inherited to pacify labour and depoliticise unemployment, the period between 1989 and 1997 saw the Conservatives advancing their class offensive against claimant autonomy. Through benefit retrenchment and more stringent work-related conditionality, state managers made the prospect of subsisting on unemployment benefits more difficult, while the embedding of training allowances for participation in low-cost training schemes marked a further step in pressing down the price of labour power and the cost to the state of managing this process. Although the new training schemes for older unemployed claimants, and the functioning of the TECs, faced difficulties in operation, the reconfiguration of the terrain of the state to privilege capital advanced the class political strategy of the New Right and co-constituted the changing composition of labour for post-industrial employment. A fuller transformation of the state's labour market policy regime would, though, await the progressive market-liberal modernisation project of the New Labour governments.

8

Inclusive employability and the progressive market-liberal turn: 1997–2004

Inclusive employability

The return of the Labour Party to Government following the 1997 General Election led to a rearticulation of class and economic order politics, with Gallas (2016: 280) making a convincing case that economic order politics moved to the fore. The new Government was more comfortable with using the power of the state, and public spending to foster social cohesion, repair dilapidated public services and expand activation, as a means to consolidate the liberal market economic model. Through reforms to social security and employment policy the New Labour Government's class politics cohered with an emergent economic order politics of extensive labour utilisation (Koch, 2006) as the means to improve medium–term conditions for accumulation. Where the following analysis demurs from the position taken by Gallas is with respect to viewing ministers' progressive market-liberal modernisation project as a resumption of a 'one nation' mode of governing.

In social security and employment policy and governance the overt, divisive political practice particular to the Conservatives was softened, but not abandoned. Rather, the contention is that ministers adopted a *progressive* two-nation mode of leadership. The then leader of the Labour Party and Prime Minister between 1997 and 2007, Tony Blair MP, self-defined as a progressive (Faucher-King and Le Galès, 2010: 8–9) and the Government's positive depiction of diversity and express support for expansive equal opportunity did challenge traditional conservative social mores and their inscription in the exclusionary practices of institutions (Sayeed, 2017).

Breaking down barriers and improving opportunity to engage in paid work, irrespective of ascribed social characteristics, also provided a means to diversify extant hierarchies and strengthen social cohesion, while leaving the market intact as the arbiter of efficient and just resource allocation. In this way progressive, socially liberal values cohered with, and supported the deepening of a competitive liberal market order in which the authority of capital remained supreme. The social liberalism of New Labour however, remained thoroughly productivist and this manifested in a discourse that lauded worker-consumers and denigrated reliance on out-of-work benefits (O'Grady, 2022: 129–35). To seek formal employment was the moral obligation of non-employed working-age benefit claimants, and a means for Government to instil the discipline required to strengthen social cohesion and the economy (Blair, 1996; Mandelson, 2002: 72; Atkins, 2011: 105). A progressive, yet disciplinary mode of governing aligned with the perception that the state apparatus continued to facilitate a degree of claimant autonomy that hampered the effective sorting and mobilisation of labour power to meet the needs of the post-industrial labour market (see Grover and Stewart, 2002; Koch, 2006).

The gradual expansion of active labour market programmes and ramping-up of benefit policing (Dwyer, 2004; Clarke, 2005) marked an attempt to close off social security, expand the labour reserve and promote quicker transitions into paid formal employment. This extraction strategy of *disciplinary inclusion* depended in turn on reconfiguring employment and social security institutions, albeit in ways commensurate with the continuing development of a market-managerialist state strategy initiated under preceding Conservative administrations. In this regard, the orientation of welfare governance accorded with ministers' broader championing of market-based policy reforms to the welfare state, including the development of new quasi-markets in employment service provision (Greener, 2008; see also Chapter 9). The combination of a desire to deepen liberal market economic practices, embrace of a politics of identity recognition, support for mild redistribution and a disciplinary approach to claimants, was reflective of what Fraser has conceptualised as 'progressive neo-liberalism' (Fraser, 2019: 13–14). Informed by this, the orientation of labour market policy and governance under New Labour is conceptualised here as progressive-market liberalism (Table 8.1).

Economic strategy, (welfare) state modernisation and paid work

Before turning to discuss specific labour market policy and governance reforms the broader intersection of welfare state modernisation, employment

Table 8.1: The progressive market-liberal labour market policy orientation

Class politics	Economic order
Progressive	Market-liberal
Extraction strategy	**Accumulation strategy**
Disciplinary inclusion	Extensive labour utilisation
Mode of leadership & domination	**State strategy**
Progressive two nations	Market-managerialism

Source: Author's creation informed by Gallas (2016: 64).

and economic strategy of the New Labour Government is considered. The ejection from office in May 1997 of the Conservative Party after 18 years in government implied that a reordering of social forces within society might usher in a transformation of state policies and institutions with respect to the management of labour commodification and social reproduction. Yet, the return of the Labour Party to government in 1997 took place on new institutional terrain. The Conservatives' successful class offensive had shattered the political and technical composition of the industrial working class and transformed the economy and society. After successive general election defeats the Labour Party had accepted the broad political economy settlement imposed by the Conservatives, which constrained the policy instruments deemed desirable and feasible by Labour politicians (Wickham-Jones, 2003: 36–8).

Yet, as Gallas (2016) argues, the very success of the New Right project had led to a destabilising rise in income inequality and material deprivation. For New Labour the accompanying increase in long-term unemployment in the early 1990s, and rise in the levels of 'economic inactivity' was a social tragedy that not only destabilised society, but also diminished the productive capacity of the economy and weakened the conditions for sustained economic growth (see Blair, 1996: 91–4; Balls, Grice and O'Donnell, 2004). Given the changed balance of forces and institutional terrain the party leadership set out to stabilise and improve the functioning of the market-liberal settlement. A sense of radical moderation was conveyed by the leadership, which affirmed class power relations were to be largely untroubled. New Labour would focus on modernising the state to enhance economic dynamism, renew the public realm and regulate the new market order to address social and economic problems as the means to generate greater labour market opportunities and economic growth (Blair, 1996: 206–7). At the core of this project was a fundamental concern with securing the subordination of labour as the necessary precondition for improving the environment for accumulation and this linked reform of benefit and employment programme settings and instruments, with overall economic policy decisions and goals. The New Labour leadership, for example, perceived an incongruence between the state apparatus and organisation of post-industrial labour markets, which hampered pursuit of low inflation and high employment, undermining Britain's economic potential and adding to social dislocation (Blair, 1996: 82–4; Brown, 2017; Grover and Stewart, 2002: 31–4).

The announcement in 1997 by the then Chancellor of the Exchequer Gordon Brown MP of operational independence for the Bank of England providing an early example of this. Bank independence and inflation targeting would insulate decisions from electoral calculations, transforming the process into a seemingly non-political technocratic deliberation, with greater transparency and predictability crafting a more propitious investment environment (Brown, 2017: 115). The Government retained authority for the strategic direction of monetary policy through setting the inflation rate target, but relinquished any role in setting the Bank of England's base rate to the new Monetary Policy Committee (MPC) (Wiggan, 2007b: 653). The target was symmetrical, implying interest rates be lowered should the rate of inflation fall below 2 per cent, and raised if sustained inflation of above 2 per cent was expected (Brown, 2017: 121). The aim being to mitigate the risk of a destabilising inflationary or deflationary spiral taking hold (Brown, 2001: C34; Balls, 2016: 147).

The configuration of operational independence for the Bank of England anchored New Labour's employment and social security policies to those commensurate with a level of worker and claimant autonomy insufficient to threaten capital's authority over wage setting, and hence price stability. The Government could point, for example, to how a struggle to raise wages in excess of productivity improvement would induce the MPC to raise interest rates, which would raise the cost of borrowing, depress business investment, dampen demand for labour and erode wages. Provided workers and employers understood this then the mere existence of an inflation target and Bank independence would discourage such action and embed low-inflation expectations. The new institutional environment was in this way an attempt to pre-empt and dampen struggle to raise wages and create greater space for a non-inflationary expansion of employment and output (Grover and Stewart, 2002: 47).

New Labour's diagnosis of the problems afflicting the economy and labour market (see Mandelson, 2002) essentially positioned the Conservatives approach to public spending and the state apparatus as a 'fetter' on the growth potential of the economy. If the the social fabric of society was to be repaired and the productive capacity of the economy improved then this also implied supply side reform of social security and employment services to promote paid work (Payne, 2017: 79). In the early 1990s Ed Balls and Paul Gregg,[1] in a submission to the Commission on Social Justice, identified how a disjuncture between the structures of social security and changes in the labour market undermined labour commodification. The treatment of partners of unemployed claimants in income maintenance and employment services in the UK post-1945 had been built around a gendered segmentation of the labour market and social reproduction work, manifest in a male-breadwinner model of the family. This institutionalised a presumption of dependency of (non-employed) women (as primary carers) upon men (primarily workers) even when temporarily unemployed (Ginsburg, 1979; Millar, 2000). Yet, as detailed in Chapter 3, the changing technical class composition of the labour force with the decline of industrial employment and rise of service jobs was accompanied by new employment opportunities and rising labour market participation among women (MacLeavy, 2007).

The problem, however, was that in the case of unemployment of the 'main' earner, the taking of a part-time job by their partner did little to raise family income, as earnings would largely be offset by reductions to, or elimination of, out-of-work benefit payments (Gregg, 1993: 54). Partners (usually women) of unemployed claimants (often men), as leading members of New Labour recognised (Mandelson, 2002: 125–6), consequently had limited incentive to seek paid work, until the 'main earner' secured a new job (see McLaughlin, 1991: 501).

Conversely, part-time, low-paid service-sector jobs were less attractive to (male) unemployed benefit claimants looking for wages that lifted their income above out-of-work social security benefits and much service work could be perceived by male claimants as ill-suited to their skills or (gendered) role in society (Balls, 1993: 21–2; Gregg, 1993: 50). This was interpreted as discouraging the commodification of the unemployed 'main earner' and their partner, contributing to a polarisation between 'job poor' and 'job rich' households (Clasen, 2002: 65), and in effect worked to reproduce a gendering of the labour reserve and relative surplus population.

Unable to produce sufficient quantities of the labour power desired by employers, the extant state apparatus made achieving price stability, social cohesion and sustained growth more difficult (Brown, 2001: C39; Balls, Grice and O'Donnell, 2004: 10–11). New Labour's problem interpretation owed much to endorsement of the concept of a Non-Accelerating Inflation Rate of Unemployment (NAIRU) (Brown, 2001: C39). The NAIRU being the level of unemployment deemed commensurate with a stable level of inflation (Grover, 2016a: 136). In this view, should unemployment fall below a particular level then pressure builds for wage rises, which in a tight labour market an employer acquiesces to, while passing on the cost to the consumer, leading to price rises. To prevent the embedding of a wage-price spiral this then necessitates intervention to raise interest rates, to depress investment and spending, slow growth and raise unemployment sufficient to reduce the inflation rate. Importantly, the NAIRU is not a fixed level, and mobilising unemployed and non-employed claimants into the labour market to increase competition for jobs diminishes worker bargaining power and the pressure on employers to accede to higher wages. Assuming that greater labour supply contains labour costs, this makes additional employment and output compatible with lower rates of inflation and interest rates (Sawyer, 2004; Grover and Stewart, 2002: 61–2).

The NAIRU informed the rationale for active labour market policy reforms, as succinctly conveyed by the Department for Education and Employment (DfEE), in evidence to the Education and Employment Select Committee in 1999:

you allow the market to work better, which enables more production basically. There is a dynamic element to it that means that you increase the productive potential of the economy if you bring more of the people who are either at the margins of the labour force or who are excluded altogether back into the labour force. (Education and Employment Select Committee, 1999: 2)

To contain wages and secure a lower NAIRU New Labour's approach would build on the preceding Conservative Government's experiments with 'workfare', work-related benefit conditionality and moderate improvements to in-work benefits (Grover and Stewart, 1999; King, 1995; Walker and Wiseman, 2003) in pursuit of 'activation for the many' (Griggs et al, 2014) (that is, extensive labour utilisation).

The New Labour leadership consequently revised social security and employment services to diminish institutional impediments to activation and labour market participation (Grover and Stewart, 2002; Balls, Grice and O'Donnell, 2004) improving the state's ability to organise and manage transitions between the secondary labour market, labour reserve and relative surplus population (Peck and Theodore, 2000; Finn, 2003a; Koch, 2006). The presumption being greater social stability, reductions in 'wasteful', rather than productive forms of public spending, and a rise in the supply of labour would improve the dynamism of the labour market and enhance the conditions for investment, growth and capital accumulation. This marked a continuation of the state's offensive against claimant's ability to exercise autonomy over labour market participation, and the ability of social security to function as an 'outside option' to paid work, and hence buffer of the collective power of labour (Altunbuken et al, 2022: 5).

The new suite of employment programmes

In the run up to the 1997 General Election it was made clear that a future Labour Government would address long-term unemployment and reduce youth unemployment by 250,000 (Brown, 1995; Labour Party, 1997). Though these groups were given priority upon taking office the Government also sought a more comprehensive engagement with the working-age non-employed claimant population that pointed to what would become an expansion of activation to other groups over time (Griggs et al, 2014). A DfEE memo to the Education and Employment Select Committee noted that the 1998 Green Paper on welfare reform, *New Ambitions for Our Country: A New Contract for Welfare*, included four key measures of success: tackling long-term unemployment; increasing the size of the labour force; reducing household worklessness; and (re-)engaging non-employed claimants to move them closer to labour market participation (DfEE, 1999). To advance these goals the Government introduced a suite of 'New Deal' employment programmes targeted at different segments of the claimant population, and began to reconfigure the social security and employment service apparatus.

The employment programmes included the: New Deal for Young People (NDYP); New Deal 25+ (ND 25+);[2] New Deal for Lone Parents (NDLP); New Deal for Disabled People (NDDP); New Deal for Partners of the Unemployed (NDPU); and New Deal 50+ (ND 50+) (Griggs et al, 2014). The NDYP and ND 25+ rolled out in 1998 and participation for 18–24-year-olds was mandatory once claiming Jobseeker's Allowance (JSA) for six months, with those aged 25–49 mandated to participate in ND 25+ at 18 (initially 24) months. The NDYP involved a period of intensified job search and advice (the Gateway) for up to 16 weeks, managed by the Employment Service. After which continuing participants were required to opt for one of the following four options: a waged job of 30 plus hours per week with a public or private sector employer for six months with the employer receiving a £60 per week subsidy[3] and £750 towards training; an education/training placement lasting up to 12 months; a six-month placement with a voluntary organisation; or community-oriented work with the Environmental Taskforce. The 'non-employment' options paid the equivalent of benefits, plus a small grant. If no movement into work was secured, then participants returned to the Employment Service for further assistance, and became eligible to participate in the NDYP again after six months if claiming JSA (Lourie, 1997a: 32; Walker and Wiseman, 2003: 11–12; Webb, 2003: 28).

The first stage of participation in the ND 25+ involved intensive job-search advice and support for six months. Participants after this point then had the option of a six-month job with an employer subsidised at £75 per week, an education or training placement for up to 12 months or a move onto other state employment service provision (Hasluck, 2000: 2–3). Revisions to the ND 25+ in 2001 firmed up the employment focus of the programme to reduce scope for claimants to passively participate and to accelerate re-engagement (Hasluck, 2002: i–ii). Mandated participation was moved to 18 months[4] and involved a 16-week Gateway period, followed by up to six months' participation in training, self-employment, subsidised employment or work experience. A period of intensified job-search assistance followed for participants completing without securing employment (Hasluck, 2002: 3–4).

The Government backstopped participation with the threat of sanctions to foster compliance and strengthen the work ethic, depicting this as a form of 'tough love' (Peck, 1999; Blunkett, 2006: 154; Hansard, 1997: col 308). A failure to apply, accept, attend or loss of an NDYP placement could trigger loss of JSA payment for two weeks, increasing to four weeks for a second sanction within a year, or 26 weeks for a third sanction within a year. Similarly, participants in the ND 25+ risked sanction of a JSA payment for failure to comply with programme conditions (Harris, 2008: 65). The expanding support for labour market reintegration and production of labour power involved then an active drive to curtail claimant autonomy and instil pliability.

Conversely, for working-age sick and disabled people in receipt of Incapacity Benefit[5] (IB), lone parents claiming Income Support (IS) and non-employed partners of JSA claimants, employment programme participation remained voluntary. The NDP was the complementary package of support accompanying the recasting of non-employed partners (mainly women) of unemployed claimants as job seekers, rather than functional dependants of JSA claimants (Beale, 2005: 48–50). Introduced in 1999, the NDP targeted partners of JSA claimants unemployed for six months plus and was subsequently made available to partners of other benefit claimants, including IS/IB and the in-work benefit, Working Families' Tax Credit (WFTC). The support available to NDP participants included: advice and guidance; access to basic training (with a top-up allowance paid for approved training); support for transitional costs with moving into employment; and potential assistance with childcare costs (Beale, 2005: 48; Coleman and Seeds, 2007: 8).

These additional supports for unwaged social reproductive work and action to address gendered presumptions of dependency were in keeping with Labour's progressive market-liberal goal of lowering the barriers to labour market participation among non-employed partners. While not dismissing the enhanced individual opportunities this helped open, this should not obscure that the functional goal was the mobilisation of a latent segment of the surplus population and their integration into the labour reserve or active army of labour. Or that this expanded and enhanced state direction of the activity of a segment of the working-age non-employed population previously excluded from its purview.

The mobilisation of IS lone parents for paid work also reflected the intersection of New Labour's class and economic order politics. The lone-parent employment rate (45.3 per cent) in 1997 lagged the overall employment rate for working age men (77.8 per cent) and women (67.6 per cent) (DWP, 2007a: 51 and 53). There was scope then for a more active engagement of lone parent IS claimants to expand labour utilisation, improve labour market flexibilisation, and mitigate the poverty and social exclusion that undermined economic stability (Blair, 1996: 93–4; Grover and Stewart, 2002). The NDLP, which was mainstreamed across Great Britain in 1998, involved inviting lone-parent IS claimants, whose youngest dependent child was aged 5 and above, to interviews with personal advisors to discuss: claimants' employment experience, preferences and plans; job-search assistance and advice; access to state supports; and 'better off in work' calculations to help identify financial returns from employment. NDLP participants could avail of various services, including childcare support and (basic) training and work experience opportunities. Participants in approved training were paid a 'top-up' (initially £10 and then £15) to their weekly IS and frontline staff in the public employment service had a discretionary fund to help with transitions into employment (Webb, 2003: 54; Beale, 2005: 78; NAO, 2007: 36).

The voluntary nature of the scheme reduced the risk of opposition and helped to construct lone-parent activation as a progressive, inclusive initiative. In practice, though, the interest of IS lone parents in the NDLP was limited. Evans et al (2003: 18) estimated that lone-parent NDLP participants as a proportion of all lone-parent IS claimants stood at 2 per cent in the first quarter of 1999 and had risen to only 8 per cent in the first quarter of 2002. Subsequently, Brown and Joyce (2007: 27) indicated 17 per cent of claimants, eligible for the NDLP, had participated in the scheme. Whether through lack of awareness, understanding, or active choice a substantial portion of IS lone-parent claimants were not reached by the voluntary approach, and in 2001 mandatory lone-parent Work-Focused Interviews (LPWFIs) were introduced. These marked the beginning of requirements for IS lone parents to engage directly with the state to discuss employment opportunities as a condition of benefit receipt. The LPWFIs were first mandated for new lone parents flowing onto IS with children aged 5 and above and for those in the existing stock of lone-parent claimants with a child 13 years of age or older. The requirement to attend LPWFIs was then gradually extended to all lone-parent IS claimants by 2004 (DWP, 2011a: 11; Rafferty and Wiggan, 2017: 513).

New Labour's enthusiasm for (re)mobilising non-employed working-age benefit claimants for employment also brought people in receipt of IB into the purview of its activation strategy. In the mid-1980s there had been around 1 million incapacity-related benefit claimants and by 1998 this had risen to 2.5 million (HM Treasury/DWP, 2003: 25). The Government was particularly concerned by the stock of IB claimants, noting that although many people moved off IB each year, around half were long-term claimants (five years plus) (DWP, 2002: 6). In addition, the employment rate for disabled people stood at 38 per cent in 1997, some 35 percentage points below the overall working-age employment rate (DWP, 2007a: 51–3). The stated belief of the Government was that rising health-related economic inactivity and low employment participation among disabled people reflected a combination of: discriminatory social views and practices (including negative employer attitudes and unsupportive working environments); weak financial incentives within social security to risk a move into paid work;

and limited specialist advice and support for condition management and labour market transitions (HM Treasury/DWP, 2003: 21–2). State managers were adamant that the absence of regular engagement and employment-oriented discussion had led to disengagement among IB claimants and with sufficient support and incentives many people could compete for jobs and enter employment (Education and Employment Select Committee, 1999; DWP, 2002: 7–15). In short, a reconfiguration of the state apparatus could increase the transition of IB claimants into the floating labour reserve or labour force, and reduce the numbers sinking into the 'pauperised' segment of the surplus population, cut off from making a direct contribution to production of value.

The NDDP[6] was rolled out in 2001 and intended to support activation of IB claimants by providing access to advice and guidance regarding job opportunities, job search and application activity, and assistance with interview preparation (Orr et al, 2007: 13). Between 2001 and August 2008, 306,000 people participated in the NDDP (Morgan, 2008), though the proportion of the eligible population engaging with NDDP was low, rising from around 1 per cent to 3 per cent (Stafford, 2007: 45). Administrative information indicated the proportion of NDDP participants gaining a job within a year of engagement was around one third in 2001–02 (32 per cent), rising to just over four in ten (44 per cent) for 2004–05 (Stafford, 2007: 111). It is less clear what proportion of jobs, irrespective of the NDDP, would have been secured, or whether the NDDP improved job sustainability, but the NDDP did little to address existing patterns of labour market segmentation and stratification. A greater proportion of participating women than men tended to enter customer-facing service occupations, with men more likely to take elementary, or skilled, trade jobs. Lower-paying occupations were more evident in the types of job secured, and the share entering management and professional occupations was lower than the share of such jobs in the broader economy (Stafford, 2004: 131).

From the Government's perspective however, evaluations suggested that once the costs had been taken into account HM Treasury made a net financial gain from the NDDP (Greenberg and Davis, 2007: 82–91; Stafford, 2007: 174–7). With research suggesting higher employment entry and cost improvements in managing this claimant population were realisable, but beset by a problem of limited engagement there was, then, a case for development and expansion of activation interventions to this segment of the non-employed claimant population. It is worth noting, however, that the voluntary nature of the scheme skewed the composition of participants. NDDP participants tended to possess higher educational qualifications, have more recent employment experience, fewer health constraints and a shorter period of benefit receipt than the broader IB population (Stafford, 2007: 47).

In contrast to the well-resourced NDYP and ND 25+ flagship schemes, the NDDP, NDLP and NDP were statements of future intent. The introduction laid a marker for the gradual emergence of an expansive, interlocking system of social security and employment policy and governance reform, which, as we return to in Chapter 9, would remake the state apparatus to improve its ability to reach into and (re)organise the non-employed working-age claimant population for (re)commodification (Walker and Wiseman, 2003; Griggs et al, 2014).

Re-regulating low-income employment

Stipulating the minimum hourly rate of pay

As a complement to reforms to social security and employment services for people not in paid work were attempts to stabilise 'in-work' incomes associated with low-paid jobs via the introduction of a National Minimum Wage (NMW)[7] and improvements to in-work benefits. Again, these aligned with Labour's particular progressive market-liberal approach to labour commodification, which positioned medium-term capital accumulation as best served by utilising moderate state intervention to better regulate exploitation in ways that did little to re-empower labour as a collective political actor. This is not to diminish the income gains that low-wage workers experienced as a consequence of the NMW or in-work benefits. Also, given the Conservatives' undermining of collective bargaining, abolition of the Wage Councils and vociferous opposition to the idea of an NMW, then New Labour's introduction of an NMW in 1999 appears a political triumph and immediate material gain for low-wage workers. Yet, by 1997, employer organisations had ceased to oppose the NMW once they came to understand it would be set at a level they regarded as manageable (Rutter et al, 2012: 62–5). This calls to mind Saville's (1957) observation that the development of social welfare has been shaped by the opposition and dissembling of the propertied classes, whose goal has been to delay reforms so that eventual concessions take a form unlikely to trouble fundamental class power relations and the profitability of capital.

New Labour's NMW was of course not intended to disrupt capitalist social relations, but rather stabilise and improve conditions for accumulation. The NMW supporting a more inclusive competitive market order and preventing excessive wage competition by placing a lower limit on the hourly price of labour power, preventing unscrupulous employers reducing wage rates in anticipation that the fall in worker incomes could be offset by higher in-work benefit entitlements (Grover and Stewart, 2002; Dillow, 2007: 104; Rutter et al, 2012; Brown, 2017).

As with interest rate setting, the Government established an arm's-length independent advisory body – the Low Pay Commission (LPC) – in

1997 to distance decisions from everyday politics (Rutter et al, 2012: 71). Charged with suggesting (though not setting) the NMW rate, the LPC was populated by employers, trade unionists and academics. Although the setting of the NMW rate was decoupled partly from the core state apparatus, deliberations and decisions prioritised business profitability and employment growth in keeping with the Government's broader economic strategy. The LPC had to take into account the issue of employer buy-in, potential effects of a given rate on employment and wage and price stability (Metcalf, 1999: 174–9; Brown, 2009: 430–3; Brown, 2017: 133). Ministers (and the LPC) were keen to avoid the risk that higher wages would price young people out of jobs and perceived lower pay an acceptable trade-off to protect jobs (Sargeant, 2010: 352), and this influenced the setting of the initial rate and a lower rate for the 18–21 age group (Metcalf, 1999: 174 and 182; Sargeant, 2010: 353).

The NMW adult rate in 1999 was set equivalent to 47 per cent of the then median wage rate (Brewer, 2008: 8). This lifted the wages in 1.2 million low-paid jobs, and by 2004 the NMW rate had increased quicker than the rate of inflation (Metcalf, 2008: 490–1), and was equivalent to about 52 per cent of the median hourly pay rate (Brewer, 2008: 8). In the absence of any discernible negative impact on employment, the NMW provided opportunity for ministers to demonstrate that social justice and economic orthodoxy could go hand-in-hand (Blair, 1999; Rutter et al, 2012; Balls, 2016: 113), buttressing the Government's progressive market-liberal project.

In-work benefit reforms

The structure of the NMW, though, affirmed age-related wage rate segmentation, complementing age-related benefit rates as a means to bolster the labour commodification of young adults, thereby re-regulating, but not departing from the moves by preceding administrations to contain the price of (youth) labour. In keeping with New Labour's articulation of a more coherent class politics of claimant subordination, and an economic order strategy of social stabilisation and extensive labour utilisation, the NMW was accompanied by changes to the in-work benefit system to improve the level of state financial assistance to low-income families (Grover and Stewart, 2002: 31–32; Millar, 2009: 234–37; Grover, 2016a: 127–32). The first change was replacement of Family Credit (FC) by the Working Families' Tax Credit WFTC in 1999. Like FC, the WFTC was a means-tested benefit available to low-income families with children, where one or more parent was in paid work of 16 hours per week. The exact level of payment varied by family income and hours worked per week, but WFTC included a lower withdrawal rate (55 per cent versus 70 per cent) as earnings increased, and a higher threshold at which support tapered away, in order to reduce high marginal taxation rates. Assistance with childcare costs was also improved, with the Childcare Tax Credit (CCTC) element of WFTC covering up to 70 per cent of formal childcare costs for two children (Inland Revenue, 2003a: 5). From under 750,000 FC recipients in May 1997, by May 2002 there were 1.3 million WFTC recipients, with lone-parent families as a proportion of total recipient families rising from around 48 per cent in November 1997 to 54 per cent in November 2002 (Inland Revenue, 2003a: 3).[8]

In April 2003 the Working Tax Credit (WTC) and Child Tax Credit (CTC) replaced the WFTC. This reform disaggregated payment of a wage top-up for low-paid workers (that is, WTC), from the financial assistance for the additional costs of children to low-income households in general (that is, CTC). The main innovation of the WTC was it extended support to lone-income childless families provided a claimant was aged 25 years old plus and worked 30 hours per week, or more. The CTC rolled together supports for child dependants within out-of-work benefits and those in the preceding WFTC, so that CTC was payable to both in-work and out-of-work households (Wiggan, 2010: 634; HM Revenue and Customs, 2012).[9] Removing the rigid separation of financial assistance for families in and out of paid work via CTC meant the financial 'risk' facing non-employed claimants transitioning into paid work diminished, enhancing the predictability of income and work incentives (Grover, 2016a: 134–5).

In 2004–05 around 1.4 million 'in-work families' were receiving WTC/CTC support, 2.8 million a CTC payment and 234,000 the WTC payment alone (HMRC, 2012: 13). The WTC/CTC was particularly important for lone parents, with Millar (2009: 242) pointing out that around four in five lone-parent families in work received both WTC and CTC, pointing to their lower wages/ intensity of labour market participation (see also HMRC, 2012: 14). The cost of in work benefits to the Exchequer was considerable, with Brewer (2008: 11) estimating that expenditure increased from under £2.5 billion in 1996–97 to more than £6 billion by 2002–03. The resourcing of in work benefits is indicative of economic order politics moving to the fore and New Labour's willingness, relative to their Conservative predecessors, to use public spending to undergird the market for low wage, flexible work, advancing an extensive labour utilisation strategy, while bolstering social cohesion.

The enhanced support via tax credits did not so much eliminate the gendering of care and paid work though, as rework the state's long-standing treatment within social security of non-employed lone parents (usually mothers) (Millar, 2000: 335). While lone parents continued to experience constraints on employment, the WFTC and then WTC/CTC system improved lone parents' ability to combine parenting and (part-time) paid work, making their commodification as labour power potentially more realisable (Wiggan, 2010). Consequently, the structure of the in-work benefit system, as it expanded the labour supply for part-time and lower-paid jobs (Brewer, 2008: 7), reflected, and worked to shape broader gendered patterns of labour market segmentation and stratification.

Blundell and Hoynes (2004) concluded that, while WFTC increased employment among low-income lone parents and stimulated job entry in previously 'workless' couples, it could disincentivise labour market engagement among employed couples. The household assessment for tax credit entitlements meaning the pay of a second earner in couple families was partly offset by lower tax credit entitlement (Brewer, 2008: 16–17) and additional work-related costs. New Labour's priority, however, was to reduce the number of households without a working-age adult engaged in paid work, and the new tax credits aligned with this goal (Finn, 2003b). Taken together, the NMW and reform in work benefit system point to how a progressive two-nation governing project of inclusion and social cohesion cohered with an accumulation strategy that involved reforms to facilitate extensive labour utilisation. Reforms to out-of-work benefits and employment services to engage the broader non-employed claimant population in work-related activity are also indicative of this, but were flanked by a more coercive approach to activating unemployed claimants (that is, an extraction strategy of disciplinary inclusion).

Reconfiguration of employment services and social security administration

Integral to New Labour's state strategy of modernisation was an embrace of the New Public Management techniques initiated by their Conservative predecessors. These had upended traditional bureaucratic practices, expectations and power relations attendant to the class settlement of Britain's social democratic productivist political economy (Considine, 2001) by instituting business logic and market rationality into the organisation and operation of public services. Public bureaucrats who regularly engaged with benefit claimants and made decisions about work availability, benefit eligibility and sanctioning were unionised, and represented an, albeit weak, potential bureaucratic centre of power within the state apparatus that could obstruct government reforms. As Considine (2001: 52–6) details, the Conservative reforms pushed back against this risk by creating an incentive system that would encourage frontline staff to govern themselves in line with Government objectives. The effect of new performance management systems was to tighten control of state managers at the centre of the state apparatus over the activity of frontline staff, by holding them more tightly to account for achieving stipulated targets and expenditure. In the case of social security and employment and training services this meant greater attention to policing benefit eligibility and job entry of claimants, while containing costs (Considine, 2001: 44). Price (2000: 296), for example, noted how, in response to concerns that frontline staff were insufficiently policing claimant availability for work, the Conservatives strengthened performance measures to drive up referral of claimants suspected of not being available to take a job.

The complex division of responsibility embedded in policymaking and performance management for unemployed and non-employed claimants (see Chapter 7) was viewed by New Labour as poorly suited, however, to mobilise all working-age claimants for labour market participation (Wiggan, 2007a: 417; Wiggan, 2007b: 660–1a). The New Labour Government's Green Paper on welfare reform, for example, had outlined a case for 'modernisation' of benefit administration and employment services, given the emergent post-industrial labour market (DSS, 1998). With the joining-up of activity between benefit administration and employment services a means to (re)prioritise and mainstream labour market participation (Hansard, 1998: cc 681), institutional reconfiguration was central to managing expansion in the population of claimants targeted for labour commodification.

The first step towards joining up the governance of benefits and employment services and transforming the organisational culture of working-age provision so as to offer a more personalised, flexible and work-first-focused system of administration was taken with the announcement of the 'ONE' service pilots (Kelleher et al, 2002). The launch of this pilot in 1999 to integrate benefits and employment services in a one-stop shop formed a staging post in New Labour's crafting of an administrative counterpart to their inclusive-productivist active labour market programmes. By the end of New Labour's first term the Government was signalling a thoroughgoing restructuring of the Employment Service and Benefits Agency, and parent departments (DSS, 2000; DfEE, 2001: 14; Wiggan, 2007a).

The full realisation of this took place with the integration from 2002 of the Employment Service and working-age components of the Benefits Agency into a new agency, named Jobcentre Plus (JCP) (DfEE/DSS, 1998: 1; Kelleher et al, 2002: 7). In parallel, the employment components of the DfEE were merged into the DSS and a new department created, the Department for Work and Pensions (DWP), which became the parent department for JCP (Wiggan, 2007a: 418; Wright, 2011: 88). The creation of the DWP and JCP replaced the deregulatory vision and narrow focus on mobilising (only) unemployed people (the labour reserve) of their New Right predecessors, with a set of institutions administratively geared towards improving the articulation of the Government's approach to labour commodification with its broader economic strategy (Wiggan, 2007a: 419; 2007b).

At the core of this was the further development of a market-managerialist state strategy with the operation of the new DWP and JCP subject to the New Labour Government's refined performance-management apparatus, in which quasi-contracts ('Public Service Agreements' (PSA)) between the centre and line ministries set targets for delivery. The PSA system enhanced the power of the Chancellor of the Exchequer and HM Treasury to direct and monitor the activity of departments and their subordinate bodies, in line with Government's overall socio-economic and political objectives (Grover and Stewart, 2002: 184; Wiggan, 2007b; Weishaupt, 2011). The key employment-related targets of the new DWP included the following: raising of the overall employment rate; reducing the gap between the overall rate and the employment rates of lone parents; disabled people; people with few or no qualifications; minority ethnic groups and people aged 50 plus; addressing worklessness in families with children; and driving down fraud and error (HM Treasury, 2002: 31).

For JCP, the Job Entry Target (JET) provided the key performance focus for the organisation (Johnson, 2003; Wiggan, 2007a). The JET set a point target for JCP, which cascaded down the organisation to local offices. Greater points for a job entry were assigned to incentivise engagement with claimants deemed likely to be 'less job ready'. A job entry for lone parents and sick and disabled inactive benefit claimants was worth 12 points, compared with 8 points for long-term JSA claimants, 4 points for short-term JSA claimants and 2 points for unemployed people not in receipt of benefit (Johnson, 2003: 27). While the New Labour Government positioned themselves as enthusiastically pro-business, the centralised control of employment and training programme content remained with the New Deals. The public employment service took the lead in the majority of New Deal areas in managing the diverse state and non-state actors engaged in delivery of these programmes (Finn, 2005: 104; Considine et al, 2015). The Prime Minster had been adamant though that space for experimentation with greater private sector involvement be provided for, and in ten locations private sector organisations were contracted to lead the delivery of the New Deal (PREM 49/43).

In keeping with this desire to explore the potential of the private sector and quasi-markets to stimulate innovation and cost savings, the Government rolled out the first iteration of the Employment Zone (EZ) pilot scheme in 15 areas in 1998 (Bruttel, 2005: 392; Griffiths and Durkin, 2007: 13–15). In the EZ, third- and private-sector providers were contracted to organise return-to-work interventions for long-term unemployed claimants aged 25 plus, with eligibility subsequently extended to JSA claimants aged

18–24 who had already completed the NDYP, lone parents and those characterised as 'disadvantaged jobseekers' (Griffiths and Durkin, 2007: 14; NAO, 2007: 38). Under the funding model for the EZ, each contracted provider was paid an: input payment per participant commencing the programme; outcome payment for securing job entry; and outcome payment for securing job sustainment for 13 weeks (Hales et al, 2003: 8; Hasluck et al, 2003: 3–4; Finn, 2005: 110). The goal was to test the replacement of state prescription with a market-based approach, whereby providers were given freedom over delivery and financial incentives were used to drive provider innovation, control costs and secure desired outcomes (Bruttel, 2005).

The growing experimentation with market mechanisms and outcome-based contracting in employment programme delivery should be viewed as a route by which the state began to tie the financial interests, practices and outlook of delivery organisations and their frontline workers more closely to the realisation of the goals of state managers. As Wright (2011) explains, New Labour's market managerialism enabled ministers to de-centralise service delivery without losing the ability to direct and impose discipline on subordinate parts of the (para-)state apparatus and secure compliance with ramping up activation pressure on programme participants. In short, a market-managerialist state strategy cohered with, and augmented, an extraction strategy of disciplinary inclusion and an accumulation strategy of extensive labour utilisation.

Navigating the activation state

Whereas the prospect of 'work for your benefit' under the Conservatives engendered opposition among organised labour during the 1980s, the TUC accepted the thrust of the New Labour Government's employment strategy, but remained critical of the payment model of benefits plus, rather than wages (TUC, 2001). That the TUC and trade unions did not seriously contest the Government's employment strategy, despite it being premised upon the containment of wages, is indicative of their diminished social weight in society and power in the labour market policymaking apparatus. As detailed in Chapter 3, union coverage of the labour force had declined, particularly among private sector workers and young people, and days lost to industrial action had collapsed. In parallel, the TUC-linked Unemployed Workers Centres (UWCs), which, irrespective of their limitations in fostering claimant self-activity, provided an organisational resource for non-employed labour (Bagguley, 1992; Richards, 2009), had decreased in number from around 200 in the mid-1980s to just over 80 by the turn of the millennium (MSS.292/PUB/4/3/240).

Outside of the mainstream of the organised labour movement, the decline of the Claimant Unions further weakened the prospect of claimant led activity. The aforementioned autonomous claimant groups of the Groundswell Network that had come together in the mid-1990s to oppose the JSA and Project Work (Groundswell, 1997) recognised that New Labour's reforms represented a development of attempts to curtail access to social security and improve the state's capacity to sort and channel claimants into the secondary labour market. At the local level, groups still active continued to disseminate information and guidance on benefits and employment programmes, and engaged in occasional direct action to aid claimants. Reflective of the broader decline in labour mobilisation though (Bailey, 2014: 35–6), by the early 2000s the network was moribund and collective opposition dissipated[10] (Counter Information, 1998: 4; Aufheben, n.d.: 18–19).

The absence of mass opposition to the ratcheting-up of work–related activity requirements (Cinalli, 2012: 185–7) should, Aufheben (2011) argued, also be understood as due to the upturn in the economy creating more opporutnities for claimants to move into employment. Even if jobs proved temporary they offered an alternative to mandatory participation in the New Deal options and respite from benefit policing. It is notable that after a year of operation just under 50 per cent of participants leaving the NDYP sustained employment of 13 weeks, falling to just under 40 per cent by October 2001 (NAO, 2002: 24). Also, although entry into employment was the single-largest recorded destination for those exiting the NYDP by October 2001, a majority (60 per cent) returned to JSA; claimed other benefits; remained unemployed or inactive, but not claiming; moved into education; or left for another unknown destination[11] (NAO, 2002: 10). By the third quarter of 2001 among those starting the NDYP around 16 per cent had participated twice and 2 per cent had been on the NDYP three times (NAO, 2002: 14). By 2003 the proportion of NDYP participants that had been in the scheme three times had reached over 9 per cent, and 3 per cent were on their fourth (or higher) round of participation. Similarly, among participants commencing the ND 25+ in 2003, around 8 per cent of all starts were third starts and 3 per cent had participated four or more times (DWP, 2011b: 2–3). Such figures are a useful reminder that while early evaluation of the NDYP suggested it contributed to a decline in youth unemployment of 25,000–45,000 over what would otherwise have occurred (NAO, 2002: 20), a large number of participants ended up cycling between out-of-work benefits, New Deals and employment.

Shildrick et al's (2010) and MacDonald's (2008) qualitative research into cycling between low-paid jobs and out-of-work benefits provides insight into the interaction between people's work ethic, grudging acceptance of poor work, limited expectations of state employment schemes and a benefit system that discouraged claims. Their research points to how claimants' motivation to take even low-paid jobs helped constitute the supply for insecure work found in the secondary labour market, encouraging its expansion and sustainment (Shildrick et al, 2010: 7). MacDonald (2008: 246) terms this a process of 'economic marginalisation', which casts our attention to how the investment in the multi-stage, multi-option NDYP/ND 25+ for unemployed people provided state managers with new tools to regulate and manage the flow of labour both between employment and unemployment and within the unemployed category itself. That is, the New Deals were not simply concerned with transitioning people into jobs, but also in transforming the nature and experience of unemployment. The New Deals worked to reduce the numbers of long-term unemployed claimants at risk of sinking into the 'pauperised' segment of the relative surplus population through extended labour market detachment, which would diminish the potential labour power that could be brought to market and offered to capital.

Repeat transitions between work and out of work benefits, while seemingly a waste of effort and resources, were however beneficial in this regard with claimants re-positioned as roving members of the floating labour reserve and secondary labour market. In the light of a decline in long-term unemployment (Van Reenan, 2004: 467), the activation strategy, from the perspective of New Labour, could reasonably be regarded as a success. The enhanced functional correspondence between the state labour commodification apparatus, flexible labour market and service-dominated economy improved the state's ability to (re)impose work, and the economy to sustain a high-employment rate and non-inflationary expansion (see Wells, 2001: 249–57; Van Reenan, 2004: 461; Nickell, 2001).

The novelty of New Labour's approach, however, was that its economic strategy necessarily implied reaching beyond unemployed claimants to activate a portion of the 'latent' relative surplus population of non-employed working-age benefit claimants. To achieve this goal required development of initiatives to engage IB and IS benefits claimants and shift social expectations of the work-related activity that could be reasonably expected of the non-employed claimant population. For lone parents, for example, a complex array of social, personal, financial and institutional factors, not least the availability of childcare and the feasibility of jobs that fitted with care work, contoured employment decisions and whether or not lone parents engaged with the NDLP (Brown and Joyce, 2007: 29–37). The structure of the social security system that New Labour inherited had also implicitly endorsed the 'value' of care work, by permitting lone parents to receive income assistance until their youngest dependent child was aged 16, with no requirement to engage in work-related activity (Millar, 2000). Having led with the carrot in terms of activating non-employed IS and IB claimants during their first two terms of office, New Labour switched to brandishing the stick in their third term in response to the seeming reluctance of claimants to act as the self-activating, enthusiastic sellers of labour power the Government deemed they should be.

9

Disciplinary inclusion and extensive labour utilisation: 2005–10

Employment programme performance and the dynamics of incremental reform

The initial active labour market reforms initiated by New Labour after 1997 could, from the perspective of ministers, be regarded as at least a partial success with respect to improving claimant transitions between unemployment and paid work and reducing the stock of (and flow into) unemployment. Evaluations of the New Deal for Young People (NDYP)/New Deal 25+ (ND 25+) pointed to participant take-up of jobs, above what would otherwise be expected in their absence, and contributing to claimants remaining in receipt of out-of-work benefits for fewer days (Hasluck and Green, 2007: 34; Beale et al, 2008). Some of the heavy lifting was likely attributable, as Griffiths and Durkin (2007: 24–5) point out, to the mandatory nature of participation in the core schemes working to discourage continuing claims. Most participants in the NDYP, for example, exited the scheme prior to entering the options phase (NAO, 2002: 10).

By the end of May 2005, 11 per cent of the 1.23 million leaving NDYP exited before an interview, with 55 per cent exiting during the Gateway stage. Only around 14 per cent left during the options stage, with a further 20 per cent exiting after this (ONS, 2005: S102). Most Jobseeker's Allowance (JSA) claimants would, in any case, have ceased claiming JSA by nine months' unemployment, but such a pattern of exit implicitly affirmed the seeming value of low-cost job-search assistance, and policing of benefit claims for driving claimants off benefits. By mid-2004, as Labour approached the end of its second term in office, around one in five unemployed people aged 16–64 were unemployed for 12 months plus. In mid-1997 this had been more than one third and very long-term unemployment had fallen from over 400,000 people to around 120,000 (ONS, 2022d).

In terms of class politics, New Labour's reforms to out of work social security benefits and employment programmes increased the pressure on claimants to sell their labour power under conditions not of their choosing, augmenting the supply of labour for lower paid jobs (Sunley et al, 2006: 74–5; Shildrick et al, 2010: 10; McCollum, 2011). The National Audit Office (NAO) (2007: 23), for example, noted higher turnover of vacancies for elementary occupations compared with highly skilled occupations. Not surprisingly, the former was more likely to be filled by long-term unemployed claimants (Bruttel, 2005: 399). Research commissioned by the NAO suggested that among those leaving NDYP/ND 25+ and Employment Zone (EZ) programmes directly for a job, only around 25–30 per cent sustained it for 12 months (NAO, 2007: 17; also Bruttel, 2005: 399–400; Griffiths and Durkin, 2007: 19–26). Davies (n.d.: 191–3) also points out that performance data for NDYP, ND 25+ and EZ showed that 13-week 'sustained' job outcomes as a proportion of programme 'starts' had declined over the period of New Labour's second term, casting doubt on their long-term efficacy.

Although, cycling between (low-)paid work and out-of-work benefits reflected changes in employer demand, this was, as McCollum's (2011, 2012) research with people engaged in work–welfare cycling indicates, also a matter of claimant and worker agency. The period of buoyant labour demand of the early to mid-2000s meant that individuals with few or no qualifications had scope to avoid applying for, or to leave, a job they deemed undesirable (McCollum, 2011: 154–5). The continued salience of gendered-employment segmentation and claimant rejection of 'poor work' for activation initiatives was clear, for example, in how some (male) claimants were reluctant to consider service-sector jobs perceived to be dominated by women, and/or associated with low wages, part-time hours or insecurity (Lindsay, 2002: 414; McQuaid and Lindsay, 2002: 622; McCollum, 2011: 151).

Activating claimants into jobs they were reluctant to take due to the terms and conditions on offer, meant state employees walked a fine line between complying with performance targets linked to the Government's drive to expand employment, output and social cohesion, and the risk of claimant disengagement from services, exit into informality or abrupt departures from jobs that disrupted business (Sunley et al, 2006: 140; Wright, 2006; Grant, 2013). Given New Labour's expressed vision of inclusion, cohesion and economic growth rested on expanding labour commodification, then it is perhaps not surprising that ministers began to hone in on 'work–welfare cycling' (McCollum, 2012: 218) during their third term, implying it was indicative of flawed institutions and insufficient imposition of 'work' obligations. A claimed 'can work, won't work culture' being discursively contrasted with responsible 'hard working families', and providing the warrant for disciplinary welfare reform (Secretary of State for Work and Pensions, 2006b), in keeping with a progressive two-nations mode of leadership.

> These repeat claimants pose a fundamental question about the design of the welfare system; for the degree of conditionality; for the contract between those out of work – and the hard-working taxpaying families who are supporting them. (John Hutton MP, Secretary of State for Work and Pensions, 2006b)

This is not to suggest claimants were, or are, anti-work, but to recognise seeking employment is not necessarily synonymous with enthusiasm for accepting any job (Wiggan, 2015a: 377). A government-commissioned survey of people with repeat JSA claims found a majority (70 per cent) of respondents thought that 'having almost any job is better than being unemployed'; a clear majority, then, but also a sizeable minority that did not agree that claimants had a responsibility to take any job (Carpenter, 2006: 60). Turning to actual job-search behaviour, the same survey reported among respondents without a job at the time, four in five had searched for work in the preceding four weeks, which conveys the centrality of a commitment to paid work. The intensity of job search though, was arguably suggestive of a compliance first approach from claimants. Just over a third (37 per cent) of respondents without work reported a total of nine or fewer job applications in the preceding six months and around one fifth (21 per cent) reported five or fewer job applications (Carpenter, 2006: 52–3). Moreover, just under one in five (18 per cent) of all respondents surveyed did express attitudes that questioned the centrality of paid work in their lives (Carpenter, 2006: 61). Such a pattern of job-search activity indicates there remained scope for claimants to continue to exercise some autonomy around labour market participation, despite the drive to curtail this by successive governments (Trickey and Walker, 2001: 186–89).

Strengthening the activation push was central to the pursuit of full employability, which now moved centre stage. Against the backdrop of an expanding economy, low unemployment and high labour demand, ministers set out an aspiration to achieve an 80 per cent employment rate for working-age people within a decade. To achieve this would require raising the work-related expectations and conditionality applied to the broader non-employed working-age claimant population (Hansard, 2005a: 232; DWP, 2006a: 3). Fewer than 5 per cent of new IB claimants had elected to join the New Deal for Disabled People (NDDP) (DWP, 2006c: Ev217) and as Millar (2003: 130) points out, New Labour initially gave priority to resourcing interventions targeting unemployed claimants, rather than the broader non-employed population of lone-parent Income Support (IS), and IB claimants. By March 2007 around four fifths of the £4.8 billion cost associated with the six New Deals related to spending on the NDYP and ND 25+ (NAO, 2007: 36–7). In keeping with New Labour's progressive market-liberal modernising project, the reform package to extend and intensify activation of non-employed claimants and address the issue of cycling between out-of-work benefits and low-paid jobs (McCollum, 2011) involved new developments in the quasi-marketisation of employment services (that is, a market managerialist state strategy), articulated with a stricter application of work-related benefit conditionality (that is, an extraction strategy of disciplinary inclusion) (Finn, 2009; Wright, 2009; Grover, 2012).

Unifying the New Deals for unemployed people

An early signal of this change was the announcement in 2004 of the 'Building on the New Deal' (BOND) proposal. Under BOND, local Jobcentre Plus (JCP) offices would have been given a menu of various services and the freedom to decide what might work best for the claimant in dialogue with them, rather than provision being prescribed by central government by particular programme; for example, NDYP; ND 25+ or New Deal 50+ (ND 50+) (DWP, 2004: 18–24). The heterogeneity of claimant capabilities meant that linking a particular intervention to a given benefit category was increasingly viewed as problematic and meta-analysis into the effectiveness of active labour market programmes added weight to the case for less prescription from the centre (Hasluck and Green, 2007).

Local flexibility, however, would remain regulated by the Department for Work and Pensions (DWP) Public Service Agreement targets and a strengthening of outcome-based performance management, with ministers flagging greater use of quasi-markets and contracted provision (DWP, 2004). Managerial direction from the centre together with market rationality would shape the priorities and behaviour of subordinate arms of the state organisation and their employees, to ensure alignment with government priorities and preferences. The BOND model was derailed before its introduction, seemingly due to spending constraints (Work and Pensions Committee, 2007: 20–2) and changes in departmental political leadership. The desire for a less prescriptive model of contracting out that placed greater weight on securing job sustainability did not go away though as the New Labour Government and the Conservative Party opposition supported marketisation, albeit to different degrees (Beale, 2005: 63).

In 2006, the then Secretary of State for Work and Pensions, John Hutton MP, commissioned the investment banker David Freud to review the organisation of employment services (Grover, 2007: 536). The subsequent paper, titled, 'Reducing dependency, increasing opportunity: options for the future of welfare to work' (Freud, 2007) (that is, the Freud Report), called for a radical reconfiguration of how employment programmes were organised, managed and funded. Discouraged from making any recommendation to privatise JCP by senior policy makers, Freud concentrated on how to make better use of non-state actors to deliver a new outcome-focused employment programme for long-term unemployed and non-employed working-age claimants (Freud, 2021: 12 and 16). In this vision, contracted third- and private-sector providers would be given operational flexibility to determine the services to provide for programme participants, while central government would direct and cohere provider activity by strengthening the connection between provider funding and achievement of sustained employment participation (Freud, 2007; also see later).

Permeating Freud's report was, as Grover (2007) notes, a determination to mainstream the inclusion of lone parents and sick and disabled people in receipt of out of work benefits in active labour market policy. The proposed competitive market order and its expanded client group was also teamed with a desire to tighten benefit conditionality for IS and IB claimants. The goal being to erode the difference in treatment of IS and IB claimants relative to JSA claimants, reducing non-employed claimants' ability to choose whether or not to participate in activation (Freud, 2007: 90). In effect, the Government was narrowing the basis on which membership of a given benefit category would translate into alleviation of the state's recommodification pressure. The state was reaching into the relative surplus population to mobilise and circulate claimants through the training segment of the labour market, topping up the labour reserve and making previously latent labour power available to employers. Although heightened conditionality recommendations were challenged by organisations such as the Child Poverty Action Group and One Parent Families, the Freud Report received cross-party endorsement at Westminster (Grover, 2007; Woodward, 2007; Griggs et al, 2014).

The 2007 DWP paper, 'Ready for Work – full employment in our generation' (DWP, 2007b), marked the partial adoption of Freud's proposals. A new employment programme – the Flexible New Deal (FND) – was announced and the case restated for provider flexibility, market competition and 'payment by results' funding to drive job-sustainability performance and reduce work–welfare cycling (DWP, 2007b; 2007c). To mitigate deadweight costs, JCP would retain responsibility for short-term unemployed claimants as the majority of claimants secured employment in fewer than six months and nine in ten by 12 months (DWP, 2007c: 9; Morgan, 2009: 5). The FND would replace the NDYP, ND 25+ and ND 50+ schemes beginning in 2009 in specific locales across Britain (phase one). After a year in receipt of JSA, all claimants would be mandated to participate in the FND for 12 months, unifying the point of mandated participation for older and younger claimants (Davies, n.d.: 199; see also DWP, 2007c: 2; Morgan, 2009).

Prior to the roll-out of FND, the benign period of economic growth sustained since the recovery from the early 1990s recession came to a shuddering halt with the financial crisis, plunging the UK economy into economic recession in 2008 (Jenkins, 2010; also see Chapter 10). With a deteriorating economic context it is perhaps not surprising that many employment programme participants were, as in earlier recessions, engaged in training and social economy activities. While the majority of NDYP participants at the end of May 2008 were in the Gateway phase, among the NDYP participants engaged in one of the four options, fewer than 2 per cent were in the employment option. Around 57 per cent were in the training and education option, while 29 per cent were in the voluntary option and 13 per cent with the environmental task force (Morgan, 2008: 4). The Trades Union Congress (TUC) and Federation of Small Business (FSB) proposed a new wage-subsidy scheme for short-time work to stem the flow of unemployment, and on a limited scale the Welsh Government introduced subsidies for short-time working in Wales, but the New Labour Government rejected a short-time working programme of its own (TUC/FSB, n.d.; Hansard, 2009b). The decision was a contrast with the willingness of the Labour Government during the late 1970s to intervene to mitigate industrial destruction and accompanying redundancies, but was consistent with a market-liberal state strategy in which employment and the price of labour power would be left to adjust to changes in employer demand.

A temporary initiative, the Young Person's Guarantee (YPG), was announced in 2009 (HM Treasury, 2009: 96) and fully rolled out in 2010 for 18–24-year-old JSA claimants. In keeping with the role of state managers in considering the long-term national conditions for accumulation and labour commodification, the YPG was aimed at mitigating the risk that the downturn would hamper the inculcation of work discipline and underdevelopment of basic employment-related skills, networks and attitudes of young people (DWP, 2009a: 38). The YPG provided for a six-month placement in a subsidised job, employment-focused training, or work experience after six months' unemployment with participation mandatory at ten months' unemployment (Children, Schools and Families Committee, 2010: 11; DWP, 2011c: 1).

The employment option was organised via the Future Job Fund (FJF) and work experience placements through the Community Taskforce (CTF). Under the FJF the Government initially allocated around £1 billion to pay employers a subsidy of up to £6,500 per FJF recruit. Ministers aimed to provide up to 150,000 subsidised employment placements, with two thirds earmarked for 18–24-year-old JSA claimants and a third for older unemployed and non-employed adults (Work and Pensions Committee, 2010: 5; DWP, 2012a: 8). FJF and CTF placements could be with public sector, third sector or private sector organisations, and to guard against substitution or displacement effects, were intended to be additional posts. The CTF placements of 25 hours a week work experience and five hours' job search paid a training allowance of the applicable benefit rate, plus a £15 top-up. Conversely, the FJF paid a wage at National Minimum Wage (NMW) rates for 25 hours' work per week (Children, Schools and Families Committee, 2010: 17; Work and Pensions Committee, 2010: 6). As in earlier periods the schemes leant heavily upon public and voluntary sector organisations to craft additional temporary jobs (Work and Pensions Committee, 2010: 20; DWP, 2012a: 9).

As initiatives to promote stability in the youth labour market, the YPG and FJF functioned as a means to warehouse temporarily surplus youth labour and stabilise the crisis-afflicted flexible labour market. This was consistent with an economic order politics of pursuing social cohesion and extensive labour utilisation as the means to create the low-inflation, low-conflict environment, regarded as propitious for improved economic growth. Yet, despite the economic crisis there was to be no turn away from the broader disciplinary approach to 'inclusion'. The pressure to take up paid work continued to be slowly ratcheted up as the real value of benefit payments declined and imposition of sanctions increased. In 1980–81, for example, the insurance-based Unemployment Benefit had been equivalent to 18.7 per cent of the average wage for a claimant aged 25 plus. By 1997–98, this had fallen to 13.4 per cent and the slide continued under New Labour, with contributory JSA worth 10.5 per cent of the average wage in 2008–09 (Hansard, 2009a, vol 490). Meanwhile, the application of JSA-benefit sanctions as a proportion of all JSA claimants rose during the first and second New Labour administrations from under 1 per cent in 1997 to just above 2 per cent in 2000 and settled around this rate until 2006. The sanctions rate then climbed to almost 4 per cent between 2006 and 2008, briefly falling back to around 2 per cent in early 2009, then rising again to 4 per cent into early 2010 (Watts et al, 2014: 5; Webster, 2014: 8).

Extending disciplinary inclusion to non-employed benefit claimants

The voluntary New Deal for Lone Parents (NDLP) and New Deal for Disabled People (NDDP) had provided an early means to experiment with activation of non-employed lone-parent IS claimants and sick and disabled IB claimants, and their performance gave little reason for ministers to pause their activation drive of non-employed claimants. The NAO noted, for example, that among a cohort of New Deal participants in 2002–03, the proportion of NDLP and NDDP participants sustaining employment for 12 months was higher than equivalent programmes for unemployed claimants (NAO, 2007: 17). Similarly, the employment additionality of the NDLP and NDDP participants in 2005–06 also compared favourably to the NDYP and ND 25+ (NAO, 2007: 9). Yet, as previously noted, the voluntary schemes skewed participation to more enthusiastic or 'job-ready' participants and limited the reach of the state into the non-employed population. As such, the extant system of out-of-work benefits and employment services was deemed to provide insufficient support, or incentives to encourage active job search (DWP, 2005: 40). For a government seeking to maximise labour market participation, the IB claimant population was a logical focus for attention. The number of claimants had risen into the late 1990s, flatlined to 2005, dipped at the beginning of New Labour's third term, before kicking up again with the run into the 2008 financial crisis (DWP, 2005: 41–42; DWP, 2006b: 4; NAO, 2010a: 14).

In recognition of this, New Labour had launched the pilot Pathway to Work (PtW) initiative in seven locales in 2003 (NAO, 2010a). The target group for the PtW included new and repeat IB claimants on a mandatory basis and existing long-term claimants on a voluntary basis (NAO, 2010a: 6–7). The PtW programme introduced the requirement for mandated claimants to undertake up to six Work-Focused Interviews (WFIs) with a dedicated personal advisor, underpinned by the threat of benefit sanction for failure to comply. In addition, the assessment that determined eligibility for IB, the Personal Capability Assessment (PCA), was moved forwards from 28 weeks to 12 weeks. The first WFI directed claimants away from participation if deemed to be relatively job-ready, or to have a severe health condition that exempted them from the PCA, with the intention being to minimise deadweight and concentrate interventions on claimants with some capacity for engaging in activity that would move them closer to employment (that is, from surplus population to labour reserve). For PtW participants a suite of training and advice services, including NDDP and a new Condition Management Programme, were available to support moves towards labour market participation. Claimants exiting IB for a job of at least 16 hours a week could also avail of a wage top-up of £40 per week – the Return to Work Credit – for the first year after moving into employment (DWP, 2008a: 1–4; Becker et al, 2010: 144).

Analysis of the early PtW pilot areas indicated that, compared with the overall six-month rate of claimants flowing off IB, the rate in the PtW areas was higher by six percentage points. Although the Work and Pensions Select Committee cautioned it was unclear what proportion were moving into employment (Work and Pensions Committee, 2006a: 54), the 'performance' of PtW pilots was sufficient for Secretary of State John Hutton MP to imply that over ten years this would contribute to reduction in the IB claimant count by 1 million (Work and Pensions Committee, 2006b: Ev229).

The NAO's subsequent report into the PtW programme suggested the 'innovation' driving programme success was a mix of bringing forward the PCA and mandated WFI. In essence, faster screening, information provision and a threat effect helped to (re)direct claimants away from IB (NAO, 2010a: 20–3). The PtW was subsequently scaled up in 2005 and 2006 as the Government moved to curtail the flow into IB as well as support re-engagement of long-term claimants. The first phase of expansion was headed by the employment service (JCP), but in keeping with the Government's market-managerialist state strategy the second phase of the roll-out from 2007 was contracted to third-sector and private sector organisations (NAO, 2010a).

Proceeding in parallel to these developments were further changes to the regime of activation for lone-parent IS claimants. From the perspective of state managers, if child poverty was to be reduced, social cohesion improved and the productive potential of the economy increased then a broader mobilisation of non-employed lone-parent claimants into the formal labour market was necessary (DWP, 2006a: 52; see also Freud, 2007). In October 2005 quarterly WFIs were introduced for lone-parent IS claimants with a youngest dependent child aged 14 and above. Subsequently, six-monthly WFIs were introduced in 2007 for lone parents with a youngest dependent child of school age, but under 14, and in April 2008 for lone parents with a youngest dependent child aged under 5 years old. From late 2008 all lone parents in the final year of their eligibility for IS were required to undertake quarterly WFIs (DWP, 2011b: 12–13; Rafferty and Wiggan, 2017).

A synthesis report of government-commissioned evaluations of lone-parent WFIs noted that they channelled lone parents with an expressed interest in employment towards interventions intended to facilitate this, such as the NDLP, but had little effect on claimants who rejected the desirability/feasibility of seeking employment at that moment in time (Thomas, 2007: 5–6). The WFI functioned as a tool for screening in/out claimants who were more/less job-ready and/or expressing pro-employment attitudes, and as such was of use for identifying and mobilising more job-ready lone parents and directing these to activity to transform them into active job seekers (that is, from the latent segment of the surplus population to the floating labour reserve). Yet, the WFI did little to prevent an instrumentalist engagement with JCP by lone parents seeking to navigate the (new) rules governing IS entitlement. In other words, a space remained within the social security system for claimants to exercise some discretion over engagement in work-related activity.

In pursuit of extensive commodification of lone parents, New Labour set about making further tweaks to improve the marginal financial value of paid work and the feasibility of combining paid work with care for children. The Childcare Act 2006 placed a duty on local authorities in England and Wales to provide formal childcare provision for parents in paid work (Rahilly, 2008: 88) and the Government continued to channel resources into the tax credit system. Given the absence of a second (potential) earner and likely lower hours of paid work, lone parents in particular benefitted from the tax credit system. In 2009–10 around eight in ten recipient lone-parent families in paid work received both the wage top-up component – that is, Working Tax Credit (WTC) – and component for children – that is, Child Tax Credit (CTC) – of tax credits, a higher proportion than among couple families with children (Millar, 2009: 242; HMRC, 2012: 14–15). As Daly (2011: 17) pointed out, New Labour's activation policy was an amalgam of treating parents in receipt of benefits as independent individuals expected to engage in their own job seeking, increasingly irrespective of care commitments, and as interdependent members of a household when it came to assessment of entitlement to assistance for in- and out-of-work benefits.

Consequently, the incentives for low-income couple families with children to engage both partners in paid work were weaker (Browne and Phillips, 2010: 29). The breadwinner model of the family might have been increasingly presented as obsolete, but New Labour's in-work benefit reforms provided incentives for a single earner – primary carer family form (Lewis, 2001; Daly, 2011). Requiring lone parents to internalise the cost of managing worker/carer commitments and incentivising couple families to specialise in paid work/care work was, it seems, an acceptable trade-off in the balance between mobilising labour for commodification, shoring up social cohesion and managing demands on public expenditure (Grover, 2016a: 140–1). The total number of families in receipt of tax credits, for example, increased from 5.7 million in 2003–04 to 6.25 million in 2009–10 (HMRC, 2012: 8). Strikingly recipient families without children numbered 482,000 in 2009–10, up from 164,000 in 2003–04, pointing to how the reform of tax credits in 2003 had also been followed by the radical expansion of coverage of low-waged childless workers during Labour's third term (HMRC, 2012: 13).

The additional level of in-work financial support was paralleled by a narrowing of eligibility conditions for out-of-work benefits and a diminishment of claimant autonomy over work–welfare transitions. In 2007 the Government signalled an intention to close off lone-parent eligibility for IS if their youngest dependent child was of school age. Lone parents with older children would only be eligible to claim JSA on grounds of unemployment, or IB, if incapable of paid work due to impairment or health condition (DWP, 2007b; 2007d). From November 2008 eligibility ceased for lone-parent claimants with a youngest dependent child aged 12 and above. The new regulations also stipulated that from October 2009 eligibility for IS was to be limited to lone parents whose youngest dependent child was aged under 10, and a year later eligibility was restricted to those with a youngest dependent child aged under 7 (Haux, 2012: 1; Rafferty and Wiggan, 2017: 515).

The IB population was itself also in the process of being remade as the Government moved to phase out the existing IB, beginning in 2008, with the introduction of the Employment and Support Allowance (ESA) (Rahilly, 2008: 81). As with JSA, the ESA took two forms: an insurance-based contributory benefit, ESA (C), and a means-tested income-related benefit, ESA (IR). The former replaced IB, while the latter replaced means-tested IS for disabled people and/or people with health conditions that limited employment (Harris and Rahilly, 2011). The ESA included a new test of eligibility – the Work Capability Assessment (WCA) – as replacement for the PCA, with assessment brought forward to the first three months of a claim, echoing the earlier PCA in the PtW. The WCA narrowed the grounds on which a limited capability for work and entitlement to ESA was established. A further 'limited capability for work-related activity' (LCWRA) test followed if entitlement had been established, with the result of the LCWRA determining placement in either the ESA Support Group (ESA SG), or the ESA Work-Related Activity Group (ESA WRAG). The ESA SG was for claimants whose condition was assessed as meaning long-term absence from the labour market. It had no work-related activity conditions attached and attracted a higher level of financial support. Conversely, the ESA WRAG positioned the claimant as temporarily incapable of paid work, provided a lower rate of payment (albeit greater at the time than the JSA payment rate) and required work-related activity (Harris and Rahilly, 2011: 56).

The ostensible rationale for ESA was the assertion that many IB claimants expressed a desire to find a job, and New Labour's expansion of 'supportive' policy instruments, such as the NDDP/PtW and in-work benefits, had weakened the barriers to, and constraints on, employment (Hansard, 2005a: c233). There was also recognition that the introduction of JSA in 1996 had made it more difficult for claimants with health conditions or impairments, who would otherwise regard themselves as unemployed, to comply with the active job-search conditions of JSA. This was held to have redirected some claimants to IB, although the proportion of people flowing off JSA and onto IB in the 1990s and early 2000s was not especially high; making up 4.2% per cent of total JSA off-flow in May 1998 and 4% per cent of JSA off-flow in May 2005 (Hansard, 2005b: c1491W). The TUC, in evidence to the Work and Pensions Committee, noted that research published by the DWP indicated moves from JSA to IB reflected deteriorations in health status, suggesting 'gaming' of IB was marginal at best (TUC, 2006: ev74). The payment structure of IB, which paid a higher rate for long-term receipt, was also perceived to discourage benefit off-flow while failing to identify how some health conditions, or the disabling structures of society, could be managed to allow labour market re-integration (Hansard, 2005a: c233; DWP, 2006a: 4; Hansard, 2005a: c233; Sainsbury, 2009: 222–24).

Absent changes to social security benefits for non-employed people, it was implied that demographic shifts over time would tighten the labour market and depress economic growth (Hansard, 2005a: 232; DWP, 2006a: 2). The seeming persistence of a high IB caseload clashed then with the pursuit of extensive labour utilisation (Koch, 2006) upon which New Labour's accumulation strategy rested. As the route to higher economic growth, lower poverty and greater social cohesion was depicted as flowing through higher employment, this meant shrinking the portion of the working-age population protected by social security from the commodifying pressure of the labour market (DWP, 2005, 2006a; Hansard, 2006; Freud, 2007: 46). Harris and Rahilly (2011: 56–7) notes that the Government initially anticipated only 10 per cent of ESA claimants would be placed in the ESA SG. With the resulting majority qualifying for assistance only deemed temporarily absent from employment (ESA WRAG), the stock of labour supported by the state as permanently detached from the labour market would decline.

With engagement in work-related activity improving employability and re-mobilising claimants, a portion of ESA WRAG claimants would always be in the process of flowing back into employment, or into the labour reserve, strengthening competition for paid work. Wright (2009: 201) characterised these developments as a shift towards treating non-employed benefit claimants 'as a functional equivalent of unemployed' (claimants). What Wright alights on here is how Labour's third-term reforms to benefits and employment programmes were, as others have noted (Grover and Piggott, 2005: 710–14; Grover and Piggott, 2010; Roulstone and Prideaux, 2012), geared towards improving the state's ability to manage a (re)allocation of (some) claimants from the relative surplus population to the reserve and active army of labour (Grover, 2012: 287). Rather than a long-term stock of IB claimants sinking into labour market detachment and hardship (that is, pauperisation), the reforms would reposition many IB claimants as a temporarily 'latent' surplus population, somewhat akin to lone-parent IS claimants with young children, while lone parents with older children were channelled into employment, or the labour reserve.

Addressing the marginalisation of claimants 'stranded' in the surplus population was, however, also consistent with a progressive mode of political leadership that sought to cohere a 'big tent' of support through an articulation of social and economic liberalism as a new hegemonic governing project. An embrace of social diversity and measures to promote individual equality of (employment) opportunity in this way remained compatible with representing out-of-work benefit claims as morally suspect, and social inclusion as synonymous with participation in relations of economic exploitation (Secretary of State for Work and Pensions, 2006a; Secretary of State for Work and Pensions, 2006b; Secretary of State for Work and Pensions, 2008; Wright, 2009: 203–4; Roulstone and Prideux, 2012).

Discursively, such changes burnished the progressive credentials of the Government, buttressing and normalising an expansive commodification drive that pressed new obligations to engage in work-related activity upon the non-employed claimant population (Piggott and Grover, 2009; Secretary of State for Work and Pensions, 2008).

The maturing of the New Labour Government's approach of disciplinary inclusion made few concessions to the disruptive impact of the financial crisis in 2008 and the onset recession in 2009. The direction of travel had been indicated in a government-commissioned report by Professor Paul Gregg (hereafter, the Gregg Report), which proposed introduction of a new three-tiered conditionality regime – a 'work-ready' group, a 'progression to work' group and a 'no conditionality' group (Gregg, 2008: 57). The Gregg Report (2008) implied a significant reduction in the proportion of non-employed benefit claimants 'excused' from any work-related activity. Only lone parents and partners of the unemployed with a youngest dependant child aged under 1, and sick and disabled people deemed not capable of any paid work, would be in the 'no conditionality' group. Lone parents with children aged up to 7 and IB claimants deemed temporarily incapable of paid work would be placed in the 'progression to work' group. The 'ready to work' group being for JSA claimants, including lone parents with older children (Gregg, 2008: 57).

Though the Government did not immediately adopt the Gregg proposals, the Welfare Reform Act 2009 echoed the desire to narrow the number of claimants not subject to 'conditionality'. The extension of work-related activity requirements to lone-parent IS claimants with a youngest dependent child aged 3 and over, and for partners of JSA claimants, effectively created a form of the 'progression to work' conditionality group. The Act also legislated for piloting of mandatory 'work for your benefit' schemes for long-term JSA claimants from 2010. The goal being to reduce repeat cycling between out-of-work benefits and employment programmes, by coercing claimants into 30 hours per week of work activity and 10 hours of job search. The pilots would ostensibly instil the discipline associated with paid work (SI, 2010: 2), rendering participants more attractive to potential employees, while mere 'threat' of enrolment would likely encourage some participants to cease their claims and seek alternative sources of subsisting. Given the planned migration of the lone-parent caseload with older children to JSA and the introduction of ESA (IR), the IS benefit was being repositioned as superfluous, as indicated by inclusion in the Act of the power to abolish IS (CPAG, 2010). These measures point to how a strategy of disciplinary inclusion to secure the domination of claimants cohered with extensive labour utilisation on which the long-term stability and competitiveness of the UK liberal-market political economy was, in part, deemed to rest. To achieve the step change in the scale and reach of claimant commodification, and strengthen control over (para-)state employees charged with delivery of activation services, the New Labour Government moved to refine its market-managerialist state strategy.

Deepening managerialism and marketisation

New Labour's reconfiguration of employment and social security institutions during its first two terms in office had brought the organisation of the state apparatus in to closer alignment with the Government's goals of expanding and intensifying the activation of working-age, out-of-work benefit claimants (Wiggan, 2007a; 2007b). Analyses of JCP performance, for example, suggested that in terms of a cost-effective expediting of benefit outflows, and improving job entries for JSA claimants, the creation of JCP had met expectations (Karagiannaki, 2007; Riley et al, 2011; Bagaria et al, 2013). Confidence in the dynamic power of the market to deliver economic and social goals and potential benefits to be gained throughout the welfare state from extending market rationality infused New Labour thinking (Gilbert, 2004: 33), and as noted, the Freud Review sought to develop this. A belief in the potential of the private sector to improve employment service delivery had though pervaded New Labour's thinking since it entered office in 1997 (see PREM 49/39), but had manifested mainly in the early pilot experiments with private sector-led Employment Zones (EZ).

The government-commissioned evaluations of the EZs indicated that, relative to NDYP and ND 25+, higher job-outcome performance could be achieved through a less prescriptive form of contracting out that rewarded providers primarily for achieving job outcomes (Bruttel, 2005: 399; Griffiths and Durkin, 2007: 25–6). Bruttel (2005: 396–7) argued that an important factor here was that the EZ model was close to a pure 'work first' programme, as it rewarded providers delivering quick job entries and sustainment for 13 weeks. The relative freedom afforded to EZ providers to use their resources flexibly provided scope to address straightforward constraints on employment. Contracted providers could, and some did, pay for goods and services intended to enhance job seeker availability, mobility and attractiveness, or offered participants financial payment for securing a job, thereby strengthening the material incentives for participants to cooperate with rapid job entry (Bruttel, 2005: 397; Griffiths and Durkin, 2007: 39).

With the commissioning of the Freud (2007) review the Government signalled an overhaul of the goals, organisation and management of the employment services quasi-market. The recommendations of Freud added technocratic weight to criticism of the existing plethora of New Deal and EZ programmes for different claimant groups and chimed with support among Government and the opposition Conservative Party that greater flexibility and marketisation of employment service provision would improve service innovation, cost-effectiveness and job outcomes (Finn, 2009: 39).

The model of employment programme provision that Freud (2007) recommended included a payment-by-results model, in which providers would receive the majority of their funding for securing participant-sustained job outcomes over a period of two to three years. In place of multiple programmes for unemployed and non-employed claimants, a single programme would serve all claimants. Higher fees for 'less job-ready' participants would be used to encourage providers to engage all participants, not just the most 'employable', and providers would largely be freed to innovate and develop their own model of delivery. To mitigate the risk that public-spending constraints would limit programme caseload, Freud also suggested that benefit 'savings' accruing from claimants moving into employment be reinvested. Success in moving claimants into sustained paid work would in this way generate a self-funding virtuous cycle of investment, activation and sustained commodification, and increase the attractiveness of the market to large for-profit and not-for-profit service providers who could take responsibility for delivery as 'Prime' contractors (Bennett, 2017: 136–7: also Freud, 2007).

The New Labour Government moved in the direction proposed by Freud, but more cautiously. Neither the invest-to-save model was adopted, nor the proposed two-to-three-year job-sustainability measure, and unification of provision was limited to unemployed claimants with the creation of the FND. A Prime provider model of contracting between the DWP and a small number of large, well-resourced non-state actors, charged with delivering their own services, and/or managing sub-contracted providers (Considine et al, 2018: 232–4) was adopted, though, along with greater emphasis on payment by results. The provider-led PtW programme, which launched in 2007–08, also involved the DWP contracting 11 Prime providers to deliver the PtW programme for IB claimants across 60 per cent of Great Britain, with payment geared towards securing job entries (NAO, 2010b: 6–10). The Prime provider model attempted to manage the tension between using competition to drive performance and contain costs. As Bennett (2017) notes, a smaller number of large providers helped mitigate the costs experienced by DWP in managing the market by limiting the number of direct contracts DWP held with providers. The Prime model was also intended to allow the state, ostensibly at least, to shift more of the risk of underperformance in securing job outcomes to providers themselves (DWP, 2007c; Finn, 2009; Bennett, 2017; Considine et al, 2018).

With the PtW serving IB claimants, the Government began replacing its NDYP/ND 25+ and EZ with the FND (Finn, 2009; Wiggan, 2015b). Phase 1 FND rolled out in 2009, with 14 providers commissioned to deliver the unified provision and participants joining the programme at 12 months' claiming of JSA. The job-outcome 'sustainability' definitions in the funding model were shorter than proposed by Freud and there was no variation in fee payment to recognise different job readiness and/or participant characteristics (that is, 'differential pricing'). The payment model for the

FND was, though, intended to place greater weight on outcomes, with Government expecting to pay four fifths of total contract value for short (13-week) and long (26-week) job outcomes and a fifth for participant starts to the programme (Wiggan, 2015b).

As analysts at the Social Market Foundation (SMF), and others noted, the payment structure in the FND encouraged providers to use resources to work with more employable participants (Mulheirn and Menne, 2008: 51–4; Work and Pension Committee, 2009: 31–2). To mitigate the risk of the least job-ready participants being ignored, the DWP retained some prescription of minimum services, including mandating provider engagement with each participant every two weeks, creation of return-to-work plans and the delivery of four weeks of mandatory work activity during enrolment (Wiggan, 2015b: 121–3). That the Government stipulated mandatory 'work' activity for all participants during their time on FND (Vegeris et al, 2010: 63–4; Vegeris et al, 2011: 54–6) indicates that provider freedom to innovate remained somewhat circumscribed by managerial direction from the centre.

Launched amid a depressed labour market, the FND was caught between the long-term goal of state managers to activate a greater portion of claimants, and the reality that employers had little need to take 'risks' in recruitment given the engorged labour supply. In implicit recognition of how rising unemployment made securing job outcomes more challenging, the Government increased the proportion of funding for participant enrolment in the PtW and FND (NAO, 2010b: 10; Wiggan, 2015b). The actual performance of Phase 1 FND did not differ significantly from preceding New Deals. Drawing on DWP performance data, Davies (n.d.: 236) calculates that, over the course of the FND contract, 18.6% per cent of participants who commenced the FND secured a 13-week sustained employment outcome and 13.4% per cent secured a 26-week sustained outcome, with no discernible improvement over comparable New Deal programmes (Davies, n.d.: 239–40). Moreover, Davies' (n.d.: 259–66) comparison of Prime provider performance and contract area labour market context suggests that weaker outcome performance was associated with a JCP area having fewer notified vacancies relative to claimant caseload, and a higher proportion of people with no qualifications.

A survey of FND participants also points to limited provider innovation in delivery form. The most common services delivered (experienced or offered to more than 70 per cent of participants) were assessment of a participant's capabilities/preferences, support with CV writing, job applications and interview skills (Vegeris et al, 2011: 39). Basic skills and motivational courses, advice on self-employment, debt counselling, support for alcohol and drug misuse, and the sourcing of temporary, short-work placements required for the mandatory activity (Vegeris et al, 2010: 61–4) were also present. In common with preceding employment programmes, the FND was geared towards (low-cost) identification of claimant job-readiness, expediting job seeking, and job entry. At a time of weak labour demand, the structure of the FND payment model reinforced the incentives for providers to identify and mobilise the most job-ready participants to compete for paid work (Wiggan, 2015b; Davies, n.d.).

New Labour's partial adoption of Freud's suggestions in the FND should not obscure that the intention was to introduce additional market mechanisms, including provider star ratings and 'customer' choice of provider at a later date. It was also the intention post-2010 to pilot the feasibility of the 'invest to save' funding approach, and experiment with an alternative 'accelerator' (outcome-based) payment model. The latter to explore whether, once a given threshold of performance had been met, increasing the payment rate for subsequent outcomes achieved would encourage providers to push deeper into their programme caseloads and activate less job-ready participants (Davies, n.d.: 209–11; Work and Pensions Committee, 2009: 34–5; DWP, 2009b, 2008c). With the labour reserve swelling there was however less demand for the labour power of claimants whose particular capabilities were deemed to mark them out as surplus to the requirments of capital.

Concluding remarks

The commitment of New Labour to a comprehensive amplification of active labour market reforms and extensive state resourcing of these was distinct from the preferences of Conservative opponents. New Labour's (albeit limited) institutionalisation of social liberal values that promoted equality of opportunity, irrespective of ascribed social characteristics as the official position of the state apparatus, marked a 'post New Right' cultural break (Power Sayeed, 2017). Attuned to the Party's ostensibly egalitarian tradition and sources of support, this progressive two-nation mode of leadership was recognition that decomposition of the industrial technical class composition of labour in the 1980s and early 1990s had transformed social attitudes, expectations and work practices. Together, with a fraying of the public realm, this created an opportunity to modernise the state apparatus to stabilise the market-liberal political economy and better support expansive labour commodification (Gilbert, 2004; Power Sayeed, 2017).

As Grover and Stewart (2002) recognised, the enhanced generosity and coverage of in-work benefits and introduction of the NMW reworked the role of the state in regulating the incomes of low- to middle-income families. This form of, what Sloman (2019: 744; see also Robertson, 2023: 94) characterises as, 'Redistributive Market Liberalism', enabled ministers to set a floor under incomes, without significantly improving the power of organised labour to bargain up wages, or enhancing protection and autonomy of unemployed claimants. Unemployed and non-employed claimants though were depicted as (unproductively) dependent and, at best, victims of circumstance, deserving of state support, but whose salvation lay in proactive engagement in seeking paid work, or engaging in work-related activity (Clarke, 2005; Wright, 2009). Where this was perceived to be in doubt New Labour converged with the Conservative Party in denigrating out-of-work social security, ratcheting-up disciplinary control and benefit retrenchment, as ministers worked to impose labour market inclusion via curtailment of claimant autonomy (Connor, 2007; O'Grady, 2022: 130–6).

The progressive two nation mode of leadership provided a warrant for, and political coherence to, the articulation of an extraction strategy of labour subordination, manifest in a disciplinary approach to claimant inclusion, with an accumulation strategy rooted in extensive labour utilisation. As discussed by Clasen and Clegg (2012) and Griggs et al (2014), the transformation of the state apparatus extended the reach of active labour market policy throughout the labour reserve and into the surplus population of working-age non-employed claimants. Enhancing the capabilities of claimants, and their willingness to make their labour power available for sale (Hansard, 2005a) was intended to impose work and facilitate sustained economic expansion, while bolstering social cohesion.

An activation model that relied on mandated job search and other work-related activity, irrespective of claimant preferences, however, generated claimant disaffection (McCollum, 2011). With the decline of claimant organisations and the absence of an organised, collective movement to oppose the new offensive steps against claimant autonomy however, individuals were left to get by within the system as best they could. Yet, as Standing (2011: 38) perceptively noted, claimant evasion, or struggle against activation measures, and state managers' perception that this was facilitated by the structure of the state, created a punitive liberal-market ratchet effect in welfare reform. Each indication of policy success or failure becoming the justification for another round of marketisation, tightening of benefit conditionality or new workfare measures.

10

Austerity and the imposition of work discipline: 2010–16

The (de)stabilisation of accumulation and the class politics of labour commodification

The onset of the financial crisis and subsequent economic recession in 2008–09 shook the UK's finance and consumption-led model of economic growth (Green and Lavery, 2015; Lavery, 2019). The UK experienced a 6 per cent decline in GDP between 2008 and 2009 (Jenkins, 2010: 30–1) and the cost of managing the financial crisis and its fallout meant the gap between state income and expenditure widened. Public sector net borrowing grew from £41 billion in 2007 to £154 billion in 2009 (ONS, 2016a), and the deficit as a proportion of GDP reached 10 per cent in 2009–10, compared with less than 3 per cent in 2006–07 (ONS, 2016b; Figure 2). Public debt as a percentage of GDP, meanwhile, rose from 36 per cent in 2006–07 to 65 per cent in 2009–10 (ONS, 2016b: Figure 3). The Conservative opposition at Westminster seized the moment to frame the financial crisis as a failure of economic management, profligate public spending and expansion of an unproductive and inefficient public sector under New Labour.

The Shadow Chancellor, George Osborne MP, argued that the deficit and public debt were imminent risks to economic stability, as purchasers of government bonds might demand a higher interest rate, while servicing higher debt repayments would leave fewer resources for public services, or tax cuts to spur economic activity (Osborne, 2010b: 210–11; Wiggan, 2016; Calvert Jump et al, 2023: 9–10). Moreover, business would begin to curtail investment in the expectation that higher levels of taxation would be required to finance the deficit, which would eat into profits and depress consumer demand. The consequence would be a further weakening of the economy and the state's ability to address the deficit and debt (Wiggan, 2016). The Conservative leadership argued that to prevent this, a programme of fiscal consolidation was required that should rest primarily on reductions in public spending. The emphasis on spending cuts would signal lower future tax pressure, reassuring financial markets and alleviating pressure on the Bank of England to raise the base rate of interest. Maintaining lower interest rates would reinvigorate the UK's finance- and consumption-led model of growth by supporting new borrowing, undergirding asset prices and inducing private sector investment and consumer spending (Osborne, 2010b: 216; Berry, 2016; Lavery, 2019).

Acknowledging that austerity posed risks to government legitimacy and social order, the Shadow Chancellor noted the public had to perceive the negative consequences of spending cuts to be fairly distributed if austerity was not to fall to popular opposition (Osborne, 2010b: 217). As Lavery (2019) argues, while the Conservative–Liberal Coalition Government, formed following the 2010 General Election, gestured to a common national interest, a regressive two-nation governing strategy was adopted as the means to manufacture division and undermine opposition to the public spending austerity that an economic strategy of 'expansionary fiscal contraction' required (Calvert Jump et al, 2023: 9). Material and discursive division between claimants and workers and public and private sector workers was actively constructed by overlaying these categories with dichotomous depictions of undeserving/deserving, dependent/ independent, irresponsible/responsible and productive/unproductive citizens (Lavery, 2019; Morrison, 2019). The crafting of insiders and outsiders, who were more or less productive or deserving of assistance from the state, was, for example, in line with the rationale for downsizing of the public sector, expansion of contracting out to non-state actors and development of market rationality in public services. The refinement of this market-managerialist state strategy worked, in turn, to further decompose the public sector as bastion of organised labour, strengthen hierarchical control over frontline (para-)state employees, and discourage sympathy or solidarity with claimants.

The Coalition continued the turn towards more expansive and directive activation that had developed under New Labour, but broke with their inclusionary orientation in favour of a harder-edged activation approach, conceptualised here as disciplinary exclusion. A regressive distributive project moved centre stage that involved a narrowing of eligibility for working-age benefits and sustained reductions in their value (Green and Lavery, 2015: 909). Accompanying this was an increase in the work-related activity requirements that unemployed and non-employed claimants were expected to meet and a more punitive policing of benefit receipt. Consequently, not only was the ability of claimants to subsist outside the labour market weakened, but also the threat of being denied access to the diminished level of state support grew (see Grover, 2012). The erosion of claimant autonomy was commensurate with continuation of policy commitments to maximise labour market flexibilisation and expand the labour supply (that is, extensive labour utilisation). A strengthening of the state's domination of labour enhanced capital's ability to repress wages and renew accumulation through an intensification of exploitation (Berry,

2016; Lavery, 2019: 133–44; Reisenbichler and Wiedemann, 2022: 234–5; Calvert Jump et al, 2023).

With the employment rate for 16–64-year-olds having fallen to 70 per cent in 2010 and remaining subdued into 2012, this appeared optimistic, but by early 2014 the employment rate had risen to 73 per cent (ONS, 2023a). In this context the Government pledged to pursue full employment, but the Chancellor of the Exchequer's conceptualisation of full employment was defined as the highest employment rate among comparable countries and did not imply full-time employment for all who wanted it (Osborne, 2014). Rather, it implied a commitment to increase the production of employable labour power, empowering employers by expanding their choice of labour for deployment in Britain's low-wage, service-heavy economy (Berry, 2016: 65). The weakening of social security and strengthening of market-driven 'work first' employment programmes accords with the argument advanced by Calvert Jump et al (2023: 10) that austerity was primarily about subordinating labour and securing wage repression, rebuilding conditions for accumulation through what Green and Lavery (2015: 894) have termed a "regressive recovery".

In broad agreement with this claim, the chapter contends that the Coalition Government embarked upon a new offensive step in the class struggle, as ministers sought to degrade social protection and reorganise the labour reserve and surplus population to expose labour to greater pressure to accede to the authority of capital and state. While accompanied by a ramping-up of divisive and denigrating discourse with respect to benefit claimants (see Morrison, 2019; O'Grady, 2022), the participation of the centrist Liberal Democrats and changed social attitudes relative to the 1990s meant the Coalition Government retained a veneer of social liberalism, relative to the more overt social conservativism of Conservative governments of the 1980s and 1990s. However, given the emphasis on benefit retrenchment, punitive activation and market-managerial reconfiguration of the state apparatus, the orientation of labor market policy and governance is conceptualised here as regressive–market liberalism (Table 10.1).

Table 10.1: The regressive market-liberal labour market policy orientation

Class politics	Economic order
Repressive-liberal	Market-liberal
Extraction strategy	**Accumulation strategy**
Disciplinary exclusion	Extensive labour utilisation
Mode of leadership & domination	**State strategy**
Regressive two nations	Market-managerialism

Source: Author's construction informed by Gallas (2016: 64).

The institutionalisation of (social) wage repression and its limits

The credibility of the Coalition's strategy was enhanced by a broad consensus among state managers in favour of public-spending retrenchment and market oriented reform, which aligned with the embedded policy paradigm of economic liberalism (Stahl, 2019: 476–7). New Labour's 2010 Fiscal Responsibility Act stipulated public sector borrowing should fall to 5.5 per cent of GDP by 2013–14 (HM Government, 2010), and going into the 2010 General Election the Conservative Party, Labour Party and the Liberal Democrats all advocated fiscal austerity (Wiggan, 2016: 147). The then Governor of the Bank of England, Sir Mervyn King (Cohen, Parker and Pimlott, 2010) also viewed spending cuts as necessary to stabilise public finances, maintain confidence and allow the Bank to combine loose monetary policy with pursuit of the 2 per cent inflation target (Pimlott, 2010; King, 2011: 3). The emphasis on public-spending austerity and supply-side reform was also in keeping with the long-standing preference for economic liberalism and supply-side policy reform embedded within the Treasury (Macpherson, 2014). The cohering of central institutions of economic governance with the objectives of the Coalition provided for a relatively stable political administrative platform (Beech, 2015) from which to enact austerity and reconfigure the state labour commodification apparatus.

The Coalition also created new institutions and policies to support austerity as a necessary and credible policy, sow inter- and intra-class division, and buffer the durability of a residualised welfare state. The Office for Budget Responsibility (OBR), for example, was established in 2010 to provide economic forecasts and assess government performance with respect to eliminating the deficit, reducing public debt as a proportion of GDP and supporting monetary policy to promote growth (Osborne, 2010a; HM Treasury, 2011: 7). Green and Lavery (2015: 912) argue that the OBR's remit implied future governments would need to exercise caution in their spending commitments, lest judgement from the OBR lead to adverse financial market reactions and imperil economic stability. In this sense, the OBR complemented the Bank of England and HM Treasury as an institutional pillar of liberal orthodoxy, and the depiction of austerity as the responsible response to the financial crisis and recession (Wamsley, 2022: 10). The OBR did identify slippage between the Government's deficit and debt reduction plans, and the actual pace of consolidation (Berry, 2016; Ellison, 2016), but this was used by the Coalition Government to legitimate continued retrenchment (Berry, 2016: 79–81). Similarly, to constrain pressure on spending and inconvenience the Labour opposition the Coalition introduced the 'Welfare Cap' policy in 2014. Excepting pensions and unemployment benefits, the Cap required benefit-expenditure forecast during a five-year period to remain below a given level of spending, with compliance monitored by the OBR (HM Treasury, 2014:87–8; Ellison, 2016: 39; Keep, 2022: 7–12), strengthening alignment of the new institutional framework with continued imposition of austerity.

The formation of a majority Conservative Government following the 2015 General Election continued the erosion of the social wage, with a £37 billion spending reduction, including £12 billion from 'welfare reform', announced in the Summer 2015 budget, with the ostensible goal of year-on-year reduction in the deficit and its elimination by 2019–20, alongside reduction in the public debt to GDP ratio (HM Treasury, 2015a: 17–21). This direction of travel was reiterated in the 2016 update to the Charter for Budget Responsibility, with the Government's fiscal policy intended to deliver a falling level of public debt relative to GDP and public sector net borrowing below 2 per cent GDP by 2020–21 (HM Treasury, 2017: 7).

The impact of public-spending reductions is indicated in the decline in public sector employees, from around 5.4 million in 2010 to around 5 million in 2016 (ONS, 2022a: Table 6a and 7a). Trade union opposition provided the opportunity for Government to depict organised labour as a sectional interest, protecting a spendthrift, overstaffed public sector (Lavery, 2019: 169–74) to the detriment of the public and economic stability. Job cuts were flanked by a public sector pay freeze imposed in 2011–12 and subsequent rises averaging 1 per cent through to 2015–16. The Institute for Fiscal Studies estimated pay restraint left real terms public sector pay 4 per cent below its 2009–10 level in 2016–17, with private sector pay also falling (5 per cent) in real terms over the same period (Cribb, 2017: 3–4). An indication of the shifting balance of power is given in the overall fall in labour's share of income from 60.5 per cent in 2010 to 58.1 per cent in 2016 (ONS, 2022b: Figure 4).

Yet, wage repression created tensions with the Government's 'two nation' lauding of hard-working families. Amid an expansion of low-wage work openings appeared for opponents to challenge the common-sense narrative of austerity and divisive policy package of successive Conservative-led administrations (Wiggan, 2016), and put forward alternatives. As Wilson (2017) points out, the flexibilisation of labour markets, erosion of social protection and the power of organised labour in liberal welfare states had, over time, seen labour recompose as a political actor to campaign around state-regulated minimum wages. Community groups and unions in the UK, for example, had been campaigning for a 'living wage' rate since New Labour's second term, and going into the 2015 General Election, the Labour Party sought to appeal to public concern with the costs of everyday life by promising a higher National Minimum Wage (NMW) rate (Johnson et al, 2019; Grover, 2016b: 694; Etherington, 2020: 55–6).

Adriotly reading the runes of public opinion the Government announced in summer 2015 a higher minimum wage rate for workers aged over 25, termed the National Living Wage (NLW). Given the antipathy of preceding Conservative administrations to regulating pay rates this was somewhat surprising, but in a context of falling real wages and growing pressure to improve living standards, ministers tactically conceded ground on pay rate regulation to preserve their authority and the durability of the austerity project (Wilson, 2017; Johnson et al, 2019). The NLW raised pay rates for the lowest paid workers, blunted opposition criticism and enabled the Government to appropriate the language of community organisations and trade unions. Furthermore, as the NLW rate was set below the level calculated to achieve a living wage and excluded young people (Johnson et al, 2019: 326–7), the additional costs for employers were limited, and remained consistent with age-related segmentation of the labour force and labour reserve, preserving young people as a particularly attractive supply of labour power for low paid, often service sector work. The NLW also reinforced moral and material divisions drawn by Government between the independence achieved via (low-)wage work and the dependence fostered by benefits (Lavery, 2019: 166), which successive bouts of benefit retrenchment and reconfiguration worked to sharpen (Ellison, 2016: 36–7; Farnsworth, 2021: 84).

The retrenchment, reconfiguration and residualisation of social security

The transformation of working-age welfare was taken forward in successive budgets, the Welfare Reform Act 2012 and the Welfare Reform and Work Act 2016 (CPAG, 2017; Hobson, 2020: 8–20). In terms of retrenchment in the value of benefits the seemingly minor technical change to uprate working-age benefits from April 2011 in line with the CPI measure of inflation was significant. The annual increase in benefit rates would consequently generate growing savings over time relative to the counterfactual of continued RPI uprating (Hobson, 2020: 7). Ministers added to this with the decision to cap increases at 1 per cent per year for 2013–16, and in 2015 the Chancellor imposed a freeze on the uprating of working age benefit payments between 2016 and 2020 (Hobson et al, 2022: 29). Politically, this form of policy 'drift' was attractive as it avoided a cut to the nominal rate of payment. Morever, it inscribed an automatic ratcheting-up each year of work incentives, as the real value of benefits declined relative to low-paid work. The changes to uprating and imposition of a freeze were, by 2020, estimated to deliver an annual saving of £4 billion (HM Treasury, 2015a: 37).

The introduction of a 12-month time limit for receipt of the contributions-based Employment Support Allowance (ESA C) also residualised state support (HM Treasury, 2010a: 28). After a year, only income related Employment Support Allowance (ESA IR) could be claimed. As this was means-tested those with higher household income and savings would be ineligible for support, or only qualify for a lower level of assistance.[1] In 2013 a cap on the social security assistance available to out-of-work families was introduced,[2] initially set at £26,000 for lone-parent and couple families, and £18,200 for childless single adults. The Welfare Reform and Work Act 2016 subsequently reduced the cap to £20,000 and £13,400 for each group, respectively (Hobson et al, 2022: 30; Welfare Reform and Work Act 2016: Ch 8). The stated goal was to keep the income of families without an adult in paid work below the income of working families (HM Treasury, 2010a: 28). Expressing a regressive two-nation governing strategy, the benefit cap was presented as a matter of fairness between hard-working taxpayers and dependent out-of-work working-age claimants (Chancellor of the Exchequer, George Osborne MP, 2014).

There was an element of political opportunism here in that the policy was pushing at an open door, with Lord David Freud subsequently suggesting that a cap on entitlements was introduced as it chimed with public opinion (Freud, 2021: 117). Enacting the cap was therefore politically attractive, and reinforced the austerity logic and welfare dependency narrative of the Coalition (Wiggan, 2012; O'Grady, 2022). Additional cuts to social security came via recalibration of the tax credit system with changes meaning that support was withdrawn more quickly from families as income rose, and a lower proportion of eligible childcare costs would be covered by the state (HM Treasury, 2010b: 34).[3] The £25,000 income disregard, which allowed in-year incomes to rise by the specified amount before triggering a reassessment of entitlement, dropped to £5,000 under the Coalition and £2,500 under the subsequent Conservative Government. The latter also announced the child element payment within tax credits – and its replacement, Universal Credit (UC) – would be limited to two children per family (CPAG, 2017: 9–13). Clegg (2015: 493) pointed out that the expected savings from changes to the tax credit system were equal to around three quarters of the £12 billion reduction in benefit spending the Conservative Government committed to seek following the 2015 General Election.

Eligibility for Income Support (IS) was also further restricted from 2012 to lone parents with a youngest dependent child aged under 5 (Rafferty and Wiggan, 2017: 515). From 2014 lone-parent IS claimants with children aged between 1 and 5 were required to have two to four Work-Focused Interviews (WFIs) per year and lone parents of children aged three to four were expected to undertake work-related activity (DWP, 2017a: 5). For unemployed claimants an expectation of 35 hours per week[4] job search became a condition of benefit receipt, ostensibly to mimic full-time employment (Work and Pensions Committee, 2014a: 15–16; DWP, 2015a; Daguerre and Etherington, 2016). The Government's reforms indicated a high-tempo class offensive in play that reworked the state apparatus so that fewer redoubts from the commodifying pressure of the market remained. As Iain Duncan Smith MP, Secretary of State for Work and Pensions between 2010 and 2016, conveyed: 'Our reforms are about reaching the residual unemployed and helping to make sure they are available for work' (Secretary of State for Work and Pensions, 2010).

The impact of the benefit changes on claimants was contoured by, and constitutive of, social divisions associated with the intersection of ascribed social characteristics with patterns of employment, benefit receipt and household income. For example, work by the Resolution Foundation indicated that Pakistani-, Bangladeshi- and Black-identifying families have lower household incomes, lower employment rates and higher average family sizes than White British-identifying families (Corlett, 2017: 5–8). It is little surprise then that assessment of the impact on family incomes of the adjustments to tax and benefits in 2010–17 indicated that while all low-income families lost out, the average annual income loss was higher among minority ethnic families than White families (Portes and Reed, 2017: 13 and 14).

Similarly, with lone-parent IS claimants being predominantly women and the gendered segmentation of the labour market, the enactment of benefit retrenchment affected low-income women in particular (Sanders et al, 2019; Andersen, 2023). That benefit residualisation left more families dependent solely on market incomes also strengthened the incentivises for (higher-income) families excluded from *any* assistance to (re)calibrate their view of social security as support for indolent others at personal cost. In this the Coalition's overall recalibration of the tax and benefit system worked to dismantle New Labour's 'progressive universalism' which extended support up the income scale to cohere support for its inclusive approach to commodification (Brown, 2017: 148). Instead, benefit reconfiguration and residualisation to foster exclusion from state support moved to the fore as the means by which labour subordination would be secured.

Benefit integration, labour market flexibility and work–welfare cycling

The broader pursuit of benefit retrenchment was cohered with the two specific welfare reform projects intended to transform working-age social security and employment programmes for unemployed and non-employed claimants. These were the single working-age benefit, Universal Credit (UC) and the single working-age employment scheme, the Work Programme (WP) (Freud, 2021; O'Grady, 2022). The former involved the replacement of means-tested Jobseeker's Allowance (JSA), ESA and IS, along with WTC/CTC and Housing Benefit with the new means-tested UC, unifying assistance to in- and out-of-work claimants into a single system (Millar and Bennett, 2017: 169).[5] The rationale for UC was that the patchwork of regulations that governed benefit entitlement increased scope for fraud and error, while the rates at which financial assistance was withdrawn as income increased blunted the incentives for claimants to take paid work, or increase their hours of employment (Grover, 2016a; Freud, 2021). The income disregard of £5/£10 for single and couple claimants in JSA,[6] for example, meant income above the disregard was offset by a corresponding deduction in payment on a pound-for-pound basis, discouraging work of a few hours per week (Hansard, 2011a: col 72ws). Yet, to qualify for WTC a claimant required 16 or 24 hours' paid work per week depending on circumstance. Senior Conservatives and centre-right think tanks, such as the Centre for Social Justice, had argued since the early 2000s that this limited incentives to take jobs of a few hours a week, or to maximise employment participation once above the hours qualifying threshold of WTC (Haddon, 2012; Grover, 2016a; Freud, 2021). This interpretation of the social security system was that it hampered the full and flexible utilisation of labour in and outside of the labour force (Minister of State for Welfare Reform, 2011a; 2011b; Freud, 2021).

To address these issues, UC did away with income disregards and hours eligibility rules, and introduced a single withdrawal rate, initially set at 65 per cent, intended to lower the numbers of people experiencing very high marginal deduction rates, as benefits were withdrawn and tax paid as incomes rose (DWP, 2012b: 24; Grover, 2016a: 158–65). The impact assessment of UC estimated that relative to the existing pre-UC tax and benefit system, one million fewer UC claimant households would experience a 70 per cent plus loss of income due to tax/NI and benefit withdrawal if taking a job of 10 hours per week (DWP, 2012b: 22). As the foreword to the 2015 *Universal Credit at Work* report attributed to Iain Duncan Smith and Lord Freud, makes clear, the intention with UC was to improve employers' ability to match labour use with (shifting) demand, contain labour costs and foster labour market dynamism and growth (DWP, 2015a: 3). Though not stated in these specific terms, through UC, the state's management of the labour reserve and surplus population would better support the work–training–employment transitions of claimants in a flexible low-wage labour market (Minister of State for Welfare Reform, 2011a; Freud, 2021).

There was a risk though, that UC claimants might respond by reducing or limiting their hours of work, which would increase costs to the state and potentially undermine employer control and value creation. To guard against this ministers extended conditionality to UC recipients in paid work if their income was below a specified level, as stipulated in the UC Administrative Earnings Threshold (AET) and Conditionality Earnings Threshold (CET). For an individual the AET was set at £338 per month in 2015, while the standard CET initially equated to 35 hours per week at the NMW rate. Given the nature of UC, conditionality requirements were related to assessment of the claimant and their placement in one of four conditionality groups. These included the following: All Work Requirements; Work Preparation; Work Focused Interviews; and a No Conditionality group (Welfare Reform Act, 2012: Ch 2; DWP, 2023i). Each conditionality category aligned in turn with one or more of six 'labour market regimes': Intensive Work Search; Light Touch; Work Preparation; Work Focused Interviews; No Work-Related Requirements; and Working Enough (DWP, 2023i).

The All Work-Related Requirements conditionality group includes claimants not in paid work and judged capable of paid work, as well as claimants in paid work with earnings below the AET, or above the AET, but below the CET. The latter group of UC claimants with earnings below the CET but above the AET, were initially subject to a softer form of labour market regime as state managers let the system bed in (Rowe, 2022: 87; DWP, 2023i). That achieving an income above the CET will, for many, require a rise in work hours points to how, what Dwyer and Wright (2014) depict as a shift to 'ubiquitous conditionality', has been geared towards enhancing state managers' ability to increase the intensity of value extraction. The AET–CET is though perhaps better understood as a mechanism for calibrating labour activation dependent on circumstance. Through tweaking the AET–CET settings, the expected intensity of job-search and paid-work engagement can be ramped up or down, in accord with the preferences of policy makers, business demand for workers or the tempo and intensity of class struggle.

Similarly, the UC system introduced a new approach to testing entitlements for self-employed claimants. The numbers of self-employed workers had been growing since the early 2000s and rose from 3.8 million people in 2008 to 4.6 million people in 2014 (SSAC, 2014: 8). Self-employment aligned with the Government's goal of raising the labour supply and a discourse that lauded hard work and entrepreneurialism, echoing their New Right forebears. Also, as Evans (2023: 98–101) eloquently argues, the material interests of self-employed people have historically been distinct from unemployed claimants and waged workers due to their different relations to production. The competitive pressure, limited resources, and relative precarity of their position making them receptive to messages denigrating welfare 'dependency', state regulation and taxation. With median earnings lower among self-employed workers than employees (Caraher and Reuter,

2019: 201–2), self-employment also induces a competitiveness compatible with flexibility, discipline and containment of one's own labour costs. To the extent income top-ups encourage self-employment, they potentially complement the (re)production of a class composition favourable to Conservative policy preferences.

Yet, they also carry a risk that in work benefits like UC can end up subsidising low-intensity self-employment that shields claimants from pressure to increase their competitiveness, work intensity, or accept waged work with an employer (Caraher and Reuter, 2019). To mitigate this risk in UC the Government included a instrument known as the Minimum Income Floor (MIF). The MIF assumes that self employed claimants have a level of earnings equal to 35 hours per week at NMW for assessment of UC entitlement after the first year of self employment (DWP, 2012b: 35). Through the inclusion of the MIF in UC we see the playing out of tensions between the ideational preferences of the Conservatives to support self-employment, with the desire to curtail the scope for claimant's to creatively make use of UC to enhance their autonomy via low-intensity self-employment (Rowe, 2022).

While in-work benefits in their modern form go back to the 1970s in Britain (Grover, 2016a), the merging of means-tested working-age benefits and the institutional innovations of UC are novel. With UC, the Conservatives sought to craft a social security structure intended to improve the fluidity of the labour reserve and relative surplus population, and state managers' ability to modulate the supply of labour power to better-fit Britain's liberal labour market and economy (Berry, 2014b: 604–5).

Employment services and disciplinary exclusion

Parallel reforms to the governance, content and delivery of employment services complemented the UC reforms with revision and development of the market-managerialist strategy that had marked New Labour's approach in office. Employment service performance-management systems, as Nunn and Morgan (2020) have argued, institutionalise political economy projects at the street level through constructing environments that shape (para-) state employee practice to conform with high-level policy objectives. In 2011 the performance-management framework for Jobcentre Plus (JCP) was revised, with the organisation directed to prioritise increased claimant exit from benefits, and securing reductions in benefit fraud and error (Nunn and Devins, 2012: 8–9). Previous targets for JCP offices that emphasised job entry and outcome performance were displaced by a focus on the 'Benefit Off flow rate' with targets to achieve a given level of JSA claimants exiting benefits at 13, 26, 39 and 52 weeks (NAO, 2013: 48).

Survey data of claimant destinations following benefit exit suggested that, in 2011, about two thirds entered employment (68 per cent), leaving a sizeable minority who did not, generating concerns about growing exclusion, and flows into inactivity (NAO, 2013: 26). Analysis of flows into JSA also indicated around four in ten new claims had made a claim within the preceding six months (Public Account Committee, 2013: Ev29) pointing to the circulation between unemployment and paid work of some claimants. Rather than a problem, senior civil servants viewed this as a feature of Britain's dynamic, flexible labour market, which active labour market policies contributed to and which helped keep employment higher, and benefit caseloads lower, than they might otherwise have been (Public Accounts Committee, 2013: Ev 8–9). Making benefit off-flow the key performance measure was also justified as a cost-effective means to direct and monitor JCP delivery that avoided the complexity and costs of tracing and checking job outcomes (Public Accounts Committee, 2013: Ev7; Work and Pensions Committee, 2014b: Q489–90).

Irrespective of the actions of employers or claimants, the new measure enhanced state managers' ability to monitor frontline compliance with the DWP's prioritisation of driving down the caseload (Nunn and Devins, 2012). Responding to a question about the effect of the Off Flow measure on JCP behaviour, the then Permanent Secretary of the DWP, Robert Devereux, commented:

> I think it has sharpened up what it is we are asking, which is actually that we would like anyone on benefits to be somewhere else – preferably in employment. (Public Accounts Committee, 2013: Ev 5–6)

The emphasis on benefit exit was paralleled, as Daguerre and Etherington (2016) point out, with a ramping-up of penalties (that is, benefit sanction) for behaviour deemed to indicate claimant non-compliance with activity required as a condition of benefit receipt. From late 2012 referral for a higher-level sanction for a JSA claimant risked a 13-week sanction of benefit payment; a second failure within a year risked a 26-week sanction and a third failure within the same year could lead to a three-year sanction of benefit. ESA claimants required to undertake work-related activity also faced stronger penalties (Oakley, 2014: 17). Redman and Fletcher's (2022) small-scale qualitative research with JCP staff indicates how the shift in performance expectations manifested in an increasingly hostile environment for claimants, as advisors sought creative ways to induce benefit exit.

The most visible example was a greater willingness to impose sanctions upon claimants, with Webster (2017: 24) calculating that between 2010 and 2015 37 per cent of claimants receiving JSA for between 12 and 24 months had been sanctioned. The number of monthly referrals for JSA claimants' to benefit sanction increased, from just under 7 per cent in early 2010 to 16 per cent in late 2013, before slowly falling back by mid-2015 (Considine et al, 2015; Webster, 2016: 14 and 28; Royston, 2017: 227–8; Redman and Fletcher, 2022: 315). Webster (2016: 4–5; 2017: 5–6) suggests this followed more demanding interpretation of the actively seeking-work condition of JSA, and instructions to Prime providers of the new Work Programme (WP) (see later) to refer participants for a sanction if failing to meet stipulated participation requirements, irrespective of the reason. While senior civil servants rejected claims that they set sanction targets, they acknowledged monitoring sanction levels in JCP offices, noting this was helpful for identifying and engaging with the (minority of) staff opposed to the practice (Work and Pensions Committee, 2014b: Q578).

Interestingly, Dunn's (2013) research into frontline workers in contracted providers of New Labour's Flexible New Deal (FND) identified some reluctance to pursue sanctions, even though a portion of the caseload were perceived as not actively seeking paid work, or unrealistic in the jobs sought. The strengthening of outcome-related funding in the contracted-out WP, together with the JCP focus on out-flow rate, point to how the reconfiguration of the market-managerialist state strategy worked to further constrain the discretion of (para-)state employees and discourage activity that would alleviate the pressure on claimants to seek paid work.

That the environment was hostile to claimant autonomy was well recognised by claimants and low-wage workers (Wright et al, 2020: 284–8). Redman's (2021) study of marginalised young men details how some claimants in this context sought to negotiate this by creating the impression of compliance, while working to evade activation into poor-quality jobs, regarded as unsuitable. Strategies included foregrounding their long-term unemployment to discourage engagement by employment agencies and job offers, condensing and finessing hours of job search, and adopting various tactics to 'hurry up' in-person interviews with advisors to limit JCP oversight of their activity (Redman, 2021).

Everyday individual 'resistance' was, however, contingent and precarious, and there are reasonable grounds to think sanctions did drive some claimants to exit benefit and/or take jobs they would otherwise avoid, contributing to repeat transitions between employment and benefits and a more liquid labour reserve. Briken and Taylor's (2018) study of low-paid and temporary workers identified that participants viewed the 'threat' of sanctions as a reason to apply for, accept and tolerate poor-quality jobs, which participants anticipated would, in due course, cycle them back to out-of-work benefits. Similarly, quantitative studies suggest sanctioning is associated with increased exit from unemployment benefits and entry to employment, though not the securing of stable, long-term jobs (Pattaro et al, 2022: 635–7).

The prospect that benefit sanctions might throw a claimant into destitution was very real, as documented by the negative impact of sanctions on the living standards and well-being of individuals and families affected (Jeffrey et al, 2018; Wright et al, 2020; Williams, 2021; Pattaro et al, 2022). Not surprisingly, the Public and Commercial Services (PCS) union argued that, given this context, claimants increasingly regarded frontline staff in JCP offices as their 'enemy' (Work and Pensions Committee, 2016: 11). The articulation of performance-management targets and ramping-up of sanctioning deepened divisions between the immediate interests of workers and claimants, and subjected both to greater pressure to comply with the preferences of the Government, indicating erosion of labour autonomy is at the core of the process of 'double activation' (see McGann, 2023: 21–2), at least in Britain. In this regard market managerialism underpinned the ramping-up of the threat, and use, of exclusion as the means to impose discipline and support extensive labour utilisation.

Varieties of work-first activation schemes: the choice is (not) yours

Complementing reforms to social security and its governance was a shake-up of employment programmes. A variety of schemes were enacted to activate claimants, including: the New Enterprise Allowance (NEA); Work Experience (WE); Sector-Based Work Academies (SBWA); and Mandatory Work Activity (MWA).[7] The Coalition also (re)introduced a wage subsidy to encourage employers to hire young unemployed claimants (DWP, 2015b) as part of its 'Youth Contract', and replaced Labour's FND with the WP.

The NEA echoed previous self-employment support schemes (Powell, 2019a; Smith et al, 2019) with their desire to foster a Thatcherite micro-entrepreneurial sensibility (Young, 1991; Freud, 2021). One can also view the NEA as a means to channel (select) claimants' desire for employment, and/or escape from state control and employer domination (Caraher and Reuter, 2019: 210) into a privatised form of autonomy, commensurate with the Government's broader labour-commodification goals. A survey of NEA participants, for example, found 52 per cent cited the opportunity to 'be your own boss' as a key reason for engagement in the scheme, greater than the three in ten citing lack of jobs locally (28 per cent), or lack of jobs suitable for their skills and experience (29 per cent) (DWP, 2016f: 24). The scheme itself involved a period of advice and guidance on creating a business plan, with proposals deemed feasible permitted to commence a business start. Participants were entitled to payment of £65 per week for 13 weeks and £33 for a further 13 weeks, along with eligibility for a business loan (DWP, 2013; DWP, 2016d; Powell, 2019a: 3–4). Although participation was voluntary, a risk of sanction remained should participants fail to work with an assigned mentor, complete activities specified or attend interviews with JCP (DWP, 2016e: 12).

The majority of business starts (81 per cent) were sole-trader operations at the time of the survey of NEA respondents (DWP, 2016f: 49), and a substantial minority were engaged in precarious self-exploitation. Of surveyed NEA respondents starting a business, 37 per cent reported an income/turnover of less than £500 per month and 21 per cent an income/turnover of less than £1,000 per month. Although women made up only 38 per cent of NEA business starts between 2011 and 2016 (DWP, 2016d), a higher proportion of women (48 per cent) reported a business income of less than £500 per month than men (31 per cent) (DWP, 2016f: 48). The NEA was, in this sense, reproductive of broader patterns of self-employment, in which men have tended to concentrate in higher-paying sectors with women making up a greater proportion of part-time self-employment (SSAC, 2014: 14–17). The stronger employment experience and access to credit and savings of older people that shapes patterns of self-employment (Hatfield, 2015: 13–14; Eurostat, 2016) also contoured NEA participation, with the majority of starts concentrated in the 25–49 age group (69 per cent) (DWP, 2016d).

The minimal participation of young people in the NEA stood in stark contrast to their engagement in the WE, SBWA and MWA schemes. The WE intended to acculturate job seekers to the work environment and provide an opportunity to gain an employer reference. Conversely, the SBWA sought to match job-ready claimants with identified demand for labour in specific occupations. Lasting up to six weeks, the SBWA incorporated two weeks of pre-work training focused on sector-related employment practices; a short period of work experience with an employer in the sector and then a guarantee of an interview at the end, though no guarantee of a job offer (DWP, 2016a; 2016b: 12–13). None of the schemes discussed here paid participants a wage, only benefits plus expenses. Grover and Piggott (2013: 556) note the state was effectively socialising the costs of recruitment and subsistence of claimants who were working to generate value for participating organisations. DWP-commissioned surveys of employers engaged with the WE and SBWA suggest a majority of SBWA employers were large employers and predominantly from the private sector. A higher proportion of WE respondent employers, in contrast, were public- and third-sector organisations and smaller businesses, indicating the nature of each scheme partly aligned with intra-employer variation (Wiggan and Knuth, 2023: 133–5). The subtle differences between the schemes provided JCP with options for sorting and channelling claimants to different types of employers and activity, depending on perceived claimant capabilities.

The focus of the WE scheme, for example, was the 18–24-year-old age group and this is where starts in the scheme were concentrated; whereas the SBWA drew a higher proportion of starts from older age groups (DWP,

2017b). The WE impact evaluation estimated that two years on from commencing a WE placement, 19–24-year-old participants recorded a longer period in paid work (47 days) and fewer days in receipt of out-of-work benefits (10 days), compared with a matched group of non-participants (DWP, 2016a: 10). The employment impact being greater for men (51 days) than women (45 days) and for the older 22–24 age group (53 days) than 19–21-year-olds (44 days) (DWP, 2016a: 34). Similarly, evaluation of 19–24-year-old JSA claimants commencing the SBWA in 2012–13 estimated that, during the 18 months following the start to SBWA, participants recorded fewer days in receipt of benefits, with this impact greater for women than men and for longer-term claimants (DWP, 2016b: 30). For participants completing all three components of the SBWA, they were estimated to have spent the equivalent of 64 additional days in paid work relative to a comparable group of non-participants (DWP, 2016b: 33). While the evaluations do not imply transition into permanent employment, they point to how the schemes fostered benefit off-flow and recommodification of claimant labour. While enrolment in these schemes was notionally 'voluntary', non-take-up after agreement to being placed or early drop-out could be grounds for benefit sanction.

In a context of higher unemployment, repressive benefit conditionality and 'work for your benefit' schemes, claimant led campaigns and groups experienced rejuvenation. New and established groups began to contest the punitive nature of 'welfare reform' and expansion of 'workfare' and sought to strengthen links with trade unions, including the PCS (Weghmann, 2019; Etherington, 2020; Coderre-LaPalme et al, 2023). The successive waves of reform to social security and employment services as noted earlier, had, however, transformed the terrain of the state apparatus in ways that encouraged compliance of frontline state employees with government policy. Reinforcing this was anti-trade union legislation that discouraged collective action to obstruct operation of conditionality and workfare, and a broader climate of antagonism towards claimants, including cross-party support for benefit conditionality (Coderre-LaPalme et al, 2023).

The PCS did vocally contest government policy in the public realm, and claimant organisations and anti-workfare campaigners, such as Boycott Workfare,[8] provided advice and guidance to push back against benefit sanctioning and undermine 'work for your benefit' schemes. Local organisations, such as Edinburgh Coalition Against Poverty and the Scottish Unemployed Workers Network, held regular stalls outside JCP offices to connect with claimants and provide advice and support to help avoid, or challenge imposition of benefit sanctions (Weghmann, 2019: 445; SUWN, 2016). More broadly, groups such as Disabled People Against Cuts[9] mounted vigorous opposition to benefit retrenchment and changes to conditions of entitlement, independently and in conjunction with sympathetic trade unions (Etherington, 2020: 84–8). The Government's willingness to supply claimant labour to private- and third-sector organisations also created an opening for claimant groups at the local level to apply pressure through targeting protests at employers hosting placements. Through occupations and demonstrations, pro-claimant groups disrupted the everyday business of participating employers and Freedom of Information requests were submitted to identify which organisations were hosting unwaged placements.[10] The generation of negative publicity around participation intended to discourage organisations from continuing their participation and thereby make the schemes unworkable (Grover and Piggott, 2013: 556; Weghmann, 2019; Coderre-LaPalme et al, 2023). This tactic had some success with companies and charities, under pressure from campaigners and adverse reactions from the public, pulling out of workfare schemes, or requesting changes to sanctioning practices (Bennett, 2014; Armour, 2015; Malik, 2012). Presented with the growing disquiet of large employers targeted by campaigners, ministers clarified that participation in WE/SBWA schemes was not mandatory and the threat of sanction was eased for these schemes (Hansard, 2012: Col. 48WH; Grover and Piggott, 2013):

'We do not mandate to go and work for private companies—they would not take it even if we did. The same is true of the Work programme. We cannot send people against their wishes to work for a big retailer'. (Minister for Employment, Chris Grayling MP, Work Experience Debate, 13 March 2012, Hansard Col. 49WH)

The self-activity of claimants[11] and claimant-supporting groups pushed the Government to clarify and alter their practice with respect to the 'voluntary' work-experience schemes. The MWA scheme in contrast was targeted at unemployed claimants deemed to lack work discipline, and was a means to test availability for work, standing behind the WE/SBWA schemes as a threat to encourage participation in voluntary schemes (Wiggan, 2015a: 380). To an extent state managers could regard the MWA as a partial success. An early survey of MWA participant views reported that among respondents under 25, around 50 per cent who had submitted a job application since commencing the scheme reported increasing job applications. For those aged over 25, an increase in job applications was reported by 31 per cent of men and 44 per cent of women, and over four in ten men and women reported broadening the jobs they considered (DWP, 2012c: 74). Young people and people not reporting a disability were also somewhat more likely to exit the MWA scheme prior to the commencement of their placement, suggesting that the scheme contributed to activating those the state deemed 'troublesome' (Wiggan, 2015a: 381; DWP, 2016g).

The campaign against workfare, however, brought to the fore the tensions state managers confront between strengthening domination over claimants and the risk that claimant disaffection will lead to disruptive activity that discourages employer engagement (Wiggan and Knuth, 2023). It is notable that the MWA scheme did not rely on the private sector to provide its unwaged four-week work placements of 30 hours per week (Wiggan, 2015a). Enaging the third sector to host MWA placements though, created the problem that mandated participation under threat of benefit sanction clashed with the softer, social image of charities and not for profit organisations, and long standing traditions of voluntary work. The involvement of the third sector in this type of scheme expanded the range of people with an interest in opposing workfare, broadening the front of opposition. Groups such as Keep Volunteering Voluntary were formed to draw attention to the clash of values workfare represented and encouraged charities to stay out, or withdraw from offering placements.[12]

Following years of disruptive opposition to workfare type schemes, the 2015 Spending Review announced the 'mandatory' schemes were to be brought to an end, albeit ostensibly on the grounds of falling unemployment and a drive for reduced spending (HM Treasury, 2015b: 89). Given this explanation, caution should be exercised in drawing the conclusion that claimant opposition influenced the decision. What is reasonable to point out however, is that the return of autonomous claimant organisations committed to direct action, as well as advice and guidance, raised the costs to organisations hosting work for your benefit placements by ensuring the value generated from unwaged claimant labour had to be weighed against business disruption and bad publicity. In this regard, the activity of claimant groups and union campaigns helped to undermine workfare and defend claimant autonomy over labour market transitions and access to income supports. The limited scale of claimant mobilisation and public opposition however, meant the broader repressive and regressive direction of labour market policy and governance persisted.

In addition to the various supply side activation measures, the Coalition did temporarily deploy a policy tool to raise demand for unemployed young people, whose unemployment post-2008–09 recession remained elevated through 2011–12 (see Chapter 3). This marked a reversal of the decision of the Coalition Government upon taking office to scrap New Labour's Future Job Fund (FJF). Following this the Government found itself with no policy lever geared towards encouraging employers to hire young people and vulnerable to criticism of inaction over youth unemployment. In this context the decision was taken to introduce a temporary wage-subsidy scheme in the form of a payment of £2,275 to employers hiring a young (six months plus) unemployed claimant for 16–30 hours a week for six months (DWP, 2015b).

Reflecting the Coalition's particular class and economic order politics, the scheme precluded many public sector bodies from participation. There was also no stipulation, as in the FJF, that the subsidy supported new additional employment. Strikingly, the estimated level of deadweight for the scheme was high (76 per cent) (Coleman et al, 2014: 47). The DWP survey of employers receiving the subsidy reported 85 per cent of respondents were private sector businesses, with the majority of surveyed organisations (68 per cent) having fewer than 50 employees. Among respondent employers the subsidised jobs tended to be in elementary, sales and customer service, personal service and administrative occupations (Coleman et al, 2014: 31–3), which record higher proportions of low-wage work (ONS, 2015: Figure 4). That subsidies are used to address unemployment is not uncommon, but the nature of this scheme reflected the particular class politics of the Coalition. Resources were channelled to the private sector and not the public sector, and absence of concern with deadweight meant the Coalition essentially socialised the recruitment costs of (small) employers hiring young people to low-paid vacancies. JCP staff themselves emphasised to employers the scheme essentially meant access to a free recruitment agency, and no requirement to spend the subsidy on developing employee capabilities (Coleman et al, 2014: 37–38). Though a demand side activation measure, the form of the scheme remained tied in this sense to a broader strategy of (repressive) underdevelopment of claimant labour power (Wiggan, 2015a). As the labour market recovered, concern with youth unemployment eased, and the wage-subsidy scheme was brought to a close.

Reconfiguring the employment service quasi-market

The most significant of the Coalition Government's employment schemes though, was the Work Programme (WP), which, overseen by Lord Freud, bore closer resemblance than Labour's FND to Freud's earlier proposals for homogenisation of working-age employment schemes, and a refined outcome-based funding model to drive improvements in a marketised system of employment programme delivery (Freud, 2007). Introduced in 2011 the WP replaced all programmes for long-term unemployed *and* non-employed claimants, and contracted directly with a small number of (largely private sector) Prime providers (2–3) in 18 Contract Package Areas (CPAs) (Wiggan, 2015b: 120–1; Dar, 2016: 19; Bennett, 2017: 136–9). Underpinning the WP was a relatively sophisticated 'Payment by Results' (PBR) quasi-market, in which provider fee payment was dependent on securing participants sustained jobs, with the payment rate varying by category of participant. To foster intra CPA competition, provider performance was periodically reviewed and the flow of new participants adjusted to reward the top performing providers with more participants at the expense of the weakest provider

(DWP, 2016c). The WP quasi-market and contracting model was intended to improve the mobilisation of unemployed and non-employed claimants for commodification, while maintaining a stable market of (competing) providers and limiting transaction costs experienced by the DWP in managing the market (Wiggan, 2015b; Bennett, 2017; Greer at al, 2017).

Entry to the WP was mandatory at nine months of a claim for young (18–24) unemployed claimants, and at 12 months for older claimants (25+). For ESA WRAG claimants, direction to participate in the WP occurred when they were expected to be capable of employment within the next few months. Other categories of claimant were eligible for voluntary participation or accelerated access if deemed 'disadvantaged' (Wiggan, 2015b: 124). The structure of the payment model for providers was based around nine payment groups, that reflected a mix of benefit category (for example, JSA, ESA, IB) and participant characteristics/experiences (for example, age, prison leaver, severity of limited capability for paid work) (DWP, 2020a: 71). Higher payments were attached to payment groups deemed to contain less job-ready participants, and/or those participants whose maintenance was associated with higher cost to the state over time (for example, IB claimants). Conversely, the funding attached to groups regarded as more job-ready and 'lower cost' (for example, JSA 18–24-year-olds) was lower as the ostensible goal was to encourage providers to spread their attention to all participants, not just the job-ready (Carter and Whitworth, 2015; Wiggan, 2015b).

A small stream of income was channelled through a service fee (payable up to year 4) to contractors to offset the costs incurred at the beginning of the contract, and via an incentive payment that rewarded job outcomes achieved above a DWP-stipulated minimum level of performance. The majority of contractor income, however, was delivered through payment of job-outcome fees and sustainment fees (NAO, 2014: 13–15; Wiggan, 2015b: 125). Continuous or cumulative employment over a defined period (for example, six months for unemployed claimants) triggered a job-outcome payment, with sustainment payments following for each subsequent four-week period in paid work up to a specified limit (DWP, 2020a: 72). Unemployed participants remained in the WP for two years, but providers were also responsible for offering up to a year of in-work support to those who secured and sustained employment (DWP, 2020a: 60).[13]

Early work on the operation of the WP drew attention to how use of benefit category as a crude proxy for job readiness, and potential benefit savings that would accrue if a claimant from the group sustained employment, was problematic. The caseloads in each group were not homogenous in capabilities, which encouraged Prime providers to sift the caseload, 'creaming' off the most employable for attention, while providing limited support to those deemed least job-ready (that is, 'parking') (Rees et al, 2014: 229–32; Carter and Whitworth, 2015). That the WP reproduced labour market inequalities is important to acknowledge,[14] but we should not conclude that stronger Prime engagement with parked participants would have been desirable. Research into WP delivery, for example, points to how the experience of some claimants was of providers ignoring constraints on labour market participation and directing them to participate in activities they regarded as detrimental to their well-being (Scholz and Ingold, 2021). Given the WP was intended to further the reach and intensity of activation to drive labour recommodification, (and by implication buffer the authority of employers), then from a class analysis perspective, there is no reason to regard a more thorough application of activation pressure as a good thing (Wiggan, 2015a; Greer, 2016).

The Government's aim for the WP was to increase the speed at which participants entered employment, the numbers and diversity of participants securing jobs and the period for which employment was sustained (NAO, 2014: 2).

Weak early performance of the WP coincided with a depressed labour market and weak economy, but with the recovery of the economy and labour market into the middle of the decade the job-outcome performance improved, indicating the pro-cyclical nature of the scheme (DWP, 2020b). The proportion of the monthly WP referral intake achieving a job outcome among the JSA 18–24 age group, for example, reached around 56 per cent in 2014, and 51 per cent for the JSA 25+ age group, with outcome performance dropping back to around 35 per cent for both payment groups by early 2017. For the New ESA payment group the proportion of the monthly WP referral intake achieving a job outcome peaked at around 36 per cent in 2015, before similarly gradually falling back to 20 per cent in 2017 (DWP, 2020b: Table 1.1). This points to how the WP, as might be expected, was less successful for payment groups whose benefit receipt was linked to disability, or health constraints on employment. Conversely, the performance of the WP shows it was particularly successful for young unemployed claimants, who as a group are particularly sensitive to upticks and downturns in the labour market, and are arguably well positioned for expansion of service sector jobs with low-entry barriers. Similarly, a subsequent evaluation of the impact of the WP on employment and benefit patterns estimated that, among a cohort of unemployed people aged 25+, participation in the WP was associated with an additional 45 days of employment and not claiming out-of-work benefit in the two years following eligibility (DWP, 2020a: 51). In short, the WP was better suited to mobilising the labour reserve than the segment of the surplus population at greater risk of long-term labour market exclusion.

Concluding remarks

Coming to power in 2010, the Coalition Government launched a new offensive step in the class struggle as they sought to renew the conditions for accumulation through public-spending austerity. A revised performance-management system and employment service quasi-market worked to encourage claimants and (para-)state employees to adhere to Government direction, generating mutual antipathy and incentivising the latter to police the behaviour of the former (Greer and Umney, 2022: 87). Ministers also took advantage of what O'Grady (2022: 278-81) identifies as a permissive moment, in which popular support for working-age out-of-work claimants was weak, to propagate division and public antagonism towards claimants, contributing to operationalisation of a regressive two-nation governing strategy (Lavery, 2019). The resulting stigmatisation of claimants in turn warranted residualisation that reinforced material divisions, undermined solidarity and discouraged recognition of social security as a common good. Complementing this was the increased use of exclusion from state support as a means to secure claimant compliance with steps to engage in work related activity (Greer, 2016; Grover, 2019: 337–9; Redman and Fletcher, 2022).

The deepening of the repressive turn encountered opposition from a recomposing claimant movement that met with some success in hampering the operation of disciplinary exclusion, but was unable to garner the strength and support necessary to alter the overall trajectory of government active labour market policy. Rather, the remaking of state institutions gradually reworked the organisation of the labour reserve and surplus population to cohere with expansion of 'a-typical' and low wage employment. Benefit retrenchment and punitive activation to strengthen domination of labour was in this way necessary to the extensive labour utilisation strategy and intensification of the exploitation of labour underpinning a regressive market liberal strategy for economic renewal, as others have detailed (Green and Lavery, 2015; Calvert-Jump et al, 2023).

The Conservatives return to office in 2015 seemed to indicate the hegemony of their particular articulation of class and economic order politics, but electoral success masked how their class politics was gradually undermining the economic order as wage stagnation fed growing disaffection with the effects of austerity upon the social fabric, sapping confidence in the political-economic settlement.

11

Consolidation and continuity in the shadow of crisis: 2016–23

Emergent instability in the political-economic order

Despite the return to office of a Conservative-majority Government at the 2015 General Election, the successful carrying through of a repressive class politics in working-age benefits under the Coalition Government was beginning to show signs of exhaustion. By the middle of the decade austerity had brought to the fore the tensions within the welfare state between controlling and reproducing labour; augmenting the profitability and power of business, and securing legitimacy of the political order (Farnsworth, 2021: 79). The British Social Attitudes survey records that the proportion of respondents favouring additional public spending and taxes touched a low of 32 per cent in 2010, but by 2016 had recovered to 48 per cent (Curtice, 2017: 77). The proportion indicating that unemployed claimants were engaged in fraud had also fallen from just under four in ten in 2011, to around one fifth in 2016 (Baumberg Geiger et al, 2017: 37). Although unemployment was only viewed as a priority for additional spending on benefits by a similar proportion in 2016 (13 per cent) as in 2010 (11 per cent), the proportion prioritising additional spending on benefits for disabled people was 67 per cent in 2016 compared with 53 per cent in 2010 (Harding, 2017: 11).

While the spectre of exclusion and destitution haunted working-age social security claimants, the implementation of public-spending austerity and 'welfare reform' had contributed to disaffection with the political class, and the nature of Britain's economy (Hopkin, 2020; Burton Cartledge, 2021). In Scotland this had found expression in a swell of support for the Scottish National Party (SNP). At the 2015 General Election, the SNP took 56 out of 59 seats in Scotland (UK Parliament, 2015), and in the 2016 Scottish Parliament Election fell two seats short of an overall majority, but returned to office (BBC, 2016; Wiggan and Grover, 2022: 726). The SNP had set out a progressive vision and messaging that was critical of austerity, and gestured to a more universalist and 'Nordic' social investment approach to the welfare state (Wiggan, 2017). Similarly, the election of Jeremy Corbyn as leader of the Labour Party in 2015 on an anti-austerity ticket upended expectations and disrupted Westminster's market-liberal policy consensus (Hopkin, 2020: 135–7; Wiggan and Grover, 2022). Intra-party division also emerged within the Conservative leadership, with the architect of

Conservative welfare reform, Iain Duncan Smith MP, resigning as Secretary of State for Work and Pensions in 2016, over the Treasury's determination to cut further into working-age benefits, while promoting tax cuts for higher earners (Duncan Smith, 2016; Mason et al, 2016).

A sense that the political consensus was falling apart increased with the 2016 referendum on membership of the European Union (EU) and the success of the Vote Leave campaign. As Benquet and Bourgeron (2022) elaborate, membership of the EU had co-constituted development of the UK's financialised liberal political economy since the 1970s. A fraction of finance capital, and fellow travellers in the Conservative Party, media and right-wing think tanks had though, come to view exit from the EU as an opportunity for further liberalisation and departure from the employment rights, and social and environmental protections that EU membership stipulated. In short, Banquet and Bourgeron (2022) suggest division had opened up within capital and its representatives in the state between the regulated 'neo-liberalism' of the EU and an insurgent libertarian-authoritarian movement struggling to advance a new political-economic strategy to reconstitute the British economy. The latter favoured (re)centralisation of power in a core executive willing to use the state apparatus to strip away social protections and rights to ratchet up the exploitation of labour and the environment, as the means to enhance international competitiveness (Banquet and Bourgeron, 2022).

With the vote to exit the EU casting Britain's long-standing trade relations and economic model into doubt, Prime Minster David Cameron MP and Chancellor George Osborne MP soon resigned, and parliamentary politics plunged into turmoil (Worth, 2023). Taking office in Summer 2016, the new Conservative Prime Minister, Theresa May MP, presented as a 'One Nation' Conservative. Untamed market liberalism was implied to be posing a threat to social cohesion and state legitimacy (Prime Minister, 2017; Pitt, 2023: 183–4), and concern was expressed that government must deliver greater support for working families, struggling to get by on low and middle incomes (Burton-Cartledge, 2021: Loc 3717; Lee, 2023: 117). Yet, while the regressive two-nation rhetoric around productive/unproductive workers/claimants was toned down, the marshalling of such division in a repressive and regressive strategy of claimant domination was not abandoned. Austerity in working-age benefits persisted, as did market-managerialism in the governance of labour activation (Burton-Cartledge, 2021; Wiggan and Grover, 2022: 726; Lee, 2023: 116).

Working-age social security consolidation: 2016–19

The decision announced in 2015 to freeze the uprating of out-of-work working-age benefits until 2020 and the two-child limit to restrict benefit payments at the expense of larger families (HM Treasury, 2015a: 38) was introduced as planned in April 2017 by the new May administration. These changes were in keeping with a regressive two-nation governing strategy denigrating 'dependent' families, and the use of financial incentives to foster higher levels of labour commodification. Research into labour market participation of large families affected by the two-child limit, however, suggests little increase in formal paid work followed, and some indication of further disengagement (Reader et al, 2023: 35–7). We might regard this as an example of how a strategy of fostering domination via division between families in and out of work and increasing hardship, arguably, undermined medium-term economic order concerns with mobilising additional labour power and fostering social stability. Of course, such tension between social security as a cost imposed on business and drag on capital accumulation, and welfare as an investment that augments and stabilises accumulation, has long been recognised as endemic to the welfare state, reflecting the contradictions of capitalist relations of production (Smyth and Deeming, 2016).

That a class politics geared towards subordination of labour via curtailment of autonomy and imposition of hardship persisted is further evidenced by changes to Employment and Support Allowance (ESA). In 2017 the 'Work-Related Activity' component of ESA was removed from new claimants in the Work-Related Activity Group (WRAG). New ESA WRAG claimants were left with the standard payment only, equivalent to that for older unemployed benefit claimants (Kennedy et al, 2017). The homogenisation of payment rates reduced the 'incentive' to claim ESA, rather than Jobseeker's Allowance (JSA), and raised the pressure on new ESA WRAG claimants to return to the labour market, implying they were part of the labour reserve rather than relative surplus population. The removal of the WRAG component was also expected to deliver £450 million per year in savings relative to the status quo by 2020–21 (Kennedy et al, 2017: 16–17; Work and Pensions Committee, 2017: 23). These developments were indicative of an accumulation strategy that remained rooted in extensive labour utilisation.

There were some indications of an attempt to shore up social cohesion, particularly in the light of growing public disquiet that new technology was encouraging employers to degrade working conditions. Seeking to buffer the 'One Nation' discourse with a material offering, the May Government commissioned a review into working practices and the future of the labour market, expressing broad support for the report's recommendations (Mason, 2016; Taylor et al, 2017). However, as Briken and Taylor (2018: 439–40) point out the review retained the assumption that Britain's labour market flexibility needed only minor tweaks to prevent egregious exploitation. While some legislative changes to promote additional 'rights' in the workplace were enacted, many recommendations remained unaddressed up to and beyond the pandemic (Ferguson, 2020: 5–11; Codd and Powell, 2022: 3).

Overall, the structure of the state labour commodification apparatus remained geared towards imposing discipline and sorting claimants for their relative employability for jobs marked by the types of poor conditions contributing to public concern (Briken and Taylor, 2018). The minor modifications to the labour market policy regime, such as the increased Universal Credit (UC) work allowance in Budget 2018 (Butler, 2018), or decision in 2019 to reduce the maximum level of benefit sanction from three years to six months, did not alter this (Secretary of State for Work and Pensions, 2019).

Employment services: varieties of (scaled-down) marketisation

Similarly, employment service delivery was marked by broad continuity, with the expansive Work Programme (WP), replaced in 2017 with the Work and Health Programme (WHP). With a smaller budget and a narrower focus (Work and Pensions Committee, 2016: 26; Powell, 2020: 7), mandatory participation[1] in the WHP was limited to claimants unemployed for two years (that is, Long-Term Unemployed Group – LTUG). Participation was voluntary for disabled people (that is, the Disability Group – DG) and 'disadvantaged' job seekers, such as care leavers, ex-offenders, refugees (that is, Early Access Group – EAG) (Powell, 2020: 4; DWP, 2023a: ch 1; DWP, 2023c). Given its small size, the WHP meant shrinkage of the employment service quasi-market. The WHP was organised into six Contract Package Areas and five Local Government Partners across England and Wales. Five private- or third-sector providers were contracted to deliver the WHP, with each area run by a single provider, meaning some providers operated in more than one area (DWP, 2023b; 2023c).

The scaling back of employment programmes had not led to any departure from the broad form of outcome oriented market managerialism proposed in the Freud Review ten years earlier. The payment model for the WHP included a delivery fee worth up to 30 per cent of estimated total contract value, and an outcome fee determined by a participant attaining the equivalent of 16 hours' work per week at the National Living Wage (NLW) rate, or six months' self-employment. Departing from the differential pricing of the WP's payment by results model, the WHP used an accelerator payment model (APM) instead, reflecting a within paradigm instrument experimentation, rather than rejection of underlying assumptions and objectives. The APM included two levels of payment (DWP, 2023a: ch 13). A standard outcome fee paid for all job outcomes secured for the first three quarters of outcomes stipulated in the contract between the provider and the DWP. Additional outcomes attracted a fee 40 per cent higher than standard, to incentivise providers to dig deeper into the caseload and mobilise claimants deemed less job-ready (DWP, 2023a: ch 13). WHP providers were responsible for service delivery to participants for 15 months with a further six months of support permissible if a participant at that point secured employment (DWP, 2023b).

Around three quarters of all referrals (77 per cent) were for people in the DG, with around one in ten being in the LTUG (9.5 per cent) and the remaining referrals for those in the EAG (13 per cent). The proportion of overall starts to the programme was just under six in ten (57 per cent) of total referrals to the WHP between November 2017 and February 2023 (DWP, 2023c: Table 1.1). The proportion of starts to referrals for the DG matched this overall figure of 57 per cent, with the proportion of starts to referrals a little lower for the EAG (55 per cent) and higher for the LTUG (62 per cent) (DWP, 2023c: Table 1.1). The level of 12-month job-outcome performance as a proportion of starts to the WHP between roll-out for each group and February 2022 was weakest for the LTUG (12 per cent), with the DG (21 per cent) and EAG (23 per cent) having similar outcomes to starts (DWP, 2023c).[2] The level of pre-programme-stipulated monthly job outcomes fell to around half the level 'expected' by the Department for Work and Pensions (DWP) following lockdown in March 2020, before recovering to exceed expected levels during 2021 (DWP, 2023c: Table 4.2). The LTUG hitting 27 per cent of starts achieving a 12-month job outcome, and the DG and EAG peaking at highs of 33–34 per cent achieving a 12-month job outcome among starts early in 2021 (DWP, 2023c).

Unlike the WP, the WHP did not operate in Scotland, as the surge of support for independence in 2014–15 led unionist politicians to concede additional powers to the Scottish Government. The passing of the Scotland Act 2016 gave the Scottish Government new authority over some aspects of working-age social security, and employability services focused on long-term unemployed people and disabled people (Wiggan, 2017; Simpson et al, 2019; Simpson, 2022).[3] The interim Work First Scotland scheme was quickly replaced with the Fair Start Scotland (FSS) employment programme from April 2018 (Scottish Government, 2019). The FSS employment programme did not mandate participation for any group of claimants, but indicative of the market liberal policy concensus among state managers remained within the familiar policy parameters of quasi-market-based delivery and economic rationality. A single public-, private- or third-sector provider functioning as the Prime in each of the nine contract areas, with the payment model built around a service fee and job outcome fees. The former represented 30 per cent of overall contract value, with the remaining 70 per cent based on jobs gained and sustained for 13, 26 and 52 weeks, with a higher proportion of fees weighted towards longer job sustainment (that is, 50 per cent for 52 weeks compared with 15 per cent for 13 weeks) (Scottish Government, 2022: 6).

In contrast to the WHP, but echoing the WP, the FSS included differential pricing, with three payment groups – Intense, Advanced and Core – as a proxy for variation in participant job-readiness. The Intense group, which had a maximum per participant fee claimable of £10,422, included disabled people, non-employed claimants with significant barriers to employment and people unemployed five years plus. The Advanced group included unemployed two years plus and 'disadvantaged' groups, with a maximum per participant fee claimable of £7,083. The maximum per participant fee for the Core group, which included people unemployed for less than two years, and those whose main employment constraints were basic skills or (lack of) childcare, was £4,626 per participant (Scottish Government, 2021: 12–13).

Though not directly comparable, job-outcome performance of the FSS was not dissimilar to other marketised programmes. Between April 2018 and December 2022 around a quarter of all participants (27 per cent) secured a 13-week job outcome, with this declining for 26 weeks (22 per cent) and 52 weeks (17 per cent) (Scottish Government, 2023: 12). As with the preceding WP, the level of job entry was greater for the youngest age group – in this case, participants aged 16–24. Around four in ten (42 per cent) started a job – nine percentage points higher than the proportion entering paid work from among the 50+ age group. Strikingly, the proportion of participants for each successive age group (for example, 16–24; 25–34; 35–49; 50+) that secured a job entry and then sustained that for 13, 26 or 52 weeks showed a progressively shallower drop-off as age increased. For example, the 'gap' between the proportion of 16–24-year-olds securing a job entry (42 per cent) and 12-month job sustainment (16 per cent) was 26 percentage points. Conversely, although the job-entry rate for the 50+ age group was 33 per cent, the drop-off was only 16 percentage points to the proportion sustaining for 12 months (17 per cent) (Scottish Government, 2023: 13), suggesting either better job matching, or less scope to exit, perhaps due to greater financial commitments, or limited alternatives relative to younger participants. In this, the performance of FSS provides a reminder of how employment programmes, irrespective of location, have reflected and helped produce and reproduce age-related divisons within Britain's labour market.

Though FSS arguably points to the consolidation of market-managerialism in employment programmes, the UK Government's ceding of additional social security powers to Scotland, to stabilise a political union destabilised by austerity, did open the door to the SNP's articulation of a progressive one nation mode of leadership that challenged, albeit in limited ways, the class politics of the Conservative UK Government. The founding charter of the new Social Security Scotland agency, for example, foregrounded the necessity of ensuring claimants are treated with dignity, respect and rights, and the Scottish Government used its powers to enhance financial support paid to families with children (Social Security Scotland, n.d.; Simpson, 2022). From a labour-oriented perspective the Scottish Government's approach has disrupted the discourse of the Conservative strategy of division and destitution in Scotland. It does not reflect a policial recomposition of labour as a powerful autonomus actor, but does point to the competition for hegemony within the British state apparatus over how best to organise the process of labour commodification to secure compliance, social cohesion and stability of the political-economic order.

Conservative instability, the COVID-19 shock and the durability of repressive market liberalism

The relative stability within the Scottish Government between 2016 and 2022 was not matched in the UK Government, despite the Conservatives being in office throughout this period. Between 2017 and 2022 the UK had four different Conservative prime ministers, as divisions over Brexit and the response to the COVID-19 pandemic that took hold in 2020 intersected with changes in class conflict occasioned by shifting socio-economic circumstances. The first to fall was Theresa May MP, who, in a ill-feted attempt to increase the Conservative majority in Parliament, and strengthen her position, called a general election to be held in June 2017. An unexpected surge of support for the Labour Party was sufficient, however, to deprive the Conservatives of a majority, leading to their reliance on the Democratic Unionist Party (DUP) to continue in Government (Burton-Cartledge, 2021). In a weakened position, the Prime Minister was unable to secure parliamentary support for her preferred EU withdrawal agreement, and with the Conservatives under electoral pressure from the UK Independence Party (UKIP), May resigned and was replaced in Summer 2019 by Boris Johnson MP (Burton-Cartledge, 2021: Worth, 2023: 820–1). Spours (2020) depicts this period as a recomposition of the (centre) right through "regressive combinational politics", cohering Brexit, strident (English) nationalism and a contradictory commitment to further liberalisation and greater state intervention. This was incorporated into the Conservative's two nations mode of leadership as a populist narrative of speaking for the (common sense of) people, against the (out of touch) political elite. The goal being to re-bind 'right' leaning voters to the Conservative Party, and attract new voters in areas deemed to have been 'left behind' by deindustrialisation, and decades of disinvestment and underdevelopment (Morrison, 2022: 5).

Under the politically flexible leadership of Johnson and seeking an electoral mandate and sufficient parliamentary majority to overcome opposition to withdrawing from the EU, a general election was called for December

2019 to 'get Brexit done', and with a promise to level up 'left behind' areas (Morrison, 2022). Returned with a majority of 80, the new Conservative Government under Johnson pressed ahead with exiting the EU, and indicated that the end of austerity was near, pledging to deliver on levelling up and actioning a return to the annual uprating of working-age benefits in 2020 (Pitt, 2023; Wiggan and Grover, 2022).

The onset of the COVID-19 pandemic, however, presented ministers with an immediate disruption to policymaking as usual and struck at the heart of capitalist relations of production. Attempting to persist with normal economic activity and social interaction risked acceleration of the spread of infection, overload of the NHS and unpredictable and damaging disruption to business. Yet, imposing restrictions on people's movement and business activity would negatively impact the economy and labour market, and require increased state support for inactive businesses and workers. An attendant expansion in public spending, while necessary to protect the productive capacity of capital, presented state managers with the risk that such spending would be difficult to roll back, would potentially distort market signals regarding business viability and labour allocation, and upend long established power relations in which labour was subordinate (Wiggan and Grover, 2022). Yet, it also offered a political opportunity to solidify the populist regressive hegemony of an emergent 'Johnsonism' (Spours, 2020) by demonstrating the state's willingness to intervene to protect people and nation. In the event, and as in other countries (Moreira and Hick, 2021), with the pandemic taking hold, economic order concerns around social cohesion, stability and state legitimacy moved to the fore. Under pressure to act the Government rolled out an expansive package of financial support for business and labour to stabilise society and protect the productive capacity of the economy, as restrictions on economic activity and people's movement were imposed as a public health measure (Wiggan and Grover, 2022).

Rather than a break with the prevailing regressive market-liberal labour market policy regime however, ministers' support to decommodify labour during the COVID-19 pandemic reflected a tactical step, intended to consolidate pre-pandemic arrangements during a period of crisis. Doing so, however, posed a risk to the politics of dominating and decomposing labour as a collective political actor. Undermining the parsimonious, disciplinary activation regime risked upsetting the balance of class power relations and hampering restoration of the favoured liberal political economy if people became accustomed to the more expansive levels of assistance and autonomy this engendered. So, while economic order concerns triggered extensive state intervention, the form this took was determined by a class politics concerned with (re)establishing labour subordination post-pandemic (Wiggan and Grover, 2022; Burton-Cartledge, 2023: 279).

Preserving class relations and productive capacity: the defensive step

The spread of COVID-19 throughout the country during March 2020, and imposition of restrictions on people's movement, gatherings and permissible business activity, was accompanied by a rise in the number of 'starts' to UC following a claim, with over 2 million between mid-March and mid-May 2020, up from around 200,000 per month prior to 'lockdown' (DWP, 2021). Minor policy adjustments, such as permitting claims for sickness- and disability-related benefits from the first day of not working due to ill health, were soon joined by more significant reforms (Harris et al, 2020: 10; Machin, 2021: 654). The support provided to claimants with rental costs for housing was improved, the benefit conditionality regime temporarily suspended and the value of UC was increased from around £75 per week for individuals to around £95 per week. The temporary removal of the 'Minimum Income Floor' (MIF) also improved access to UC entitlements for self-employed people (Harris et al, 2020; Machin, 2021: 653; Wiggan and Grover, 2022).

The increase in the value of UC contrasted with the real-terms erosion in the value of means-tested working-age benefits during the preceding four years, but contributory JSA and ESA benefits did not receive an equivalent uplift in payment rate. This incentivised claims to the new UC system, marginalised contributory benefits and reinforced residualisation of social security (Hick and Murphy, 2021: 318). This is indicated by the retention of the benefit cap during the pandemic, which meant families already at or close to the cap did not gain from the additional income support provided. Similarly, ministers chose not to alter how savings/investments were treated in calculation of UC entitlement, meaning that any household with £6,000–£16,000 in savings/investments would receive a lower level of assistance, while those with £16,000 plus in investments or savings would be entitled to nothing (Wiggan and Grover, 2022: 728). By not altering these eligibility conditions the Government limited claims to UC from higher-income, asset-holding households, and maintained out-of-work benefits as a safety net for poorer groups, rather than an expansive system of insurance against unpredictable risk.

The defence of residual social security was politically feasible because it was flanked by an, albeit temporary, policy innovation in the form of the Coronavirus Job Retention Scheme (CJRS), introduced in April 2020. The practice of subsidising companies to retain workers in jobs during temporary economic difficulties as an alternative to mass redundancy, was not unprecedented in Britain, but was largely abandoned in the mid-1980s by the New Right (see Chapter 5; Wiggan and Grover, 2022). Given this, the return of state subsidisation of the wages of non-working employees, by a Conservative Government, was a striking development. With the CJRS the state effectively rented the labour power of eligible workers in order to deactivate their engagement in the production or provision of goods and services.

Run by HM Revenue and Customs (HMRC) rather than the DWP, the first iteration of the CJRS met employer National Insurance and minimum auto-enrolment pension contributions in addition to 80 per cent of wage costs, up to a cap of £2,500 per month, for each employee of a company placed on 'furlough' (that is, not working) for a period of at least three weeks. Claims could be backdated to the beginning of March 2020, with the scheme expected to cease by the end of May 2020, given the expected emergence from 'lockdown' and reopening of businesses, but was quickly extended (Ferguson, 2021: 4; Leary et al, 2022: 8).

During its operation the CJRS was accompanied by numerous tweaks to its structure. From July 2020 it was altered to enable part-time employment for any worker previously furloughed during March–June 2020 with days not worked eligible for furlough subsidy. A requirement for employers to begin paying pension and National Insurance contributions was then introduced in late summer, with the proportion of state subsidy up to a maximum of £2,190 dropping to 70 per cent in September and 60 per cent up to a maximum of £1,875 in October. Employers were left to fill in the difference to reach the 80 per cent of wages paid, as ministers sought to taper away support and transition slowly back to employers being responsible for wages (HMRC, 2021d; Wiggan and Grover, 2022: 729).

The replacement of the CJRS from November 2020 by the less generous Job Support Scheme (JSS) was also planned, with the expectation that, for a lower cost, this would help mitigate unemployment as the economy opened up, state assistance was withdrawn, and market forces were restored (Ferguson, 2021: 6; Wiggan and Grover, 2022: 729). The resurgence of COVID-19, however, meant that by the beginning of November the scheme had been cancelled. The CJRS, reverting to its previous form, was again extended, first to January and then April 2021, as a new lockdown was imposed. A final extension was granted in March 2021, with the state subsidy dropping in July to 70 per cent and then 60 per cent in August 2021 with the scheme closed in September (Ferguson, 2021: 7; Leary et al, 2022: 9; Wiggan and Grover, 2022: 729).

In terms of scale, the CJRS cost £70 billion (Francis-Devine et al, 2021: 20) and the initial lockdown period saw the number of jobs furloughed daily peaking at around nine million (Francis-Devine et al, 2021: 9). As the wave of infections receded and Government encouraged business reopening this fell to under three million, before a new wave of infections and lockdowns pushed this up to five million daily employments on furlough, which tailed off through Summer 2021 to just over one million jobs furloughed daily as the scheme approached closure in

September (Francis-Devine et al, 2021: 9–10; HMRC, 2021c: Table 2; Wiggan and Grover, 2022: 730).

A survey of employers using the CJRS reported that in its absence 56 per cent would have made a greater number of redundancies than they did, with this closer to 70 per cent among small- and medium-sized businesses (Dabhi et al, 2022: 71). Qualitative research with employers indicated the importance of the CJRS in preventing business collapse, and helping to avoid loss of skilled staff (Leary et al, 2022: 34–5). The nature of the pandemic-induced lockdown affected the distribution of furlough, with HMRC calculation of take-up among CJRS-eligible employers indicating this was lower across industry relative to services (HMRC, 2021c; Francis-Devine et al, 2021: 12).

On 31 May 2021 the highest take-up rate (52 per cent) among employers was in the accommodation and food services sector, followed by arts, entertainment and recreation (45 per cent) (HMRC, 2021c: Table 10). Reflective of the diverse nature of work tasks in services, the employer take-up of CJRS among the information and communication (22 per cent) and finance and insurance (21 per cent) sectors was much lower (HMRC, 2021c: Table 10). Given the concentration of younger workers employed in accommodation, food, entertainment and recreation businesses, it is perhaps not surprising that while around one quarter of all employees (26 per cent) had been furloughed at some point between March 2020 and June 2021, for those aged up to 24 this was around 30–35 per cent (ONS, 2021a: 3; ONS, 2021b: Tables 1 and 3). The proportion of male (27 per cent) and female employees (25 per cent) during the pandemic who were furloughed was broadly similar (ONS, 2021b: Table 2), but experience of furlough was contoured by how qualification and skill levels intersected with labour market position.

The Office for National Statistics (ONS) calculated that, whereas 16 per cent of employees during the pandemic with a degree-level qualification or higher had been furloughed, the proportion was more than double for those whose highest qualification was GCSEs (35 per cent), or who had no qualifications (37 per cent) (ONS, 2021a: 4; ONS, 2021b: Table 5). The take-up of furlough was also greater among lower-paying jobs than higher-income jobs (Francis-Devine et al, 2021: 15–16; HMRC, 2021c: Table 20). The types of service sector jobs occupied by many highly qualified workers no doubt being more amenable to work-from-home requirements and so not necessitating furlough. The majority of employees furloughed were supported for a period of one to six months, but over one fifth of the people were furloughed for a period of six months plus (ONS, 2021b: Table 12).

With CJRS targeting employees, a new policy intervention to protect the incomes of self-employed people, the Self-Employment Income Support

Scheme (SEISS), was also introduced in April 2020, and also brought to a close in September 2021. The SEISS was also managed by HMRC, indicating how these extraordinary interventions were kept separate from the DWP, the department charged with management of mainstream employment services and social security provision. The SEISS was initially intended to deliver only one round of support in Spring 2020, but there were eventually five rounds of grant awards (Seely, 2023). The first grant in the SEISS based assessment for eligibility on trading profits during the 2018–19 tax year as a means to guard against fraud and target resources. People who had gone self-employed after April 2019 were initially excluded from SEISS, as were people with profits above £50,000 per year, and those with more than half their income deriving from activity other than self-employed trading. The first round of SEISS paid out a grant to the value of 80 per cent of previous earnings, averaged over three months up to a maximum of £2,500 with the conditions and amount payable varying over the five rounds during 2020–21[4] (Seely, 2023: 4–9).

As with the CJRS, the SEISS represented a monumental intervention in the labour market, with £28 billion paid out in grants between May 2020 and October 2021, and 2.9 million individuals receiving at least one grant during this period (HMRC, 2021a). Yet, not all benefitted, and the uneven impact of the pandemic upon different industrial sectors and its intersection with the patterning of self-employment with ascribed social characteristics is shown in the distribution of claims to SEISS.

The largest number of individuals (974,000) claiming SEISS were located in the (male-dominated) construction sector, equivalent to one third (34 per cent) of all individual claimants (HMRC, 2021b: Table 3), with take-up particularly high for the first grant (that is, the first lockdown) (HMRC, 2021a: Table 12). As analysis by the Women's Budget Group (WBG) argued, women's pattern of engagement in (part-time) self-employment meant criteria for the SEISS left them at greater risk of exclusion from support (WBG, 2021: 6). The WBG also noted that take-up of SEISS by those meeting the eligibility conditions was lower among women than men (WBG, 2021: 6), suggesting SEISS was less protective of self-employed women in practice.

So while the layering on of the SEISS to the existing social security institutions enhanced protection of self-employed people's income, the extent to which this was so reflected broader inequalities. Among people ineligible for SEISS due to not earning more than 50 per cent of income from self-employment, analysis by the Institute for Fiscal Studies estimated that around half had a total income below £25,000, with a majority below this level having profits of £5,000 or less (Cribb et al, 2021: 6–8). Lack of access to SEISS could be devastating for financial stability during the pandemic and plunged some families into considerable hardship (Cameron et al, 2022: 101–2; Dickerson et al, 2022: 77).

Overall though, the CJRS (and SEISS) made the short-term powering down of value extraction economically and politically feasible. Prevention of mass redundancies, in a concentrated period of time, prevented a collapse of worker income, helping stabilise demand and enable companies to maintain capacity for post-pandemic expansion of activity, while mitigating pressure to expand the generosity and coverage of out-of-work benefits. In effect, state managers used the CJRS to partially socialise the costs of lockdown as economic order concerns with social cohesion, and long-term productive capacity, moved to the fore at the beginning of the pandemic (Wiggan and Grover, 2022).

The scale of the intervention that the CJRS and SEISS represented, though, rapidly led to concerns that elevated public spending was unsustainable, would hamper future growth and risked a misallocation of labour by supporting unproductive companies that, left to the market, would go out of business. In protecting the income of furloughed workers and keeping unemployment low (Francis-Devine et al, 2021: 23), the state was also distorting the labour market in a way that tightened the labour supply and risked making it more difficult to restore the authority of employers and state post-pandemic. The desire of ministers to avoid such a state of affairs is indicated in their repeated attempts to bring the CJRS to a close, and swift reintroduction of coercive activation measures (Wiggan and Grover, 2022).

Employment services and the re-mobilisation and sorting of the labour reserve

As early as July 2020 the Government's announced 'Plan for Jobs' signalled renewal of the activation drive (HM Treasury, 2020) and drew on a familiar panoply of pre-pandemic work-first measures. These included: increasing the number of Work Coaches; additional spending on basic job-search activity (for example, CV development; interview coaching); a £3,000 wage subsidy for employers hiring 'apprentices' and a £1,000 subsidy for employers providing work experience for 16–24-year-olds. Funding was also made available to expand the Sector-Based Work Academies (SBWA) scheme and WHP and a £1,000 Job Retention Bonus was introduced for each 'furloughed' employee an employer retained to the beginning of 2021 (HM Treasury, 2020). The Plan for Jobs also heralded two new supply-side employment programmes, Kick Start and Restart (HM Treasury, 2021).

The Coalition's WP had demonstrated that maximising competition between (potential) Primes could deliver lower-cost employment programme provision and ramp up pressure on para-state employees to prioritise job-ready participants for rapid commodification. Retaining a confidence in market rationality, the Restart scheme nonetheless adopted some differences in approach, as state managers sought to improve engagement of less job-ready claimants, and increase market capacity, which had fallen away with the end of the WP, and move to the smaller WHP (NAO, 2022). State managers limited price competition to mitigate incentives for potential providers to underbid for contracts, and relative to the WP, the Restart Programme (RP) involved greater managerial direction by the centre. Government stipulated all Prime providers were to meet nine 'customer service standards' and backed this with threat of financial penalties for non-compliance (NAO, 2022: 41–2). Scheduled to run for a period of three years with each participant supported for a year, the RP began in July 2021 with £2.9 billion allocated to mobilise one million claimants into paid work (DWP, 2023d: ch 1). The initial target being UC claimants of 12 months plus (later nine months plus) subject to the Intensive Work Search (UC IWS) regime, and subsequently extended to means-tested JSA claimants (DWP, 2022a). Participation was mandatory if referred, but referral was at the discretion of a Jobcentre Plus (JCP) Work Coach (NAO, 2022: 23). The RP was contracted to eight non-state providers (Primes) organised into 12 Contract Package Areas (CPAs) across England and Wales, with one Prime per CPA and each overseeing sub-contractors (NAO, 2022: 38).

Echoing the WHP, the payment model was balanced between delivery fees, worth 30 per cent of total contract value[5] and job-outcome fees, which made up the majority of the total contract payment that could be claimed. The latter were achieved when a participant either sustained self-employment for six months, or secured and sustained a job, earning equivalent to 16 hours per week at the NLW rate for six months (DWP, 2022a). An accelerator model of payment was also used, with a standard fee paid by the DWP for a specified proportion (21 per cent) of outcomes secured. For outcomes achieved above this level, contractors were paid a higher rate (140 per cent of standard) per outcome achieved to encourage providers to continue to reach further into the caseload (DWP, 2023d: ch 17). The proportion of participants attaining a six-month job outcome between July 2021 and March 2022 was 11 per cent, though this had fallen to 8 per cent in March (DWP, 2022a; 2022b: Table 1.2). As with similar programmes the RP may function primarily to mobilise claimants to engage in work-related activity, that is to move people into the 'training' segment of the labour market and support retention in the labour reserve and only secondarily serve as a mechanism for securing transition into employment.

Participation in Restart was lowest for those in the under-25 age group, who were also eligible for the Kickstart scheme targeted at 16–24-year-olds. Developed in 2020 amid projections of high youth unemployment post-pandemic (Public Accounts Committee, 2022: 10), the Kickstart scheme was resourced with £1.9 billion to support 250,000 young UC claimants into jobs, and ran in 2020–22 (NAO, 2021: 3; Public Accounts Committee, 2022: 3-4). A wage-subsidy equivalent to 25 hours per week at the NMW rate for six months was provided to employers recruiting a young person to an entry-level job, with an additional £1,500 potentially available for costs of employability support (DWP, 2021). Again, unlike New Labour's Future Jobs Fund (FJF), the Kickstart scheme did not include a 'community benefit' condition (NAO, 2021: 23). In contrast to the Coalition's wage subsidy for young people, however, the subsidy was ostensibly intended to support 'additional' jobs (NAO, 2021: 8; Public Accounts Committee, 2022: 12–13; Public Accounts Committee, 2021: Q22–7). A hire under Kickstart also remained eligible post-programme for recruitment to an apprenticeship or to a traineeship. Shrewd employers could potentially sequence state support to further lower their labour costs (NAO, 2021: 24), illustrating how the intersection of pandemic-era active labour market policy partially provided for a socialisation of the costs of employing young people, as ministers sought to prevent a long-term reduction in the supply of labour.

In total 429,000 individuals had been referred and 152,000 individuals had started a job with Kickstart by 2023 (Davies, 2023). Of total job starts by April 2022, the highest proportions were located in administration (25 per cent); retail and sales (16 per cent); creative media (10 per cent); and hospitality and food (9 per cent)[6] (Davies, 2022). Together with previous schemes, such as New Labour's FJF and the youth wage subsidy of the Coalition, Kickstart shows how state managers have developed the art of turning to expansive (youth) employment subsidies to moderate unemployment during moments of (feared) crisis in the commodification of youth labour. In this way, wage subsidies have become a temporary but regular feature of how activation policy in Britain is cyclically adjusted. As moments of crisis subside, state managers marginalise subsidises and revert back to low-cost, coercive, supply-side incentive reinforcement that is oriented to fostering entry into existing vacancies. Whether individual employers welcome this one dimensional approach is less evident (Ingold and Stuart, 2015; Wiggan and Knuth, 2023).

Social security and the renewal of class struggle

The emergence from the pandemic was accompanied by a roll-back of the uplift in the value of UC, despite cross-party and civil society support. Under political pressure, ministers instead lowered the withdrawal rate for UC to 55 per cent, which raised the amount of income that would flow to claimants moving into paid work, or increasing their earnings. The strengthening of financial incentives to take any job or increase hours of work, while diminishing support for out-of-work claimants was consistent with a pivot back to a repressive class politics (Wiggan and Grover, 2022: 728). The imposition of benefit sanctions also returned with a vigour, pointing to continuity in the pursuit of a strategy of disciplinary exclusion as the means to secure the compliance of labour. Analysis by the Institute for Public Policy Research (IPPR) think tank showed that the proportion of 'full conditionality' UC claimants being sanctioned rose from under 1 per cent of the caseload in Summer 2021 to 4 per cent by the end of that year, before reaching around 8 per cent towards the end of 2022 (Parkes, 2023: 3; Webster, 2023: 20–1). As noted in preceding chapters, and pointed out by Jones and Kumar (2022: 71), sanctioning has a deleterious effect on claimant wellbeing, but is low cost and drives (short-term) benefit exit.

The DWP evaluation of the effect of benefit sanctions on UC IWS claimants suggested that sanctioned claimants were more likely to exit UC and move into lower earnings than non-sanctioned claimants (DWP, 2023h: 6.2). Whether or not this has provided for an optimal allocation of labour has been less of a concern for state managers than restoring labour supply (see HM Treasury, 2023: 18). Similarly, the 'Way to Work' campaign announced at the beginning of 2022 (DWP, 2022c) dialled down job matching as a goal and dialled up the pressure for claimants to accept 'any job', by reducing from 13 weeks to four weeks the period during which a claimant could focus on job-search activity in their usual occupation (Secretary of State for Work and Pensions, 2022a). Such approaches point to how reconfiguration of the state apparatus has peeled away the autonomy enhancing aspects of social security and increased claimant exposure to the 'mute compulsion' structurally embedded within capitalism to sell one's labour power (Mau, 2023: Loc 1030–41).

The problem that this return to repressive class politics sought to address was that the post-pandemic surge in demand for labour enhanced individual autonomy and recomposed labour as an important collective political actor. Job vacancies were running above pre-pandemic levels throughout 2021–23 (ONS, 2023i) and the unemployment rate had fallen from 5.3 per cent in the final quarter of 2020 to 3.6 per cent in the third quarter of 2022 (Figure 3.3). Compounding this was a rise in the economic inactivity rate for the 16–64 age group during the pandemic and which remained above its pre-pandemic level through 2022 (ONS, 2023a). With a depleted labour reserve amid high demand, workers' ability to leverage job switching or (threat of) industrial action to raise or defend pay and conditions increased.

In nominal terms the growth in regular average weekly earnings was running at 3–4 per cent in 2019, but then fell with the onset of the pandemic. Wage growth gradually recovered, and during 2022–23 accelerated from 4.3 per cent in January–March 2022 to 7.3 per cent in March–May 2023 (ONS, 2023h), with growth higher in the private than public sector. The nominal growth in wages, however, began to be outpaced by a rise in the rate of inflation, with the quarterly CPI rate rising from a low of 0.5 per cent in the fourth quarter of 2020 to a high of 10.7 per cent in the fourth quarter of 2022 (ONS, 2023j). Given the Bank of England's mandate to maintain a rate of 2 per cent CPI, the Monetary Policy Committee (MPC) responded by increasing the Bank's base rate, which trended upwards throughout 2022 to 3.5 per cent by the end of the year and 5 per cent during Summer 2023 (Bank of England, n.d.).

The commitment to ratcheting up punitive activation through 2022–23 persisted, irrespective of the turmoil engulfing the Conservative Party, and turnover in its leadership. In the summer of 2022 Boris Johnson MP resigned as Prime Minister and was replaced by Liz Truss MP (Clarke, 2023: 159), who appointed Kwasi Kwarteng MP as Chancellor of the Exchequer. Under this partnership, further restriction on labour rights and curtailment of social protection moved to the fore, alongside an aggressive tax-cutting agenda and determination to sidestep extant institutional 'constraints' regulating Britain's economy, in a libertarian-tinged strategy to accelerate economic growth (Benquet and Bourgeron, 2022; Parker et al, 2022; Russell, 2022). The class politics of the Government's fiscal statement in Autumn 2022 were transparent, with a lifting of the cap on banker pay bonuses and removal of the 45 per cent tax rate on income above £150,000 announced, along with expansion in the proportion of UC claimants subject to intensive work-search activity and new constraints on trade unions' ability to pursue (effective) industrial action (HM Treasury, 2022).

In the event, the fiscal statement proved controversial and politically and economically damaging. An absence of clear information on how the proposed rise in borrowing would be financed, and concern that the strategy would add to existing inflationary pressures and further destabilise the economy, generated a negative reaction from financial markets and the guardians of fiscal orthodoxy (that is, the Bank of England and Conservative opponents of Truss) (Parker et al, 2022; Partington, 2022a; Russell, 2022).

The preceding dismissal of the Permanent Secretary of HM Treasury, shortly after the new Prime Minister took office, and decision to prevent the Office for Budget Responsibility (OBR) providing a forecast of the economic implications of the fiscal statement added to a sense of ministers recklessly breaking with accepted policy parameters (Bartrum, 2022; Pope, 2022; Partington, 2022b). Financial disruption ensued, with rapid rises in the cost of borrowing translating into political destabilisation and ebbing of confidence in the Government (Romei, 2022; Russell, 2022; Stubbington et al, 2022). The resignation of Kwasi Kwarteng as Chancellor was followed shortly after by the resignation of Truss as Prime Minister, after around six weeks in office (Walker et al, 2022).

The subsequent ascent of Rishi Sunak MP to the position of Prime Minister and Jeremy Hunt MP as Chancellor was accompanied by renewed commitment to fiscal orthodoxy and the role of core economic policymaking institutions. Public-spending constraint moved back to the centre of the Government's accumulation strategy, as ministers moved to reassure the markets that fiscal conservatives were back in charge, and alleviate upward pressure on interest rates (Clarke, 2023: 181–2). The policy combination of interest rate rises, austerity and demands for wage restraint (Bailey, 2022; Hunt, 2023) undermined the political authority and popularity of the Conservative Government, but were coherent in terms of attempting to defend a pro-capital political-economic order at the expense of labour.

The Government's commitment to bolstering its regressive market-liberal labour market policy regime continued through 2022–23 as ministers responded to worker militancy and labour shortages. New anti-trade union legislation was enacted to allow employers to hire agency workers to replace those on strike, and the Government pressed ahead with legislation to require that unions maintain a minimum level of services during industrial action in various sectors (DBEIS, 2022; Crerar and Stacy, 2023). Government and media discourse again denigrated trade unions as out of touch and holding the public to ransom (Ellery, 2022). The spectre of the benefit cheat and the skiver discourse was revivified, along with attempts to elide the difference between economic inactivity on grounds of ill health and disability, and unemployment (DWP, 2022d; Chan and Martin, 2023; Ryan, 2023; Webster, 2022, Webster, 2023).

In parallel, the coercive activation of unemployed, underemployed and non-employed labour was intensified and broadened, as mobilising the labour reserve and segments of the surplus population came to be deemed a pressing economic matter (that is, extensive labour utilisation as accumulation strategy). To increase the intensity of labour market participation among working UC claimants, the Administrative Earnings Threshold (AET) in UC was raised in September 2022 to the equivalent of 12 or 19 hours a week at NLW for single or couple claimants respectively (DWP, 2023e). In raising the threshold, ministers set eligibility for the 'light touch' regime at a higher level, meaning claimants with earnings below this became subject to a more onerous job search regime geared towards increasing hours and/or pay rates. The DWP Equality Impact Assessment (DWP, 2023e) noted this meant younger people not entitled to the NLW would need to work a greater number of hours to clear the AET. In early 2023 the AET was adjusted upwards again to the equivalent of 15 or 24 hours work per week at the NLW for single and couple claimants respectively (DWP, 2023e) with expectations that this AET adjustment would draw 120,000 claimants into the purview of intensive work-search requirements (Hansard, 2023 col 8WS).

The 2023 Spring Budget announced that the AET was to be raised to the equivalent of 18 hours per week at the NLW for single people and removed the couple AET (HM Treasury, 2023: 99). The earnings of one member of a couple would no longer elevate a low- or non-earning partner into the 'light touch' regime. Instead, escaping a more intense job search regime became dependent on the individual earnings of each partner alone lifting them clear of the AET (DWP, 2023f). We can conceptualise this as a form of intensive and extensive activation as it raises the level of work activity required for recipients and extends the purview of activation, using the threat of removing assistance to secure the domination of labour (that is, an extraction strategy of disciplinary exclusion) and mobilise a latent surplus population (that is, extensive labour utilisation).

As alluded to earlier, the post-pandemic fall in unemployment was not matched by a similar fall in economic inactivity and the caseload of non-employed claimants on grounds of sickness or disability. A review of the interaction of health-related economic inactivity and the operation of social security by the OBR (2023) suggested that the introduction of the Work Capability Assessment (WCA) accompanying the introduction of ESA had initially reduced access to benefits on health grounds. The OBR suggested, however, that the effect diminished after 2015, identifying claimant and claimant organisations' familiarity with the claims process, and struggles to have the WCA better reflect needs, as partly responsible. From the perspective of ministers the pandemic had then exacerbated this 'problem', as the approval rate of new claimants taking a WCA approached 100 per cent during the pandemic, before declining back to its immediate pre-pandemic rate of around 80 per cent (OBR, 2023: 45–7).

From a class-analysis perspective, the pandemic had opened up access to decommodifying benefits that expanded the relative surplus population, while the labour reserve then began to be depleted by rising employer demand, tightening the labour market and adding impetus to the (re) emergence of a militant political class composition of labour. The shutting-down of this route to decommodification was consequently attractive to the Government and the Spring 2023 Budget announced the intention to abolish the WCA and 'personalise' assessment via JCP Work Coaches (HM Treasury, 2023; DWP, 2023g: 34). Given the market-oriented and managerialist reconfiguration of employment services and benefit administration, this is unlikely to favour claimants, with state managers likely to use incentives to direct and constrain frontline delivery to align with their coercive activation imperatives. The Additional Jobcentre Support programme pilot, requiring daily meetings of claimants with a Work Coach included, for example, the testing of £250 bonus payments to staff in JCP offices deemed high performers (PCS, 2023; Secretary of State for Work and Pensions, 2023; Webster, 2023: 7–8).

Concluding remarks

With respect to active labour market policy, the period up to 2020 was largely marked by consolidation. Continuation of austerity in working-age benefits, conjoined with a relative slackening of the imposition of sanctions, and downgrading of the size and scope of the employment service quasi-market, amid declines in unemployment and a shift in focus to the roll-out of UC. A 'One Nation' rhetoric was resurrected and combined with populist discourse pitching an undifferentiated 'people' against an EU-supporting 'elite', as successive prime ministers sought to cohere support from voters impacted by working-age benefit retrenchment and post-industrial economic decline (Fetzer, 2019: 3884; Hopkin, 2020: 145; Morrison, 2022; Worth, 2023).

The rhetoric belied the persistence in practice of a regressive two-nation governing strategy, which the pandemic did not fundamentally alter. The layering-on of the CJRS, alongside modest changes to regular social security and employment services, crafted a division in generosity of support, dependent on position in the labour force, or labour reserve and relative surplus population. The temporary 'crisis' innovations and modest tweaks to existing benefits reinforced the pre-pandemic drift to residualisation of social security. It also moderated the risk of inadvertently generating support for pathbreaking change, and facilitated path reversion to the more punitive market-liberal labour market policy approach (Wiggan and Grover, 2022).

The post-pandemic demand for labour in 2021–23 and its effect in bolstering the power of workers, as indicated in rising industrial action (ONS, 2023d), suggests the preference of the Conservative leadership to quickly restore coercive activation measures was an astute reading of the risks the pandemic response posed to the continued domination of labour. The return to a more aggressive two-nation mode of leadership, with its denigration of unemployed and non-employed claimants, again sought to deepen intra-class division and warrant the accompanying attempt to close off social security as a potential 'outside option' to formal employment, or low-intensity paid work (that is, hours just above the UC AET).

The revivification of a repressive extraction strategy does, of course, have costs. Increased economic hardship and negative labour market experience risk calling into doubt the legitimacy of the social order and/ or fostering the sub-optimal allocation of available labour power. Jones and Kumar (2022: 104) and Umney et al (2018) have noted that employers are critical of the inefficiencies and resource costs they experience, due to the inappropriate job applications and interview candidates that accompany claimant compliance with benefit conditionality. State managers, though, concern themselves with the general conditions for the reproduction of capital (Banks, 2012: 98–9). While this may take different forms depending on specific conditions and balance of forces, in Britain the successive recomposing of labour as a weak collective political actor and the low-wage, flexible labour market of a liberal economic model have provided ample incentive for Government to adopt a coercive approach (Umney et al, 2018). For all the disruption between 2016 and 2023, the regressive market-liberal labour market policy regime initiated under the Coalition persisted; successive governments deepening the 'structural entrenchment of class domination' (Jessop, 2015: 15) in, and through the state, in order to impose work and control over labour in the drive to expand capital's collective share of value (Calvert Jump et al, 2023: 16).

12

Concluding remarks

The preceding chapters have detailed the class and economic order politics informing, and informed by, the remaking of the state labour commodification apparatus under successive British governments since the early 1970s. The chapters elaborate how the remaking of labour market policy and governance did not simply follow a shift to post-industrial employment, but actively shaped (while also being shaped by) the type of post-industrial labour market and class composition of labour brought into being. Following the arguemt put forward by Gallas' (2016: 48), that securing the domination of labour is a necessary precursor to commodification, value extraction and capital accumulation, the analysis sets out how the development of active labour market policy under successive British Governments has sought to erode the autonomy enhancing potential of working age social security benefits and employment services. In this the the work draws on, and adds support to, Aufheben's notion of 'dole autonomy', which conceptualised how, as full employment collapsed, the welfare arrangements of industrial society buttressed the collective and individual autonomy of claimants and workers and hampered the ability of state managers to (re) impose ('make') work and labour discipline (Aufheben, 1998).

The form and tempo of the development of active labour market policy and its relationship to the gradual embedding of an institutional orientation to fostering full employability, is in turn understood here as entwined with the shifting intensity of class struggle over time. Which was itself influenced by, and fed into, the remaking of the technical and political class composition of labour into a form less capable of contesting the authority of capital and state, embedding a cycle of autonomy eroding reforms and progressive weakening of the collective power of labour. To parse the particularities of this process as it has unfolded in Britain the framework developed by Gallas (2016) to analytically separate out the strategies governments use to pursue domination from those used to support accumulation, has been applied to labour market policy and governance in Chapters 4 through 11. From the analysis, five distinct orientations were identified (Table 12.1), providing an indication of changes in how class order politics manifested specifically in labour market policy and governance over time, and their relationship to the intensity of struggle.

Table 12.1: The changing orientation of labour market policy and governance 1973–2023

Orientation	Class politics (extraction strategy and mode of leadership)	Economic order (state strategy & accumulation strategy)	Step in struggle	Period
Social democratic-pacificatory	Labourist	Weak corporatist	Defensive	1974–79
Conservative transitional-pacificatory	Cautious conservative	Transitional	Cautious offensive	1979–85
Conservative-emergent market-liberal	Social conservative	Emergent market-liberal	Offensive	1985–97
Progressive market-liberal	Progressive	Market-liberal	Consolidation/ offensive	1997–2010
Regressive market-liberal	Regressive	Market-liberal	Offensive/ consolidation/ offensive	2010–23

Source: Author creation informed by, and adapted from Gallas (2016: 290).

The emergence of active labour market policy amid the stagnation and conflict that marked the end times of Britain's social democratic industrial society (Ross and Jenson, 1986) marked a defensive step. Amid rising unemployment, state managers rejected reflationary fiscal policy (Wickham-Jones, 1996; Lopez, 2014), turning instead to corporatist institutions to expand low-cost Special Employment Measures (SEMs) (Metcalf, 1982) to placate organised labour amid concern at its capacity to obstruct the Government's pursuit of wage repression as the core of its economic strategy. This was paralleled by a relatively well-organised broader claimant movement, whose activities helped to support claimants to access entitlements, and contest pernicious benefit policing (Marsland, 2018), in what remained a relatively benevolent institutional environment geared to the development of labour. The proto-activation measures, for example, remained anchored in the economic logics and class power relations sedimented in the (weakly) social democratic corporatist state of post-war industrial society. The role of subsidised short-term work schemes and temporary waged employment schemes, cohering with an economic order politics rooted in intensive labour utilisation to maximise productivity and output of the core labour force. Unemployment benefits and employment services intended to improve efficient (re)allocation of labour also reinforced this logic, creating greater space for unemployed claimants to exercise autonomy over job search, and timing of labour market participation (Aufheben, 1998; Koch, 2006).

The first half of the 1980s saw state managers pivot to a cautious offensive step. The new (Right) Conservative Government abandoned full (male) employment and state intervention as disruptive of employer authority, and market distorting (Joseph, 1980; Thatcher, 1995). Yet, amid rapid de-industrialisation and an engorged labour reserve the corporatist governance and pacificatory type employment programmes of social democracy were retained. Though moderate retrenchment in the value and coverage of social security pointed to the beginning of the stripping back of working age benefits as an outside option to paid work. The cautious approach to watering down and then rescinding such developmental measures is indicated by the persistence of a (market-distorting) subsidised short-time working scheme into the beginning of the second Thatcher Government (Wiggan and Grover, 2022).

By the end of this period the SEMs were flanked by new policies geared towards individual employability and lowering the price of unemployed labour power, indicating the transition underway to a liberal apparatus geared towards bolstering employer authority. The complex articulation of continuity and change reflected the contingent balance of social forces with (New Right) ministers keen to secure their ascendancy and dominance within, and outwith the state, pragmatically deploying familiar policy forms to occupy the attention of some unemployed people, and 'depoliticise' unemployment as an electoral issue amid public disquiet (Moon and Richardson, 1985; Tebbit, 1989).

With electoral dominance at Westminster, the Conservatives renewed the scale and tempo of their offensive in the struggle over labour commodification, though moves to strengthen activation of claimants remained focused on unemployed people, to the exclusion of the broader (surplus) population of non-employed claimants. The future extensive labour utilisation accumulation strategy in labour market policy was signalled, as ministers attempted to respond to and shape the (emergent) post-industrial labour market by remaking the structures of social security that facilitated 'dole autonomy' and bolstered the power of labour (Aufheben, 1998). The remaining institutionalised influence of organised labour in labour market policymaking and delivery was removed with abolishment of the Manpower Services Commission (MSC) as ministers responded to trade union opposition to the phasing out of subsidised waged social economy jobs in favour of unwaged employment and training programmes (Ryan, 1995; Jones, 1996; Price, 2000).

With the remaking of the state labour commodification apparatus the terrain of class struggle had shifted in favour of capital, with business leaders inserted into leadership positions in the governance of employment programmes for unemployed people via the Training and Enterprise Councils (TECs). The entrepreneurialism, competitive market pressure and local business knowledge in the TECs were intended to raise the performance of the state in equipping unemployed people with skills relevant to the new labour market, improving claimant transitions between the labour reserve and secondary labour market (Jones, 1999). The new unwaged training schemes though were met by a lack claimant enthusiasm, manifesting in lower than expected participation levels at times. With unemployment rising following the recession of the early 1990s (Jenkins, 2010), and the Conservative Government's desire to curtail spending on 'training schemes', the approach floundered (Jones, 1999), but pointed to the growing importance of market rationality for directing (para) state employees. The development of a market-liberal and incentive-reinforcement approach to labour market policy (Clasen, 2002) intersected with the articulation of a more stridently socially conservative, two-nations mode of governing. Conservative ministers increasingly depicting claimants as dependent, and a source of disorder when claimant behaviour and life choices did not align with those deemed conducive to productive formal employment, and (conservative) notions of social stability (Jones and Novak, 1999; O'Grady, 2022; also see Chapter 7).

Yet, as Gallas (2016) and others (Aufheben, 1998; Power Sayeed, 2017) have suggested, the social conservativism of Conservative ministers was increasingly out of place with public social mores. Together with their expressed ideological distaste for public spending and state intervention, this had become an obstacle to improving the coherence between economic strategy, the state labour commodification apparatus and the utilisation of claimant labour. With the exhaustion of the Conservatives in office the opportunity opened for a reconditioned Labour Party to renew the state apparatus. More at ease with the changed social relations of post-industrial society, and willing to use public spending to overhaul the organisation of labour commodification, the progressive market-liberals of New Labour articulated a consolidatory and offensive step in their development of a progressive market liberal, active labour market policy.

An offensive step was taken against claimant autonomy, with employment programme participation for unemployed claimants made mandatory, work-related activity requirements for non-employed claimants increased and delivery governed increasingly through (job-)outcome-oriented managerial targets and marketisation (Wiggan, 2007b; Wright, 2011). The offensive manoeuvre was teamed with a consolidatory step where additional support and regulations (for example, minimum wages, in-work benefits, childcare) were intended to place limits on the intensity of exploitation, bolster social reproduction and strengthen cohesion to create an 'inclusive' competitive labour market order (Byrne, 2005; Dwyer, 2008). In the early 2000s, for example, the New Labour governments expressed a desire to mobilise a higher proportion of working-age non-employed people to enter the labour market and compete for waged work, setting an aspiration to achieve an overall employment rate of 80 per cent (Gregg and Gardiner, 2016: 22). The pursuit of domination encoded in the conditional, work-first approach, cohering with an accumulation strategy of extensive labour utilisation rooted in a shift to what Griggs et al (2014) term 'activation for all', as the means to combine expansion of employment and value extraction in ways that did not threaten to undermine employer authority, or induce wage-push inflation (Grover and Stewart, 2002).

In the propitious economic circumstances of the late 1990s to mid-2000s the activation of unemployed claimants, from the perspective of state managers, could be regarded as a moderate success (Wells, 2001). The strengthening of a disciplinary but inclusive form of activation however, was accompanied by the cycling of unemployed claimants between benefits, employment programmes and the labour market. A consequence of the nature of the jobs available, and what was implied to be claimants 'gaming' the system (Secretary of State for Work and Pensions, 2006b). Or what we might reasonably regard as (some) individual's creative use of social security to exercise autonomy over the conditions under which one's labour power is sold, to whom, and when.

With the formation of the Conservative–Liberal Coalition Government, state managers intensified the offensive against claimant autonomy as part of a drive to repress social and money wages. Austerity in working-age benefits was combined with a strengthening of benefit conditionality, and greater use of market rationality in delivery of employment programmes, as state managers worked to strengthen control over (para) state employees and reach into the labour reserve *and* surplus population to identify, and activate claimants deemed to be most employable (Wiggan, 2015a; 2015b; Farnsworth, 2021). The incentive to seek even low-paid work, was Grover (2012; 2019) argues, backstopped by the threat of destitution that benefit removal, or reduction implied. The intense stigmatisation of benefit claimants accompanied this, marking a shift to a more expressly divisive, confrontational and regressive two-nations governing strategy (Lavery, 2019; Morrison, 2019). The pivot to a strategy of disciplinary exclusion was also found in the drive to expand work for your benefit schemes for the short term unemployed. In a defensive response the claimant movement and pro-claimant campaigns began to recompose as an organised oppositional force, harrying the operation of workfare and sanctioning at the local level (see SUWN, 2016), undermining the feasibility of work for your benefit schemes (see Chapter 10).

The turn of the punitive market-liberal ratchet and expansion of the labour supply was connected to the strategy for renewal of accumulation that, Calvert Jump et al (2023) argue, was realised through disciplining workers to repress wage growth (see also Green and Lavery, 2015).

The Government, for example, expressed the intention to achieve the highest employment rate among the countries of the G7, depicted as the modern interpretation of 'full employment' (Berry, 2014a). Yet, as this full employability goal did not discern between full-time paid work and marginal labour market attachment (Osborne, 2014; also Berry, 2014a, 2014b), it implied the key aim was to improve the liquidity of the labour market. The parallel introduction of the new Universal Credit (UC) aligned with this, as it aimed to erode divisions between being in and out of paid work and in receipt of benefits, encouraging greater flexibility in hours, wages and workers employed.

The aggressive pursuit of austerity, however, gradually destabilised the political and social order, contributing to the fall from office of its principal architects and a period of intense instability post-2016 (Burton Cartledge, 2023; Clarke, 2023). In response, the intensity of coercive measures applied to activate claimants was eased as the tempo of class struggle shifted to a period of consolidation. At the same time the move away from the expansive employment programmes of the Coalition era to smaller schemes under successive Conservative governments after 2016, reflected the overall decline in unemployment, and signalled that the new UC was expected to do the heavy lifting of activation via financial incentives, irrespective of its various flaws (Millar and Bennett, 2017).

The COVID-19 pandemic immediately disrupted the extraction of value and accumulation of capital as state managers were forced to shut down businesses and demobilise millions of workers to mitigate spread of the virus. Recognising the inadequacy of Britain's social protection system to mitigate hardship, protect productive capacity, bolster social cohesion and compliance with lockdown, ministers engaged in (constrained) policy innovation. The repressive class politics encoded in social security was eased and extensive labour utilisation temporarily abandoned. Temporary improvement of support for low-income households via the existing benefit system was combined with new instruments, notably the Coronavirus Job Retention Scheme (CJRS), which provided generous protection to workers 'furloughed' during the crisis (Wiggan and Grover, 2022; Clegg et al, 2023). Marketised employment programmes and wage subsidies for young people were once again expanded, indicating their use as infrequent, but regular tools in the cyclical management of expansion in the labour reserve.

The abeyance of a repressive class politics in labour market policy as ministers maintained an orientation to consolidating social cohesion ceased as the pandemic eased. A roll back of increases in benefit payments and return to coercive activation via increased sanctioning (Wiggan and Grover, 2022: 733; Webster, 2023) marking the latest iteration of attempts to rework the state, and class power relations, so as to secure the domination of labour.

In the post-pandemic environment this became a pressing political concern as a tight labour market and rising inflation began to recompose labour as a more militant political actor. Workers enjoying new exit options and/or greater industrial strength began to press their demands on employers individually and collectively, and to some success. In response to the outbreak of worker autonomy, state managers doubled down on their regressive strategies to expose claimants to greater pressure to take paid work, or increase hours of work. The raising of the UC earnings threshold altered the point at which a claimant is exempt from in work conditionality, for example, respresenting an intensification and extension of conditionality among the UC claimant population.

Through UC, state managers have developed an instrument with which to fine tune the availability of labour power, through creation of what Wright and Dwyer (2022: 23) have termed a 'coerced-worker-claimant'. Moreover, its operation incentivises employers to increase atypical work as low-income and insecure workers search for additional hours, or jobs to boost their income to escape UC conditionality. Whether or not this does occur is an empirical question that cannot be answered here, but it points to how social security structures can favour particular developments in the labour market and technical class composition of labour.

Yet, there are some indications that the repressive class politics embedded in contemporary active labour market policy may be on the verge of exhaustion. Some claimants continue to try and carve out space within the system to exercise autonomy around labour market participation (Redman, 2021), while others disengage (Jones et al, 2024), with negative effects on income, that arguably undermine labour reproduction, social cohesion and the medium-term stability of capital accumulation. Wells (2022: 4) also suggests that the introduction of UC has been accompanied by a focus of DWP and its employees on activating unemployed, and in-work UC claimants below the CET (that is, the labour reserve), at the expense of engaging with the larger group of inactive claimants (that is, relative surplus population). In this regard, the nature of the activation drive may itself have contributed to enlarging a space within social security in which activation pressure has been weaker.

The actions of the Conservative Government of Rishi Sunak MP indicate that they are sensitive to the risk this may pose to the labour supply, claimant subordination and control of public spending. In September 2023 there were murmurs that the Government might again impose real-terms cuts in working-age benefits (Parker and Giles, 2023), and ministers announced consultation on reform of the Work Capability Assessment. This was underpinned by the claim that the rise in working from home had created new opportunities for claimants of incapacity-related benefits to engage in paid work (DWP, 2023a). The proposed changes, though, were primarily concerned with lowering the 'points' that particular conditions attract, making it more difficult during assessment for people to achieve the tally required for entitlement (Murphy, 2023). The intent to narrow eligibility for out-of-work social security on grounds of sickness and disability and reduce welfare spending was then reiterated at the beginning of 2024 (Daly, 2024; Parker, 2024). Once again, as demand for labour increased, ministers moved to alter the conditions that permit categorisation as a 'non-employed' claimant excused from work related activity, in order to divert people to the labour reserve.

Rather than additional support, the proposals are part of the Government's broader offensive step. The post-pandemic reinforcement of a residualised social security system and work-first employment services (Redman and Fletcher, 2022; Wiggan and Grover, 2022) has been accompanied by new anti-trade union legislation in the form of the Strikes (Minimum Service Levels) Act 2023. The Act provides ministers with the power to specify a minimum level of provision in public services during industrial action (DBT, 2023a). Despite the relative weakness of trade unions and pro-claimant organisations, the post-pandemic labour market gave state managers a fright, as the spectre of autonomy returned to haunt the state's organisation of labour commodification. As of early 2024 the Conservative Government show no indication of departing from their post-pandemic policy path. While disappointing, such a development is commensurate with the dynamic that has been elaborated through successive chapters here. That is, the struggle over labour autonomy has driven the co-evolution of particular forms of active labour market policy, and changes in the class composition of labour that have favoured a strengthening of the authority of capital in general. In this regard at least, labour in Britain has lost out from the activation turn in social security and employment policy and governance.

Appendix

Short note on sources

The material drawn upon for this study included secondary academic and policy-related literature, government policy documents and research publications, official statistics, debates, speeches and written questions from Hansard, party and union documents, cabinet papers and literature by, and about, claimant organisations. Some of the Labour and TUC material was sourced from the Labour History Archive of the People's History Museum, and cabinet papers from The National Archives. Many of the cabinet papers from the 1980s are available online, courtesy of the Margaret Thatcher Foundation, an excellent resource for material related to the Conservative governments of the period. Literature relating to claimant organisations was sourced online from Libcom.org; from the holdings of the Scottish Radical Library/Autonomous Centre Edinburgh; and from the Sparrows Nest Archive and Library.

My understanding of organised claimant activity around unemployment, workfare and benefit reform benefitted from interviews, conducted during 2017–18, with 14 people active in claimant-related organisations, or as workers and trade unionists in social security and employment services. I thank each interviewee for their time, and the insights they provided into local and national activity. The one or more organisations that interviewees were involved with at some point during the 1980s, 1990s, 2000s and 2010s included the following:

- Boycott Workfare; Civil and Public Services Association; Counter Information Newsletter; Edinburgh Coalition Against Poverty; Edinburgh Unemployed Workers Centre; Haringey Solidarity Group; Haringey Unemployed Workers Centre; Lothian/Edinburgh Claimants Union; Keep Volunteering Voluntary; London Coalition Against Poverty; National Coalition for Independent Action; Nottingham Against the JSA; Public and Commercial Services Union; Scottish Unemployed Workers Network; Tottenham Claimants Union.

Where an interviewee is quoted in the text, a pseudonym is used to maintain confidentiality. Ethics clearance was provided by the School of Social and Political Science, University of Edinburgh.

Notes

Chapter 1

[1] The unemployment rate cited here is based upon administrative data concerning the number of people registered with the state as seeking employment. This is not the same as the Labour Force Survey measure which is based upon the International Labour Organisation's (ILO) definition of unemployment as including those who are 'without a job, have been actively seeking work in the past four weeks, and are available to start work in the next two weeks', or who are, 'out of work, have found a job and are waiting to start it in the next two weeks' (ONS, 2019a).

[2] The exact nature of 'activation' policy can vary with particular policy goals (human capital development/ rapid job entry/benefit off flow), types of programmes (for example, training, subsidised employment, work experience) and settings of specific instruments (voluntary/mandatory programme participation; general or advanced/ sector-related training; low/high benefit payments and/or sanctions) (Bonoli, 2010; Dinan, 2018).

[3] Financialisation here refers to the increased importance of financial services and the proliferation of financialised ways of thinking and acting across the economy, state and society (Norfield, 2016; Dorre, 2015).

Chapter 2

[1] Core and 'peripheral' are used here as analytical abstractions rather than as a definitive categorisation for all jobs in a sector of industry. As Peck (1996) notes, workers in secondary jobs are not peripheral to their employer, nor to the economy as a whole and sub-contracting means peripheral workers are often integral to organisations providing 'core' jobs.

[2] For example, Gallas (2016: 290) depicts neo-liberalism as founded upon an EOP of free-market authoritarianism, cohered with a class politics bifurcated between a Thatcherite offensive, and a Blairite period of consolidation.

Chapter 3

[1] Until April 2010 the State Pension Age for women was 60, but was then raised in stages to be equalised with the State Pension Age for men (also gradually rising) (DWP, 2023j).

Chapter 4

[1] The MSC employment initiatives were located in the Special Programmes Division (that is, separate to the Training Services Division and the Employment Services Division). Department for Employment schemes were referred to in a review of services for unemployed people as 'Special Measures' (MSC 1981b: 23). Hereafter I follow Brown (1990) and use 'Special Employment Measures' to encompass both (also see MSC, 1981a: 27; Metcalf, 1982; Walker, 1988; King, 1995).

[2] The post-2010 Sector-Based Work Academies and Work Experience schemes are strikingly similar (see Chapter 9) and point to the recurring nature of such measures to regulate problems in labour commodification.

Chapter 5

[1] A briefing by the Conservative Research Department to ministers warned against being dismissive of the marchers, but suggested public sympathy and concern for unemployment did not equate to opposition to broader government policy (THCR 2/7/3/40 f47).

[2] Striking workers could apply for a lower level of money to meet urgent needs (Ginsburg, 1979: 77), though this was only permissible if no family, charity or union support was available (Carson, 1981: 101; Mesher, 1981: 124).

[3] As a dispute wore on, eligibility could be expected to rise. See Booth and Smith (1985: 369) on take-up among striking mineworkers in 1972.

[4] Gallas (2016) details the complementarities of the New Right's diagnosis of the role of the trade unions in the political and economic problems of Britain and the steps required to confront organised labour and overturn the social democratic 'common sense' of the period (see also THCR 2/6/1/248; Thatcher MSS (2/1/1/39)).

[5] Two ex-frontline state employees working in the DE/DHSS during the 1980s, who were interviewed by the author, recalled frontline staff exercising discretion around benefit policing, and forging links with local claimant organisations to try to build solidarity and obstruct punitive policy (see also Chapters 6 and 7).

[6] Later appointed Secretary of State for Employment.

[7] Young people who joined the scheme, but chose to leave the scheme prior to completion and who became unemployed risked reduction of their Supplementary Benefit (Finn, 1987: 183).

[8] Placements were arranged by managing agents contracted to the MSC who could be public, private or community organisations and who either provided the placement themselves and claimed all the funding, or alternatively acted as an organiser of placements provided by other employers in exchange for the management fee (House of Commons Employment Committee, 1985: 45).

[9] Standard Industrial Classification 1980. Other services included national and local public sector organisations, voluntary and community welfare organisations, and the recreational, creative and personal services industries.

Chapter 6

[1] Three volumes (Secretary of State for Social Services, 1985a, 1985b, 1985c).

[2] Discussion of the application for assistance for a 'minor household item' did not define what 'minor' meant, leading to debates over the scope and nature of entitlement (Secretary of State for Social Services, 1985b: 22 para 2.62).

[3] The Social Fund included regulated support and discretionary support. The former were entitlement-based grant payments for maternity, funeral expenses and cold weather. The latter included: budgeting loans to meet unpredictable one-off expenses; crisis loans to meet unexpected emergency costs; and community care grants to facilitate transitions from institutional care and/or in response to exceptional circumstances (Huby and Whyley, 1996: 2).

[4] With David Young in the House of Lords, Ken Clarke as Paymaster General spoke for the Secretary of State in the House of Commons (Young, 1991: 159).

[5] Supports Aufheben's (1998) observation regarding the operational problem facing state managers in bringing additional pressure to bear upon claimants.

[6] The administrative and clerical and the health, community and personal service occupations made up 60 per cent of the placements of young female YTS participants at the end of October 1988 (Hansard, 1988a: col 144).

Chapter 7

[1] The subsequent passing of the Criminal Justice and Public Order Act 1994 increased police powers to prevent gatherings, remove and seize vehicles, and eroded the rights of travellers to be provided with sites by local authorities (see Halfacree, 1996: 43).

[2] Exceptions included disabled people and those with caring responsibilities (Department of Employment/Department of Social Security, 1994: 26).

[3] The Network included groups in Bradford, Bridgewater, Brighton, Bristol, Cambridge, Edinburgh, Exeter, Greater Manchester, Huddersfield, Liverpool, Greater London, Newcastle, Norwich, Nottingham, Oxford, Plymouth, Sheffield and Wrexham (Groundswell, 1997: 4; Aufheben, 1998).

[4] An ex CPSA member interviewed by the author similarly recalled the tactic as divisive and self-defeating, while interviewees who had been active in Nottingham and Edinburgh at the time noted this was a new tactic to challenge coercive administration, but was rarely used.

[5] ET participants were dependent on contracted providers so there was no guarantee that preferred training/placement was met (Unemployment Unit, 1990).

[6] Jones (1999: 135) suggests the term originated with Ralph Howells MP – the Conservative parliamentarian who advocated for workfare.

[7] Community Action was introduced in 1993 alongside TfW. The CA resurrected part-time work in a community project, alongside job-search support for up to 60,000 long-term (12 months plus) unemployed claimants on a benefit-plus basis (Hansard, 1993a; Webb, 2003: 101). One can view this as a temporary measure to soak up claimant unemployment. As the labour market improved the CA was wound up at the end of 1995, and low-cost policing of job search moved to the fore (Hansard, 1996a: cols 603–10; Employment Committee, 1996b: xl–xli).

[8] Senior Conservatives, including the Prime Minister John Major MP, in 1993 had expressed a growing interest in placing greater obligations upon unemployed claimants, though stopped short of calling expressly for mass 'work for your benefit' schemes (that is, workfare) (Tonge, 1999: 221). As the Unemployment Unit noted, in a memorandum to the House of Commons Employment Committee investigation of Workfare (1996: 15), the government's hesistancy came at a time of high unemployment and could be regarded as pragmatic recognition of the political opposition and resource implications that a mass workfare programme implied. Rather than one 'big bang' of reform the shift to workfare type employment programmes would proceed more gradually, the intensity of the offensive against claimant autonomy increasing as the economy recovered and demand for labour grew.

[9] The TECs/LECs were abolished in 2001 (Ramsden et al, 2007: 228).

[10] The inequities built into this market signalled the issues that would affect subsequent employment service quasi-markets in the 2000s, particularly post-2010 (see Greer et al, 2017; Wiggan, 2015a).

Chapter 8

[1] Ed Balls, would go on to become Economic Advisor to the Chancellor and then Secretary of State for Children, Families and Schools in the New Labour governments. An expert on labour market economics, Paul Gregg would go on to advise the Labour governments and produce the influential 'Gregg Report' on benefit conditionality (Gregg, 2008).

[2] Originally New Deal for Long-Term Unemployed.

[3] For 'part-time' jobs of 24–30 hours the subsidy was £40 (Webb, 2003: 28).

[4] Access to the ND 25+ was permissible at 12 months for ex-offenders, disabled claimants and people with weak literacy, numeracy or English-language skills (see Hasluck, 2000).

[5] The term is used here to refer to the contribution-based Incapacity Benefit and means-tested Income Support paid on grounds of ill health or disability (Sainsbury, 2009: 215).

[6] Other working-age disability-related benefits also gave eligibility for the NDDP (Greenberg and Davis, 2007: 10).

[7] The NMW set a minimum price for labour power per hour, rather than a wage and excluded 16–17-year-olds and self-employed people (Metcalf, 1999).

[8] New Labour also introduced the Disabled Persons Tax Credit (DPTC) for disabled people working 16 hours plus a week. Recipient numbers rose from just over 12,500 in April 1997 to around 35,000 in October 2002 (Inland Revenue, 2003b: 2).

[9] From April 2003 the DPTC was integrated into the WTC (HMRC, 2012: 2).

[10] Former members of Groundswell Network affiliated groups in Nottingham, Edinburgh and London interviewed by the author reported a refocusing of their campaigning activity on other social issues, including housing and anti-war/gloablisation activity and/or a narrower focus on benefit advice work.

[11] Some participants with unknown destinations will have entered employment (NAO, 2002: 10; Coleman et al, 2004: 23).

Chapter 10

[1] See Hobson et al (2022: 31) for information on how savings above a given threshold reduced payments.

[2] Benefits providing additional help with costs of disability, caring or topping up low wages were exempt (HM Treasury, 2010a: 28; see also www.gov.uk/benefit-cap/).

[3] Reduced from 80 per cent to 70 per cent, but subsequently raised in 2016 to 85 per cent for working family claimants of Universal Credit.

[4] Expected hours were lower for claimants with caring responsibilities or other constraints.

[5] The insurance-based JSA and ESA benefits remain separate.

[6] Refers to standard rates set for 2012.

[7] Claimants deemed to have 'gaps' in basic employability could be mandated to participate in the Skills Conditionality scheme (DWP, 2016g).

[8] www.boycottworkfare.org/about/

[9] https://edinburghagainstpoverty.org.uk/; https://scottishunemployedworkers.net/; https://dpac.uk.net/

[10] The DWP contested releasing the names of organisations participating in workfare schemes. In 2016 the Court of Appeal ruled the information be made publicly available (Staufenberg and Stone, 2016).

[11] A challenge to workfare on grounds of human rights and inadequate information on conditions of participation was also brought by claimants during this period with partial success (Grover and Piggott, 2013; Daguerre, 2020: 27–8).

[12] This is not to say charities necessarily saw a clash between workfare and their values or objectives, but as an activist involved in KVV conveyed to the author the seeming disjuncture was a weak point in Government policy. Physical locations could be protested and leafletted, potentially leading a charity's supporters and customers to contact local managers or head office to express opposition to workfare.

[13] Work Programme completers leaving without a job entered the Help to Work scheme. The proportion of the Help to Work monthly intake spending at least some time in paid work varied from 30 per cent to 43 per cent, with those sustaining 26 weeks' employment much lower – 12 per cent to 23 per cent (DWP, 2018).

[14] Whitworth's (2020) spatial analysis also indicates the WP payment model channelled fewer resources to local authorities with higher levels of deprivation, reproducing the economic disparities and uneven development within Britain.

Chapter 11

[1] Mandatory referral was paused during the pandemic. After restarting referrals in May 2022 the LTU were from November of that year considered instead for the 'Restart' Programme, first rolled out during the COVID-19 pandemic (DWP, 2023c: see 'Guidance').

[2] Author calculation based on Table 1.2b.

Notes

3   Refer to Simpson (2022) for a broader discussion of devolution and variations in social security.

4   The final grant awarded a maximum £7,500 if turnover had dropped by 30 per cent plus with a payment of £2,850 available if turnover had fallen by less than 30 per cent (Seely, 2023: 5). The final two rounds of SEISS in 2021 based assessment on 2019–20 tax returns.

5   The delivery fee was paid over 48 months, but a greater portion was allocated to the first 12 months (DWP, 2023e: ch 17).

6   Author calculation derived from "Table 2: Number of Kickstart total available jobs and job starts, Great Britain, by Sector (figures rounded to the nearest 10★)" (Davies, 2022).

References

Adkins, L. (2017) 'Disobedient workers, the law and the making of unemployment markets', *Sociology*, 51(2): 290–305.

Aglietta, M. (2000) *A Theory of Capitalist Regulation: The US Experience*, London: Verso.

Ainley, P. (2013) 'Education and the reconstitution of social class in England', *Research in Post-Compulsory Education*, 18(1): 46–60.

Ainley, P. and Corney, M. (1990) *Training for the Future: The Rise and Fall of the Manpower Services Commission*, London: Cassell Educational Limited.

Alcock, P. (1985) 'The Fowler reviews: social policy on the political agenda', *Critical Social Policy*, 5(14): 93–102.

Alcock, P. (1990) 'The end of the line for social security: the Thatcherite restructuring of welfare', *Critical Social Policy*, 10(30): 88–105.

Allen, D. and Hunn, A. (1985) 'An evaluation of the Enterprise Allowance Scheme', *Employment Gazette*, 93: 313–17, Department of Employment.

Altunbuken, U. Bukowski, P. Machin, S. and Slaughter, H. (2022) Power plays: the shifting balance of employer and worker power in the UK labour market, Resolution Foundation, https://economy2030.resolutionfoundat ion.org/reports/page/2/?inquiry-theme=people

Andersen, K. (2023) 'Promoting fairness? Exploring the gendered impacts of the benefit cap and the two-child limit', *Journal of Poverty and Social Justice*, online first.

Armour, R. (2015) 'Glasgow charity abandons work-for-benefits scheme', Third Force News, 3 March, Third Force News, https://tfn.scot/news/ glasgow-charity-abandons-work-for-benefits-scheme

Atkins, J. (2011) *Justifying New Labour Policy*, Basingstoke: Palgrave MacMillan.

Atkinson, A.B. (1990) 'Income maintenance for the unemployed in Britain and the response to high unemployment', *Ethics*, 100(3): 569–85.

Aufheben (n.d.) 'Unemployed recalcitrance-and welfare restructuring in the UK today', *Stop the Clock: critiques of the new social workhouse*, Sparrows Nest Archive, https://www.thesparrowsnest.org.uk/collections/public_arch ive/4810.pdf

Aufheben (1998) 'Dole autonomy versus the re-imposition of work: analysis of the current tendency to workfare in the UK', https://libcom.org/libr ary/dole-autonomy-aufheben

Aufheben (2011) 'The renewed imposition of work in the era of austerity: prospects for resistance', 19, https://libcom.org/article/aufhe ben-19-2011

Axelrad, H., Malul, M. and Luski, I. (2018) 'Unemployment among younger and older individuals: does conventional data about unemployment tell us the whole story?', *Journal of Labour Market Research*, 52(3): 1–12.

Bagaria, N., Petrongolo, B. and Van Reenen, J. (2013) 'Incentives, disruption and jobs: evidence from a public employment service reform', https://conference.iza.org/conference_files/PolicyEval_2013/bagaria_n8718.pdf

Bagguley, P. (1991) *From Protest to Acquiescence? Political Movements of the Unemployed*, London: Macmillan Ltd.

Bagguley, P. (1992) 'Protest, acquiescence and the unemployed: a comparative analysis of the 1930s and 1980s', *British Journal of Sociology*, 43(3): 443–61.

Bailey, A. (2022) 'Monetary policy and financial stability interventions in difficult times', speech to G30 37th Annual International Banking Seminar, Washington, DC, 15 October, www.bankofengland.co.uk/speech/2022/october/andrew-bailey-opening-remarks-and-panellist-37th-annual-intern ational-banking-seminar

Bailey, D.J. (2014) 'Contending the crisis: what role for extra-parliamentary British politics?', *British Politics*, 9: 68–92.

Bailey, D.J., Clua-Losadab M., Hukec, N., Ribera-Almandozd, O. and Rogers, K. (2018) 'Challenging the age of austerity: disruptive agency after the global economic crisis', *Comparative European Politics*, 16(1): 9–31.

Balls, E. (1993) 'Danger: men not at work – unemployment and non-employment in the UK and beyond', in E. Balls and P. Gregg (eds) *Work and Welfare: Tackling the Jobs Deficit*, London: IPPR, pp 2–30.

Balls, E. (2016) *Speaking Out*, London: Arrow Books.

Balls, E., Grice, J. and O'Donnell, G. (2004) *Microeconomic Reform in Britain: Delivering Opportunities for All*, Basingstoke: Palgrave Macmillan.

Bank of England (n.d.) 'Official bank rate history data from 1694', www.bankofengland.co.uk/monetary-policy/the-interest-rate-bank-rate

Bank of England (2017) 'Table A52b–Union membership, replacement ratios and other statistics', *A millennium of macroeconomic data*, Version 3.1, https://www.bankofengland.co.uk/statistics/research-datasets

Banks, M. (2012) 'Producing workfare', *Journal of Australian Political Economy*, 70: 87–109.

Barrow, C. (1993) *Critical Theories of the State: Marxist, Neo-Marxist, Post-Marxist*, Madison, WI: University of Wisconsin Press.

Bartrum, O. (2022) 'Blocking OBR forecasts undermines the credibility of Liz Truss's economic plans', *Comment*, 22 September, Institute for Government, www.instituteforgovernment.org.uk/article/comm ent/blocking-obr-forecasts-undermines-credibility-liz-trusss-econo mic-plans

Baumberg, B. (2012) 'Re-evaluating trends in the employment of disabled people in Britain', in S. Vickerstaff, C. Phillipson and R. Wilkie (eds) *Work, Health and Wellbeing: The Challenges of Managing Health at Work*, Bristol: Policy Press, pp 79–94.

Baumberg Geiger, B., Reeves, A. and de Vries, R. (2017) 'Tax avoidance and benefit manipulation', in E. Clery, J. Curtice and R. Harding (eds) *British Social Attitudes: The 34th Report*, London: NatCen Social Research, pp 12–37, www.bsa.natcen.ac.uk/latest-report/british-social-attitudes-34/key-findings/context.aspx

BBC (2016) 'Results – Scotland Election 2016', www.bbc.co.uk/news/election/2016/scotland/results

Beale, E. (2005) *Employment and Training Programmes for the Unemployed*, Vol 1, Research Paper 05/61, Economic Policy and Statistics Section, House of Commons Library, https://commonslibrary.parliament.uk/research-briefings/rp05–61/

Beale, I., Bloss, C. and Thomas, A. (2008) *The Longer-Term Impact of the New Deal for Young People*, Department for Work and Pensions, Working Paper No. 23, HMSO.

Becker, E., Hayllar, O. and Wood, M. (2010) *Pathways to Work: programme engagement and work patterns: findings from follow-up surveys of new and repeat and existing incapacity benefits customers in the Jobcentre Plus pilot and expansion areas*, Department for Work and Pensions, Research Report No. 653, HMSO.

Beech, M. (2015) 'The ideology of the Coalition: More Liberal than Conservative', in M. Beech and S. Lee (eds) *The Conservative–Liberal Coalition: Examining the Cameron–Clegg Government*, Basingstoke: Palgrave Macmillan, pp 1–15.

Bell, A. (1984) 'RABBITS and the unemployed', *Unemployment Unit Bulletin No. 11*: 5–6, London: Unemployment Unit.

Bell, S. and Hindmoor, A. (2014) 'The structural power of business and the power of ideas: the strange case of the Australian Mining Tax', *New Political Economy*, 19(3): 450–86.

Benanav, A. (2019a) 'Automation and the future of work – 1', *New Left Review*, 119: 5–38, September–October 2019.

Benanav, A. (2019b) 'Automation and the future of work – 2', *New Left Review*, 120: 117–46, November–December 2019.

Bennett, A. (2014) 'IT firm pull out of Workfare scheme after George Osborne visit', The Huffington Post UK, 24 July, https://www.huffingtonpost.co.uk/2014/07/24/george-osborne-it-firm-workfare_n_5616281.html

Bennett, F. and Millar, J. (2009) 'Social security: reforms and challenges', in J. Millar (ed) *Understanding Social Security: Issues for Policy and Practice* (2nd edn), Bristol: Policy Press, pp 11–29.

Bennett, H. (2017) 'Re-examining British welfare to work contracting using a transaction cost perspective', *Journal of Social Policy*, 46(1): 129–48.

Bennett, R.J., Wicks, P. and McCoshan, A. (1994) *Local Empowerment and Business Services: Britain's Experiment with Training and Enterprise Councils*, London: UCL Press.

Benquet, M. and Bourgeron, T. (2022) *Alt-Finance: How the City of London Bought Democracy*, London: Pluto Press.

Berry, C. (2014a) 'The perversion of "full employment"', 15 May, Sheffield Political Economy Research Institute, http://speri.dept.shef.ac.uk/2014/05/15/perversion-full-employment/

Berry, C. (2014b) 'Quantity over quality: a political economy of active labour market policy in the UK', *Policy Studies*, 35(6): 592–610.

Berry, C. (2016) *Austerity Politics and UK Economic Policy*, London: Palgrave Macmillan.

Berthoud, R. (2006) *The Employment Rates of Disabled People*, Department for Work and Pensions, Research Report No. 298, Leeds: CDS.

Blackmore, M. (2001) 'Mind the gap: exploring the implementation deficit in the administration of the stricter benefits regime', *Social Policy and Administration*, 35(2): 145–62.

Blair, T. (1996) *New Britain: My Vision of a Young Country*, London: Fourth Estate.

Blair, T. (1999) 'Beveridge Lecture' by the Prime Minister, 18 March, Toynbee Hall, London, www.bristol.ac.uk/poverty/downloads/backgro und/Tony%20Blair%20Child%20Poverty%20Speech.doc

Block, F. (1977) 'The ruling class does not rule: notes on the Marxist theory of the State', *Socialist Revolution*, 33 (May–June): 6–28.

Blundell, R. and Hoynes, H. (2004) 'Has "in-work" benefit reform helped the labor market?', in D. Card, R. Blundell and R.B. Freeman (eds) *Seeking a Premier Economy: The Economic Effects of British Economic Reforms, 1980–2000*, Chicago, IL: National Bureau of Economic Research, University of Chicago Press, pp 411–60.

Blunkett, D. (2006) *The Blunkett Tapes: My Life in the Bear Pit*, London: Bloomsbury.

Bonoli, G. (2010) 'The political economy of active labor-market policy', *Politics and Society*, 38(4): 435–57.

Bonoli, G. (2013) *The Origins of Active Social Policy: Labour Market and Childcare Policies in a Comparative Perspective*, Oxford: Oxford University Press.

Booth, A. and Smith, R. (1985) 'The irony of the iron fist: social security and the coal dispute 1984–85', *Journal of Law and Society*, 12(3): 365–74.

Bowman, P. (2012) 'Rethinking class: from recomposition to counter-power', *Irish Anarchist Review*, 6 (Winter), www.wsm.ie/c/class-recomp osition-counterpower

Bradley, S. (1995) 'The Youth Training Scheme: a critical review of the evaluation literature', *International Journal of Manpower*, 16(4): 30–56.

Brand, U. (2013) 'State, context and correspondence. Contours of a historical-materialist policy analysis', *Österreichische Zeitschrit für Poliikwissenschat* (ÖZP), 42(4): 425–42.

Brewer, M. (2008) *Welfare Reform in the UK: 1997–2007*, Working Paper, No. 2008: 12, Uppsala: Institute for Labour Market Policy Evaluation (IFAU), www.econstor.eu/bitstream/10419/45770/1/573610452.pdf

Briken, K. and Taylor, P. (2018) 'Fulfilling the British way: beyond constrained choice – Amazon workers' lived experiences of workfare', *Industrial Relations Journal*, 49(5–6): 438–58.

Brosnan, P., Rea, D. and Wilson, M. (1995) 'Labour market segmentation and the state: the New Zealand experience', *Cambridge Journal of Economics*, 19(5): 667–96.

Brown, G. (1995) 'Shadow Chancllor's speech, Brighton', Labour Party Conference, http://www.britishpoliticalspeech.org/speech-archive.htm?speech=266

Brown, G. (2001) 'The conditions for high and stable growth and employment', *The Economic Journal*, 111(471): C30–44.

Brown, G. (2017) *My Life, Our Times*, London: Vintage.

Brown, J. (1990) *Victims or Villains? Social Security Benefits in Unemployment*, York: Joseph Rowntree Memorial Trust/Policy Studies Institute.

Brown, R. and Joyce, L. (2007) *New Deal for Lone Parents: Non-Participation Qualitative Research*, Research Report No. 408, Department for Work and Pensions, https://webarchive.nationalarchives.gov.uk/ukgwa/20100208134416/http://research.dwp.gov.uk/asd/asd5/rrs-index.asp

Brown, W. (2009) 'The process of fixing the British National Minimum Wage, 1997–2007', *British Journal of Industrial Relations*, 47(2): 429–43.

Browne, J. and Phillips, D. (2010) *Tax and Benefit Reforms Under Labour – 2010 Election Briefing Note No. 1*, Institute for Fiscal Studies (IFS BN88), https://ifs.org.uk/sites/default/files/output_url_files/bn88.pdf

Bruttel, O. (2005) 'Are Employment Zones successful? Evidence from the first four years', *Local Economy*, 20(4): 389–403.

Bryson, A. and Jacobs, J. (1992) *Policing the Workshy: Benefit Controls, the Labour Market and the Unemployed*, Aldershot: Avebury.

Bryson, A. and Marsh, A. (1996) *Leaving Family Credit*, Department of Social Security, Research Report No. 48, London: HMSO.

Buck T. (1993) 'New Age Travellers: actively seeking work?', *Industrial Law Journal*, 22(3): 227–34.

Buck, T. and Smith, R. (2005) *A Critical Literature Review of the Social Fund: Final Report for the National Audit Office*, National Audit Office, www.nao.org.uk/wpcontent/uploads/2005/01/0405179_Lit_Rev_Full.pdf

Burgmann, V. (2013) 'The multitude and the many-headed hydra: autonomist Marxist theory and labor history', *International Labor and Working Class History*, 83: 170–90.

Burton-Cartledge, P. (2021) *Falling Down: The Conservative Party and the Decline of Tory Britain*, London: Verso.

Burton-Cartledge, P. (2023) *The Party's Over: The Rise and Fall of the Conservatives from Thatcher to Sunak*, London: Verso.

Butler, P. (2018) 'Philip Hammond says Universal Credit is here to stay', *The Guardian*, 21 October, www.theguardian.com/society/2018/oct/29/philip-hammond-universal-credit-is-here-to-stay

Butler, P. (2019) 'Tories ditch "ineffective" three-year benefit sanctions', *The Guardian*, 9 May, www.theguardian.com/society/2019/may/09/tories-ditch-ineffective-three-year-benefit-sanctions

Byrne, D. (2005) *Social Exclusion* (2nd edn), Maidenhead: Open University Press.

CAB/129/196/15 *The Medium Term Prospect: Memorandum by the Chancellor of the Exchequer*, CP (77) 65, 23 June 1977, Cabinet Office, The National Archives, http://discovery.nationalarchives.gov.uk/ [last accessed 30 June 2017].

CAB/128/63/2 *Conclusions of a Meeting of the Cabinet Held at 10 Downing Street*, CM (78), Thursday 26 January, The National Archives, Cabinet Office, The National Archives http://discovery.nationalarchives.gov.uk/ [last accessed 24 March 2020].

CAB/129/203/1 *Pay Policy after July: Note by the Chancellor of the Exchequer*, CP (78) 76, 11 July 1978, Cabinet Office, The National Archives, http://discovery.nationalarchives.gov.uk/ [last accessed 30 June 2017].

CAB/129/183/16 *Development of the Social Contract on Pay*, C (75) 66, 12 June 1975, Memorandum by the Secretary of State for Employment, Cabinet Office, The National Archives, http://discovery.nationalarchives.gov.uk/ [last accessed 30 June 2017].

CAB/129/184/20 *Unemployment Measures*, C (75) 95, 18 September 1975, Memorandum by the Secretary of State for Employment, Cabinet Office, The National Archives, http://discovery.nationalarchives.gov.uk/ [last accessed 30 May 2017].

CAB/129/184/21 *Measures to Alleviate Unemployment*, C (75) 96, 18 September 1975, Memorandum by the Chancellor of the Exchequer, Cabinet Office, The National Archives, http://discovery.nationalarchives.gov.uk/ [last accessed 11 June 2017].

CAB/134/4442 (a) *Minutes of Ministerial Committee on Economic Strategy – E (80) 36th (Special Employment Measures, Industrial Training, Industrial Support Measures)*, 15 October 1980, Margaret Thatcher Foundation, www.margaretthatcher.org/document/117345

CAB/134/4442 (b) *CPRS Note Circulated to E Committee – E (80) 116 (Industrial Support and Employment Measures)*, 13 October 1980, Margaret Thatcher Foundation, www.margaretthatcher.org/document/117345

CAB/134/4446 *Prior Memo Circulated to E Committee – E (80) 110 (Special Employment Measures)*, 9 October 1980, Margaret Thatcher Foundation, www.margaretthatcher.org/document/117461

CAB/129-219b *Fowler Memo Circulated to Cabinet – C (85) 27 (Review of Social Security: Final Decisions)*, 25 November 1985, Margaret Thatcher Foundation, www.margaretthatcher.org/document/136990

CAB/129-219a *Fowler Memo Circulated to Cabinet – C (85) 9 (Social Security Review)*, 19 April 1985, Margaret Thatcher Foundation, www.margarett hatcher.org/document/136977

Calvert Jump, R., Michell, J., Meadway, J. and Nascimento, N. (2023) *The Macroeconomics of Austerity*, Progressive Economy Forum, https://progress iveeconomyforum.com/wp-content/uploads/2023/03/pef_23_macroeco nomics_of_austerity.pdf

Cameron, C., Hauari, H., Heys, M., Hollingworth, K., O'Brien, M., O'Toole, S. and Whitaker, L. (2022) 'A tale of two cities in London's East End: impacts of COVID-19 on low- and high-income families with young children and pregnant women', in K. Garthwaite, R. Patrick, M. Power, A. Tarrant and R. Warnock (eds) *COVID-19 Collaborations: Researching Poverty and Low-Income Family Life during the Pandemic*, Bristol: Policy Press, pp 88–105.

Caraher, K. and Reuter, E. (2019) 'Mind the gaps: Universal Credit and self-employment in the United Kingdom', *Journal of Poverty and Social Justice*, 27(2): 199–217.

Carpenter, H. (2006) *Repeat Jobseeker's Allowance Spells*, Research Report No. 394, Leeds: Department for Work and Pensions, Corporate Document Services.

Carson, D. (1981) 'Recent legislation – Supplementary Benefit (Trades Disputes and Recovery from Earnings) Regulations 1980 (SI 1980 No. 1641)', *Journal of Social Welfare Law*, 3(1): 101–20.

Carter, E. and Whitworth, A. (2015) 'Creaming and parking in quasi-marketised welfare-to-work schemes: designed out of or designed into the UK work programme?', *Journal of Social Policy*, 44(2): 277–96.

Carter, E. and Whitworth, A. (2017) 'Work activation regimes and well-being of unemployed people: rhetoric, risk and reality of quasi-marketization in the UK work programme', *Social Policy and Administration*, 51(5): 796–816.

Casson, M. (1979) *Youth Unemployment*, London: Macmillan.

Chan, S.P. and Martin, D. (2023) 'Millions paid benefits without ever having to find a job', *The Telegraph*, 24 May.

Child Poverty Action Group (2010) 'Welfare Reform Act 2009 – a quick guide', *Welfare Rights Bulletin*, Issue 215, April, https://cpag.org.uk/welfare-rig hts/resources/article/welfare-reform-act-2009-%E2%80%93-quick-guide

Child Poverty Action Group (2017) *The Austerity Generation: The Impact of a Decade of Cuts on Family Incomes and Child Poverty*, London: CPAG, https://cpag.org.uk/policy-and-campaigns/report/austerity-generation-impact-decade-cuts-family-incomes-and-child-poverty

Children, Schools and Families Committee (2010) *Young People not in Education, Employment or Training*, Eighth Report of Session 2009–10, House of Commons, Vol HC 316-I, London: The Stationery Office, https://publications.parliament.uk/pa/cm200910/cmselect/cmchilsch/316/31607.htm

Choonara, J. (2019) *Insecurity, Precarious Work and Labour Markets: Challenging the Orthodoxy*, London: Palgrave Macmillan.

Chorlton, P. and Dunn, A. (1985) 'Thousands join children's classroom strike for jobs / Protest against the Government Youth Training Scheme', *The Guardian*, 26 April, Guardian Newspapers, Lexis Library News.

Cinalli, M. (2012) 'Contention over unemployment in Britain: unemployment politics versus the politics of the unemployed', in D. Chabanet and J. Faniel (eds) *The Mobilisation of the Unemployed in Europe: From Acquiescence to Protest?*, New York: Palgrave Macmillan, pp 175–94.

Cirillo, V. (2018) 'Job polarization in European industries', *International Labour Review*, 157(1): 39–63.

Clark, C. (1997) 'New Age Travellers: identity, sedentarism and social security', in T. Acton (ed) *Gypsy Politics and Traveller Identity*, Hatfield: University of Hertfordshire Press, pp 125–41.

Clark C. (1999) 'Race, ethnicity and social security: the experience of gypsies and travellers in the UK', *Journal of Social Security Law*, 6(4): 186–202.

Clarke, J. (2005) 'New Labour's citizens: activated, empowered, responsibilized, abandoned?', *Critical Social Policy*, 25(4): 447–63.

Clarke, J. (2023) *The Battle for Britain: Crises, Conflict and the Conjuncture*, Bristol: Bristol University Press.

Clarke, S. and Cominetti, N. (2019) *Setting the Record Straight: How Record Employment Has Changed the UK*, Resolution Foundation, www.resolutionfoundation.org/app/uploads/2019/01/Setting-the-record-straight-full-employment-report.pdf

Clasen, J. (2002) 'Unemployment and unemployment policy in the UK: increasing employability and redefining citizenship', in J. Goul Andersen, J. Clasen and W. van Oorschot (eds) *Europe's New State of Welfare: Unemployment, Employment Policies and Citizenship*, Bristol: Policy Press, pp 59–74.

Clasen, J. (2011) 'The United Kingdom: towards a single working age benefit system', in J. Clasen, and D. Clegg (eds) *Regulating the Risk of Unemployment*, Oxford: Oxford University Press, pp 15–32.

Clasen, J. and Clegg, D. (2006) 'Beyond activation: reforming European unemployment protection systems in post-industrial labour markets', *European Societies*, 8(4): 527–53.

Clasen, J. and Clegg, D. (2012) 'Adapting labour market policy to a transformed employment structure', in G. Bonoli and D. Natali (eds) *The Politics of the New Welfare State*, Oxford: Oxford University Press.

Cleaver, H. (1977) 'Malaria, the politics of public health and the International crisis', *Review of Radical Political Economics*, 9(1): 81–103.

Cleaver, H. (1993) 'Marxian categories, the crisis of capital and the constitution of social subjectivity today', *Common Sense*, 14: 32–57.

Cleaver, H. (1994) 'Kropotkin, self-valorisation and the crisis of Marxism', *Anarchist Studies*, 2(2): 119–36.

Cleaver, H. (2000) *Reading Capital Politically*, Leeds and Edinburgh: Anti/ Theses and AK Press [1979 original publication].

Cleaver, H. (2017) *Rupturing the Dialectic: The Struggle against Work, Money and Financialisation*, Edinburgh: AK Press.

Clegg, D. (2015) 'The demise of tax credits', *The Political Quarterly*, 8(4): 493–99.

Clegg, D., Durazzi, N., Heins, E. and Robertson, E. (2023) 'Policy, power and pandemic: varieties of job and income protection responses to COVID-19 in Western Europe', *Journal of European Public Policy*, 1–24.

Cockburn, C. (1987) *Two-Track Training: Sex Inequalities and the YTS*, London: Macmillan.

Codd, F. and Powell, A. (2021) *Implementing the Taylor Review of Modern Working Practices*, Number CDP-2022-0011, House of Commons Library, https://commonslibrary.parliament.uk/research-briefings/cdp-2022-0011/

Coderre-LaPalme, G., Greer, I. and Schulte, L. (2023) 'Welfare, work and the conditions of social solidarity: British campaigns to defend healthcare and social security', *Work, Employment and Society*, 37(2): 352–72.

Coffield, F. (1990) 'From the decade of the Enterprise Culture to the decade of the TECs', *British Journal of Education and Work*, 4(1): 59–78.

Coffield, F. (1992) 'Training and Enterprise Councils: the last throw of voluntarism?', *Policy Studies*, 13(4): 11–32.

Cohen, N., Parker, G. and Pimlott, D. (2010) 'King denies crossing line over Coalition', *The Financial Times*, 10 November, www.ft.com/content/ 63239eee-ed04-11df-9912-00144feab49a

Coleman, N. and Seeds, K. (2007) *Work Focused Interviews for Partners and enhanced New Deal for Partners evaluation: Synthesis of findings*, Research Report No. 417, Department for Work and Pensions.

Coleman, N., Wapshott, J. and Carpenter, H. (2004) *Destination of Leavers from NDYP and ND25 Plus, 3rd Draft Report*, Working Age and Employment Reports 1998–2004, No. 206, Department for Work and Pensions, https:// webarchive.nationalarchives.gov.uk/ukgwa/20100208143950/http://resea rch.dwp.gov.uk/asd/asd5/working_age/index_2004.asp

Coleman, N., Seeds, K. and Edwards, G. (2006) *Work Focused Interviews for Partners and Enhanced New Deal for Partners: Quantitative Survey Research*, Research Report No. 335, Department for Work and Pensions.

Coleman, N., McGinigal, S., Thomas, A., Fu, E. and Hingley, S. (2014) *Evaluation of the Youth Contract Wage Incentive: Wave Two Research*, Research Report, Department for Work and Pensions, www.gov.uk/government/publications/youth-contract-wage-incentive-wave-2-research

Commission on Social Justice/Institute for Public Policy Research (1994) *Social Justice: Strategies for national renewal*, The Report of the Commission on Social Justice, London: Vintage.

Connor, S. (2007) 'We're onto you: a critical examination of the Department for Work and Pensions' "Targeting Benefit Fraud" campaign', *Critical Social Policy*, 27(2): 231–52.

Conservative Party (1977) *The Right Approach to the Economy*, London: Conservative Central Office, Margaret Thatcher Foundation, www.margaretthatcher.org/document/112551

Conservative Party (1979) *General Election Manifesto*, 11 April, Margaret Thatcher Foundation, Archive, www.margaretthatcher.org/document/110858

Conservative Party (1987) *The Next Moves Forward*, General Election Manifesto, www.ukpol.co.uk/general-election-manifestos-1987-conservative-party/

Considine, M. (2001) *Enterprising States: The Public Management of Welfare to Work*, Cambridge: Cambridge University Press.

Considine, M., Lewis, J.M., O'Sullivan, S. and Sol, E. (2015) *Getting Welfare to Work: Street Level Governance in Australia, the UK, and the Netherlands*, Oxford: Oxford University Press.

Considine, M. O'Sullivan, S. and Nguyen, P. (2018) 'The policy maker's dilemma: the risks and benefits of a 'Black Box' approach to commissioning active labour market programmes', *Social Policy & Administration*, 52(1): 229–51.

Corlett, A. (2017) *Diverse Outcomes: Living Standards by Ethnicity*, Resolution Foundation Briefing, www.resolutionfoundation.org/app/uploads/2017/08/Diverse-outcomes.pdf

Counter Information (1995/96) 'Brighton Rocked', No. 44 November/December/January, https://libcom.org/library/counter-information

Counter Information (1996) 'JSA No Way', No. 45, March/April/May, https://libcom.org/library/counter-information

Counter Information (1996/97) 'Make the JSA unworkable!' No. 47, November/ December/ January, https://libcom.org/library/counter-information

Counter Information (1998) 'Dead Toad Hits Back', No. 50, Spring–Summer, The Sparrows Nest Library and Archive, www.thesparrowsnest.org.uk/collections/public_archive/4191.pdf

Crerar, P. and Stacey, K. (2023) 'Union fury as Rishi Sunak unveils anti-strike laws for "minimum service levels"', *The Guardian*, 5 January.

Cribb, J. (2017) *Public Sector Pay: Still Time for Restraint?*, IFS Briefing Note BN216, Institute for Fiscal Studies, https://ifs.org.uk/publications/pub lic-sector-pay-still-time-restraint

Cribb, J. Delestre, I. and Johnson, P. (2021) *Who is excluded from the government's Self Employment Income Support Scheme and what could the government do about it?* IFS Briefing Note BN316, https://ifs.org.uk/ sites/default/files/output_url_files/BN316-Who-is-excluded-from-SEISS.pdf

Croxford, L., Raffe, D. and Surridge, P. (1996) *The Early Impact of Youth Credits in England and Wales*, CES Briefing, Vol 7, Centre for Educational Sociology, www.pure.ed.ac.uk/ws/portalfiles/portal/25056765/Brief 007.pdf

Cuninghame, P. (2015) 'Mapping the terrain of struggle: autonomist movements in 1970s Italy', *Viewpoint Magazine*, 1 November, www.viewp ointmag.com/2015/11/01/feminism-autonomism-1970s-italy/

Curtice, J. (2017) 'Role of Government', in E. Clery, J. Curtice and R. Harding (eds) *British Social Attitudes: The 34th Report*, London: NatCen Social Research, pp 67–84, www.bsa.natcen.ac.uk/latest-report/british-soc ial-attitudes-34/key-findings/context.aspx

Dabhi, K., McHenry, D., Tu, T. and Klahr, R. (2022) *Coronavirus Job Retention Scheme Employer and Agent Quantitative Research*, HM Revenue and Customs Research Report: 611, HMRC, www.gov.uk/governm ent/publications/coronavirus-job-retention-scheme-quantitative-resea rch-with-employers-and-agents

Daguerre, A. (2020) 'Policy styles and welfare reform in Britain and the US: the Conservative-led Coalition Government and the Obama Administration compared', *Journal of Social Security Law*, 3: 1–38, https:// ssrn.com/abstract=3595399

Daguerre, A. and Etherington, D. (2016) 'Welfare and active labour market policies in the UK: the Coalition Government approach', in H. Bochel and M. Powell (eds) *The Coalition Government and Social Policy: Restructuring the Welfare State*, Bristol: Policy Press, pp 201–20.

Dale, I. (1994) 'Recent trends in skill shortages', *Employment Gazette*, 102(4): 123–7, London: Department of Employment.

Dalla Costa, M. and James, S. (1972) 'Women and subversion of the community', https://libcom.org/library/power-women-subversion-community-della-costa-selma-james

Daly, M. (2011) 'What adult worker model? A critical look at recent social policy reform in Europe from a gender and family perspective', *Social Politics: International Studies in Gender, State and Society*, 18(1): 1–23.

Daly, P. (2024) 'Welfare reforms to fund pre-election tax cuts about "fairness", Sunak suggests', *The Independent*, 7 January, www.independ ent.co.uk/news/uk/prime-minister-rishi-sunak-government-laura-kue nssberg-jeremy-hunt-b2474515.html

Dar, A. (2016) *Work Programme: Background and Statistics*, Briefing paper, No. 6340, House of Commons Library, http://researchbriefings.files.par liament.uk/documents/SN06340/SN06340.pdf

D'Arcy, C. (2018) *Low Pay in Britain*, Resolution Foundation, www.resol utionfoundation.org/app/uploads/2018/05/Low-Pay-Britain-2018.pdf

Das, R.J. (1996) 'State theories: a critical analysis', *Science and Society*, 60(1): 27–57.

Davies, M. (2022) *Kickstart Scheme Question for Department for Work and Pensions*, UK Parliament, Written Answer UIN 159037, tabled on 25 April, https://questions-statements.parliament.uk/written-questions/det ail/2022-04-25/159037

Davies, M. (2023) *Kickstart Scheme Question for Department for Work and Pensions*, Uk Parliament, UIN 143749, tabled on 9 February, https:// questions-statements.parliament.uk/written-questions/detail/2023-02-09/143749

Davies, W. (n.d.) 'For neither love nor money: was the Flexible New Deal a more effective and efficient active labour market policy than those it replaced?', PhD Thesis, Department of Politics, University of Liverpool, https://ethos.bl.uk/OrderDetails.do?uin=uk.bl.ethos.579370

Deeming, C. (2015) 'Foundations of the workfare state – reflections on the political transformation of the welfare state in Britain', *Social Policy and Administration*, 49(7): 862–86.

Denman, J. and McDonald, P. (1996) 'Unemployment statistics from 1881 to the present day', *Labour Market Trends*, 104(1): 5–18, www.ons.gov.uk/ ons/rel/lms/labour-market-trends--discontinued-/january-1996/unemp loyment-since-1881.pdf

Department of Employment (1984) *Training for Jobs*, Cmnd 9135, London.

Department of Employment (1990) *Labour Market and Skills Trends 1991/ 92*, Sheffield: Employment Department Group.

Department of Employment/Department of Social Security (1994) Jobseeker's Allowance, Cm2687, House of Commons Parliamentary Papers Online.

Department for Business, Energy and Industrial Strategy (2022) *New Law in Place to Allow Businesses to Hire Agency Workers to Plug Staffing Gaps Caused by Strike Action*, 21 July, www.gov.uk/government/news/new-law-in-place-to-allow-businesses-to-hire-agency-workers-to-plug-staffing-gaps-caused-by-strike-action

Department for Business and Trade (2023a) *Strikes Bill Becomes Law*, Press Release, 20 July, www.gov.uk/government/news/strikes-bill-becomes-law

Department for Business and Trade (2023b) *Trade Union Membership, UK 1995–2022: Statistical Bulletin*, 24 May, www.gov.uk/government/collecti ons/trade-union-statistics

Department for Education and Employment/Department for Social Security (1998) *A New Contract for Welfare: The Gateway to Work*, Cm 4102, https:// webarchive.nationalarchives.gov.uk/ukgwa/20040105093458/http:// www.dwp.gov.uk/publications/dss/1998/gateway/pdfs/gateway.pdf

Department for Education and Employment (1999) 'Employability and jobs: Is there a jobs gap?', *Memorandum by the Department for Education and Employment*, Select Committee on Education and Employment, Minutes of Evidence, 3 November 1999, HC 886-I, https://publications.parliam ent.uk/pa/cm199899/cmselect/cmeduemp/cmeduemp.htm

Department for Education and Employment (2001) *Towards Full Employment in a Modern Society*, Cm 5084.

Department for Social Security (1998) *New Ambitions for Our Country: A New Contract for Welfare*, Cm 3805, House of Commons, Parliamentary Papers online.

Department for Social Security (2000) *Prime Minister Unveils Modern Agency to Provide 21st Century Service to People of Working Age*, Press Release 2000/ 070, 16 March, https://webarchive.nationalarchives.gov.uk/ukgwa/200 10701112158/http://www.dss.gov.uk:80/mediacentre/pressreleases/2000/ mar/00070.htm

Department for Work and Pensions (2002) *Pathways to Work: Helping People into Employment*, Cm 5690, HMSO. https://webarchive.nationalarchives. gov.uk/ukgwa/20090210223517mp_/http://www.dwp.gov.uk/consultati ons/consult/2002/pathways/pathways.pdf

Department for Work and Pensions (2004) *Building on New Deal: Local Solutions Meeting Individual Needs*, DWP, https://webarchive.nationalarchi ves.gov.uk/ukgwa/20071204162316/http://www.dwp.gov.uk/publicati ons/dwp/2004/buildingonnewdeal/index.asp

Department for Work and Pensions (2005) *Five Year Strategy: Opportunity and Security Throughout Life*, Cm 6447, HMSO.

Department for Work and Pensions (2006a) *A New Deal for Welfare: Empowering People to Work*, Cm 6730, HMSO. https://assets.publishing.service.gov. uk/government/uploads/system/uploads/attachment_data/file/272235/ 6730.pdf

Department for Work and Pensions (2006b) *Quarterly Statistical Summary*, 16 August.

Department for Work and Pensions (2006c) Memorandum, Work and Pensions Committee: Evidence, *Incapacity Benefit and Pathways to Work*, 3rd Report, Session 2005–06, Vol 2 Oral and Written Evidence, 6 March, HC616-II.

Department for Work and Pensions (2007a) *Opportunity for All: Indicators Update 2007*, https://webarchive.nationalarchives.gov.uk/ukgwa/2009060 5204505/http://www.dwp.gov.uk/ofa/reports/latest.asp

Department for Work and Pensions (2007b) *Ready for Work: Full Employment in Our Generation*, Cm 7290, Norwich: HMSO, https://assets.publishing. service.gov.uk/government/uploads/system/uploads/attachment_data/ file/243122/7290.pdf

Department for Work and Pensions (2007c) *Flexible New Deal Evidence Paper*, https://webarchive.nationalarchives.gov.uk/ukgwa/20130128102031/http:// www.dwp.gov.uk/welfarereform/readyforwork/flexible-new-deal.pdf

Department for Work and Pensions (2007d) *In Work, Better Off: Next Steps to Full Employment*, Cm 7130, HMSO. https://assets.publishing.service. gov.uk/government/uploads/system/uploads/attachment_data/file/243 257/7130.pdf

Department for Work and Pensions (2008a) *Pathways to Work Performance Summary (Jobcentre Plus)*, December 2008, https://webarchive.nationalarchi ves.gov.uk/ukgwa/20100208152238/http://research.dwp.gov.uk/asd/wor kingage/p2w_jc_arc.asp

Department for Work and Pensions (2008b) *No One Written Off: Reforming Welfare to Reward Responsibility*, Norwich: The Stationery Office.

Department for Work and Pensions (2008c) *Raising Expectations and Increasing Support: Reforming Welfare for the Future*, Cm 7506, London: The Stationery Office, https://assets.publishing.service.gov.uk/government/uploads/sys tem/uploads/attachment_data/file/238683/7506.pdf

Department for Work and Pensions (2009a) *Building Britain's Recovery: Achieving Full Employment*, Cm 7751, Norwich: The Stationery Office, https://ass ets.publishing.service.gov.uk/government/uploads/system/uploads/atta chment_data/file/238506/7751.pdf

Department for Work and Pensions (2009b) 'Second supplementary memorandum submitted by the Department for Work and Pensions', EV160, Written Evidence, Work and Pensions Committee, *DWP's Commissioning Strategy and the Flexible New Deal*, Vol II, 2nd Report of Session 2008–09, House of Commons, HC 59-II, London: The Stationery Office, https://publications.parliament.uk/pa/cm200809/cmselect/cmwor pen/59/9780215528933.pdf

Department for Work and Pensions (2011a) *Income Support Lone Parent Regime: Official Statistics*, May, www.gov.uk/government/collections/inc ome-support-lone-parent-regime-figures-on-sanctions-and-work-focu sed-interviews--2

Department for Work and Pensions (2011b) *The Number of Starts on New Deal for Young People and the New Deal 25 Plus, and the Number of Times They Have Started Each Programme*, Ad-hoc statistical analysis, www.gov.uk/ government/statistics/new-deal-for-young-people-and-new-deal-25plus

Department for Work and Pensions (2011c) *Young Person's Guarantee Official Statistics*, October, https://assets.publishing.service.gov.uk/media/5a7c0 374ed915d01ba1ca96d/ypg_oct2011.pdf

Department for Work and Pensions (2012a) *Ad Hoc Statistical Analysis 2012 Quarter 4: Impacts and Costs and Benefits of the Future Jobs Fund*, https://ass ets.publishing.service.gov.uk/government/uploads/system/uploads/atta chment_data/file/223120/impacts_costs_benefits_fjf.pdf

Department for Work and Pensions (2012b) *Universal Credit: Impact Assessment*, www.gov.uk/government/publications/universal-credit-imp act-assessment

Department for Work and Pensions (2012c) *Evaluation of Mandatory Work Activity*, Research Report No. 823, www.gov.uk/government/publicati ons/evaluation-of-mandatory-work-activity-rr823

Department for Work and Pensions (2013) *New Enterprise Allowance – Analysis of Benefit Status of Participants*, www.gov.uk/government/statistics/new-ent erprise-allowance-analysis-of-benefit-status-of-participants

Department for Work and Pensions (2015a) *Universal Credit at Work*, Spring, www.gov.uk/government/publications/universal-credit-at-work

Department for Work and Pensions (2015b) *Youth Contract Official Statistics: April 2012 to November 2014*, www.gov.uk/government/statist ics/youth-contract-starts-and-payments-april-2012-to-november-2014

Department for Work and Pensions (2016a) *Work Experience: A Quantitative Impact Assessment*, Research Report No. 917, www.gov.uk/government/ publications/work-experience-a-quantitative-impact-assessment

Department for Work and Pensions (2016b) *Sector-Based Work Academies: A Quantitative Impact Assessment*, Research Report No. 918, www.gov.uk/ government/publications/sector-based-work-academies-a-quantitative-impact-assessment

Department for Work and Pensions (2016c) *Work Programme Adjustment of Referrals Data for September 2016*, www.gov.uk/government/publications/ work-programme-adjusting-referrals

Department for Work and Pensions (2016d) *New Enterprise Allowance Statistics*, 21 December, www.gov.uk/government/statistics/new-enterprise-allowa nce-april-2011-to-september-2016

Department for Work and Pensions (2016e) *New Enterprise Allowance Provider Guidance – Version v8.0*, www.gov.uk/government/uploads/system/uplo ads/attachment_data/file/524508/nea-provider-guidance.pdf

Department for Work and Pensions (2016f) *New Enterprise Allowance Survey*, www.gov.uk/government/publications/new-enterprise-allowance-survey

Department for Work and Pensions (2016g) *Mandatory Programmes Official Statistics: May 2011 to August 2016*, www.gov.uk/government/statistics/ pre-work-programme-support-mandatory-programmes-may-2011-to-aug ust-2016

Department for Work and Pensions (2017a) *Income Support Lone Parent Regime: Official Statistics*, Quarterly Official Statistics Bulletin, www.gov.uk/government/statistics/income-support-lone-parent-regime-data-to-september-2016

Department for Work and Pensions (2017b) *Employment Schemes Statistics: Work Experience, Sector-Based Work Academy and Skills Conditionality Starts to November 2017*, www.gov.uk/government/statistics/employment-schemes-work-experience-sector-based-work-academy-and-skills-conditionality-starts-to-november-2017

Department for Work and Pensions (2018) *Help to Work Statistics to December 2017*, www.gov.uk/government/statistics/help-to-work-quarterly-statistics

Department for Work and Pensions (2020a) *The Work Programme: A Quantitative Impact Assessment*, www.gov.uk/government/publications/the-work-programme-impact-assessment

Department for Work and Pensions (2020b) *Work Programme Statistics: Data to June 2020*, www.gov.uk/government/statistics/work-programme-statistical-summary-data-to-june-2020/work-programme-statistical-summary-data-to-june-2020

Department for Work and Pensions (2021) *Universal Credit Statistics, 29 April 2013 to 8 July 2021*, www.gov.uk/government/statistics/universal-credit-statistics-29-april-2013-to-8-july-2021/universal-credit-statistics-29-april-2013-to-8-july-2021

Department for Work and Pensions (2022a) *Summary: Restart Scheme to September 2022*, www.gov.uk/government/statistics/restart-scheme-statistics-to-september-2022

Department for Work and Pensions (2022b) *Restart Scheme Statistics: Demographics, Individuals Referred, Starts, First Earnings from Employment and Job Outcomes up to September 2022*, Tables, www.gov.uk/government/statistics/restart-scheme-statistics-to-september-2022

Department for Work and Pensions (2022c) *New Jobs Mission to Get 500,000 into Work* – Press Release, 27 January, www.gov.uk/government/news/new-jobs-mission-to-get-500-000-into-work

Department for Work and Pensions (2022d) *Fighting Fraud in the Welfare System*, Policy Paper, CP 679, www.gov.uk/government/publications/fighting-fraud-in-the-welfare-system/fighting-fraud-in-the-welfare-system--2

Department for Work and Pensions (2023) *Government Announces New Welfare Reforms to Help Thousands into Work*, Press Release, 5 September, www.gov.uk/government/news/government-announces-new-welfare-reforms-to-help-thousands-into-work

Department for Work and Pensions (2023a) *Work and Health Programme Including JETS Provider Guidance*, May 2023, www.gov.uk/government/publications/work-and-health-programme-including-jets-provider-guidance

Department for Work and Pensions (2023b) *Work and Health Programme Statistics: Background Information and Methodology*, www.gov.uk/governm ent/publications/work-and-health-programme-statistics-background-info rmation-and-methodology/work-and-health-progamme-statistics-backgro und-information-and-methodology

Department for Work and Pensions (2023c) *Work and Health Programme Statistics: Referrals, Starts, First Earnings from Employment and Job Outcomes up to February 2023*, www.gov.uk/government/statistics/work-and-hea lth-programme-statistics-to-february-2023

Department for Work and Pensions (2023d) *Restart Scheme Provider Guidance*, updated February 2023, www.gov.uk/government/publications/restart-provider-guidance

Department for Work and Pensions (2023e) *Impact Assessment Equality Analysis: Raising the Administrative Earnings Threshold (Spring Budget 2023 Announcement)*, www.gov.uk/government/publications/changes-relating-to-in-work-progression-equality-analysis

Department for Work and Pensions (2023f) *Impact Assessment Equality Analysis: Removing the Couple Administrative Earnings Threshold (Spring Budget 2023 Announcement)*, www.gov.uk/government/publications/changes-relat ing-to-in-work-progression-equality-analysis

Department for Work and Pensions (2023g) *Transforming Support: The Health and Disability White Paper*, CP 807, www.gov.uk/government/publications/ transforming-support-the-health-and-disability-white-paper

Department for Work and Pensions (2023h) *The Impact of Benefit Sanctions on Employment Outcomes*, Draft Report, Research and Analysis, www.gov. uk/government/publications/the-impact-of-benefit-sanctions-on-emp loyment-outcomes-draft-report/the-impact-of-benefit-sanctions-on-emp loyment-outcomes#fn:29

Department for Work and Pensions (2023i) *Universal Credit Statistics: Background Information and Methodology*, Guidance, updated 14 February, www.gov.uk/ government/publications/universal-credit-statistics-background-informat ion-and-methodology/universal-credit-statistics-background-informat ion-and-methodology

Department for Work and Pensions (2023j) *Policy Paper: State Pension Age Review 2023*, www.gov.uk/government/publications/state-pension-age-review-2023-government-report/state-pension-age-review-2023

De Sousa, E. (1987) 'Racism in the YTS', *Critical Social Policy*, 7(20): 66–73.

De Sousa, E. (1989) 'YTS – The Racism Riddle', *Unemployment Bulletin*, Issue 29 Spring, London: Unemployment Unit, pp 23–4.

Devine, F. and Sensier, M. (2017) 'Class, politics and the progressive dilemma', *Political Quarterly*, 88(1): 30–8.

Dickerson, J., Lockyer, B., McIvor, C., Bingham, D.D., Crossley, K.L., Endacott, C., Moss, R.H., Smith, H., Pickett, K.E. and McEachan, R.R.C. (2022) 'The impact of the COVID-19 pandemic on families living in the ethnically diverse and deprived city of Bradford: findings from the longitudinal Born in Bradford COVID-19 research programme', in K. Garthwaite, R. Patrick, M. Power, A. Tarrant and R. Warnock (eds) *COVID-19 Collaborations: Researching Poverty and Low-Income Family Life during the Pandemic*, Bristol: Policy Press, pp 73–87.

Dillow, C. (2007) *The End of Politics: New Labour and the Folly of Managerialism*, Petersfield: Harriman House.

Dilnot, A. and Webb, S. (1988) 'The 1988 social security reforms', *Fiscal Studies*, 9(3): 26–53.

Dilnot, A. and McCrae, J. (1999) *The Family Credit System and the Working Families' Tax Credit in the United Kingdom*, Briefing Note 3, London: Institute for Fiscal Studies, www.ifs.org.uk/bns/bn3.pdf

Dinan, S. (2018) 'A typology of activation incentives', *Social Policy and Administration*, 53(3): 1–15, online first.

Disney, R., Bellmann, L., Carruth, A., Franz, W., Jackman, R., Layard, R., Lehmann, H.F. and Philpott, J. (1992) *Helping the Unemployed: Active Labour Market Policies in Britain and Germany*, London: Anglo-German Foundation.

Dorey, P. (2013) '"It was just like arming to face the threat of Hitler in the late 1930s". The Ridley Report and the Conservative Party's preparations for the 1984–85 miners' strike', *Historical Studies in Industrial Relations*, (34): 173–214.

Dorey, P. (2022) 'Neo-liberalism in Britain: from origins to orthodoxy', in N. Lévy, A. Chommeloux, N.A. Champroux, S. Porion, S. Josso and A. Damiens (eds) *The Anglo-American Model of Neo-Liberalism of the 1980s*, Cham: Palgrave Macmillan, pp 97–116.

Dorre, K. (2015) 'The new Landnahme: dynamics and limits of financial market capitalism', in K. Dorre, D. Lessenich and H. Rosa (eds) *Sociology, Capitalism, Critique*, London: Verso, pp 11–66.

Dowling, E. (2016) 'Valorised but not valued? Affective remuneration, social reproduction and feminist politics beyond the crisis', *British Politics*, 11(4): 452–68.

Drakeford, M. and Davidson, K. (2013) 'Going from bad to worse? Social policy and the demise of the Social Fund', *Critical Social Policy*, 33(3): 365–83.

Droy, L.T., O'Connor, H. and Goodwin, J.D. (2019) *Inequity in the School to Work Transitions of YTS participants*, Occasional Papers, School of Media, Communication and Sociology, University of Leicester, DOI: 10.13140/RG.2.2.11060.71046

Duncan Smith, I. (2010) 'Our contract with the country for the 21st century', speech to the Conservative Party conference, 5 October.

Duncan Smith, I. (2016) '"A compromise too far": Iain Duncan Smith's resignation letter in full', *The Guardian*, www.theguardian.com/politics/2016/mar/18/iain-duncan-smith-resignation-letter-in-full

Dunn, A. (2013) 'Activation workers' perceptions of their long-term unemployed clients' attitudes towards employment', *Journal of Social Policy*, 42(4): 799–817.

Dwyer, P. (2004) 'Creeping conditionality in the UK: from welfare rights to conditional entitlements?', *Canadian Journal of Sociology*, 29(2): 265–87.

Dwyer, P. (2008) 'The conditional welfare state', in M. Powell (ed) *Modernising the Welfare State: The Blair Legacy*, Bristol: Policy Press, pp 199–218.

Dwyer, P. and Wright, S. (2014) 'Universal Credit, ubiquitous conditionality and its implications for social citizenship', *Journal of Poverty and Social Justice*, 22(1): 27–35.

Dyer-Witheford, N. (2015) *Cyber-Proletariat: Global Labour in the Digital Vortex*, London: Pluto Press.

Edgell, S. and Duke, V. (1991) *A Measure of Thatcherism*, London: Harper Collins.

Education and Employment Select Committee (1997) 'Question 16 ("GROUNDSWELL") in Appendix 9', *Appendices to the Minutes of Evidence*, 1–28, Security of Staff in Jobcentres, House of Commons Report, 5 March, Session 1996–97, HC 149, https://parlipapers.proquest.com/parlipapers/docview/t70.d75.1996-097737/usgLogRstClick!!?accountid=10673

Education and Employment Select Committee (1999) 'Examination of Witnesses Mr Bill Wells, Economy and Labour Markets, and Mr Mark Neale, Structural Unemployment Policy, Department for Education and Employment', 1–30, *Minutes of Evidence*, 3 November, HC 60-II, Session 1998–99, https://publications.parliament.uk/pa/cm199899/cmselect/cmeduemp/886/9110301.htm

Edwards, D. (1985) 'The history and politics of the Youth Opportunities Programme 1978–1983', PhD thesis, Institute of Education, University of London, http://eprints.ioe.ac.uk/19227/

Ehrenreich, B. and Ehrenreich, J. (1977) 'The professional-managerial class', *Radical America*, 11(2): 7–32, https://library.brown.edu/pdfs/1125403552886481.pdf

Ellery, B. (2022) 'Health unions accused of colluding on strikes to "hold UK to ransom"', *The Times*, 24 December.

Ellison, N. (2016) 'The Coalition Government, public spending and social policy', in H. Bochel and M. Powell (eds) *The Coalition Government and Social Policy: Restructuring the Welfare State*, Bristol: Policy Press, pp 27–52.

Employment Committee (1980) *The Manpower Services Commission's Corporate Plan 1980–84: Observations by the Government and Manpower Services Commission on the First Report of the Committee in Session 1979–80*, HC 817, House of Commons, 29 October.

Employment Committee (1985) *The Training of Young People for Employment*, Session 1984–85, Minutes of Evidence, 27 March 1985, House of Commons 209-iii, Parliamentary Papers Online.

Employment Committee (1986) *The Work of the Department of Employment Group*, Minutes of Evidence, Session 1986–87, 3 December, House of Commons.

Employment Committee (1988) *The Work of the Department of Employment Group*, Minutes of Evidence, Session 1987–88, 27 January, HC 290-I, House of Commons.

Employment Committee (1989) *Employment Training and the Youth Training Scheme*, Minutes of Evidence, Session 1989–90, 6 December, HC 69, House of Commons.

Employment Committee (1995) *The Work of TECs: Minutes of Evidence – Equal Opportunities Commission; Commission for Racial Equality*, HC 99-I, 12 December 1995, Session 1995–96, House of Commons.

Employment Committee (1996a) *The Work of TECs: Report and Proceedings of the Committee together with Appendices*, First Report Session 1995–96, HC 99, 6 February 1996, House of Commons.

Employment Committee (1996b) *The Right to Work/Workfare*, Report of the proceedings of the committee together with the Appendices, 13 February, Second Report, Session 1995–96, London: HMSO.

Etherington, D. (2020) *Austerity, Welfare and Work: Exploring Politics, Geographies and Inequalities*, Bristol: Policy Press.

Evans, B. (1992) *The Politics of the Training Market: From Manpower Services Commission to Training and Enterprise Councils*, London: Routledge.

Evans, D. (2023) *A Nation of Shopkeepers: The Unstoppable Rise of the Petite Bourgeoisie*, London: Repeater Books.

Evans, G. and Tilley, J. (2017) *The New Politics of Class: the Political Exclusion of the British Working Class*, Oxford: Oxford University Press.

Evans, M., Eyre, J., Millar, J. and Sarre, S. (2003) *New Deal for Lone Parents: Second Synthesis Report of the National Evaluation*, Working Age and Employment Reports 1998–2004, No. 163, Department for Work and Pensions, https://webarchive.nationalarchives.gov.uk/ukgwa/20100208134427/http://research.dwp.gov.uk/asd/asd5/wae-index.asp

Farnsworth, K. (2021) 'Retrenched, reconfigured and broken: the British welfare state after a decade of austerity', *Social Policy and Society*, 20(1): 77–96.

Faucher-King, F. and Le Galés, P. (2010) *The New Labour Experiment: Change and Reform Under Blair and Brown*, Stanford: Stanford University Press.

Fawcett, H. (1999) 'Jack Jones, the social contract and social policy 1970–74', in H. Fawcett and R. Lowe (eds) *Welfare Policy in Britain: The Road from 1945*, London: Macmillan, pp 158–83.

Felstead, A. (1994) 'Funding government training schemes: mechanisms and consequences', *British Journal of Education and Work*, 7(3): 21–42.

Felstead, A. (1995) 'The gender implications of creating a training market: alleviating or reinforcing inequality of access', in J. Humphries and J. Rubery (eds) *The Economics of Equal Opportunities*, Manchester: Equal Opportunities Commission, pp 177–202.

Felstead, A. (1998) *Output-Related Funding in Vocational Education and Training: A Discussion Paper and Case Studies*, Thessaloniki: European Centre for the Development of Vocational Training, www.cedefop.europa.eu/files/5080_en.pdf

Felstead A. and Unwin, L. (2001) 'Funding post-compulsory education and training: a retrospective analysis of the TEC and FEFC systems and their impact on skills', *Journal of Education and Work*, 14(1): 91–111.

Ferguson, D. (2020) *Insecure Work: The Taylor Review and the Good Work Plan*, Research Briefing No. CBP 8817, House of Commons Library, https://commonslibrary.parliament.uk/research-briefings/cbp-8817/

Ferguson, D. (2021) *FAQs: Coronavirus Job Retention Scheme*, Briefing Paper, No. CBP 8880, House of Commons Library, https://commonslibrary.parliament.uk/research-briefings/cbp-8880/

Fetzer, T. (2019) 'Did austerity cause Brexit?', *American Economic Review*, 109(11): 3849–86.

Finn, D. (1987) *Training Without Jobs: New Deals and Broken Promises*, London: Macmillan.

Finn, D. (1989) 'Employment training – success or failure', *Unemployment Bulletin 31*, Unemployment Unit and Youthaid, pp 9–16.

Finn, D. (1995) 'The jobseeker's allowance – workfare and the stricter benefit regime', *Capital and Class*, 19(3): 7–11.

Finn, D. (2000) 'From full employment to employability: a new deal for Britain's unemployed?', *International Journal of Manpower*, 21(5): 384–99.

Finn, D. (2003a) 'Modernisation or workfare? New Labour's work-based welfare state', *Competition and Change*, 5(4): 355–37.

Finn, D. (2003b) 'Employment policy', in N. Ellison and C. Pierson (eds) *Developments in British Social Policy*, Basingstoke: Palgrave Macmillan, pp 111–29.

Finn, D. (2005) 'The role of contracts and the private sector in delivering Britain's "employment first" welfare state', in E. Sol and M. Westerveld (eds) *Contractualism in Employment Services*, The Hague: Kluwer Law International, pp 101–18.

Finn, D. (2009) 'The welfare market and the Flexible New Deal: lessons from other countries', *Local Economy*, 24(1): 38–45.

Finn, D. (2011) 'Welfare to work after the recession: from New Deals to the Work Programme', in C. Holden, M. Kilkey and G. Ramia (eds) *Social Policy Review 23*, Bristol: Policy Press, pp 127–46.

Fletcher, D.R. (1997) 'Evaluating special measures for the unemployed: some reflections on recent UK experience', *Policy and Politics*, 25(2): 173–84.

Fletcher, D.R. (2019) 'British public employment service reform: activating and civilising the precariat?', *Journal of Poverty and Social Justice*, 27(3): 407–21.

Fletcher, D.R. and Wright, S. (2018) 'A hand up or a slap down? Criminalising benefit claimants in Britain via strategies of surveillance, sanctions and deterrence', *Critical Social Policy*, 38(2): 323–44.

Fowler, N. (1991) *Ministers Decide: A Personal Memoir of the Thatcher Years*, London: Chapmans.

Foxton, D. (1982) 'The specialist claims control', *Unemployment Unit Bulletin*, November, No. 6: 6–7.

Francis-Devine, B., Powell, A. and Clark, H. (2021) *Coronavirus Job Retention Scheme: Statistics*, Research Briefing, No. CBP 9152, House of Commons Library, https://commonslibrary.parliament.uk/research-briefings/cbp-9152/

Fraser, N. (2016) 'Contradictions of capital and care', *New Left Review*, 100, July–August.

Fraser, N. (2019) *The Old Is Dying and the New Cannot Be Born*, London: Verso.

Freathy, P. (1991) 'Black workers and the YTS: A case of discrimination?', *Critical Social Policy*, 11(32): 82–97.

Freedland, M. (1983) 'Labour law and leaflet law: the Youth Training Scheme of 1983', *Industrial Law Journal*, 12: 220–35.

Freud, D. (2007) *Reducing Dependency, Increasing Opportunity: Options for the Future of Welfare to Work*, an independent report to the Department for Work and Pensions, HMSO.

Freud, D. (2021) *Clashing Agendas: Inside the Welfare Trap*, London: Nine Elm Books.

Furlong, A., Goodwin, J., O'Connor, H., Hadfield, S., Hall, S., Lowden, K. and Plugor, R. (2017) *Young People in the Labour Market: Past, Present, Future*, London: Routledge.

Gallas, A. (2016) *The Thatcherite Offensive: A Neo-Poulantzasian Analysis*, Haymarket Books.

Gardiner, L. and Corlett, A. (2015) *Looking through the Hourglass: Hollowing out of the UK Jobs Market Pre- and Post-Crisis*, Resolution Foundation, www.resolutionfoundation.org/app/uploads/2015/03/Polarisation-full-slide-pack.pdf

GB243 T/SOR C.197 Claimant Union National Address List, May 1979, John Cooper Collection, The Spirit of Revolt Archive, https://dn790007.ca.archive.org/0/items/ClaimantsUnionPapers/Claimants%20Union%20Papers.pdf

George, A., Metcalf, H., Tufekci, L. and Wilkinson, D. (2015) *Understanding Age and the Labour Market*, Joseph Rowntree Foundation, www.jrf.org.uk/report/understanding-age-and-labour-market

Gilbert, J. (2004) 'The second wave: the specificity of New Labour neo-liberalism', *Soundings*, 26.

Ginsburg, N. (1979) *Class, Capital and Social Policy*, London: Macmillan.

Goos, M. and Manning, A. (2007) 'Lousy and lovely jobs: the rising polarisation of work in Britain', *Review of Economics and Statistics*, 89(1): 118–33.

Goos, M., Manning, A. and Salomons, A. (2014) 'Explaining job polarisation: routine-based technological change and offshoring', *American Economic Review*, 104(8): 2509–26.

Gough, I. (1981) *The Political Economy of the Welfare State*, London: Macmillan.

Grant, A. (2013) 'Welfare reform, increased conditionality and discretion: Jobcentre Plus advisers' experiences of targets and sanctions', *Journal of Poverty and Social Justice*, 21(2): 165–76.

Gray, A. (2000) 'The comparative effectiveness of different delivery frameworks for training of the unemployed', *Journal of Education and Work*, 13(3): 307–25.

Green, J. and Lavery, S. (2015) 'The regressive recovery: distribution, inequality and state power in Britain's post-crisis political economy', *New Political Economy*, 20(6): 894–923.

Greenberg, D. and Davis, A. (2007) *Evaluation of the New Deal for Disabled People: The Cost and Cost-Benefit Analyses*, Research Report No. 431, Department for Work and Pensions, HMSO, CDS.

Greene, F.J. (2002) 'An investigation into enterprise support for younger people, 1975–2000', *International Small Business Journal*, 20(3): 315–36.

Greener, I. (2008) 'The stages of New Labour', in M. Powell (ed) *Modernising the Welfare State: The Blair Legacy*, Bristol: Policy Press, pp 219–34.

Greer, I. (2016) 'Welfare reform, precarity and the recommodification of labour', *Work, Employment and Society*, 30(1): 162–73.

Greer, I. and Umney, C. (2022) *Marketization: How Capitalist Exchange Disciplines Workers and Subverts Democracy*, London: Bloomsbury.

Greer, I., Breidahl, K.N., Knuth, M. and Larsen, F. (2017) *The Marketization of Employment Services: The Dilemmas of Europe's Work First Welfare States*, Oxford: Oxford University Press.

Gregg, P. (1990) 'The evolution of Special Employment Measures', *National Institute Economic Review*, 132(1): 49–58.

Gregg, P. (1993) 'Jobs and justice: why job creation alone will not solve unemployment', in E. Balls and P. Gregg (eds) *Work and Welfare: Tackling the Jobs Deficit*, London: IPPR, pp 31–65.

Gregg, P. (2008) *Realising Potential: A Vision for Personalised Conditionality and Support*, Department for Work and Pensions.

Gregg, P. and Gardiner, L. (2016) *The Road to Full Employment: What the Journey Looks Like and How to Make Progress*, The Resolution Foundation, www.resolutionfoundation.org/app/uploads/2016/03/Full-employment.pdf

References

Griffin, P. (2021) 'Expanding labour geographies: resourcefulness and organising amongst "unemployed workers"', *Geoforum*, 118: 159–68.

Griffin, P. (2023a) 'Unemployed Workers' Centres (1978–): Spatial Politics, "Non-Movement", and the Making of Centres', *Antipode*, 55(2): 393–414.

Griffin, P. (2023b) 'Solidarity on the move: imaginaries and infrastructures within the People's March for Jobs (1981)', *Transactions of the Institute of British Geographers*, https://doi.org/10.1111/tran.12637

Griffiths, R. and Durkin, S. (2007) *Synthesising the Evidence on Employment Zones*, Research Report No. 449, Leeds: Department for Work and Pensions, Corporate Document Services.

Griggs, J., Hammond, A. and Walker, R. (2014) 'Activation for all: welfare reform in the United Kingdom 1995–2009, in I. Lodemel and A. Moreira (eds) *Activation or Workfare? Governance and the Neo-liberal Convergence*, Oxford: Oxford University Press, pp 73–100.

Grimshaw, D., Fagan, C., Hebson, G. and Tavora, I. (2017) 'A new labour market segmentation approach for analysing inequalities: introduction and overview', in D. Grimshaw, C. Fagan, G. Hebson and I. Tavora (eds) *Making Work More Equal: A New Labour Market Segmentation Approach*, Manchester: Manchester University Press, pp 1–32.

Groundswell (n.d.) *Signing On: A Survival Guide for Signing on under the Job Seekers Allowance*, London: Haringey Solidarity Group/Groundswell, The Sparrows Nest Library and Archive, www.thesparrowsnest.org.uk/collecti ons/public_archive/14863.pdf

Groundswell (1997) 'Brighton claimants cripple project work', News and Information August/September, Occasional Newsletter, Groundswell.

Grover, C. (2005) 'The national childcare strategy: the social regulation of lone mothers as a gendered reserve army of labour', *Capital and Class*, 29(1): 63–90.

Grover, C. (2007) 'The Freud Report on the future of welfare to work: some critical reflections', *Critical Social Policy*, 27(4): 534–45.

Grover, C. (2008) 'Loaning supplementary benefit and the introduction of the social fund', *Social Policy and Administration*, 42(5): 470–86.

Grover, C. (2011) *The Social Fund 20 Years On: Historical and Policy Aspects of Loaning Social Security*, Farnham: Ashgate Publishing.

Grover, C. (2012) '"Personalised conditionality": observations on active proletarianisation in late modern Britain', *Capital and Class*, 36(2): 283–301.

Grover, C. (2016a) *Social Security and Wage Poverty: Historical and Policy Aspects of Supplementing Wages in Britain and Beyond*, Basingstoke: Palgrave Macmillan.

Grover, C. (2016b) 'From wage supplements to a 'living wage'? A commentary on the problems of predistribution in Britain's summer budget of 2015', *Critical Social Policy*, 36(4): 693–703.

Grover, C. (2019) 'Violent proletarianisation: social murder, the reserve army of labour and social security "austerity" in Britain', *Critical Social Policy*, 39(3): 335–55.

Grover, C. and Stewart, J. (1999) '"Market Workfare": social security, social regulation and competitiveness in the 1990s', *Journal of Social Policy*, 28(1): 73–96.

Grover, C. and Stewart, J. (2002) *The Work Connection: The Role of Social Security in British Economic Regulation*, Basingstoke: Palgrave Macmillan.

Grover, C. and Piggott, L. (2005) 'Disabled people, the reserve army of labour and welfare reform', *Disability and Society*, 20(7): 705–17.

Grover, C. and Piggott, L. (2010) 'From Incapacity Benefit to Employment and Support Allowance: social sorting, sickness and impairment, and social security', *Policy Studies*, 31(2): 265–82.

Grover, C. and Piggott, L. (2013) 'A commentary on resistance in the UK's Work Experience programme: capitalism, exploitation and wage work', *Critical Social Policy*, 33(3): 554–63.

Hacker, J.S. and Pierson, P. (2010) 'Winner-take-all politics: public policy, political organisation and the precipitous rise of top incomes in the United States', *Politics and Society*, 38(2): 152–204.

Haddon, C. (2012) *Making Policy in Opposition: The Development of Universal Credit, 2005–2010*, Institute for Government, www.instituteforgovernm ent.org.uk/sites/default/files/publications/Universal%20Credit%20fi nal.pdf

Hales, J., Taylor, R., Mandy, W. and Miller, M. (2003) *Evaluation of Employment Zones: Report on a Cohort Survey of Long-Term Unemployed People in the Zones and a Matched Set of Comparison Areas*, Working Age and Employment Reports 1998–2004, No. 176, Department for Work and Pensions, https://webarchive.nationalarchives.gov.uk/ukgwa/20100208134 427/http://research.dwp.gov.uk/asd/asd5/wae-index.asp

Halfacree, K.H. (1996) 'Out of place in the country: travellers and the rural idyll', *Antipode*, 28(1): 42–72.

Hansard (1944) *House of Commons Debate on Employment Policy*, Ernest Bevin MP, Minister of Labour, 21 June, Vol 401, cc211–310, https://api.parliam ent.uk/historichansard/commons/1944/jun/21/employment-policy

Hansard (1976) *Young People (Employment), House of Commons Debate*, 21 June, Vol 913, cc1103-241, https://api.parliament.uk/historic-hansard/ commons/1976/jun/21/young-people-employment

Hansard (1978) *Temporary Employment Subsidy*, House of Commons Debate, 31 January 1978, vol 943, cc416–28, https://api.parliament.uk/historic-hansard/commons/1978/jan/31/temporary-employment-subsidy

Hansard (1979) *Budget Statement*, Chancellor of the Exchequer Geoffrey Howe, 12 June 1979, House of Commons, Vol 968, cc 235–63.

Hansard (1980a) *Budget statement*, Chancellor of the Exchequer Geoffrey Howe MP, House of Commons Debate 26 March, Vol 981 cc1457–63, https://api.parliament.uk/historic-hansard/commons/1980/mar/26/bud get-statement

Hansard (1980b) *Employment Schemes*, House of Commons Debate, James Prior MP, 14 February 1980, Vol 978, cc 1755–66.

Hansard (1980c) *Social Security Benefits (Uprating)*, House of Commons, 27 March 1980, Vol 981, cc 1659–77, https://bit.ly/2Rla 87U

Hansard (1981a) *Industrial Disputes (Benefits)*, Written Answers, House of Commons Debate, 21 May 1981, Vol 5, cc 162–3W.

Hansard (1981b) *Unemployment Statistics and Job Creation*, House of Commons Debate, 15 December 1981, Vol 15, cc 148–9.

Hansard (1981c) *Employment and Training*, House of Commons Debate, 15 December 1981, Vol 15, cc153–65.

Hansard (1982a) *Unemployment*, House of Commons Debate, 27 July 1982, Vol 28, cc 938–1008.

Hansard (1982b) *Employment Subsidies*, House of Commons Debate, 17 November 1982, Vol 32, cc 370–88.

Hansard (1984a) *Regional Benefit Investigation Teams*, Written Answers, Employment, Mr Alan Clark, 13 February, Vol 53.

Hansard (1984b) *Special Training And Employment Measures*, Written Answers: Employment, 5 June 1984, Vol 61, House of Commons, https://hansard.parliament.uk/Commons/1984-06-05

Hansard (1985a) *Social Security (Reform)*, House of Commons Debate, 18 June 1985, Vol 81, cc187–269, https://api.parliament.uk/historic-hansard/commons/1985/jun/18/social-security-reform-2

Hansard (1985b) *Social Security: Review*, House of Lords Debate, 19 June 1985, Vol 465, cc265–342, https://api.parliament.uk/historic-hansard/lords/1985/jun/19/social-security-review

Hansard (1985c) *Budget*, 19 March 1985, House of Commons, Vol 75, cc789, https://hansard.parliament.uk/Commons/1985-03-19

Hansard (1985d) *Engagements*, Oral answers to Questions, Prime Minister, 21 March 1985, House of Commons, Vol 75, cc981–3, https://hansard.parliament.uk/Commons/1985-03-21

Hansard (1985e) *Budget Resolutions and Economic Situation*, House of Commons Debate, 21 March 1985, Vol 75, cc1014–79, https://hansard.parliament.uk/Commons/1985-03-21

Hansard (1985f) *Training and Special Employment (Cost)*, Written Answers, Mr Peter Morrison MP, House of Commons Debate, 15 January 1985, vol 71, cc76–7W, https://hansard.parliament.uk/Commons/1985-01-15/debates/6a61cce6-67d1-4eec-99ea-d5f141ec3201/TrainingAndSpecia lEmployment(Cost)?highlight=training#contribution-55eba721-9495-4430-ab92-b6591f61088f

Hansard (1986a) *Restart Scheme*, House of Commons Debate, 19 November 1986, Vol 105, cc211–13W, https://hansard.parliament.uk/Commons/1986-11-19

Hansard (1986b) *Availability For Work (Test)*, House of Commons Debate, 28 October 1986, Vol 103, cc175–87, https://hansard.parliament.uk/Commons/1986-10-28

Hansard (1986c) Work Test, House of Commons Debate, 18 November 1986, Vol 105, cc422–4, https://hansard.parliament.uk/Commons/1986-11-18

Hansard (1987a) *Benefits*, Oral Answers to Questions, House of Commons, 3 February 1987, Vol 109, cc 801, https://hansard.parliament.uk/Commons/1987-02-03

Hansard (1987b) *YTS*, Written answers – Employment, House of Commons, 8 April 1987, Vol 114, cc295–306, https://hansard.parliament.uk/Commons/1987-04-08col

Hansard (1987c) *YTS*, Written answers – Employment, House of Commons, 8 April 1987, Vol 114, cc307–28, https://hansard.parliament.uk/Commons/1987-04-08

Hansard (1987d) *Training And Employment Measures*, House of Commons, 28 January 1987, Vol 109, cc337–54, https://hansard.parliament.uk/Commons/1987-01-28

Hansard (1987e) *Job Training Scheme*, Written answers – Employment, House of Commons, 3 February 1987, Vol 109, cc607, https://hansard.parliament.uk/Commons/1987-02-03

Hansard (1987f) *Unemployed People (Training)*, House of Commons, 18 November 1987, Vol 122, cc1067–82, https://hansard.parliament.uk/Commons/1987-11-18

Hansard (1987g) *Employment And Training Measures*, 28 January 1987, Vol 483, cc1332–44, House of Lords, https://hansard.parliament.uk/Lords/1987-01-28

Hansard (1988a) *YTS*, Written answers – Employment, House of Commons, 6 December 1988, Vol 143, cc144–5, https://hansard.parliament.uk/Commons/1988-12-06

Hansard (1988b) *Job Training Scheme*, Written answers – Employment, House of Commons, 5 February 1988, Vol 126, cc791, https://hansard.parliament.uk/Commons/1988-02-05

Hansard (1988c) *Adult Employment and Youth Training*, Estimates Day, House of Commons, 21 July 1988, Vol 137, cc1357–89, https://hansard.parliament.uk/Commons/1988-07-21

Hansard (1989a) *Job Start*, Written answers – Employment, House of Commons, 27 July 1989, Vol 157, cc870, https://hansard.parliament.uk/Commons/1989-07-27

Hansard (1989b) *Enterprise Allowance Scheme*, Written answers – Employment, 31 October 1989, Vol 159, House of Commons, https://hansard.parliam ent.uk/Commons/1989-10-31

Hansard (1989c) *Youth Training*, Written answers – Employment, House of Commons, 5 December 1989, Vol 163, cc196, https://hansard.parliam ent.uk/Commons/1989-12-05/debates/bf3555b0-2687-49f4-93a7-f5aaa dd119e6/YouthTraining

Hansard (1989d) *Training*, Written answers – Employment, House of Commons, 27 July 1989, Vol 157, cc 865–9, https://hansard.parliament. uk/Commons/1989-07-27

Hansard (1990a) *Training Credits*, House of Commons Debate, 27 March 1990, Vol 170, cc 209–21, https://hansard.parliament.uk/Commons/1990-03-27/debates/cb5d2a91-e772-4890-a2b3-cd16aec44d5f/TrainingCredits

Hansard (1990b) Under Secretary of State for Social Security, Gillian Shepard MP, *Actively Seeking Employment*, House of Commons Debate, 3 April 1990, Vol 170, cc1086–94, https://publications.parliament.uk/pa/cm198 990/cmhansrd/1990-04-03/Debate-5.html

Hansard (1991) Secretary of State for Employment, Michael Howard, *Unemployed People*, House of Commons Debate, 19 June 1991, Vol 193, Col 293–307, https://hansard.parliament.uk/Commons/1991-06-19/ debates/82ce2578-2b34-4f4b-8396-32a30297102f/UnemployedPeople

Hansard (1992a) *Employment*, House of Commons oral questions to answer, 1 December 1992, Vol 215, https://hansard.parliament.uk/Commons/ 1992-12-01/debates/1fe366e0-a6f1-4dbf-bee0-57612d86a2d5/OralAns wersToQuestions

Hansard (1992b) Secretary of State for Social Security, Peter Lilley MP, *Social Security*, House of Commons Debate, 12 November 1992, Vol 213, cc1017–33, https://publications.parliament.uk/pa/cm199293/cmhansrd/ 1992-11-12/Debate-3.html

Hansard (1992c) *New Age Travellers*, Written answers – Social Security, 30 November 1992, Vol 215, https://hansard.parliament.uk/Commons/ 1992-11-30#undefined

Hansard (1993a) Chancellor of the Exchequer Mr Norman Lamont, *Budget Statement*, House of Commons, Tuesday 16 March 1993, Vol 221, Col 193–4, https://hansard.parliament.uk/Commons/1993-03-16/debates/ 2036f730-3dfe-4ea4-9641-80e95aa00d09/BudgetStatement

Hansard (1993b) *Social Security and the Welfare State*, House of Commons Debate, 20 July 1993, Vol 229, cc201–94, https://publications.parliament. uk/pa/cm199293/cmhansrd/1993-07-20/Debate-2.html

Hansard (1993c) *Benefit Payments*, House of Commons Debate, 6 June 1993, Vol 226, cc1–4, https://hansard.parliament.uk/Commons/1993-06-07/ debates/6a2c8e37-f39b-4e57-9371-d520d947c567/BenefitPayments

Hansard (1994) *Jobseeker's Allowance*, House of Commons Debate, 24 October 1994, Vol 248, cc 631–48, https://hansard.parliament.uk/comm ons/1994-10-24/debates/51edb96b-1e3f-46d0-80c4-c289e80787f1/JobS eekerSAllowance#635

Hansard (1995a) *Education and Employment*, House of Commons, Written answers to questions, 26 October 1995, Vol 264, Col 805-8, https:// publications.parliament.uk/pa/cm199495/cmhansrd/1995-10-26/Writt ens-7.html

Hansard (1995b) *Training and Enterprise Councils*, House of Commons Written answers to questions, 19 January 1995, Vol 252, cc615–19W, http://hans ard.millbanksystems.com/written_answers/1995/jan/19/training-and-ent erprise-councils

Hansard (1996a) *Training and Community Action*, House of Commons Debate, 16 January 1996, Vol 269, Col 603–10, https://publications.parliament. uk/pa/cm199596/cmhansrd/vo950116/debtext/60116-23.htm

Hansard (1996b) *Training and Enterprise Councils*, House of Commons written answers, 17 October 1996, Vol 282, cc1129–30W, https://api.parliament. uk/historic-hansard/sittings/1996/oct/17

Hansard (1996c) *Departmental Expenditure*, Written answers – Education and Employment, House of Commons, 26 November 1996, Vol 286, 175–9, https://hansard.parliament.uk/Commons/1996-11-26/debates/ee87e b84-b44e-4268-9d7f-82286e4ad7df/DepartmentalExpenditure

Hansard (1996d) *Training (Expenditure)*, Written answers – Education and Employment, House of Commons, 26 February 1996, Vol 272, c373, https://hansard.parliament.uk/Commons/1996-02-26/debates/a298c b3d-8d19-43dd-8b51-06d2edf7ab6a/Training(Expenditure)

Hansard (1997) *Budget Statement*, House of Commons Debate, 2 July, Vol 297, cc 304–16, https://hansard.parliament.uk/Commons/1997-07-02/ debates/9faeb6f7-5d0e-44e4-bc7f-fbd4db86b779/BudgetStatement

Hansard (1998) *Welfare Reform*, House of Commons Debate, 26 March, Vol 309, cc681–98, https://api.parliament.uk/historic-hansard/commons/ 1998/mar/26/welfare-reform

Hansard (2005a) *Department for Work and Pensions – Five Year Plan*, House of Lords Debate, 2 February, Vol 669, cc231–47, https://api.parliament. uk/historic-hansard/lords/2005/feb/02/department-for-work-and-pensi ons-five

Hansard (2005b) *Incapacity Benefit, Work and Pensions*, Written question, House of Commons Debate, 28 June, www.theyworkforyou.com/wrans/ ?id=2005-06-28a.7993.h

Hansard (2006) *Child Poverty*, Written answer, House of Commons Debate, 10 July, Vol 448, col 1575WA, https://hansard.parliament.uk/Commons/ 2006-07-10/debates/06071128000026/ChildPoverty?highlight=new%20d eal%20partners#contribution-06071128000423

Hansard (2009a) *Jobseeker's Allowance, Work and Pensions*, Written answer, House of Commons, 2 April, Vol 490, https://hansard.par liament.uk/Commons/2009-04-02/debates/09040272000026/Jobsee ker%E2%80%99SAllowance

Hansard (2009b) *Unemployment, Work and Pensions*, Oral answers to questions, House of Commons Debate, 7 December, Vol 502: col 15, https://hans ard.parliament.uk/Commons/2009-12-07/debates/09120712000024/ Unemployment

Hansard (2011a) *Social Security Benefits Uprating*, Written statements, House of Commons, Work and Pensions, 12 December, Vol 537, Col 72WS, https://hansard.parliament.uk/commons/2011-12-12/debates/111212 3000019/SocialSecurityBenefitsUprating

Hansard (2011b) *Universal Credit, Work and Pensions*, Oral answers to questions, 28 March, Vol 526, Col 3, https://hansard.parliament.uk/Comm ons/2011-03-28/debates/1103288000006/WorkAndPensions

Hansard (2012) *Work Experience*, debated on March, Westminster Hall, Vol 542, Col WH25–49, https://hansard.parliament.uk/Commons/2012-0313/debates/12031353000001/WorkExperience

Hansard (2023) *Universal Credit Administrative Earnings Threshold Level*, Written statements, House of Commons, Work and Pensions, 30 January, Vol 727: HCWS530, https://hansard.parliament.uk/commons/2023-01-30/deba tes/2301309000011/UniversalCreditAdministrativeEarningsThresholdLevel

Harding, R. (2017) 'Key findings', in E. Clery, J. Curtice and R. Harding (eds) *British Social Attitudes: The 34th Report*, London: NatCen Social Research, pp 1–12, www.bsa.natcen.ac.uk/latest-report/british-social-attitudes-34/key-findings/context.aspx

Harris, N. (1988) 'Raising the minimum age of entitlement to Income Support: Social Security Act 1988', *Journal of Law and Society*, 15(2): 201–15.

Harris, N. (2008) 'From unemployment to active job-seeking: changes and continuities in social security law in the UK', in S. Stendahl, T. Erhag and S. Devetzi (eds) *A European Work-First Welfare State*, Göteborg: Centre for European Research at Göteborg University, pp 49–77, https://gupea.ub.gu. se/bitstream/2077/20227/1/gupea_2077_20227_1.pdf

Harris, N. and Rahilly, S. (2011) 'Extra capacity in the labour market?: ESA and the activation of the sick and disabled in the UK', in S. Devetzi and S. Stendahl (eds) *Too Sick to Work? Social Security Reforms in Europe for Persons with Reduced Earnings Capacity*, Alphen aan den rijn: Kluwer Law International, pp 43–76.

Harris, N., Fitzpatrick, C., Meers, J. and Simpson, M. (2020) 'Coronavirus and social security entitlement in the UK', *Journal of Social Security Law*, 27(2): 55–84.

Harrison, B. and Sum, A. (1979) 'The theory of dual or segmented labour markets', *Journal of Economic Issues*, 13(3): 687–706.

Harrison, E. and Scott, J. (2020) 'Class and stratification', in Payne, G. Harrison, E. (eds) *Social Divisions: Inequality and Diversity in Britain* (4th edn), Bristol: Policy Press, pp 19–50.

Harper, K. (1988) 'DHSS youth training scheme deferred after union protest', *The Guardian*, 18 March, Guardian Newspapers.

Hasluck, C. (2000) *The New Deal for the Long-term Unemployed: A Summary of Progress*, Working Age and Employment Reports 1998–2004, No. 49, Department for Work and Pensions, https://webarchive.nationalarchives. gov.uk/ukgwa/20100208134427/http://research.dwp.gov.uk/asd/asd5/ wae-index.asp

Hasluck, C. (2002) *The Re-Imagined New Deal 25 Plus: A Summary of Recent Evaluation Evidence*, Working Age and Employment Reports 1998–2004, No. 137, Department for Work and Pensions, https://webarchive.natio nalarchives.gov.uk/ukgwa/20100208134427/http://research.dwp.gov.uk/ asd/asd5/wae-index.asp

Hasluck, C. and Green, A.E. (2007) *What Works for Whom? A Review of Evidence and Meta-Analysis for the Department for Work and Pensions*, Research Report No. 407, Department for Work and Pensions, Corporate Document Services.

Hasluck, C., Elias, P. and Green, A. (2003) *The Wider Labour Market Impact of Employment Zones*, Working Age and Employment Reports 1998–2004, No. 175, Department for Work and Pensions, https://webarchive.natio nalarchives.gov.uk/ukgwa/20100208143429mp_/http://research.dwp.gov. uk/asd/asd5/working_age/wa2003/175rep.pdf

Hassle (1992) Bulletin of the National Claimants Federation, No. 16, June, source – Autonomous Centre Edinburgh, Edinburgh.

Hatfield, I. (2015) *Self-Employment in Europe*, Report, Institute for Public Policy Research, http://www.ippr.org/files/publications/pdf/self-emp loyment-Europe_Jan2015.pdf?noredirect=1

Haux, T. (2012) 'Awaiting lone parents: an evidence-based policy appraisal of welfare to work reform in Britain', *Social Policy and Society*, 11(1): 1–14.

Healey, D. (1975) *Attack on Inflation*, col 51, House of Commons Debate, 21 July 1975, vol 896, cc46–174, Hansard, http://hansard.millbanksyst ems.com/commons/1975/jul/21/attack-on-inflation

Hick, R. and Murphy, M. (2021) 'Common shock, different paths? Comparing social policy responses to COVID-19 in the UK and Ireland', *Social Policy and Administration*, 55(2): 312–25.

HM Government (2010) *Fiscal Responsibility Act 2010*, www.legislation.gov. uk/ukpga/2010/3/enacted

HM Revenue and Customs (2012) *Child and Working Tax Credits – Finalised Annual Awards: 2010–11*, https://assets.publishing.service.gov.uk/governm ent/uploads/system/uploads/attachment_data/file/634342/Main_tables_ _1112_-_Final_.pdf

HM Revenue and Customs (2021a) *Self-Employment Income Support Scheme (SEISS) Statistics: December 2021*, www.gov.uk/government/statistics/self-employment-income-support-scheme-statistics-december-2021

HM Revenue and Customs (2021b) *Self-Employment Income Support Scheme (SEISS) Statistics: December 2021 – Data Tables*, www.gov.uk/governm ent/statistics/self-employment-income-support-scheme-statistics-decem ber-2021

HM Revenue and Customs (2021c) *CJRS Statistics 16 December 2021 – Extension 2 Reference Tables*, www.gov.uk/government/statistics/coronavi rus-job-retention-scheme-statistics-16-december-2021

HM Revenue and Customs (2021d) *Changes to the Coronavirus Job Retention Scheme from July 2021*, Policy Paper, updated 3 March, https://www.gov. uk/government/publications/changes-to-the-coronavirus-job-retention-scheme/changes-to-the-coronavirus-job-retention-scheme

HM Treasury (2009) *Budget 2009: Building Britain's Future*, HC 407, London: The Stationery Office.

HM Treasury (2002) *2002 Spending Review: Public Service Agreements*, https:// webarchive.nationalarchives.gov.uk/ukgwa/20091204142025/http:// www.hm-treasury.gov.uk/spend_sr02_psaindex.htm

HM Treasury/Department for Work and Pensions (2003) *Full Employment in Every Region*, https://webarchive.nationalarchives.gov.uk/ukgwa/200802 05213835mp_/http://www.hm-treasury.gov.uk/media/1/7/employm ent_372.pdf

HM Treasury (2010a) *Spending Review 2010*, Cm 7942, HM Stationery Office, www.gov.uk/government/publications/spending-review-2010

HM Treasury (2010b) *Budget 2010*, HC 61, June, HM Stationery Office, www.gov.uk/government/publications/budget-june-2010

HM Treasury (2011) *Charter for Budget Responsibility: Presented to Parliament Pursuant to Section 1 of the Budget Responsibility and National Audit Act 2011*, April, https://obr.uk/docs/dlm_uploads/charter_budget_responsibility040411.pdf

HM Treasury (2012) *Budget 2012*, HC114, HM Stationery Office, www. gov.uk/government/publications/budget-2014-documents

HM Treasury (2014) *Budget* 2014, HC 1104, March, HM Stationery Office, https://www.gov.uk/government/publications/budget-2014-documents

HM Treasury (2015a) *Summer Budget*, HC 264 July, HM Stationery Office, www.gov.uk/government/publications/summer-budget-2015

HM Treasury (2015b) *Spending Review and Autumn Statement*, CM9162, HM Stationery Office, https://www.gov.uk/government/publications/ spending-review-and-autumn-statement-2015-documents

HM Treasury (2017) *Charter for Budget Responsibility: autumn 2016 update*, January, https://www.gov.uk/government/publications/charter-for-bud get-responsibility-autumn-2016-update

HM Treasury (2020) *A Plan for Jobs 2020*, CP 261, www.gov.uk/governm ent/publications/a-plan-for-jobs-documents

HM Treasury (2021) *Plan for Jobs: Progress Update*, 13 September, www.gov. uk/government/publications/plan-for-jobs-progress-update

HM Treasury (2022) 'The Growth Plan 2022', speech by Chancellor of the Exchequer, Kwasi Kwarteng MP, 23 September, www.gov.uk/governm ent/speeches/the-growth-plan-2022-speech

HM Treasury (2023) *Spring Budget 2023*, HC 1183, 15 March, www.gov. uk/government/publications/spring-budget-2023

Hobson, F. (2020) *The Aims of Ten Years of Welfare Reform (2010–2020)*, Briefing Paper 9090, House of Commons Library, https://researchbriefi ngs.files.parliament.uk/documents/CBP-9090/CBP-9090.pdf

Hobson, F., Kennedy, S. and Mackley, A. (2022) *How Benefit Levels Are Set*, Research Briefing CBP9498, House of Commons Library, https://resear chbriefings.files.parliament.uk/documents/CBP-9498/CBP-9498.pdf

Hodkinson, P. and Sparker, A. (1994) 'The myth of the market: the negotiation of training in a youth credits pilot scheme', *British Journal of Education and Work*, 7(3): 5–19.

Holland, G. (1981) 'A progress report and statement on policy on youth unemployment, long-term adult unemployment', *Industrial and Commercial Training*, 13(9): 292–6.

Holloway, J. (1995) 'From scream of refusal to scream of power: the centrality of work', in W. Bonefeld, R. Gunn, J. Holloway and K. Psychopedis (eds) *Open Marxism: Emancipating Marx*, Vol 3, pp 155–81, https://libcom.org/ library/open-marxism-volume-3-emancipating-marx

Holloway, J. (2010) 'Cracks and the crisis of abstract labour', *Antipode*, 42(4): 909–23.

Holmes, M. (1985) *The First Thatcher Government 1979–1983*, Brighton: Wheatsheaf Books.

Hopkin, J. (2020) *Anti-System Politics: The Crisis of Market Liberalism in Rich Democracies*, New York: Oxford University Press.

Hoynes, H. and Blundell, R. (2001) *Has In-Work Benefit Reform Helped the Labour Market?* NBER Working Paper No. 8546, www.nber.org/papers/ w8546, DOI: 10.3386/w8546

Huby, M. and Dix, G. (1992) *Evaluating the Social Fund*, Research Report No. 9, Department of Social Security, HMSO, London.

Huby, M and Whyley, C. (1996) 'Take-up and the social fund: applying the concept of take-up to a discretionary benefit', *Journal of Social Policy*, 25(1): 1–18.

Hunt, J. (2023) 'Mansion House', speech 20 July, www.gov.uk/governm ent/speeches/chancellor-jeremy-hunts-mansion-house-speech

Huws, U. (2014) *Labour in the Digital Economy*, New York: Monthly Review Press.

Ingold, J. and Stuart, M. (2015) 'The demand-side of active labour market policies: a regional study of employer engagement in the work programme', *Journal of Social Policy*, 44(3): 443–62.

Inland Revenue (2003a) *Working Families' Tax Credit Statistics*, Summary Statistics, February, https://webarchive.nationalarchives.gov.uk/ukgwa/20110202195410/http://www.hmrc.gov.uk/wftctables/index.htm

Inland Revenue (2003b) *Disabled Person's Tax Credit Statistics*, Summary Statistics, January, https://webarchive.nationalarchives.gov.uk/ukgwa/20110202181737/http://www.hmrc.gov.uk/dptctables/index.htm

James, O. (2003) *The Executive Agency Revolution in Whitehall*, Basingstoke: Palgrave Macmillan.

Jamil Jonna, R. and Bellamy Foster, J. (2016) 'Marx's theory of working class precariousness – and its relevance today', *Alternate Routes – A Journal of Critical Social Research*, 27: 21–45.

Jeffrey, B. Devine, D. and Thomas, P. (2018) '"There's nothing": unemployment, attitudes to work and punitive welfare reform in post-crash Salford', *Sociological Research Online*, 23(3): 795–811.

Jenkins, J. (2010) 'The labour market in the 1980s, 1990s and 2008–09 recessions', *Economic and Labour Market Review*, 4(8): 29–36, Office for National Statistics.

Jessop, B. (2002a) *The Future of the Capitalist State*, Cambridge: Polity Press.

Jessop, B. (2002b) 'The changing governance of welfare: recent trends in its primary functions, scale, and modes of coordination', *Social Policy and Administration*, 33(4): 348–59.

Jessop, B. (2015) 'Margaret Thatcher and Thatcherism: dead but not buried', *British Politics*, 10(1): 16–30.

Johns, S. (2015) *The UK School Students' Strike, 1985*, Libcom, https://libcom.org/history/uk-school-students-strike-1985-steven-johns

Johnson, M., Koukiadaki, A. and Grimshaw, D. (2019) 'The Living Wage in the UK: testing the limits of soft regulation?', *Transfer*, 2 (3): 319–33.

Johnson, S. (2003) *Jobcentre Plus Performance Targets: A Review of the Evidence, 2000–2002*, Working Age and Employment Reports 1998–2004, No. 153, Department for Work and Pensions, https://webarchive.nationalarchives.gov.uk/ukgwa/20100208134427/http://research.dwp.gov.uk/asd/asd5/wae-index.asp

Jones, C. and Novak, T. (1999) *Poverty, Welfare and the Disciplinary State*, Routledge: London.

Jones, K. and Kumar, A. (2022) *Idleness – The Five Giants: A New Beveridge Report*, Newcastle-Upon-Tyne: Agenda Publishing.

Jones, K., Wright, S. and Scullion, L. (2024) 'The impact of welfare conditionality on experiences of job quality', *Work, Employment and Society*, 1–22.

Jones, M. (1996) 'Full steam ahead to a workfare state? Analysing the UK Employment Department's abolition', *Policy and Politics*, 24(2): 137–57.

Jones, M. (1999) *New Institutional Spaces: TECs and the Remaking of Economic Governance*, London: Jessica Kingsley Publishers.

Jordan, B. (1973) *Paupers: The Making of a New Claiming Class*, London: Routledge and Kegan Paul Books.

Joseph, K. (1980) 'Conditions for fuller employment', speech to the Bow Group, August 1978, Royal Commonwealth Society, Centre for Policy Studies, London.

Kalecki, M. (1943) 'Political aspects of full employment', *Political Quarterly*, 14(4): 322–30.

Karagiannaki, E. (2007) 'Exploring the effects of integrated benefit systems and active labour market policies: evidence from Jobcentre Plus in the UK', *Journal of Social Policy*, 36(2): 177–95.

Keep, M. (2022) *The Welfare Cap*, Research Briefing SN06852, House of Commons Library, https://researchbriefings.files.parliament.uk/docume nts/SN06852/SN06852.pdf

Kelleher, J., Youll, P., Nelson, A., Hadjivassiliou, K., Lyons, C. and Hills, J. (2002) *Delivering a Work-Focused Service: Final Findings from ONE Case Studies and Staff Research*, Research Report No. 166, Leeds: Department for Work and Pensions, CDS.

Kennedy, S., Murphy, C., Keen R. and Bate, A. (2017) *Abolition of the ESA Work-Related Activity Component*, Research Briefing CBP 7649, House of Commons Library, https://commonslibrary.parliament.uk/research-briefi ngs/cbp-7649/

King, D. (1993) 'The Conservatives and training policy: from a tripartite to a neo-liberal regime', *Political Studies*, 41(2): 214–35.

King, D. (1995) *Actively Seeking Work: The Politics of Unemployment and Welfare Policy in the United States and Great Britain*, Chicago, IL: University of Chicago Press.

King, D. (1997) 'Employers, training policy, and the tenacity of voluntarism in Britain', *Twentieth Century British History*, 8(3): 383–411.

King, M. (2011) *Speech given by Governor of the Bank of England at the Lord Mayor's Banquet for Bankers and Merchants of the City of London at the Mansion House*, Bank of England, 15 June, www.bankofengland.co.uk/spe ech/2011/speech-by-mervyn-king-at-the-lord-mayors-banquet-at-mans ion-house

Knotz, C. and Nelson, M. (2018) *United Kingdom Country Summary*, The Comparative Unemployment and Benefits Conditions and Sanctions dataset, 10 July, https://cknotz.github.io/benefitconditionalitydata/

Koch, M. (2006) *Roads to Post-Fordism: Labour Markets and Social Structures in Europe*, Aldershot: Ashgate.

Koslowski, A. and McLean, C. (2015) 'Variation in the prevalence of temporary contracts across occupations in the UK', in W. Eichhorst and P. Marx (eds) *Non-Standard Employment in Post-Industrial Labour Markets: An Occupational Perspective*, Cheltenham: Edward Elgar, pp 217–39.

Labour Party (1975) 'Monday afternoon—incomes and jobs', *Report of the Seventy Fourth Annual Conference of the Labour Party, Blackpool 1975*, London: The Labour Party.

Labour Party (1997) *New Labour because Britain deserves better*, Labour Party General Election Manifesto, https://web.archive.org/web/20110927045 458/http://www.politicsresources.net/area/uk/man/lab97.htm

Lasko, R. (1975) 'The payment of supplementary benefit for strikers' dependants: misconception and misrepresentation', *Modern Law Review*, 38(1): 31–8.

Lavery, S. (2019) *British Capitalism after the Crisis*, Cham: Palgrave Macmillan.

Lawson, N. (1980) *The New Conservatism (Lecture to the Bow Group)*, 4 August, Margaret Thatcher Foundation, www.margaretthatcher.org/document/109505

Leary, K., Maguire, K. and Gallacher, I. (2022) *Coronavirus Job Retention Scheme: Employer Qualitative Research*, HM Revenue and Customs Research Report: 632, HMRC, www.gov.uk/government/publications/coronavi rus-job-retention-scheme-qualitative-research-with-employers

Lee, S. (2023) 'Two steps backwards: UK economic policy in the ages of austerity and Brexit, 2015–2020', in M. Beech and S. Lee (eds) *Conservative Governments in the Age of Brexit*, Cham: Palgrave Macmillan, pp 107–24.

Lewis, J. (2001) 'The decline of the male breadwinner model', *Social Politics: International Studies in Gender, State and Society*, 8(2): 153–69.

Lindblom, C. (1977) *Politics and Markets*, New York: Basic Books.

Lindley, R. (1987) 'British employment measures: policy and evidence', *Labour*, 1(2): 3–27.

Lindsay, C. (2002) 'Long-term unemployment and the "employability gap": priorities for renewing Britain's New Deal', *Journal of European Industrial Training*, 26(9): 411–19.

Lindsay, C. and Pascual, A.S. (2009) 'New perspectives on employability and labour market policy: reflecting on key issues', *Environment and Planning C: Government and Policy*, 27(1): 951–7.

Lister, R. (1991) 'Social security in the 1980s', *Social Policy and Administration*, 25(1): 91–107.

Lopez, T.M. (2014) *The Winter of Discontent: Myth, Memory and History*, Liverpool: Liverpool University Press.

Lourie, J. (1997a) *Employment and Training for the Unemployed*, House of Commons Library, Research Paper 97/98, 8 August, https://researchbr iefings.files.parliament.uk/documents/RP97-98/RP97-98.pdf

Lourie, J. (1997b) *Training and Enterprise Councils*, House of Commons Research Paper 97/48, House of Common Library.

MacDonald, R. (1991) 'Risky business? Youth in enterprise culture', *Journal of Education Policy*, 6(3): 255–69.

MacDonald, R. (1996) 'Welfare dependency, the enterprise culture and self-employed survival', *Work, Employment and Society*, 10(3): 431–47.

MacDonald, R. (2008) 'Disconnected youth? Social exclusion, the 'underclass' and economic marginality', *Social Work and Society*, 6(2): 236–48.

MacDonald, R. and Coffield, F. (1993) 'Young people and training credits: an early exploration', *British Journal of Education and Work*, 6(1): 5–21.

Machin, R. (2021) 'COVID-19 and the temporary transformation of the UK social security system', *Critical Social Policy*, 41(4): 651–62.

Machin, S. and Manning, A. (1994) 'The effects of minimum wages on wage dispersion and employment: evidence from the U.K. Wages Councils', *Industrial and Labour Relations Review*, 47(2): 319–29.

MacLeavy, J. (2007) 'Engendering New Labour's workfarist regime: exploring the intersection of welfare state restructuring and labour market policies in the UK', *Gender, Place and Culture*, 14(6): 721–43.

Macpherson, N. (2014) 'The Treasury view: a testament of experience', speech by the Permanent Secretary to the Treasury to the Mile End Group, 17 January, www.gov.uk/government/speeches/speech-by-the-perman ent-secretary-to-the-treasury-the-treasury-view-a-testament-of-experience

Malik, S. (2012) 'Tesco asks government to change flagship jobless scheme', *The Guardian*, 18 February, https://www.theguardian.com/business/2012/ feb/18/tesco-jobless-scheme-work-experience?CMP=share_btn_url

Mandelson, P. (2002) *The Blair Revolution Revisited*, Westminster: Politico's Publishing.

Manning, A. (2009) 'You can't always get what you want: the impact of the UK Jobseeker's Allowance', *Labour Economics*, (16): 239–50.

Manpower Services Commission (1977) *Towards a Comprehensive Manpower Policy*, London: MSC.

Manpower Services Commission (1979) *Review of the First Year of Special Programmes*, London: MSC.

Manpower Services Commission (1980) *Annual Report 1979–80*, London: MSC.

Manpower Services Commission (1981a) *Manpower Review 1981*, London: MSC.

Manpower Services Commission (1981b) *Review of Services for the Unemployed*, London: MSC.

Manpower Services Commission (1983) 'Community programme', *Industrial and Commercial Training*, 15(6): 184–8.

Marren, B. (2016) *We Shall Not Be Moved: How Liverpool's Working Class Fought Redundancies, Closures and Cuts in the Age of Thatcher*, Manchester: Manchester University Press.

Marsland, J. (2018) 'We'll help ourselves: the English working-class struggle to remake itself, ca. 1968–1985', PhD thesis, State University of New York, www.proquest.com/docview/2056874821?pq-origsite=gscholarandfromopenview=true

Martin, G. (1998) 'Generational differences amongst New Age Travellers', *Sociological Review*, 46(4): 735–56.

Martin, G. (2002) 'New Age Travellers: uproarious or uprooted?', *Sociology*, 36(3): 723–35.

Marx, K. (2004) *Capital: A Critique of Political Economy*, Vol 1 (Kindle version), translated by B. Fowkes, Penguin Classics.

Marx, K. (2013) *Capital: A Critique of Political Economy*, Vol 1, Ware: Wordsworth Editions Ltd.

Marx, K. and Engels, F. (1985) *The Communist Manifesto*, London: Penguin Books Ltd.

Mason, R. (2016) 'Theresa May hires former Blair policy boss to review workers' rights', *The Guardian*, 1 October, www.theguardian.com/money/2016/oct/01/theresa-may-hires-former-tony-blair-policy-boss-to-review-workers-rights

Mason, R., Stewart H. and Asthana A. (2016) 'Iain Duncan Smith resigns from cabinet over disability cuts', *The Guardian*, 19 March, www.theguardian.com/politics/2016/mar/18/iain-duncan-smith-resigns-from-cabinet-over-disability-cuts

Matthews, D. (2018) 'The working-class struggle for welfare in Britain', *Monthly Review*, 69(9): 33–45.

Mau, S. (2023) *Mute Compulsion: A Marxist Theory of the Economic Power of Capital* (e-book edn), London: Verso.

McCollum, D. (2011) '"An acceptance that it's just your lot, I suppose": reflections on turbulent transitions between work and welfare', *People, Place and Policy Online*, 5(3): 149–60.

McCollum, D. (2012) 'Towards unsustainable employment? Exploring policy responses to work–welfare cycling', *Policy Studies*, 33(3): 215–30.

McGann, M. (2023) *The Marketisation of Welfare-to-Work in Ireland: Governing Activation at the Street-Level*, Bristol: Policy Press.

McLaughlin, E. (1991) 'Work and welfare benefits: social security, employment and unemployment in the 1990s', *Journal of Social Policy*, 20(4): 485–508.

McQuaid, R. and Lindsay, C. (2002) 'The "employability gap": long-term unemployment and barriers to work in buoyant labour markets', *Environment and Planning C: Government and Policy*, 20(4): 613–28.

McQuaid, R.W. and Lindsay, C. (2005) 'The concept of employability', *Urban Studies*, 42(2): 197–219.

McTier, A. and McGregor, A. (2018) 'Influence of work–welfare cycling and labour market segmentation on employment histories of young long-term unemployed people', *Work, Employment and Society*, 32(1): 20–37.

Mesher, J. (1981) 'The 1980 social security legislation: the great welfare state chainsaw massacre?', *British Journal of Law and Society*, 8(1): 119–27.

Metcalf, D. (1982) *Alternatives to Unemployment: Special Employment Measures in Britain*, London: Policy Studies Institute/Anglo-German Foundation.

Metcalf, D. (1999) 'The British National Minimum Wage', *British Journal of Industrial Relations*, 37(2): 171–201.

Metcalf, D. (2008) 'Why has the British National Minimum Wage had little or no impact on employment?', *Journal of Industrial Relations*, 50(3): 489–512.

Millar, J. (1989) 'Social security, equality and women in the UK', *Policy and Politics*, 17(4): 311–19.

Millar, J. (2000) 'Lone parents and the New Deal', *Policy Studies*, 21(4): 333–45.

Millar, J. (2003) 'The art of persuasion? The British New Deal for lone parents', in R. Walker and M. Wiseman (eds) *The Welfare We Want? The British Challenge for American Reform*, Bristol: Policy Press, pp 115–42.

Millar, J. (2009) 'Tax credits', in J. Millar (ed) *Understanding Social Security: Issues for Policy and Practice* (2nd edn), Bristol: Policy Press, pp 233–51.

Millar, J. and Bennett, F. (2017) 'Universal Credit: assumptions, contradictions and virtual reality', *Social Policy and Society*, 16(2): 169–82.

Minister of State for Welfare Reform (2011a) *Welfare reform and flexible working*, Speech by Lord Freud, Top Employers for Working Families 2011 Benchmark and Awards Ceremony, 25 September, Department for Work and Pensions, https://www.gov.uk/government/speeches/welfare-reform-and-flexible-working

Minister of State for Welfare Reform (2011b) *The Welfare revolution*, Speech by Lord Freud, 6 December, Edinburgh, Department for Work and Pensions, https://www.gov.uk/government/speeches/the-welfare-revolution

Mizen, P. (1994) 'In and against the training state', *Capital and Class*, 18(2): 99–121.

Moon, J. (1983) 'Policy change in direct government responses to UK unemployment', *Journal of Public Policy*, 3(3): 301–30.

Moon, J. and Richardson, J.J. (1985) *Unemployment in the UK*, Aldershot: Gower Publishing.

Moreira, A. and Hick, R. (2021) 'COVID-19, the Great Recession and social policy: Is this time different?', *Social Policy and Administration*, 55(2): 261–79.

Morel, N. (2015) 'Servant in the knowledge-based economy? The political economy of domestic services in Europe', *Social Politics*, 22(2): 170–92.

Morgan, B. (2008) *New Deal Statistics*, Standard Note, SN/EP/4867, House of Commons Library.

Morgan, B. (2009) *Flexible New Deal*, Standard Note, SN/EP/4849, House of Commons Library.

Morris, R. (2020) 'Disabled people and employment: A UK perspective', in N. Watson and S. Vehmas (eds) *Routledge Handbook of Disability Studies* (2nd edn), Abingdon: Routledge, pp 250–64.

Morrison, J. (2019) *Scroungers: Moral Panics and Media Myths*, London: Zed Books.

Morrison, J. (2022) *The Left Behind: Reimagining Britain's Socially Excluded*, London: Pluto Press.

MSS.292/PUB/4/3/240 *Unemployed Workers' Centres: A Directory of Centres Recognised by the TUC*, Economic and Social Affairs Department, March 2000. Modern Records Centre, University of Warwick.

Mukherjee, S. (1974) *There's Work to Be Done: Unemployment and Manpower Policies*, London: Manpower Services Commission, HM Stationery Office.

Mulheirn, I. and Menne, V. (2008) *The Flexible New Deal: Making it Work*, London: The Social Market Foundation.

Murphy, L. (2023) 'Reassessing the Work Capability Assessment', *Spotlight*, Resolution Foundation, 6 September, www.resolutionfoundation.org/publications/reassessing-the-work-capability-assessment/

Murphy, P.M. (2016) 'Low road or high road? The post-crisis trajectory of Irish activation', *Critical Social Policy*, 36(3): 432–52.

Muysken, J. and Mitchell, W.F. (2009) *Full Employment Abandoned: Shifting Sands and Policy Failures* (METEOR Research Memorandum; No. 006), Maastricht: METEOR, Maastricht University School of Business and Economics.

National Audit Office (1985) *Department of Employment and Manpower Services Commission: Vocational Education and Training for Young People*, Report by the Comptroller and Auditor General, 497, 9 July, House of Commons, Parliamentary Papers Online.

National Audit Office (1987) *Department of Employment and Manpower Service Commission: Adult Training Strategy*, Report by the Comptroller and Auditor General, 23 January, 149, London: HMSO.

National Audit Office (2002) *The New Deal for Young People*, Report by the Comptroller and Auditor General, HC639, Session 2001–02, www.nao.org.uk/report/the-new-deal-for-young-people/

National Audit Office (2007) *Sustainable Employment: Supporting People to Stay in Work and Advance*, HC 32 Session 2007–2008, Comptroller and Auditor General, London: The Stationery Office.

National Audit Office (2010a) *Department for Work and Pensions – Support to Incapacity Benefits claimants through Pathways to Work*, HC 21 Session 2010–2011, Comptroller and Auditor General, London: The Stationery Office.

National Audit Office (2010b) *The Pathways to Work Prime Contractor Delivery Model*, London: NAO.

National Audit Office (2013) *Responding to Change in Jobcentres*, HC 965, Session 2012–13, London: The Stationery Office.

National Audit Office (2014) *The Work Programme*, HC 266 Session 2014–15, London: NAO.

National Audit Office (2021) *Employment Support: The Kickstart Scheme*, Session 2021–22, HC801, www.nao.org.uk/wp-content/uploads/2021/11/Employment-support-the-Kickstart-Scheme.pdf

National Audit Office (2022) *The Restart Scheme for Long-Term Unemployed People*, Session 2022–23 HC 936, www.nao.org.uk/reports/restart-scheme-for-long-term-unemployed-people/

Navarro, V. (1991) 'Production and the welfare state: the political context of reforms', *International Journal of Health Services*, 21(4): 585–614.

Negri, A. (1988) *Revolution Retrieved: Writings on Marx, Keynes, Capitalist Crisis and New Social Subjects 1967–83*, London: Red Notes.

Negri, A. (1991) *Marx beyond Marx: Lessons on the Grundrisse*, London: Autonomedia/Pluto Press.

Neilson, D. and Stubbs, T. (2011) 'Relative surplus population and uneven development in the neo-liberal era: theory and empirical application', *Capital and Class*, 35(3): 435–53.

Nickell, S. (2001) 'Has UK labour market performance changed?', speech given at the Society of Business Economists, 16 May, www.bankofengland.co.uk/speech/2001/has-uk-labour-market-performance-changed

NOMIS (2021) TS062 – NS-SeC, Census 2021 dataset, https://www.nomisweb.co.uk/datasets/c2021ts062

Norfield, T. (2016) *The City: London and the Global Power of Finance*, London: Verso.

Normington, D., Brodie, H. and Munro, J. (1986) *Value for Money in the Community Programme*, Department of Employment/Manpower Services Commission.

Notes from Below (2023) 'Chapter 3: an overview of work', *The Class Composition Project*, Issue 16, https://notesfrombelow.org/issue/class-composition-project

Nottinghamshire Jobs not JSA (1996) 'Three Strikes ...', Issue 4, September 1996, The Sparrows Nest Archive and Library, https://thesparrowsnest.org.uk/

Novak, T. (1997) 'Hounding delinquents: the introduction of the Jobseeker's Allowance', *Critical Social Policy*, 17(50): 99–109.

Nunn, A. (2016) 'The production and reproduction of inequality in the UK in times of austerity', *British Politics*, 11(4): 469–87.

Nunn, A. and Devins, D. (2012) *Process Evaluation of the Jobcentre Plus Performance Management Framework*, Research Report No. 801, Department for Work and Pensions, www.gov.uk/government/publications/process-evaluation-of-the-jobcentre-plus-performance-management-framework-rr801

Nunn, A. and Morgan, J. (2020) 'The political economy of public employment services: measurement and disempowered empowerment?', *Policy Studies*, 41(1): 42–62.

Oakley, M. (2014) *Independent Review of the Operation of Jobseeker's Allowance Sanctions Validated by the Jobseekers Act 2013*, Department for Work and Pensions, www.gov.uk/government/publications/jobseekers-allowance-sanctions-independent-review

Offe, C. (1984) 'Social policy and the theory of the state', in C. Offe and J. Keane (eds) *Contradictions of the Welfare State*, London: Hutchinson, pp 88–118.

Office for Budget Responsibility (2023) *Fiscal Risks and Sustainability*, CP 870, https://obr.uk/frs/fiscal-risks-and-sustainability-july-2023/

Office for National Statistics (ONS) (1998) *Social Trends 28*, London: ONS.

Office for National Statistics (2005) *Labour Market Trends*, December, 113(12): 465–516.

Office for National Statistics (2015) *Low Pay: April 2015*, www.ons.gov.uk/employmentandlabourmarket/peopleinwork/earningsandworkinghours/bulletins/lowpay/april2015

Office for National Statistics (2016a) *The Debt and Deficit of the UK Public Sector Explained*, www.ons.gov.uk/economy/governmentpublicsectorandtaxes/publicsectorfinance/articles/thedebtanddeficitoftheukpublicsectorexplained/2016-03-16

Office for National Statistics (2016b) *Public Sector Finances, UK: January 2016*, Statistical Bulletin, www.ons.gov.uk/economy/governmentpublicsectorandtaxes/publicsectorfinance/bulletins/publicsectorfinances/january2016

Office for National Statistics (2016c) *Trends in Self-Employment in the UK: 2001–2015*, www.ons.gov.uk/releases/trendsinselfemployment [last accessed 21 January 2020].

Office for National Statistics (2017) *Economic Review: October 2017*, released 19 October, www.ons.gov.uk/releases/ukeconomicreviewoctober2017 [last accessed 21 January 2020].

Office for National Statistics (2018a) *Families and the Labour Market, England: 2018*, www.ons.gov.uk/employmentandlabourmarket/peopleinwork/employmentandemployeetypes/articles/familiesandthelabourmarketengland/2018

Office for National Statistics (2018b) *Low and High Pay in the UK: 2018*, www.ons.gov.uk/employmentandlabourmarket/peopleinwork/earningsandworkinghours/bulletins/lowandhighpayuk/2018 [last accessed 21 January 2020].

Office for National Statistics (2018c) *Trends in Self-Employment in the UK: Analysing the Characteristics, Income and Wealth of the Self-Employed,* www.ons.gov.uk/employmentandlabourmarket/peopleinwork/employm entandemployeetypes/articles/trendsinselfemploymentintheuk/2018-02-07 [last accessed 21 January 2020].

Office for National Statistics (2018d) *A03 SA: Employment, Unemployment and Economic Inactivity for Men Aged from 16 to 64 and Women Aged from 16 to 59 (Seasonally Adjusted),* www.ons.gov.uk/employmentandlabourmar ket/peopleinwork/employmentandemployeetypes/datasets/employmen tunemploymentandeconomicinactivityformenagedfrom16to64andwome nagedfrom16to59seasonallyadjusteda03sa/current

Office for National Statistics (2018e) *UNEM02 All and Long-Term Unemployment Rates by Occupation of Last Job People (Not Seasonally Adjusted),* 15 May, www.ons.gov.uk/employmentandlabourmarket/peoplenotinw ork/unemployment/datasets/unemploymentbypreviousoccupationune m02/current

Office for National Statistics (2019a) *A Guide to Labour Market Statistics: Explanation of the Major Concepts that Exist Within the Labour Market and Their Relationship to Each Other,* www.ons.gov.uk/employmentandlabou rmarket/peopleinwork/employmentandemployeetypes/methodologies/ aguidetolabourmarketstatistics#unemployment

Office for National Statistics (2019b) *Disability and Employment, UK: 2019,* release date 2 December, www.ons.gov.uk/peoplepopulationandcommun ity/healthandsocialcare/disability/bulletins/disabilityandemploymen tuk/2019

Office for National Statistics (2019c) *Disability Pay Gaps in the UK: 2018,* release date 2 December, www.ons.gov.uk/peoplepopulationandcommun ity/healthandsocialcare/disability/articles/disabilitypaygapsintheuk/2018

Office for National Statistics (2019d) *Summary of Analysis: 2-digit Occupation at UK level by Sector, Industry, Age and Ethnicity,* Annual Population Survey April 2018 to March 2019, User Requested Data, 07/10/19, www.ons. gov.uk/aboutus/whatwedo/statistics/requestingstatistics/alladhocs?:uri= aboutus/whatwedo/statistics/requestingstatistics/alladhocsandsize=10an dsortBy=release_dateandpage=475

Office for National Statistics (2020) *RPI All Items: 1948 to 2020 Percentage Change over 12 Months,* Table 37, Consumer Price Inflation Tables Dataset, www.ons.gov.uk/economy/inflationandpriceindices/datasets/consume rpriceinflation

Office for National Statistics (2021a) *An Overview of Workers Who Were Furloughed in the UK: October 2021,* www.ons.gov.uk/employmentandl abourmarket/peopleinwork/employmentandemployeetypes/articles/ anoverviewofworkerswhowerefurloughedintheuk/october2021

Office for National Statistics (2021b) *Characteristics of People Who Have Ever Been Furloughed in the UK*, Data set 1 October, www.ons.gov.uk/employ mentandlabourmarket/peopleinwork/employmentandemployeetypes/ datasets/characteristicsofpeoplewhohavebeenfurloughedintheuk

Office for National Statistics (2022a) *Public Sector Employment, UK: September 2022*, released 13 December 2022, www.ons.gov.uk/employmentandlabou rmarket/peopleinwork/publicsectorpersonnel/datasets/publicsectoremplo ymentreferencetable

Office for National Statistics (2022b) *Labour Costs and Labour Income, UK: 2022*, Statistical bulletin, www.ons.gov.uk/economy/economicou tputandproductivity/productivitymeasures/bulletins/labourcostsandlab ourincomeuk/latest

Office for National Statistics (2022c) *Earnings and Hours Worked, Industry by Two-Digit SIC: ASHE Table 4*, 26 October, www.ons.gov.uk/employ mentandlabourmarket/peopleinwork/earningsandworkinghours/datasets/ industry2digitsicashetable4

Office for National Statistics (2022d) *UNEM01 SA: Unemployment by Age and Duration (Seasonally Adjusted), Dataset ID: UNEM01 SA*, www.ons.gov. uk/employmentandlabourmarket/peoplenotinwork/unemployment/datas ets/unemploymentbyageanddurationseasonallyadjustedunem01sa

Office for National Statistics (2023a) *A02 SA: Employment, Unemployment and Economic Inactivity for People Aged 16 and Over and Aged from 16 to 64 (Seasonally Adjusted)*, www.ons.gov.uk/employmentandlabourmarket/peopl einwork/employmentandemployeetypes/datasets/employmentunemploy mentandeconomicinactivityforpeopleaged16andoverandagedfrom16to64 seasonallyadjusteda02sa

Office for National Statistics (2023b) *Table EMP01: Full-time, Part-Time and Temporary Workers: People (Seasonally Adjusted)*, 15 August, www.ons. gov.uk/employmentandlabourmarket/peopleinwork/employmentandem ployeetypes/datasets/fulltimeparttimeandtemporaryworkersseasonallyadju stedemp01sa

Office for National Statistics (2023c) *EMP17: People in Employment on Zero Hours Contracts*, 15 August, www.ons.gov.uk/employmentandl abourmarket/peopleinwork/employmentandemployeetypes/datasets/ emp17peopleinemploymentonzerohourscontracts

Office for National Statistics (2023d) *Labour Disputes;uk;sic 07;total Working Days Lost;All Inds. and Services (000's)*, 15 August, www.ons.gov.uk/employ mentandlabourmarket/peopleinwork/employmentandemployeetypes/tim eseries/bbfw/lms

Office for National Statistics (2023e) *JOBS02: Workforce Jobs by Industry (Seasonally Adjusted)*, 12 December, www.ons.gov.uk/employmentandlabou rmarket/peopleinwork/employmentandemployeetypes/datasets/workfo rcejobsbyindustryjobs02

Office for National Statistics (2023f) *JOBS03: Employee Jobs by Industry (Not Seasonally Adjusted)*, 12 December 2023, www.ons.gov.uk/employment andlabourmarket/peopleinwork/employmentandemployeetypes/datasets/ employeejobsbyindustryjobs03

Office for National Statistics (2023g) *Table UNEM01: Unemployment by Age and Duration: People (Seasonally Adjusted)*, 12 September, www.ons.gov.uk/ employmentandlabourmarket/peoplenotinwork/unemployment/datasets/ unemploymentbyageanddurationseasonallyadjustedunem01sa

Office for National Statistics (2023h) *Average Weekly Earnings in Great Britain: July 2023*, www.ons.gov.uk/employmentandlabourmarket/peopl einwork/employmentandemployeetypes/bulletins/averageweeklyearning singreatbritain/july2023

Office for National Statistics (2023i) *Vacancies and Jobs in the UK: June 2023*, www.ons.gov.uk/employmentandlabourmarket/peopleinwork/employm entandemployeetypes/bulletins/jobsandvacanciesintheuk/june2023

Office for National Statistics (2023j) *CPI Annual Rate 00: All Items 2015= 100*, Consumer Price Inflation Time Series (MM23) dataset, 19 July, www. ons.gov.uk/economy/inflationandpriceindices/timeseries/d7g7/mm23

O'Grady, T. (2022) *The Transformation of British Welfare Policy: Politics, Discourse, and Public Opinion*, Oxford: Oxford University Press.

Oren, T. and Blyth, M. (2019) 'From big bang to big crash: the early origins of the UK's finance led growth model and the persistence of bad policy ideas', *New Political Economy*, 24(5): 605–22.

Organisation for Economic Cooperation and Development (n.d.) *Incidence of FTPT employment - common definition: Table H1 – Incidence and composition of part-time employment*, OECD.Stat, https://stats.oecd.org/Index.aspx?Data SetCode=FTPTC_I#

Orr, L.L., Bell S.H. and Lam, K. (2007) *Long-Term Impacts of the New Deal for Disabled People*, Research Report No. 432, Department for Work and Pensions, HMSO.

Osborne, G. (2010a) *Speech by the Chancellor of the Exchequer, Rt Hon George Osborne MP, on the OBR and spending announcements*, 17 May, www.gov. uk/government/speeches/speech-by-the-chancellor-of-the-exchequer- rt-hon-george-osborne-mp-on-the-obr-and-spending-announcements

Osborne, G. (2010b) 'A new economic model', in F. Capie and G.E. Wood (eds) (2012) *Policy Makers on Policy: The Mais Lectures* (2nd edn), Abingdon: Routledge, pp 209–20.

Osborne, G. (2014) *Speech by the Chancellor at the Start of an Important Week of Tax and Benefit Changes*, 31 March, Tilbury Port: HM Treasury, www. gov.uk/government/speeches/chancellor-speaks-on-tax-and-benefits

Paine, J. (1983) 'Community Programme – a battle lost?', *Unemployment Unit Bulletin*, November, No. 10: 1–8, London: Unemployment Unit.

Parker, G. (2024) 'Rishi Sunak pins hopes of revival in Tory fortunes on UK tax cuts', The *Financial Times*, 7 January, https://www.ft.com/content/0a6422f0-dc45-48bd-bc77-ec50ab83d52f

Parker, G. and Giles, C. (2023) 'UK ministers explore cutting working-age benefits in real terms – senior Conservatives say move would create space for tax cuts ahead of election', *The Financial Times*, 8 September, www.ft.com/content/87954077-da72-4977-aed7-ac264dafe9af

Parker, G., Payne, S. and Hughes, L. (2022) 'The inside story of Liz Truss's disastrous 44 days in office', *FT Magazine*, 9 December, www.ft.com/content/736a695d-61f6-4e84-a567-fb92ed2a3dca

Parkes, H. (2023) *The Sanctions Surge: Shining a Light on the Universal Credit Sanctions Regime*, Institute for Public Policy Research, www.ippr.org/research/publications/the-sanctions-surge

Partington, R. (2022a) 'The mini-budget that broke Britain – and Liz Truss', *The Guardian*, 20 October, www.theguardian.com/business/2022/oct/20/the-mini-budget-that-broke-britain-and-liz-truss

Partington, R. (2022b) 'Why OBR forecast is being held back until Kwarteng's next fiscal plan', *The Guardian*, 30 September, www.theguardian.com/business/2022/sep/30/why-obr-forecast-held-back-kwarteng-fiscal-plan

Pattaro, S., Bailey, N., Williams, E., Gibson, M., Wells, V., Tranmer, M. and Dibben, C. (2022) 'The impacts of benefit sanctions: a scoping review of the quantitative research evidence', *Journal of Social Policy*, 51(3): 611–53.

Payne, G. (2013) 'Models of contemporary social class: the Great British Class Survey', *Methodological Innovations Online*, 8(1): 3–17.

Payne, G. (2017) *The New Social Mobility: How the Politicians Got It Wrong*, Bristol: Policy Press.

Peck, J. (1996) *Workplace: The Social Regulation of Labor Markets*, New York: The Guilford Press.

Peck, J. (1999) 'New labourers? Making a new deal for the "workless class"', *Environment and Planning C: Politics and Space*, 17(3): 345–72.

Peck, J. (2001) *Workfare States*, New York: Guilford Press.

Peck, J. and Jones, M. (1995) 'Training and Enterprise Councils: Schumpeterian workfare state or what?', *Environment and Planning A*, 27(9): 1361–96.

Peck, J. and Theodore, N. (2000) '"Work first": workfare and the regulation of contingent labour markets', *Cambridge Journal of Economics*, 24(1): 119–38.

Peden, G.C. (1988) *Keynes, The Treasury and British Economic Policy*, London: Macmillan.

Phillipson, C., Vickerstaff, S. and Lain, D. (2016) 'Achieving fuller working lives: labour market and policy issues in the United Kingdom', *Australian Journal of Social Issues*, 51(2): 187–203.

Piggott, L. and Grover, C. (2009) 'Retrenching Incapacity Benefit: Employment and Support Allowance and paid work', *Social Policy and Society*, 8(2): 159–70.

Pimlott, D. (2010) 'King welcomes faster deficit reduction plans', *The Financial Times*, 10 May, www.ft.com/content/9b275072-5daa-11df-b4fc-00144feab49a

Pitt, D. (2023) 'Conservative welfare policies: ideational oscillation in the age of Brexit', in M. Beech and S. Lee (eds) *Conservative Governments in the Age of Brexit*, Cham: Palgrave Macmillan, pp 171–94.

Pitt, F.H. (2022) 'Contemporary class composition analysis: the politics of production and the autonomy of the political', *Capital & Class*, online first, https://doi.org/10.1177/03098168221139284

Plunkett, J. and Pessoa, J.P. (2013) *A Polarising Crisis? The Changing Shape of the UK and US Labour Markets from 2008 to 2012*, Resolution Foundation, www.resolutionfoundation.org/app/uploads/2014/08/A-polarising-crisis.pdf

Pope, T. (2022) 'Kwarteng and Truss show the perils of disregarding economic institutions', *Comment*, 29 September, Institute for Government, www.instituteforgovernment.org.uk/article/comment/kwarteng-and-truss-show-perils-disregarding-economic-institutions

Portes, J. and Reed, H. (2017) *Distributional results for the impact of tax and welfare reforms between 2010–17, modelled in the 2021/22 tax year*, Interim Findings, November 2017, Research Report, Equality and Human Rights Commission, https://www.equalityhumanrights.com/sites/default/files/impact-of-tax-and-welfare-reforms-2010-2017-interim-report_0.pdf

Poulantzas, N. (2014 (1978)) *State, Power, Socialism*, London: Verso.

Powell, A. (2019a) *New Enterprise Allowance*, House of Commons Briefing paper No. 05878, https://commonslibrary.parliament.uk/research-briefings/sn05878/

Powell, A. (2019b) *Women and the Economy*, Briefing paper No. CBP06838, House of Commons Library, https://researchbriefings.parliament.uk/ResearchBriefing/Summary/SN06838

Powell, A. (2019c) *People with Disabilities in Employment*, Briefing paper No. 7540, House of Commons Library, https://researchbriefings.parliament.uk/ResearchBriefing/Summary/CBP-7540

Powell, A. (2020) *Work and Health Programme*, Briefing paper No. 7845, House of Commons Library, https://commonslibrary.parliament.uk/research-briefings/cbp-7845/

Powell, A. (2022) *Coronavirus: Getting People Back into Work*, No. CBP 8965, House of Commons Library, https://researchbriefings.files.parliament.uk/documents/CBP-8965/CBP-8965.pdf

Power Sayeed, R. (2017) *1997: The Future that Never Happened*, London: Zed Books.

PREM 16/ 1483 *Letter Recounting Main Points of Meeting between the Prime Minister, the Secretary of State for Industry, Mr Henry Ford II and My H.A. Poling of Ford Europe, 25 August 1977*; Correspondence with Mr Ford II about Planning Agreements with Ford of Great Britain, Prime Minister's Office, The National Archives.

PREM 19-293 f7 *Hoskyns Minute to MT (Industrial Training: E Committee)*, 15 October 1980, Margaret Thatcher Foundation, www.margaretthatcher.org/document/120530

PREM 19-0837 f346 *Tebbit Letter to Brittan ('YOP allowance for 16 year olds') [proposal to end supplementary benefit]*, 23 November 1981, Margaret Thatcher Foundation, www.margaretthatcher.org/document/140961

PREM 19-1841 f116 *No. 10 Minute to MT ('Rayner Study on Unemployment Benefit')*; 20 February 1981, Margaret Thatcher Foundation, www.margaretthatcher.org/document/152314

PREM 19-121 f88 *Department of Industry Letter to HMT 'Strikers and Supplementary Benefit') [paper by Joseph]*, Prime Ministerial Private Office files, 20 November 1979, Margaret Thatcher Foundation, www.margaretthatcher.org/document/118003

PREM 19-525 f5 *No. 10 Letter to HMT (Walters paper on unemployment measures)*, 10 July, Margaret Thatcher Foundation, www.margaretthatcher.org/document/126408

PREM 19-524 f52 *Employment: Hoskyns Minute to MT ('Unemployment and Young People: E on 24 February')*, Prime Ministerial Private Office files, Policy Unit to Prime Minister, 21 February 1981, Margaret Thatcher Foundation, www.margaretthatcher.org/document/126385

PREM 19-526 f113 *Chancellor of the Exchequer Minute to MT ('Employment Measures') [further ideas for tackling unemployment]*, 11 August 1981, Margaret Thatcher Foundation, www.margaretthatcher.org/document/126427

PREM 19-525 f30 *Le Cheminant Briefing for MT ('Measures Against Unemployment (E (81) 74, 75, 76 and 77)')*, 8 July 1981, Margaret Thatcher Foundation, www.margaretthatcher.org/document/126406

PREM 19-1839 f366 *No. 10 Policy Unit Minute to MT ('Jobs') [unemployment statistics; fostering enterprise; creating jobs through schemes]*, 18 September 1985, www.margaretthatcher.org/document/152354

PREM 19-1839 f327 *Lord Young Minute to MT ('A Strategy for Enterprise and Employment')*, 1 November 1985, www.margaretthatcher.org/document/152350

PREM 19-1839 f376 *No. 10 Policy Unit Minute to MT ('Jobs Strategy')*, 4 September 1985, Margaret Thatcher Foundation, www.margaretthatcher.org/document/152357

PREM 19-1839 f400 *Tom King Minute to MT (the Community Programme and Tackling Unemployment)*, 7 August 1985, Margaret Thatcher Foundation, www.margaretthatcher.org/document/152359

PREM 19/4733 *Home Affairs, Gypsy Site Policy, January 1992–1 May 1997*, The National Archives, www.nationalarchives.gov.uk/documents/cabinet/prem-19-4733.pdf

PREM 49/43 'New Deal: Private Sector Involvement, Prime Minister to Secretary of State for Education and Employment, 16th October, 1997', *Employment Policy: Part 5*, 18 September – 31 October, Kew: The National Archives.

PREM 49/39 'Memo to the Prime Minister by Geoff Mulgan, Welfare to Work, 15th May', Labour Administration, 2–30 May 1997, The National Archives.

Price, D. (2000) *Office of Hope: A History of the Employment Service*, London: Policy Studies Institute.

Prime Minister (2017) *The Shared Society: Article by Theresa May*, 8 January, www.gov.uk/government/speeches/the-shared-society-article-by-theresa-may

Public Accounts Committee (1983) 'Special Employment Measures administered by the Department of Employment and the Manpower Services Commission: Memorandum by the Comptroller and Auditor General', 1–29, *Session 1982–83 Minutes of Evidence*, 28 February, 235-i, House of Commons Parliamentary Papers Online.

Public Accounts Committee (2013) *Department for Work and Pensions: Responding to Change in Jobcentres*, Fifth Report of Session 2013–14, HC 136 [Incorporating HC 1028 of Session 2012–13], House of Commons, London: The Stationery Office.

Public Accounts Committee (2021) *Oral evidence: DWP Employment Support 2: Kickstart scheme*, HC 655, Monday 6 December, House of Commons, https://committees.parliament.uk/oralevidence/3158/default/

Public Accounts Committee (2022) *DWP Employment Support: Kickstart Scheme Thirty-Ninth Report of Session 2021–22*, HC 655, House of Commons, https://publications.parliament.uk/pa/cm5802/cmselect/cmpubacc/655/summary.html

Public and Commercial Services Union (2023) *PCS Condemns DWP's Latest Attacks on Universal Credit Claimants*, 27 February, www.pcs.org.uk/news-events/news/pcs-condemns-dwps-latest-attacks-universal-credit-claimants

Raffass, T. (2017) 'Demanding activation', *Journal of Social Policy*, 46(2): 349–65.

Raffe, D. (1987) 'The context of the Youth Training Scheme: an analysis of its strategy and development', *British Journal of Education and Work*, 1(1): 1–31.

Rafferty, A. and Wiggan, J. (2017) 'The time-related underemployment of lone parents during welfare reform, recession and austerity: a challenge to in-work conditionality?', *Social Policy and Administration*, 51(3): 511–38.

Rahilly, S. (2008) 'Activating benefit claimants of working age in the UK', in S. Stendahl, T. Erhag and S. Devetzi (eds) *A European Work-first Welfare State*, Göteborg: Centre for European Research, University of Gothenburg, pp 79–94.

Ramsden, M., Bennett, R. and Fuller, C. (2007) 'Local economic development initiatives and the transitions from Training and Enterprise Councils to new institutional structures in England', *Policy Studies*, 28(3): 225–45.

Reader, M. Andersen, K. Patrick, R. Reeves, A. and Stewart, K. (2023) *Making work pay? The labour market effects of capping child benefits in larger families*, CASE paper 229, London School of Economics, https://sticerd. lse.ac.uk/dps/case/cp/casepaper229.pdf

Redman, J. (2021) '"Chatting shit" in the Jobcentre: navigating workfare policy at the street-level', *Work, Employment and Society*, 1–21.

Redman, J. and Fletcher, D. (2022) 'Violent bureaucracy: a critical analysis of the British public employment service', *Critical Social Policy*, 42(2): 306–26.

Rees, J., Whitworth, A. and Carter, E. (2014) 'Support for all in the UK Work Programme? Differential payments, same old problem', *Social Policy and Administration*, 48(2): 221–39.

Rees, T. (1988) 'Education for enterprise: the state and alternative employment for young people', *Journal of Education Policy*, 3(1): 9–22.

Reigler, B. (2018) 'Making Britain work again: unemployment and the remaking of British Social Policy in the eighties', *The English Historical Review*, 133(562): 634–66.

Reisenbichler, A. and Wiedemann, A. (2022) 'Credit driven and consumption led growth models in the United States and United Kingdom', in L. Baccaro, M. Blyth and J. Pontusson (eds) *Diminishing Returns: The New Politics of Growth and Stagnation*, New York: Oxford University Press, pp 213–37.

Renga, S. (1991) 'Unemployment, the social security system and the development of new working patterns in the 1980s: a theoretical perspective', *Anglo-American Law Review*, 20(2): 149–82.

Richards, A. (2009) 'Trade unions and the unemployed in the interwar period and the 1980s in Britain', in M. Guigni (ed) *The Politics of Unemployment in Europe: Policy Responses and Collective Action*, London: Routledge, Chapter 5, pp 83–100.

Richards, J. (1987) 'The Temporary Short Time Working Compensation Scheme', *Applied Economics*, 19: 111–25.

Richardson, J.J. and Moon, J. (1984) 'The politics of unemployment in Britain', *Political Quarterly*, 55(1): 39–37.

Riley, R., Bewley, H., Kirby, S., Rincon-Aznar, A. and George, A. (2011) *The Introduction of Jobcentre Plus: An Evaluation of Labour Market Impacts*, Research Report No. 781, Department for Work and Pensions, https:// assets.publishing.service.gov.uk/government/uploads/system/uploads/atta chment_data/file/214567/rrep781.pdf

Roberts, K. and Parsell, G. (1992) 'The stratification of youth training', *British Journal of Education and Work*, 5(1): 65–83.

Robertson, B.D. (1986) 'Mrs Thatcher's employment prescription: an active neo-liberal labor market policy', *Journal of Public Policy*, 6(3): 275–96.

Robertson, E. (2023) 'Wage supplements in mature welfare states: accounting for in-work benefit reforms in France and the United Kingdom, 1995-2020', PhD Thesis, University of Edinburgh, https://era.ed.ac.uk/handle/1842/40594

Rogers, C. (2009) 'From Social Contract to "social contrick": the depoliticisation of economic policy-making under Harold Wilson, 1974–75', *British Journal of Politics and International Relations*, 11: 634–51.

Rogers, R. (2002) 'Discourses of resistance and the "hostile jobseeker"', *Benefits – the Journal of Poverty and Social Justice*, 10(1): 19–23.

Romei, V. (2022) 'The FT's quick guide to the UK fiscal statement', *The Financial Times*, 23 September, www.ft.com/content/98595e6c-77ea-4247-8dc9-6c685a8cd99f

Rooksby, E. (n.d.) *Towards a Better Theory of the Capitalist State: Combining Poulantzas' and Block's Approaches*, Academica.edu, www.academia.edu/693189/Towards_a_Better_Theory_of_the_Capitalist_State_Combining_Blocks_and_Poulantzas_Approaches

Rose, H. (1973) 'Up against the welfare state: the claimant unions', *Socialist Register 1973*, 10: 179–203, https://socialistregister.com/index.php/srv/article/view/5354/2255

Ross, G. and Jenson. J. (1986) 'Post-war class struggle and the crisis of left politics', *Socialist Register 1985–86*, 22: 23–49, https://socialistregister.com/index.php/srv/article/view/5520

Roulstone, A. and Prideaux, S. (2012) *Understanding Disability Policy*, Bristol: Policy Press.

Rowe, C. (2022) 'Self-employed surfers, Universal Credit and the minimally decent life', *Legal Studies*, 42: 81–98.

Royston, S. (2017) *Broken Benefits: What's Gone Wrong with Welfare Reform*, Bristol: Policy Press.

Rubery, J. (1978) 'Structured labour markets, worker organisation and low pay', *Cambridge Journal of Economics*, 2: 17–36.

Rubery, J. and Piasna, A. (2016) *Labour Market Segmentation and the EU Reform Agenda: Developing Alternatives to the Mainstream*, Working Paper 2016, 10, Brussels: ETUI, www.etui.org/Publications2/Working-Papers/Labour-market-segmentation-and-the-EU-reform-agenda-developing-alternatives-to-the-mainstream

Russell, M. (2022) 'The constitutional causes and consequences of the Truss–Kwarteng budget crisis', *The Constitution Unit*, UCL, 5 October, https://constitution-unit.com/2022/10/05/the-constitutional-causes-and-consequences-of-the-truss-kwarteng-budget-crisis/

Rutter, J., Marshall, E. and Sims, S. (2012) *The 'S' Factors: Lessons from IFG's Policy Success Reunions*, Institute for Government, www.instituteforgov ernment.org.uk/sites/default/files/publications/The%20S%20Factors.pdf

Ryan, F. (2023) 'A decade after the Tories demonised disabled people on benefits, it's happening again', *The Guardian*, 30 May, www.theguardian. com/commentisfree/2023/may/30/tories-disabled-people-benefits

Ryan, P. (1995) 'Trade unions policies towards the YTS: patterns and causes', *British Journal of Industrial Relations*, 33(1): 1–33.

Sage, D. (2019) 'Unemployment, wellbeing and the power of the work ethic: implications for social policy', *Critical Social Policy*, (39)2: 205–28.

Sainsbury, R. (2009) 'Sickness, incapacity and disability', in J. Millar (ed) *Understanding Social Security: Issues for Policy and Practice* (2nd edn), Bristol: Policy Press, pp 213–32.

Salvatori, A. and Manfredi, T. (2019) *Job Polarisation and the Middle Class: New Evidence on the Changing Relationship Between Skill Levels and Household Income Levels from 18 OECD Countries*, OECD Social, Employment and Migration Working Papers No. 232, OECD, www.oecd-ilibrary.org/social-issues-migration-health/job-polarisation-and-the-middle-class_4bf722db-en

Sanders, A., Annesley, C. and Gains, F. (2019) 'What did the Coalition Government do for women? An analysis of gender equality policy agendas in the UK 2010–2015', *British Politics*, 14(2): 162–80, https://doi.org/10.1057/s41293-018-00103-2

Sargeant, M. (2010) 'The UK National Minimum Wage and age discrimination', *Policy Studies*, 31(3): 351–64.

Saville, J. (1957) 'The welfare state: an historical approach', *The New Reasoner*, 3: 5–25, www.marxists.org/archive/saville/1957/xx/welfare.htm

Sawyer, M. (2004) 'The NAIRU, labour market flexibility and full employment', in J. Stanford and L. Vosko (eds) *Challenging the Market: The Struggle to Regulate Work and Income*, Montreal, Canada: McGill-Queens University Press, pp 33–50.

Scholz, F. and Ingold, J. (2021) 'Activating the "ideal jobseeker": experiences of individuals with mental health conditions on the UK Work Programme', *Human Relations*, 74(10): 1604–27.

Schwander, H. and Hausermann, S. (2013) 'Who is in and who is out? A risk-based conceptualisation of insiders and outsiders', *Journal of European Social Policy*, 23(3): 248–69.

Scottish Government (2019) *Fair Start Scotland: Annual Report Year 1*, www. gov.scot/publications/fair-start-scotland-annual-report-year-1/

Scottish Government (2021) *Fair Start Scotland Evaluation Report 4: Overview of Year 3*, www.gov.scot/publications/fair-start-scotland-evaluation-rep ort-4-overview-year-3/

Scottish Government (2022) *Economic Evaluation of Fair Start Scotland*, www.gov.scot/publications/fair-start-scotland-economic-evaluation/documents/

Scottish Government (2023) *Scotland's Devolved Employment Services: Statistical Summary, Economy and Labour Market*, 22 February, www.gov.scot/publications/scotlands-devolved-employment-services-statistical-summary-17/documents/

Scottish Unemployed Workers Network (2016) *Righting Welfare Wrongs: dispatches from the frontline of the fight against austerity*, Common Print, Glasgow.

Secretaries of State for Employment, Scotland and Wales (1992) *People, Jobs and Opportunities*, CM 1810, HMSO.

Secretary of State for Employment (1988) *Training for Employment*, Cm 316, February, London: HMSO.

Secretary of State for Social Services (1985a) *Reform of Social Security*, Volume 1, Cmnd 9517, HMSO, House of Commons Parliamentary Papers Online.

Secretary of State for Social Services (1985b) *Reform of Social Security: Programme for Change*, Volume 2, Cmnd 9518, HMSO, House of Commons Parliamentary Papers Online.

Secretary of State for Social Services (1985c) *Reform of Social Security: Background Papers*, Volume 3, Cmnd 9519, HMSO, House of Commons Parliamentary Papers Online.

Secretary of State for Work and Pensions (2006a) *Speech on the Active Welfare State*, by John Hutton MP, 16 January, www.ukpol.co.uk/john-hutton-2006-speech-on-the-active-welfare-state/

Secretary of State for Work and Pensions (2006b) 'Welfare reform: 10 years on, 10 years ahead', speech by John Hutton MP, 18 December, https://webarchive.nationalarchives.gov.uk/ukgwa/20081023232331/http://www.dwp.gov.uk/aboutus/2006/18-12-06.asp

Secretary of State for Work and Pensions (2008) *James Purnell MP - Speech to Employers Conference*, 28 January, UKPol.co.uk, www.ukpol.co.uk/james-purnell-2008-speech-to-employers-conference/

Secretary of State for Work and Pensions (2010) *Iain Duncan Smith MP, IPPR speech – 7 December 2010*, www.gov.uk/government/speeches/institute-for-public-policy-research

Secretary of State for Work and Pensions (2019) 'The future of the labour market', speech by Amber Rudd MP at the Recruitment and Employment Confederation, 9 May, www.gov.uk/government/speeches/the-future-of-the-labour-market

Secretary of State for Work and Pensions (2022a) *Way to Work – Regulations*, 3 February, Correspondence between the Secretary of State for Work and Pensions and the SSAC on amendments to regulations to support the Way to Work campaign, www.gov.uk/government/publications/way-to-work-amendments-to-regulations

Secretary of State for Work and Pensions (2022b) *Thérèse Coffey MP, Speech: Movement to Work CEO Summit*, 28 March, www.gov.uk/gov ernment/speeches/work-and-pensions-secretary-speech-movement-to-work-ceo-summit

Secretary of State for Work and Pensions (2023) *Additional Jobcentre Support – Pilot rollout*, Mel Stride MP, Statement made on 27 February, UIN HCWS582, https://questions-statements.parliament.uk/written-sta tements/detail/2023-02-27/hcws582

Seely, A. (2023) *Coronavirus: Self-Employment Income Support Scheme*, Research Briefing No. 8879, House of Commons Library, https://commonslibrary. parliament.uk/research-briefings/cbp-8879/

Shildrick, T., MacDonald, R., Webster, C. and Garthwaite, K. (2010) *The Low Pay, No Pay Cycle: Understanding Recurrent Poverty*, Joseph Rowntree Foundation, www.jrf.org.uk/sites/default/files/jrf/migrated/files/unemp loyment-pay-poverty-full.pdf

Simpson, M. (2022) *Social Citizenship in an Age of Welfare Regionalism: The State of the Social Union*, Oxford: Hart Publishing.

Simpson, M., McKeever, G. and Gray, A. (2019) 'From principles to practice: social security in the Scottish laboratory of democracy', *Journal of Social Security Law*, 26(1): 13–31.

Sloman, P. (2019) 'Redistribution in an age of Neoliberalism: market economics, 'Poverty Knowledge', and the growth of working-age benefits in Britain, c. 1979–2010', *Political Studies*, 67(3): 732–51.

Smith, M.J.A., Galloway, L., Jackman, L., Danson, M. and Whittam, G. (2019) 'Poverty, social exclusion and enterprise policy: a study of UK policies' effectiveness over 40 years', *International Journal of Entrepreneurship and Innovation*, 20(2): 107–18.

Smyth, P. and Deeming, C. (2016) 'The social investment perspective in social policy: a long durée perspective', *Social Policy and Administration*, 50(6): 673–90.

Social Security Advisory Committee (2014) *Social security provision and the self employed*, Occasional Paper No. 13, https://assets.publishing.service. gov.uk/media/5a7edc6ded915d74e6226ebd/Social_security_provision_a nd_the_self-employed__FINAL_24_SEPT__.pdf

Social Security Scotland (n.d.) *Our Charter*, www.socialsecurity.gov.scot/ about/our-charter

Solomos, J. (1985) 'Problems, but whose problems: the social construction of black youth unemployment and state policies', *Journal of Social Policy*, 14(4): 527–55.

Soss, J., Fording R. and Schram, S.F. (2011) 'The organization of discipline: from performance management to perversity and punishment', *Journal of Public Administration Research and Theory*, 21(2): 203–32.

Sotiropoulos, D.P. (2011) 'Kalecki's dilemma: towards a Marxian political economy of neo-liberalism', *Rethinking Marxism*, 23(1): 100–16.

Spicer, A. and Fleming, P. (2016) 'Resisting the 24/7 work ethic – shifting modes of regulation and refusal in organised employment', in D. Courpasson and S. Vallas (eds) *The SAGE Handbook of Resistance*, London: SAGE Publications, pp 121–36.

Spours, K. (2020) *Shapeshifters: the evolving politics of modern Conservatism*, Compass, https://www.compassonline.org.uk/publications/shapeshift ing-the-evolving-politics-of-modern-conservatism/

Stafford, B. (2004) *New Deal for Disabled People (NDDP): First Synthesis Report*, Working Age and Employment Reports 1998–2004, No. 199, Department for Work and Pensions, https://webarchive.nationalarchives. gov.uk/ukgwa/20100208134427/http://research.dwp.gov.uk/asd/asd5/ wae-index.asp

Stafford, B. (2007) *New Deal for Disabled People: Third Synthesis Report – Key Findings from the Evaluation*, Research Report No. 430, Department for Work and Pensions, HMSO.

Stahl, R.M. (2019) 'Economic liberalism and the state: dismantling the myth of naïve laissez-faire', *New Political Economy*, 24(4): 473–86.

Standing, G. (2011) 'Workfare and the precariat', *Soundings*, 47: 35–43.

Statutory Instrument (2010) *Explanatory Memorandum to the Jobseeker's Allowance (Work for your Benefit Pilot Scheme Regulations 2010*, No. 1222, www.legislation.gov.uk/uksi/2010/1222/pdfs/uksiem_20101222_en.pdf

Staufenberg, J. and Stone, J. (2016) 'Revealed: The High Street firms that used benefits claimants for free labour', *The Independent*, 31 July, https:// www.independent.co.uk/news/uk/politics/benefits-department-for-work-and-pensions-mandatory-work-activity-government-major-compan ies-free-labour-welfare-a7163646.html

Stevenson, G. (2020) *The Women's Liberation Movement and the Politics of Class in Britain*, London: Bloomsbury.

Stubbington, T., Cumbo, J. and Flood, C. (2022) 'How Kwasi Kwarteng's mini-Budget broke the UK bond market', *The Financial Times*, 28 September, www.ft.com/content/4e6b89a3-a63e-49df-8a04-0488b 69e84f5

Stutzle, I. (2011) 'The order of knowledge: the state as knowledge apparatus', in A. Gallas, L. Bretthauer, J. Kannankulam and I. Stutzle (eds) *Reading Poulantzas*, Pontypool: Merlin Press, pp 170–85.

Subversion (1996a) 'The JSA and the dole workers' strike', https://libcom. org/article/subversion-20

Subversion (1996b) '3 strikes and a funeral: comments on the anti-JSA struggle', Subversion, No. 20 https://libcom.org/article/subversion-20

Sunley, P., Martin, R. and Nativel, C. (2006) *Putting Workfare in Place: Local Labour Markets and the New Deal*, Oxford: Blackwell Publishing.

Talbot, C. (2001) 'UK public services and management (1979–2000): evolution or revolution?', *International Journal of Public Sector Management*, 14(4/5): 281–303.

Talbot, C. (2004) 'Executive agencies: have they improved management in Government?', *Public Money and Management*, 24(2): 104–12.

Taylor, M., Marsh, G., Nicol, D. and Broadbent, P. (2017) *Good Work: The Taylor Review of Modern Working Practices*, https://assets.publishing.service. gov.uk/government/uploads/system/uploads/attachment_data/file/627 671/good-work-taylor-review-modern-working-practices-rg.pdf

Taylor, R. (1982) *Workers and the New Depression*, London: Macmillan Press.

Tebbit, N. (1989) *Upwardly Mobile*, London: Futura Publications.

Tepe-Belfrage, D. and Steans, J. (2016) 'The new materialism: re-claiming a debate from a feminist perspective', *Capital and Class*, 40(2): 303–24.

Thatcher, M. (1989) *Speech Launching Training and Enterprise Councils (TECs)*, Gosforth Park Hotel, Newcastle, 10 March, Margaret Thatcher Archive, www.margaretthatcher.org/document/107601

Thatcher, M. (1995) *The Downing Street Years*, London: Harper Collins.

Thatcher MSS: 1/5/1 *Employment Policy, Presented by the Minister of Reconstruction to Parliament*, May 1944, Cmd 6527, reprinted 1947, HM Stationery Office, Margaret Thatcher Foundation, www.margaretthatcher. org/document/110368

Thatcher MSS (2-1-1-39) *Sir Keith Joseph to MT (encloses draft speech on unions) [depth of change needed above & beyond legal framework]*, www. margaretthatcher.org/document/111880

Thatcher MSS (2/6/1/156) *Joseph, K. (1975) Notes Towards the Definition of Policy, Leader's Consultative Committee*, 4 April, Conservative Research Department, LCC/75/71, Margaret Thatcher Foundation, www.marga retthatcher.org/document/110098

THCR 2/11/9/32 f119 *Britto Note to Derek Howe ('Public Opinion Background Note 72') [weekly survey note – attitudes to the riots]* 12 July 1981, Margaret Thatcher Foundation, www.margaretthatcher.org/document/121453

THCR 2/7/3/40 f47 *CRD Briefing ('People's March for Jobs '83') [G7 Williamsburg, General Election*, 1 June 1983, Margaret Thatcher Foundation, www.margaretthatcher.org/document/132470

THCR 2/11/9/37 f4 *Harris Research Centre Report ('Summary of Main Findings of a Survey of the National Political Mood: Fieldwork 6–7 May 1983')*, Margaret Thatcher Foundation, www.margaretthatcher.org/document/131501

THCR 1/14/4 (153) *Hoskyns Minute to Whitmore ('Censure Debate') [unemployment]*, 25 July 1980, Margaret Thatcher Foundation, www.marga retthatcher.org/document/119219

THCR 2/6/1/248 *Stepping Stones Report (final text)*, 14 November 1977, Margaret Thatcher Foundation, www.margaretthatcher.org/document/111771

THCR 1/15/6 f3 *Walker Minute to MT ('Memorandum on a Conservative Strategy for the Next Two Years')*, 16 February 1982, Margaret Thatcher Foundation, www.margaretthatcher.org/document/122920

The New Scrounger (1988a) Bulletin of the Federation of Claimant Unions, No. 5, Autonomous Centre Edinburgh.

The New Scrounger (1988b) Bulletin of the Federation of Claimant Unions, No. 6, Autonomous Centre Edinburgh.

The Times (1988a) 'YTS staff strike rather than work with trainee', *The Times*, 20 January, Times Newspapers.

The Times (1988b) 'Training scheme coercion unlawful; law report', *The Times*, 12 November, Times Newspapers.

Thomas, A. (2007) *Lone Parent Work Focused Interviews: Synthesis of findings*, Research Report No. 443, Leeds: Department for Work and Pensions, Corporate Document Services.

Thomson, L.C. and Hunter, A.W.J. (1978) 'Great Britain', in J. Dunlop, and W. Galenson (eds) *Labor in the Twentieth Century*, New York: Academic Press, pp 85–148.

Tomlinson, J. (2017) *Managing the Economy, Managing the People: Narratives of Economic Life in Britain: From Beveridge to Brexit*, Oxford: Oxford University Press.

Tonge, J. (1999) 'New packaging, old deal? New Labour and employment policy innovation', *Critical Social Policy*, 19(2): 217–32.

Towers, B. (1994) 'Unemployment and labour market policies and programmes in Britain: experience and evaluation', *Journal of Industrial Relations*, 36(3): 370–93.

Trades Union Congress (n.d.) *The UK's Low Pay Recovery*, Trades Union Congress, www.tuc.org.uk/sites/default/files/Lowpayreport.pdf

Trades Union Congress – Labour Party Liaison Committee (1973) *Economic Policy and the Cost of Living*, 30 January, NEC Minutes and Papers, Archive of the People's History Museum, Salford.

Trades Union Congress – Labour Party Liaison Committee (1974) *Collective Bargaining and the Social Contract, Draft statement attached to Liaison Committee meeting 22/1*, 24 June, NEC Minutes and Papers, Labour History Archive of the People's History Museum, Salford.

Trades Union Congress – Labour Party Liaison Committee (1975a) *Report of the twenty-seventh meeting to the TUC–Labour Party Liaison Committee*, 21 April 1975, NEC Minutes and Papers, Labour History Archive of the People's History Museum, Salford.

Trades Union Congress – Labour Party Liaison Committee (1975b) *Report of the twenty-eighth meeting to the TUC–Labour Party Liaison Committee*, 19 May 1975, NEC Minutes and Papers, Labour History Archive of the People's History Museum, Salford.

Trades Union Congress (2001) 'Memorandum from the Trades Union Congress (TUC): Appendix 22', *Recruiting Unemployed People*, Third Report 2000–01, HC 48, House of Commons Select Committee on Education and Employment, Minutes of Evidence, https://publications.parliament. uk/pa/cm200001/cmselect/cmeduemp/48/48ap28.htm

Trades Union Congress (2006) 'Memorandum', *Incapacity Benefit and Pathways to Work, Work and Pensions Committee*, 3rd Report of Session 2005–06, Vol 2, Oral and Written Evidence, 13 February, House of Commons, HC616-II, London: The Stationery Office, https://publicati ons.parliament.uk/pa/cm200506/cmselect/cmworpen/cmworpen.htm

Trade Union Congress (2015) *TUC Directory*, https://www.tuc.org.uk/ sites/default/files/TUC_Directory_2015_A5_Flyer_Order_Form_LR.pdf

Trade Union Congress/Federation of Small Businesses (n.d.) *A TUC and FSB Proposal for a Short-Term Working Subsidy*, www.tuc.org.uk/sites/defa ult/files/extras/wagesubsidies.pdf

Treasury Select Committee (2010) *Examination of Witnesses (Questions 728– 815)*, Minutes of Evidence – Spending Review 2010, Oral Evidence, 4 November, https://publications.parliament.uk/pa/cm201011/cmselect/ cmtreasy/544/10110402.htm

Trickey, H. and Walker, R. (2001) 'Steps to compulsion within British labour market policies', in Lødemel, I. and Trickey, H. (eds) *'An Offer You Cannot Refuse': Workfare in International Perspective*, Bristol: Policy Press, pp 181–213.

Tronti, M. (1964) 'Lenin in England', English language translation of article first published in *Classe Operaia*, 1 1964 and republished in 1966 in Tronti's book *Operai e Capitale*, 89–95, www.marxists.org/reference/subject/phi losophy/works/it/tronti.htm [last accessed 4 April 2017].

Tronti, M. (2008 [1966]) 'The strategy of refusal', in S. Lotringer and C. Marazzi (eds) *Autonomia – Post Political Politics*, Semiotext Intervention Series 1, New York, pp 28–35, http://libcom.org/library/autonomia-post-political-politics [last accessed 4 April 2017].

Turner, D.S., Wallis, K.F. and Whitley, J.D. (1987) 'Evaluating special employment measures with macroeconomic models', *Oxford Review of Economic Policy*, 3(3): xxv–xxxvi

UK Parliament (2015) *Scotland*, 2015 General Election results, https://elec tionresults.parliament.uk/election/2015-05-07/results/Location/Coun try/Scotland

Umney, C. (2018) *Class Matters: Inequality and Exploitation in 21st Century Britain*, London: Pluto Press.

Umney, C., Greer, I., Onaran, O. and Symon, G. (2018) 'The state and class discipline: European labour market policy after the financial crisis', *Capital and Class*, 42(2): 333–51.

Unemployment Unit (1987) *Unemployment Unit Briefing: Statistical Supplement, October/November*, London: Unemployment Unit.

Unemployment Unit (1988a) 'Why train school leavers', *Unemployment Bulletin*, Issue 28 Autumn, London.

Unemployment Unit (1988b) 'Characteristics of entrants to the Community Programme', *Unemployment Unit Briefing*, Statistical Supplement, July 1988, London.

Unemployment Unit (1988c) 'The new adult training programme', *Unemployment Bulletin*, Issue 26 Spring: 1–5, London.

Unemployment Unit/Youthaid (1990) 'ET – the real results', 1–2, *Working Brief*, November 1990.

Valocchi, S. (1989) 'The relative autonomy of the state and the origins of British welfare policy', *Sociological Forum*, 4(3): 349–65.

Van Reenan, J. (2004) 'Active labor market policies and the British New Deal for the young unemployed in context', in D. Card, R. Blundell and R.B. Freeman (eds) *Seeking a Premier Economy: The Economic Effects of British Economic Reforms, 1980–2000*, Chicago, IL: National Bureau of Economic Research, University of Chicago Press, pp 461–96, www.nber.org/system/files/chapters/c6754/c6754.pdf

Vegeris, S., Adams, L., Oldfield, K., Bertram, C., Davidson, R., Durante, L., Riley, C. and Vowden, K. (2011) *Flexible New Deal evaluation: Customer Survey and Qualitative Research Findings*, Research Report No. 758, Department for Work and Pensions, https://webarchive.nationalarchives.gov.uk/ukgwa/20160116140759/www.gov.uk/government/publications/flexible-new-deal-evaluation-rr758

Vegeris, S., Vowden, K., Bertram, C., Davidson, R., Durante, L., Hudson, M., Husain, F., Mackinnon, K. and Smeaton, D. (2010) *Jobseekers Regime and Flexible New Deal Evaluation: A Report on Qualitative Research Findings*, Research Report No. 706, Department for Work and Pensions, https://webarchive.nationalarchives.gov.uk/ukgwa/20160116160730/www.gov.uk/government/publications/jobseekers-regime-and-flexible-new-deal-evaluation-rr706

Vlandas, T. (2019) 'The political consequences of labor market dualisation: labor market status, occupational unemployment and policy preferences', *Political Science Research and Methods*, 1–7.

Waddington, D. and King, M. (2009) 'Identifying common causes of UK and French riots occurring since the 1980s', *Howard Journal*, 48(3): 245–56.

Walker, B. (1988) 'From dole college to Youth Training Scheme: the development of state intervention in training unemployed youth', *Journal of Further and Higher Education*, 12(1): 20–41.

Walker, P., Crerar, P. and Elgot, J. (2022) 'Liz Truss resigns as PM and triggers fresh leadership election', *The Guardian*, 20 October, www.theguardian.com/politics/2022/oct/20/liz-truss-to-quit-as-prime-minister

Walker, R. and Wiseman, M. (2003) 'Making welfare work: UK activation policies under New Labour', 'Making welfare work: UK activation policies under New Labour', *International Social Security Review*, 56(1): 3–29.

Walters, A. (1986) *Britain's Economic Renaissance*, Oxford: Oxford University Press.

Wamsley, D. (2022) 'Crisis management, new constitutionalism, and depoliticisation: recasting the politics of austerity in the US and UK, 2010–16', *New Political Economy*, DOI: 10.1080/13563467.2022.2153358

Watts, B., Fitzpatrick, S., Bramley, G. and Watkins, D. (2014) *Welfare Sanctions and Conditionality in the UK*, Joseph Rowntree Foundation Report, www.jrf.org.uk/report/welfare-sanctions-and-conditionality-uk

Webb, D. (2003) *Employment and Training Programmes for the Unemployed*, House of Commons Library, Research Paper 03/13, 10 February, https://researchbriefings.files.parliament.uk/documents/RP03-13/RP03-13.pdf

Webster, D. (2014) *The DWP's JSA/ESA Sanctions Statistics Release*, Briefing, 19 February, www.welfareconditionality.ac.uk/wp-content/uploads/2013/12/sanctions-stats-briefing-d-webster-19-feb-2014.pdf

Webster, D. (2016) *Explaining the Rise and Fall of JSA and ESA Sanctions 2010–16, Briefing: The DWP's JSA/ESA Sanctions Statistics Release*, 17 August 2016 – Supplement, https://cpag.org.uk/policy-and-campaigns/briefing/david-webster-university-glasgow-briefings-benefit-sanctions

Webster, D. (2017) *Benefit Sanctions Statistics: JSA, ESA and Universal Credit*, Briefing, February, https://cpag.org.uk/policy-and-campaigns/briefing/david-webster-university-glasgow-briefings-benefit-sanctions

Webster, D. (2023) *Briefing: Benefit Sanctions Statistics February 2023*, https://cpag.org.uk/policy-and-campaigns/briefing/david-webster-university-glasgow-briefings-benefit-sanctions

Webster, L. (2022) 'Suella Braverman complains too many people are on benefits despite Tory cuts', *The National*, 11 July, www.thenational.scot/news/20271462.suella-braverman-complains-many-people-benefits-despite-tory-cuts/

Weeks, K. (2011) *The Problem with Work: Feminism, Marxism, Antiwork Politics, and Postwork Imaginaries*, London: Duke University Press.

Weghmann, V. (2019) 'The making and breaking of solidarity between unwaged and waged workers in the UK', *Globalisations*, 16(4): 441–56.

Weishaupt, T. (2011) *From the Manpower Revolution to the Activation Paradigm: Explaining Institutional Continuity and Change in an Integrating Europe*, Amsterdam: Amsterdam University Press.

Welfare Reform Act 2012, c. 5, *Claimant Responsibilities*, Chapter 2, www.legislation.gov.uk/ukpga/2012/5/contents/enacted

Welfare Reform and Work Act 2016, *Benefit Cap*, Chapter 8, www.legislation.gov.uk/ukpga/2016/7/section/8/enacted

Wells, B. (2001) 'From Restart to the New Deal in the United Kingdom', in OECD *Labour Market Policies and the Public Employment Service: Lessons from Recent Experience and the Directions for the Future*, Proceedings of the Prague Conference, July 2000, Paris: OECD, pp 241–62.

Wells, B. (2022) 'Box A: full employment and the "office of hope"', *UK Economic Outlook*, National Institute of Economic and Social Research, Summer 2022, Series A, No. 7: 15–18.

White, M. and Lakey, J. (1992) *The Restart Effect Evaluation of a Labour Market Programme For Unemployed People*, London: Policy Studies Institute.

Whiteley, P. and Winyard, S. (1983) 'Influencing social policy: the effectiveness of the poverty lobby in Britain', *Journal of Social Policy*, 12(1): 1–26.

Whiteside, N. (1991) *Bad Times: Unemployment in British Social and Political History*, London: Faber and Faber.

Whitworth, A. (2020) 'Activating spatial inequality: the case of the UK Work Programme', *Journal of Poverty and Social Justice*, 28(2): 207–26.

Wickham-Jones, M. (1996) *Economic Strategy and the Labour Party: Politics and Policy-Making 1970–83*, London: Macmillan Press.

Wickham-Jones, M. (2003) "From reformism to resignation and remedialism? labour's trajectory through British politics', *The Journal of Policy History*, 15(1): 26–45.

Wiggan, J. (2007a) 'Reforming the United Kingdom's public employment and social security agencies', *International Review of Administrative Sciences*, 73(3): 404–24.

Wiggan, J. (2007b) 'Administering economic reform: New Labour and the governance of social security', *Policy and Politics*, 35(4): 651–66.

Wiggan, J. (2010) 'Managing time: the integration of caring and paid work by low-income families and the role of the UK's tax credit system', *Policy Studies*, 31(6): 631–45.

Wiggan, J. (2012) 'Telling stories of 21st century welfare: the UK Coalition Government and the neo-liberal discourse of worklessness and dependency', *Critical Social Policy*, 32(3): 383–405.

Wiggan, J. (2015a) 'Reading active labour market policy politically: an autonomist analysis of Britain's Work Programme and Mandatory Work Activity', *Critical Social Policy*, 35(3): 369–92.

Wiggan, J. (2015b) 'Varieties of marketisation in the UK: examining divergence in activation markets between Great Britain and Northern Ireland 2008–2014', *Policy Studies*, 36(2): 115–32.

Wiggan, J. (2016) 'Austerity politics', in P. Alcock, T. Haux, M. May and S. Wright (eds) *The Student's Companion to Social Policy* (5th edn), Chichester: Wiley-Blackwell, Chapter 21.

Wiggan, J. (2017) 'Contesting the austerity and "welfare reform" narrative of the UK Government: forging a social democratic imaginary in Scotland', *International Journal of Sociology and Social Policy*, 37(11/12): 639–54.

Wiggan, J. and Grover, C. (2022) 'The politics of job retention schemes in Britain: the Coronavirus Job Retention Scheme and the Temporary Short Time Working Compensation Scheme', *Critical Social Policy*, 42(4): 716–39.

Wiggan, J. and Knuth, M. (2023) 'Active labour market programmes and employer engagement in the UK and Germany', in J. Ingold and P. McGurk (eds) *Employer Engagement: Making Active Labour Market Policies Work*, Bristol: Bristol University Press, pp 126–45.

Williams, E. (2021) 'Punitive welfare reform and claimant mental health: the impact of benefit sanctions on anxiety and depression', *Social Policy and Administration*, 55(1): 157–72.

Williams, F. (2015) 'Towards the Welfare Commons: contestation, critique and criticality in social policy', in Z. Irving, M. Fenger and J. Hudson (eds) *Social Policy Review 27*, Bristol: Policy Press, pp 94–111.

Wilson, H. (1975a) 'Parliamentary Report – Tuesday morning', *Report of the 74th Annual Conference of the Labour Party*, Blackpool, 29 September – 3 October 1975, pp 178–88.

Wilson, H. (1975b) *Attack on Inflation*, Prime Minister Harold Wilson to the House of Commons, 11 July 1975, Col. 901–7, House of Commons Debates, 11 July 1975, Vol 895, cc 901–28, Hansard, http://hansard.mill banksystems.com/commons/1975/jul/11/attack-on-inflation#S5CV089 5P0_19750711_HOC_20

Wilson, L. (2019) 'The gendered nature or employment and insecure employment in Northern Ireland: a story of continuity and change', *Journal of Research in Gender Studies*, 9(1): 39–70.

Wilson, S. (2017) 'The politics of "minimum wage" welfare states: the changing significance of the minimum wage in the liberal welfare regime', *Social Policy and Administration*, 51(2): 244–64.

Witheford, N. (1994) 'Autonomist Marxism and the information society', *Capital and Class*, 18(1): 85–125.

Women's Budget Group (2021) *Gender Differences in Access to Coronavirus Government Support*, https://wbg.org.uk/media/self-employed-women-are-losing-out-on-government-support/

Woodall, J. (1986) 'The dilemma of youth unemployment: trade union responses in the federal republic of Germany, the UK and France', *West European Politics*, 9(3): 429–47.

Woodward, W. (2007) 'Blueprint for big welfare shakeup gets backing of Blair and Brown', *The Guardian*, 6 March, www.theguardian.com/polit ics/2007/mar/06/uk.socialexclusion

Work and Pensions Committee (2006a) *Incapacity Benefits and Pathways to Work*, Third Report Session 2005–06, Vol I, HC 616-I, London: The Stationery Office, https://publications.parliament.uk/pa/cm200506/cmsel ect/cmworpen/616/61602.htm

Work and Pensions Committee (2006b) *Incapacity Benefits and Pathways to Work*, Third Report Session 2005–06, Vol I, HC 616-II, London: The Stationery Office.

Work and Pensions Committee (2007) *The Government's Employment Strategy*, Third Report of Session 2006–07, HC 63-I, House of Commons, London: The Stationery Office.

Work and Pensions Committee (2009) *DWP's Commissioning Strategy and the Flexible New Deal*, Vol I, 2nd Report of Session 2008–09, House of Commons, HC 59-I, London: The Stationery Office, https://publicati ons.parliament.uk/pa/cm200809/cmselect/cmworpen/59/9780215526 656.pdf

Work and Pensions Committee (2010) *Youth Unemployment and the Future Jobs Fund,* First Report of 2010–11, House of Commons, Vol I, HC 472, London: The Stationery Office, https://publications.parliament.uk/pa/ cm201011/cmselect/cmworpen/472/472.pdf

Work and Pensions Committee (2014a) *The Role of Jobcentre Plus in the Reformed Welfare System*, Second Report of Session 2013–14, HC 479, Vol I, House of Commons, London: The Stationery Office.

Work and Pensions Committee (2014b) Minutes of Evidence, 13 November 2013, *The Role of Jobcentre Plus in the Reformed Welfare System*, Second Report of Session 2013–14, HC 479, Vol 1, House of Commons, London: The Stationery Office.

Work and Pensions Committee (2016) *The Future of Jobcentre Plus*, Second Report of Session 2016–17, HC 57, House of Commons, London: The Stationery Office.

Work and Pensions Committee (2017) *Disability Employment Gap*, Seventh Report of Session 2016–17, HC 56, House of Commons, London: The Stationery Office.

Worth, O. (2023) 'The great moving Boris show: Brexit and the mainstreaming of the far right in Britain', *Globalizations*, 20(5): 814–28.

Wren, A. (2013) 'The political economy of the service transition', *Renewal*, 21(1): 67–76.

Wrench, J. (1986) *YTS, Racial Equality and the Trade Unions*, Policy paper for Ethnic Relations No. 6, Centre for Research in Ethnic Relations, University of Warwick.

Wright, E.O. (2023) *Classes*, Verso, London.

Wright, S. (2002) *Storming Heaven: Class Composition and Italian Autonomist Marxism*, London: Pluto Press.

Wright, S. (2006) 'The administration of transformation: a case study of implementing welfare reform in the UK', in P. Henman and M. Fenger (eds) *Administering Welfare Reform: International Transformations in Welfare Governance*, Bristol: Policy Press, pp 161–82.

Wright, S. (2009) 'Welfare to work', in J. Millar (ed) *Understanding Social Security: Issues for Policy and Practice* (2nd edn), Bristol: Policy Press, pp 193–212.

Wright, S. (2011) 'Steering with sticks, rowing for rewards: the new governance of activation in the UK', in R. van Berkel, W. de Graaf and T. Sirovátka (eds) *The Governance of Active Welfare States in Europe*, Basingstoke: Palgrave Macmillan, pp 85–109.

Wright, S. and Dwyer, P. (2022) 'In-work Universal Credit: claimant experiences of conditionality mismatches and counterproductive benefit sanctions', *Journal of Social Policy*, 51(1): 20–38.

Wright, S., Fletcher, D.R. and Stewart, A.B.R. (2020) 'Punitive benefit sanctions, welfare conditionality, and the social abuse of unemployed people in Britain: transforming claimants into offenders?', *Social Policy and Administration*, 54(2): 278–94.

Yamamori, T. (2014) 'A feminist way to unconditional basic income: claimants unions and women's liberation movements in 1970s Britain', *Basic Income Studies*, 9(1–2): 1–24.

Young, A.K. Banerjee, T. and Schwartz, M. (2018) 'Capital strikes as a corporate political strategy: the structural power of business in the Obama era', *Politics and Society*, 46(1): 3–28.

Young, D. (1991) *The Enterprise Years: A Businessman in the Cabinet*, London: Headline Book Publishing.

Youthaid (1985) 'Memorandum – The Youth Training Scheme', 42–70, Employment Committee, *The Training of Young People for Employment*, Minutes of Evidence, 27 March, Session 1984–85, 209-iii, House of Commons.

Index

Note: The following abbreviations have been used: ch denotes chapter number; *f* denotes figures; n denotes notes; *t* denotes tables.

Printed and bound by CPI Group (UK) Ltd, Croydon, CR0 4YY

23/04/2025

14661025-0004